# The Official Book of the Basset Hound

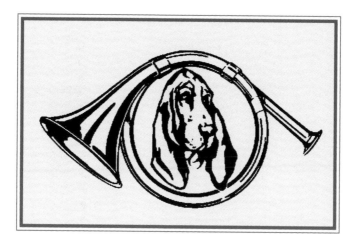

TS-304

## © by T.F.H. Publications, Inc.

Distributed in the UNITED STATES to the Pet Trade by T.F.H. Publications, Inc., One
T.F.H. Plaza, Neptune City, NJ 07753; on the Internet at www.tfh.com; in CANADA
Rolf C. Hagen Inc., 3225 Sartelon St. Laurent-Montreal Quebec H4R 1E8; Pet Trade
by H & L Pet Supplies Inc., 27 Kingston Crescent, Kitchener, Ontario N2B 2T6; in
ENGLAND by T.F.H. Publications, PO Box 15, Waterlooville PO7 6BQ; in AUSTRA-
LIA AND THE SOUTH PACIFIC by T.F.H. (Australia), Pty. Ltd., Box 149, Brookvale
2100 N.S.W., Australia; in NEW ZEALAND by Brooklands Aquarium Ltd. 5 McGiven
Drive, New Plymouth, RD1 New Zealand; in SOUTH AFRICA, Rolf C. Hagen S.A.
(PTY.) LTD. P.O. Box 201199, Durban North 4016, South Africa; in Japan by T.F.H.
Publications, Japan—Jiro Tsuda, 10-12-3 Ohjidai, Sakura, Chiba 285, Japan. Published
by T.F.H. Publications, Inc.

MANUFACTURED IN THE
UNITED STATES OF AMERICA
BY T.F.H. PUBLICATIONS, INC.

# The Official Book
## of the
# Basset Hound

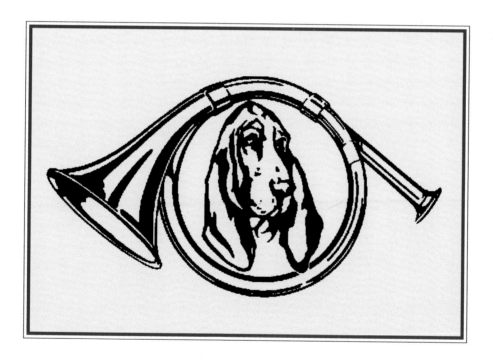

## Robert E. Booth

# Dedication

*To Mary Jane Booth, my wife of forty-five years and my partner in Hiflite Kennels, Reg.*

*This book was deprived of her considerable expertise in the breed by Alzheimer's disease.*

*Mary Jane Booth, judging at the Penn-Ridge Kennel Club in 1972.*

B.O.B.

photo by Ashbey

# Acknowledgments

For their help in the research and writing of this book, I am especially indebted to the following individuals, all of whom are members of the Basset Hound Club of America. All are recognized experts in the areas in which they contributed to the book. To **Marge Cook** for her input on Tracking with the Basset Hound, to **Chris Wallen** for her input on Obedience, to **Marge Skolnick** for the section on Field Trailing, to **Carolyn Young** for her section on Health and the Basset Hound, and to **Randy Frederiksen** for all of his polished work on the Origins, History and Modern Basset Hound Breed Development sections, as well as that of The Pack Bassets.

Last, but by no means least, **Sandra Launey** for her capable editing of the manuscript, and all of the other BHCA members who sent me their treasured photos and the information on their kennels, without which this book would not have been possible. You all have contributed significantly to a reference work for the Basset Hound breeders of the future.

*Bob Booth*

*Mary Jane Booth, awarding Best of Breed at the BHCA National in 1991.*

The author, Bob Booth, is shown here in
the yard of his retirement home in the
Texas Hill country.

# Contents

# ABOUT THE AUTHOR

Bob Booth and his wife, Mary Jane, met their first Basset Hound during a Christmastime visit to Mary Jane's aunt's home in Cross River, New York in 1956. Her aunt, Betty Stone, was at that time a well-known Cairn Terrier breeder. As luck would have it, one of her married children and family were at home for a holiday visit and had their pet Basset Hound with them. Impressed by the appearance and particularly the temperament of this unique breed, this short visit was the beginning of their lasting involvement in the "dog world."

Unable to acquire a pet for themselves at the time, due to an impending transfer to Hawaii early the following year, they promised themselves that they would pursue that endeavor upon their return to the mainland in 1960. They had anticipated that Bob would terminate his service as a pilot in the United States Air Force at that time. As it turned out, the Air Force career did not terminate as planned, but the long-awaited purchase of a Basset Hound was accomplished anyhow.

Typical of the uninitiated, they responded to a classified ad in the Champaign/Urbana, Illinois newspaper of the time for "Bassett Hound pups, pure bred, no papers, $25 " (for those who may have noticed, the two t's in Basset are intentional!). Well, they certainly had no requirement for papers, so about two hours later they were the proud owners of this delightful little black blanket "Basset Hound?" male pup. Unfortunately, a quick trip around the neighborhood, showing off their prized possession to some obviously more knowledgeable folks rapidly convinced them that the use of the word "pure" in the ad was suspect! Not to worry...back to the paper. Another ad, "Basset Hound Pups, 7 wks., AKC Reg., $50." Immediate inquiry revealed that there was only one tri-colored male left for sale. Not for long! They owned it some 45 minutes later. Well, at least most of the neighbors were able to identify this one as a Basset Hound. They named it Baron Von Gustav. The next day, much impressed with the appearance of "Gus," the breeder of their original "pure bred" purchase, agreed to take back the dog and refund their $25. Ah, for the good 'ol days!

Some months later, Judy and Lomax Teal, who were also owned by a Basset, (Lomax, at the time, was the base veterinarian), asked the Booths if they'd ever been to a dog show. They hadn't and they all agreed that the four of them should visit the upcoming Indianapolis show. In those days Indianapolis was a benched show. The dogs were kept on their individual bench spaces all day except for when they were actually being shown. There are few of these shows left today, the world famous Westminster Kennel Club dog show being one of them. What a great way to see the dogs, meet the breeders/exhibitors, and above all, learn about the breed.

It was readily apparent to the Booths, from the first pass of the benches in the Basset section that day, that poor old "Gus" just wouldn't measure up. In their eagerness to come by a really good specimen of the breed, they found that one of the Canadian exhibitors at that show had a litter of pups from which they might be able to "find something they'd like." Since these folks had what appeared to be, to their still-untrained eyes, some fine-looking dogs, agreement was made to visit their kennels, just outside Detroit, in the very near future to "have a look." And the Bassets hadn't even been judged yet that day! The day wore on and it was finally time for the Basset Hound classes to be judged by the great Alva Rosenberg. While not exactly sure of what was going on during the judging, they were able to discern that some little blonde lady, showing her dogs under the name of Kazoo kennels, Reg., won WD, WB, BOB, and BOS and that day's five-point major. At any rate, as promised, two weekends later they were on their way to Canada to "have a look." While driving on IH 94W in the area of Kalamazoo, Michigan, they happened to notice a sign on the side of the interstate for Kazoo Kennels, Reg. They took the next exit, found Kazoo, and never did make it to Canada.

For those who may not know the Kazoo kennel prefix, it is owned by Mary Jo Shields, currently a Life Member of the Basset Hound Club of America. Among many other notable dogs, Mary Jo back in that era had already produced the first Dual Champion in the breed, Dual Ch. Kazoo's Moses the Great, owned by Pat and Jim Dohr. While no longer maintaining a very large kennel, Mary Jo is still active in the breed.

On that visit to Kazoo, the Booths were able to purchase a solid red bitch, Kazoo's Effie. Though very well bred, (only one dog in a five-generation pedigree had failed to achieve a conformation championship), she did not do well in the show ring herself, due mainly to the development of a poor topline. She also was not destined to make her mark in the whelping box. Two outcrosses to champion studs failed to produce anything of show quality. Effie was retired to house-dog status, the Booths returned to Kazoo and were fortunate to be able to purchase Kazoo's Question Mark, a lovely tri-colored bitch sired by Ch. Manor Hill Top Spot and out of Ch. Kazoo's Frances. A typey, sound, and good moving bitch, "Questy" quickly finished her championship under the able hand of Mr. Roy Murray, PHA. At that point, the Booths selected the Hiflite kennel prefix (pronounced *high-flight,* with the prefix being meaningful by virtue of Bob's flying career and the John Magee poem of the same name). This established Hiflite Kennels, Reg., and Question Mark became their foundation bitch. She went on to distinguish herself in the whelping box by producing a total of 11 champions from her first two breedings to Ch. Glenhaven's Butcher Boy, a son of the outstanding producer Ch. Sir Tomo of Glenhaven. Questy died a relatively early death due to what the Booths have always considered to be a clear-cut case of veterinary incompetence. But for this misfortune, surely she would have made an even greater contribution to the breed.

The Vietnam War kept Hiflite kennels operating in a much reduced mode during the 1967–1969 time frame while Bob served as a "Jolly Green" Rescue Helicopter Pilot at DaNang Air Base, Republic of Vietnam. Always a small kennel, their breeding and showing activities increased somewhat after his return from Southeast Asia and they enjoyed success in the breed until 1973 when Bob's promotion to the rank of Colonel and his subsequent re-assignment to Williams AFB, Arizona required that they live on the base. This necessitated the placement of all of the dogs that they currently owned, since it was impossible to maintain the kennel in the "on-base environment." Another overseas assignment followed and the Booths were without dogs, but not without continuing interest in the breed, until after Bob's retirement from the Air Force in September, 1977.

Establishing a custom-home construction business (Hiflite Homes, Inc.) in San Antonio, Texas in 1978, the Booths were soon in a position to re-establish themselves in Bassets. They built a small kennel and were given the dog Switchbark's Ashmore and the bitch Switchbark's Promise T' Hiflite by Jerry and Carol O'Bryant in 1981. Both these youngsters rapidly finished their championships and Ashmore, "Moe," as he came to be known, went on to become BOB at the 1984 National Specialty and became an ROM sire as well. It was gratifying to the Booths that both these dogs could be traced back to their original stock. In limited breeding and showing since then they have been fortunate enough to have produced two more National Specialty winners: Hiflite's Rags to Riches (Style) was WD at the 1992 Nationals, and Hiflite Ultrabrite (Duchess) was WB and BW to finish her championship at the 1995 Nationals. This exciting win was the "icing on the cake," so to speak, since she had gone WB for five points at the BHCA Regional Specialty on the preceding day. Duchess was superbly handled to these wins by Vicki Steedle and is now owned by Doc and Vicki Steedle, owners of the Halcyon Basset kennel.

Both of the Booths have been AKC-approved judges of Basset Hounds since 1971. Mary Jane judged the Regular classes at the National Specialty in 1978 and judged the Intersex competition at the 1991 Nationals. She resigned from judging in 1995. Bob judged the Bitch Regular classes at the 1987 Nationals and the Intersex at the 1996 Nationals. He is currently approved to judge 11 Hound breeds. Retired from the home-building business at the end of 1995, Bob has served two terms as Vice President of BHCA and as Chairman of the BHCA Video Committee. They have shown a number of other breeds as well as having made significant contributions to the establishment of the Petit Basset Griffon Vendeén in this country.

# Introduction

What makes the Basset Hound a Basset Hound? Most who go in search of this delightful breed start by looking for the most obvious requirements: loose skin, profuse wrinkles, long ears, a soft, sad expression, and very heavy bone. Those fortunate enough to find all of these attributes on their first attempt soon come to be further captivated by the mild temperament of the animal. Well known as great pets for the children, they are equally loved by adults. In addition to their most common role, that of a household companion, many owners of this breed enjoy the challenges of competing in the show ring, working their dogs in obedience, tracking, and agility, as well as utilizing the Basset Hound's keen scenting abilities in the field.

The purpose of this book is to give you a broad overview of the Basset Hound. You will learn the historical origins of the breed and how it became what it is today. You'll be introduced to the Basset Hound standard, a verbal blueprint that attempts to describe the ideal specimen of the breed. You'll be introduced to the guardian of the breed, the Basset Hound Club of America, and to the regional breed clubs as well. If you should become interested in showing your Basset, or if you become interested in one or more of the other disciplines that many people enjoy, helpful information will be provided for those endeavors as well. While this book is intended to be a comprehensive volume on the breed, particularly covering the past 30 years, special attempt was made not to excessively overlap the breeder recognition provided in the final (fourth) edition, (now out of print), of *The New Complete Basset Hound* by Mercedes Braun. Long considered "the bible" of the breed, it continues to be a book that should be a part of every serious Basset breeder's or judge's library. This new book will, in the main, limit the majority of breeder, kennel, and hound recognition from the mid-1960s to the present. It should also be noted that there are a number of fine current-day breeders, kennels or dogs that are conspicuous by their absence. It is well to note that in such cases it was by their owners' own choice. All members of the Basset Hound Club of America were encouraged to participate.

Last, but certainly not least, some information is made available to those becoming interested in engaging in a limited amount of breeding of the Basset. This is an awesome responsibility, not to be undertaken lightly or without extensive knowledge of the breed.

Mostly, the reader should come away with a significantly improved general knowledge of the Basset Hound and learn how to go about obtaining a good specimen for the purpose desired, be it pet, show, or working dog.

# Origins of the Basset Hound

In the development of the Basset Hound breed, maybe more so than in many other breeds, it is its interdependence upon what has been done to it by individuals in different parts of the globe throughout relatively recent history that make it the special animal that it has become. Decisions taken by one kennel or another to aid in their own success have tended to impact this breed on a worldwide scale. An understanding of this will help in the full realization of the Basset Hound's origins, present structure, and future direction.

Natural evolutionary history of the Basset Hound has very little historical documentation before the 1500s. We know, however, that the breed is a man-made breed and that it may have been started by genetic mutations that were then exploited by man for their best uses. We do have good information showing the historical development of the basset-sized hounds in France. There is a real distinction between the two, basset-sized and Basset Hound. The difference will become apparent as we explore the origins of the Basset Hound. The first true canine-type animal on the earth, after many millions of years of nature's selective evolution process, was the *Tomarctus* animal. It was "a short-legged, long bodied, long-tailed predator and roamed the earth about fifteen million years ago and was the direct ancestor of wolves, coyotes, jackals, foxes, and dogs." From this animal descended four prototype canines from which came *Canis familiaris metris-optimae, Canis familiaris intermedius, Canis familiaris leineri* and *Canis familiaris inostranzewi.* It is thought that... "From

the *metris-optimae* came the sheep-herding breeds; from the *intermedius*, working and hunting dogs; from *leineri,* hounds and later terriers, and from *inostranzewi,* heavy-jawed fighting dogs and some retrievers." It was from this base that all types of dogs on earth were then developed in many shapes and sizes to either match nature's grand plan or to serve the preferences of mankind.

Around 2000 BC dog drawings were made on the monument of Thothmes III who ruled over Egypt. These drawings resembled Pharaoh Hounds, Salukis, Whippets, Basenjis, and Greyhounds, but there was also a drawing of a female hound that was drawn with very short legs...half the length of the other hounds shown. While she resembled the other hounds pictured in most other

*Egyptian tomb drawings, circa 2000 BC, show the existence of a basset-like creature.*

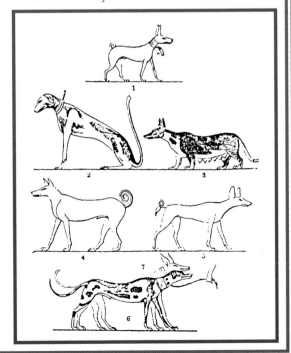

12

respects, she was definitely short legged. If by genetic fault or by man-made design, we can only assume that there must have been a purpose for this size of hound or it might not have been depicted on the monument drawings. The hounds in the drawings seem to be the ancestors of several of today's recognized sight hounds. Considering, however, the common ancestry of all canines, it was left for man to exploit the many differing attributes of the canine species.

With the development of canines there were several ways to go, i.e., giant-sized, midget-sized, regular and smaller canine sizes, as well as the dwarfs. Within the human species, achondroplasia, or dwarfing, occurs about one in every ten thousand. This condition produces smaller size in which the cartilage of the bone ends grows improperly. While the cartilage on the bone ends of normal-sized individuals turns to bone in later life, it turns to bone very early with an achondroplastic dwarf. The results are stunted limbs, curved bones, large joints, stubby paws, and large heads. In the wild, most of these types of individual canines would have died off, however, because of man's intervention we have many dwarfed breeds of which the Basset Hound is one.

Then, as now, hounds whose scenting abilities were particularly strong were used to hunt. Around 500 BC the mastiff type of heavier hounds were being bred with the hounds that made particular use of their scenting ability. Around 125 AD an ancient writer, Arrian, described dogs sent out by the Roman procurator Cynnegi as Segusian hounds. These smaller hounds were named after a Celtic tribe on the western banks of the Rhone district in western France. They resembled the modern description of the Basset Griffon varieties.

Later, around 200 AD, another writer, Oppian, tells of a variety of dog that was also sent out from the Rhone region of France; Agasaeus dogs. Even later, Spartan Hounds are described in the writings of Darcius as long, low scenting hounds with smooth coats. It must be remembered that

"low" was anything less than about 28 inches at the withers!

Circa 700 AD, the monks of the Abbey of St. Hubert at Mouson (in the Ardennes area of France) succeeded in creating the St. Hubert Hounds. These were a strain of hounds of which there were at least two varieties. The strain was most likely developed under the supervision of Hubert (656–727 AD), the son of Duc de Guiene. Hubert was, as legend goes, converted to a life of service to God when he saw a stag with a cross between its horns during a hunt on a Sunday. While devoting his life to God, he still was able to continue his breeding pursuits. The St. Hubert Hounds are thought to be the forerunners of all modern scenting hound breeds. St. Hubert was one of the first breeders to keep records. He would take his pack on visits with him to other monasteries and they were all very welcomed guests. It usually meant that the monastery would have meat on the table that night! St. Hubert is the patron saint of hunters.

It is generally accepted that the black, dark brown, and black-and-tans were the larger of the main two types of St. Hubert Hounds, while the white and multi-colored hounds were approximately 28 inches high. These mostly white hounds later became known as the Talbot Hound. It was a possible English misnomer for "Taillebois," who was abbot of St. Hubert's monastery after 727 AD. In England, they were also sometimes referred to as the Southern Hound. The hounds of St. Hubert had a great and famous supporter in the early part of the eighth century, the Bishop of Liege. It is said that "He had a passion for a good hound and for hunting on a hot trail."

French author Jacques Du Fouilloux in his work called *La Venerie* (*The Art of Hunting*) published in 1561, fully described bassets. It is the first time the word "basset" appears in a hound classification. In France and Belgium, "Bas" means low; therefore, "bas-set" means low-set. Some interpret it as "dwarfed." They are then classified by coat varieties, i.e., smooth-coated, rough-coated, and the half rough, half smooth. They are further divided by the degree of crook in the forelegs. The divisions are: the *Basset a jambes droites* or straight-legged basset; the *Basset a jambes tores* or full-crooked basset; and the *Basset a jambes demi-torses* or half-crooked basset. Another author during 1576, George Turbeville, in his *Art of Venerie* said that "...the St. Huberts are mighty of body, legs low and short, not swift, but very good on scent..." and that "...they come in all colours."

In England around 1591, Sir Thomas Cockaine recommended that a breed known as the Southern Hound from Southern France be bred to the Kibble Hound of the crook-legged basset type. These were to be used as Lymehounds. Lymehounds were used to harbor the stag or boar intended as the quarry on the morning before the hunt. They were worked on a long leash connected to a type of harness about them. Another spelling is that of "Limier" hound, possibly speaking of the Southern Hound, or more particularly of the Spartan hound, earlier described by Darcius in 200 AD. William Shakespeare wrote in *A Midsummer-Night's Dream*:
*"My hounds are bred of the Spartan kind,*
*So flew'd, so sanded and their heads are hung.*
*With ears that sweep away the morning dew;*
*Crooked-knee'd, and dew lapped, like Thessalian bulls;*
*Slow in pursuit, but match'd in mouth like bells*
*Each under each. A cry more tuneable*
*Was never holla'd to nor cheer'd with horn."*
In Mr. T. B. Johnson's *Hunting Directory*, this is said of the origin of English breeds of hounds:
*"All the ramifications of the hound which we at present possess sprung from one and the same-source, namely the Talbot, or Old English Bloodhound. These dogs are noticed by our immortal bard, who represents them as "crook-knee'd" and "dewlapped, like Thessalian bulls."*

In a French-English dictionary published in 1632, the St. Hubert Hound is described as: "Chein de St. Hubert, a kind of strong

short-legged hound, and deep-mouthed." So what we have by now is a hound described as the St. Hubert Hound, the Spartan Hound, the Southern Hound, and by some as the Talbot Hound. All of these hounds are supposed to be "short-legged and deep-mouthed." Remembering that short-legged did not mean the same as it does today, we can begin to understand that the basset-sized hounds (in France, any hound shorter than 16 inches) and the Basset Hound are not one in the same. However, during the 16th through 18th centuries, hounds were not selectively bred down to the size of the Basset Hound known to us today. The Talbot or Southern Hound could have been used to introduce the dwarf size or, through the breeding of unintentional mutations, many hound breeds could have developed their own basset-sized varieties. In fact, in France, several large hunting hound breeds developed their own basset-sized counterparts: Artesien, Normand, Bleu de Gascogne, and the Griffon breeds are but a few.

By 1785 we have written record of General George Washington having received basset-sized hounds from his friend in France, the Marquis de la Fayette. George Washington's diary records that the Basset Hounds were sent to him by his friend from France shortly after the Revolutionary War. More than likely, this accounts for the common tale of the "Old Virginian Bench-Legged Beagle" since bassets could have been crossed with the then-popular Beagle.

## CONTINUING DEVELOPMENT OF THE BREED

The stage is now set for the main developmental changes that gave us the breed that we today know as the Basset Hound. While this breed developed with the aid of the American side of the ocean, it is sad to say that no hounds from the kennels of soon-to-be President George Washington had any impact on the breed.

In France, hounds were divided into three major classifications:
1. Large-sized hounds of over 23 inches or *Chiens d'orde.*

2. Medium-sized hounds between 16–22 inches or *Chiens briquets.*

3. Low-set hounds under 16 inches or *Chiens bassets.*

During the 19th century in France there were several basset-sized hounds or *Chiens bassets.* These were the Basset d'Artois from the Artois region, Basset de Normandie from the region of Normandy, Basset d'Ardenais or Basset St. Hubert au Ardenais. The Gascogne region produced the Basset Bleu de Gascogne and there were also the Basset Griffon Vendéen, Basset Fauve de Bretagne, and the Basset de Saintonge.

It was in 1863 when the first basset-sized hound was shown at the first dog show ever held in Paris. There were classifications for bassets that were divided by straight-legged short-haired, straight-legged long-haired, crooked-legged short-haired, crooked-legged long-haired, as well as Baden Bassets, Burgos, St. Domingos, Illyrian, and Hungarian Bassets. It is assumed that some hounds must have been from either of the Couteulx or the Lane strain of bassets. Both strains refer to their breeders' names: Comte le Couteulx de Canteleu of Etrepagny and Monsieur Louis Lane of Francquevilli, near Boos. Each of these breeders was reported to have "scientifically" bred Artois and Normand basset-sized hounds.

As is evident, there were many, many basset varieties, depending on which region of Europe you were in. Even Scandinavia had Stovers and Drevers and in Switzerland there were the Neiderlaufhunden. While the intense breeding of the types of hounds that eventually formed the foundations for the Basset Hound breed begets appreciation directed toward the original French breeders, there were certainly lots of other short crooked-legged hounds and other dwarfed canines in the world at the time.

These facts also seem to disprove the terrible medieval Forest Laws, an oft-mentioned version of history addressing why the basset-sized hounds came about. Forest Laws present a cruel practice of brutally and systematically mutilating hounds to keep them from being used in hunting, a sport of the nobility and not for the commoners. The commoners, therefore, had to set about breeding a deformed hound in order to have a hound that could still hunt smaller game and not the larger quarry of the Royals. Frankly, this sounds ridiculous and is likely an old folk tale invented to explain why these smaller hounds were used in the forests.

It is interesting to note that most scholars give the St. Hubert Hounds direct credit for the development of the Basset Hound and Bloodhound breeds. According to the evidence presented by Sir John Buchanan-Jardine in his book *Hounds of the World,* it was the combination of the Normand Hound and the St. Hubert Hound that provided the Old English Bloodhound (Talbot) with its size, loose skin or wrinkles, and its varying colors. None of these traits was typical of the descriptions of the original St. Huberts of the Abbey hounds. True enough, the St. Hubert Hound came prior to the Normand Hound but it was the "Normandized" St. Hubert Hound that reached English shores to become the Old English Bloodhound, while in France the Normand Hound went on to develop its basset counterpart.

## CONTINUED FRENCH AND ENGLISH INFLUENCE

Most historical accounts of Basset Hounds make mention of Monsieur Lane at the same time as Comte le Couteulx, but then go on to emphasize the Couteulx strain. Another breeder, by the name of Monsieur Mason, also bred the Couteulx strain, but with different results. Those hounds also went on to be exported to England where they became known as the "Termino" type, whereas the Comte's hounds became known as the "Fino de Paris" type, referring to the respective names of their famous stud hounds. Therefore, even the original Couteulx strain was sub-divided into two different styles.

Monsieur Lane's hounds, however, held truer to the old Normand Hound type and, consequently, closer to the look of today's heavier Basset Hound. They did, however, have somewhat larger heads and loaded shoulders, not too different from some Bassets today! The hounds bred by Mons. Lane were large, short-legged, heavily boned animals with classic Normand Hound heads (although somewhat wide) adorned with deep muzzles and flews. The Couteulx hounds, on the other hand, when originally imported, usually had better domes and longer noses, highset but long ears and were relatively slighter in build. It must be noted that the probable first use of the term describing bassets as "large hounds on short legs" was by the French writer De la Blanchere in his description of the hounds bred by Comte Couteulx.

One of the earliest French authorities, Jacques Du Fouilloux, in his book *La Venerie*, gives two pictorial examples of the bassets he called "bassets d'Artois." It's amusing to note that while Du Fouilloux claims these illustrations to be the "basset d'Artois," Dachshund fanciers claim them as ancestors of their breed. It is currently accepted that the Dachshund breeds have some relation to the ancient basset-sized hounds. The basset-sized hounds that were to eventually become the Dachshund breed were to be mixed with some terrier breeds to give them that individual courage that seems to be lacking in most Bassets. Today's Basset Hounds are not particularly brave! Du Fouilloux describes the "basset d'Artois" as "full-crooked legs, smooth coats, brave, and having double rows of teeth like wolves." This reference to double rows of teeth is very interesting as these had been seen popping up in some modern European Basset Hound breeding during the 1980s.

Sir Everett Millais, of the South Kensington area of London, who thought that he had actually imported the first Basset into England in 1874, is quoted as saying, "As in Germany anything with crooked legs is called a Dachshund, so in France for the same reason 'the anything' is called Chien Basset, for the simple reason that the people do not know better. In England it is the same; the Terrier is good enough for the whole race, whether pure or mongrel."

To ask a French sportsman for a "basset" would be as much as asking for a horse without specifying whether one wanted a cart-horse, a racehorse or a pony! Since the phrase "dwarf dog" was taken to mean basset, it was liberally applied to any hound with short crooked legs. The ancestors of the German Dachshund are known as the Basset Allemand (referring to the region of origin). This only offers more to the confusion of the true lineage of the Basset Hound. To quote an Anglicized Frenchman and sports writer, as well as Basset Hound owner Mr. Lewis Clements, who wrote under the pen name of "Wildflower": "Any hound which stands lower than 16 inches (no matter his 'provincial breed') is called in France and in Belgium a Basset."

In 1866, the first pair of basset-sized hounds was sent to Lord Galway in England by his friend, Comte de Tournon in France. Lord Galway called them "Basset" and "Belle." The first litter of basset-sized hounds bred in England was whelped in 1867 from the mating of "Basset" and "Belle." The sire, dam, and the entire litter were sold by Galway in 1872 to Lord Onslow. In a letter to Major Godfrey Heseltine, Lord Galway gave the following description of the events:

*"In July 1866, I was staying at Royat, Pay de Dome, France, where I met the Marquis de Tournon and his son the Comte de Tournon. The latter promised me a couple of Basset Hounds from his pack, which duly arrived later in the autumn at Serlby. They were a dog and a bitch, and I called them 'Basset' and 'Belle.' They were long, low hounds, shaped much like a Dachshund with crooked forelegs at the knees with much more bone and larger heads than our Beagles. They were not the dark tan colour of the Dachshund but the colour of Fox-hounds with a certain amount of white about them. They had deep, heavy bones, more like Foxhounds than Beagles. I mated these two in 1867, and had a litter of five, all of which survive. I remember I called one 'Bellman.' I sold these three and a half couples to the late Lord Onslow in, I think, 1872, but I am not quite sure of the date."*

It was three years later, however, that the English would see their first basset-type hounds in a dog show. The hound was "Model," owned by Sir Everett Millais. He had bought the hound while at the Paris dog show, The Jardin d'Acclimation in 1874. Model's first English showing was in a variety class at the Wolverhampton dog show in 1875.

Millais was not yet titled when he decided to do an experimental breeding of Model to a Beagle bitch. This breeding was justified as there were not enough bassets in the country to breed. Later, after other imports entered the country, Millais gave up the idea of Beagle ex Basset breeding.

sets. Later, Flo, Dina, and the second-generation whelps, sired by Model out of Flo, all died from an outbreak of distemper. There was time, however, to have shown one of the second-generation puppies and it was also said to have been indistinguishable from a purebred basset.

About this same time, Lord Onslow imported three hounds from the Comte de Couteulx strain of hounds in France. They were named "Fino," "Nester," and "Finette." Within a year, Lord Onslow and Millais bred Finette to Model. Two puppies were whelped": "Proctor," a large lemon and white male (first of this color in England) and a small tri-colored bitch named "Gareene."

*Mr. E. Millais's French Basset "Model" (K.C.S.B. 7854), from a heretofore unknown etching. Donated by Mr. Len Abraham.*

Another reason stated by Millais was: "I was young then, little more than a boy, and it never occurred to me then as it would now, that it would be better to try and import a bitch of the breed from France than try to breed one myself from another species. I have, however, always had the knack of making something do, if the right thing is not at hand, and I do not think I should be wrong in saying that I succeeded." At any rate, the results of that mating were two crossbred bitches named "Flo" and "Dina." Dina was bred back to her sire Model. One of the pups was shown and it was said to be not distinguishable from purebred bas-

Most of these hounds, and the many that followed, carried the characteristics of the original hounds: shorter ear leather, high rears, and downhill top lines.

In 1880, the "Basset Hound" was officially recognized by the Kennel Club in England. (The English were not to know that the use of the term "Basset Hound" as a distinct breed reference was still a bit premature.) The first separate classes for "Basset Hounds" were offered at the Wolverhampton Show in the same year.

About the same time, a Mr. George Krehl, who worked closely with Mr. Lewis Clements, imported "Fino de Paris." This hound became the pillar of the breed in British Basset Hound history. He was one of Comte de Couteulx's bassets from France. A couple of years later, Lord Onslow sold his pack of 15 hounds to Sir Everett Millais and George Krehl. During the ten years between 1872 and 1882, the pack was strengthened by more direct imports from the kennels of the Comte de Couteulx.

In France it was the Lane hounds that continued in greater demand. It was believed that they had purer blood than the Couteulx strain within which it was suspected that Beagle crosses were used. The Lane hounds, however, did not have the head preferred by most basset breeders. The Lane heads were heavier and more apple-headed. They also had big prominent eyes and were inclined to cheek bumps. The Couteulx strain hound had a down-faced look, a deeply sunken darker eye with a prominent haw, all of which contributed to a sad expression. The heads were longer, domed and narrower than the Lane hounds. In England, where the Beagle crossbred idea was not a new one, the Lane hounds were not bred true. Perhaps because of what they envisioned as the heavier bone structure being a hindrance to the hound's hunting abilities and, of course, to clean up the look of the heavier head.

In 1884 the American Kennel Club was formed, although the first real dog show had been held ten years prior in 1874 near Mineola, New York. The Basset Hound Club of Great Britain was also formed in 1884. Aware of the importance of Royal sponsorship for the club, Mr. George Krehl presented H.R.H. the Prince of Wales a gift of some basset puppies. The puppies were sired by "Ch. Jupiter," a hound bred by Comte le Couteulx. In France, the same hound went under the name of "Ch. Bosquet." He was a tri-colored hound, born in 1878. In his book *This is the Basset Hound,* Ernest Hart reports the following: "Intrigued by the 'quaintness' of the puppies, His Royal Highness expressed his delight in the new additions to his kennels by presenting Mr. Krehl with a scarf pin in the design of the Prince's Plumes."

Another Englishman, Lord Aylesford, owned a ranch near Big Spring, Texas. He took a brace of bassets to his ranch to use as rabbit hounds. They too were sired by Mr. Krehl's Ch. Jupiter. In 1883, a Mr. Chamberlain bought a basset hound named "Nemours" from Mr. Krehl and took him to the Maizeland kennels of Mr. Lawrence Timson, located in Red Bank, New Jersey. Nemours was shown at the Westminster Kennel Club show and was the first "basset hound" to be shown in an American dog show ring and he became a champion. Sired by Ch. Jupiter and out of "Vivian," Nemours was whelped March 21, 1883 by breeder Mr. Krehl and sold to Maizeland kennels. While Nemours was the first basset to be shown in the US, the first American Kennel Club registered basset hound was "Bouncer," owned by Collin Cameron of Bickerville, Pennsylvania. He was bred by Mr. Pottinger Dorsey of New Market, Virginia and whelped in March 1881. His registration number was #3234. At just about the same time, Monsieur Lane bred bitches, "Blanchette" and "Oriflamme," which were imported into England to help

*Drawing of Mr. George Krehl's "Fino de Paris."*

strengthen the intensely inbred stock there, most of which was of the Couteulx strain from France.

Mrs. K. Ellis of Brettenham Park, Billesden, England purchased her first basset bitch called "Venus II" around 1886. Mrs. Ellis would emerge as one of the leading breeders in England. From a breeding of Mr. Muirland's "Ch. Forester" to "Ch. Psyche II," a daughter of her "Venus II" bitch, Mrs. Ellis produced "Ch. Bowman," "Ch. Paris," "Ch. Xena," "Napoleon II," and "Miriam." Four years later, in 1890, Major Godfrey Heseltine and Lt. Col. Christopher Heseltine formed the famous "Walhampton Pack," the first organized basset pack in England. In the US, Charles Porter started his Upland kennels by obtaining and showing a bitch called "Babette," sired by "Merlin," and Cornelius Stevenson was showing "Chasseur," sired by "Farmer," in New York.

On the other side of the world, J. C. Anderson and J. McLoughlin had been influenced by Sir Everett Millais, who had lived in Australia for a few years, and they imported several British basset-sized hounds. Sir Everett was able to engineer the importation of "Diana II" ("Fino VI" ex "Venus II"), "Amazon" ("Comus" ex "Busybody"), "Jessay" ("Justine" ex "Jocely"), and "Chloe II" and her daughter "Viva," both by "Bourbon." Later came "Wanda" and "Levity." These bitches, as well as the dogs "Ch. Merlin" and "Chilworth" formed the core of the new Basset Hound pack for the Melbourne Hunt Club.

Around 1892, Mrs. Mabel Tottie of Coniston Hall in the Yorkshire area of England became interested in bassets in an active way. She owned and showed the dog "Ch. Louis le Beau" ("Ch. Paris" ex "Ch. Gravity"). He earned 18 CC's (Challenge Certificates) during his show career. Also interested in the "rough-coats" (Basset Griffon Vendéen), Mrs. Tottie purchased "Ch. Tambour" and "Ch. Pervenche," which she saw at the 1892 Crufts dog show. From this pair she produced Ch. Puritian" and Ch. "Priscilla," whelped February 6, 1897. A few breeders, Mrs. Tottie in particular, experimented with crossbreeding of the "rough-coats" with the "smooths," but this concept was short-lived. Some crossbreds (Basset Griffon Vendéen x Basset Hounds) were used by the Walhampton Pack, but since they had a completely different manner of hunting, more like terriers, they had to be drafted out or they would spoil the pack.

Not satisfied, Mrs. Tottie experimented again. This time she bred one of Capt. Owen Swaffield's bitches, "Bella," a crossbred Basset ex Bloodhound offspring, to Mrs. Ellis's "Napoleon II" and produced "Belladona." This bitch was later owned by the Walhampton Pack, which also used Millais's "Cromwell" and "Ada" (both Basset ex Bloodhound). In 1895, Cromwell produced a dog hound named "Walhampton Jollyboy," while Ada was bred to "Capt. Evan's Music" to produce "Walhampton Merryman" and "Walhampton Maisie" in 1897. Pack histories are difficult to follow

## PEDIGREE OF BASSET/BLOODHOUND CROSS "ADA" (ALSO "RICKEY" AND "CROMWELL")

Ch. Forester (Basset Hound)

Nicholas (Basset Hound)

Ch. Psyche II (Basset Hound)

Ada (cross-bred)

Chorister (Bloodhound)

Inoculation (Bloodhound and littersister to Protection)

Artemis (Bloodhound)

because of their continued use of the same names for different hounds. These hounds are differentiated by the use of a number signifying the year when the hound was "entered" into the pack; i.e., "Walhampton Maisie '99" and "Walhampton Maisie '09."

Sir Everett Millais was of the opinion that the breed had succumbed to the problems of inbreeding so much that it could not be revived by French imports. Therefore, he also decided to crossbreed to the Bloodhound breed. He reasoned that the Basset Hound head should resemble that of a Bloodhound and since previous experimental breeding with the Beagle proved that he could accomplish the size downgrade, there was only color to be concerned about. The first cross was between the basset "Nicholas," a son of Ch. Forester and Ch. Psyche II, to the Bloodhound bitch "Inoculation" ("Chorister" ex "Artemis"). To help end the controversy over whether or not the Bloodhound bitch was actually named "Inoculation" or whether it was just a word put in old pedigrees to mean that an inoculation (artificial breeding) had occurred can be put to rest with the knowledge that, as George Johnston put it: "She was a littersister of Protection." The next cross was between one of the 12 born in the original cross and was what could be described as a medium-sized hound with Bloodhound color. The union of Ch. Forester and his granddaughter, Rickey, produced seven puppies. One was black and tan and six were tri-colored hounds, all with basset anatomy.

"Dulcie," one of the Ch. Forester ex Rickey crossbred puppies was bred to the Basset Hound Ch. Bowman. A bitch from this union was then bred to the Basset Hound, "Guignol." This litter produced hounds that were indistinguishable from purebred bassets and indeed, were as pure as any "basset hound" could have been. Ch. Bowman was sired by Ch. Forester ex Ch. Psyche II. In later years there would be other breeders who followed the same path. One such kennel was that of Mrs. N. E. Elms, of the famous Reynalton kennels of Bassets, Beagles, and Bloodhounds in the early 1930s.

The two brothers, Major Godfrey Heseltine and Lt. Col. Christopher Heseltine started their Walhampton Basset Hound Pack in England around 1890. For the next 42 years the Walhampton Pack was one of the most successful of the show and hunt packs in England. The brothers and the Walhampton Pack were a steady and important influence on the breed. They kept in close contact with French breeders and in 1920 they made their last French imports, "Meteor" and "Pameute" from Mons. Mallort. These imports helped in the impressive succession of champions from the Walhampton kennels.

In a letter of reply to Major Godfrey Heseltine, Monsieur Leon Verrier of Rouen, France made several comments concerning some photos of basset bitches sent to him by the Major. They are as follows: "that they were too big, the ears too rounded at the tips; i.e., not sufficiently pointed at the tips!" He then adds: "that they have magnificent limbs, perfect stance of legs and feet, and heads typical of the bloodhound." Of course, the British had already crossbred to the Bloodhound by this time.

Mons. Verrier also added that they (in France) have found it difficult to produce the type that the British were successful in producing and mentioned the fact that the British hounds seemed to revert back to their long-legged ancestors *les chiens de chasse* by having long-legged puppies. How little did he know of just how recently those longer British basset legs got there or that they were directly from the Bloodhound. It must be remembered that the French had taken larger hounds and continued to develop their basset-sized counterparts rather than bringing in other breeds. Mons. Verrier was successful in combining the two basset strains of Mons. Couteulx and Lane. From this combination, and his own particular refinements, the Basset Artesian-Normand was developed. These hounds did not carry the well-known features of the heavy bone and heavily wrinkled skin, however, the Basset Artesian-Normand would later be used in the development of today's Basset Hound breed.

# Early History in America

In America, the brothers Carl E. and George Smith of Xenia and Spring Valley, Ohio, respectively, acquired their first bassets around 1908. The hounds were "Old Deck" and "Dolly M." From these hounds of so-called Russian ancestry, they bred "Smiths's Major D." In order not to inbreed they crossbred "Old Major" to a Beagle bitch and produced their hunting basset-type hounds which were much lighter in bone, predominately dark red in color and strong, aggressive hunters. Years later the Smith brothers would obtain English and French hounds to breed to Old Major's descendants.

According to Mr. Carl Smith in his book *Training the Rabbit Hound,* written in 1926, a few imports from Russia, around 1899, brought to America a high-quality and "hardy" type of basset. He believed that these basset-sized hounds had originally made their way from France to Russia, and there were bred as hunting hounds, before the "overthrow of the old social order." Mr. Smith did not give the following account, which instead was passed on by an American in an article written for the English magazine *Dog World*, but nonetheless it has endured:

*"Apparently, one of the first of these hounds to America was imported by a relative of Carl Smith who visited a Grand Duke of Russia (while in America) and purchased a bitch in whelp. The bitch was of Russian descent and was imported prior to the first world war. The bitch whelped satisfactorily in a New York apartment, but there were no records as to where the pups went apart from the few which were taken by Mr. Smith's relatives."*

While not trying to imply that these are not the true facts, it does seem strange that so colorful a tale should not have been included in Mr. Smith's own book.

In describing these Russian hounds, Mr. Smith says:

*"In appearance, the Russians were much like the present English type with the half crooked legs, except that in coloring and marking the dark blanket seemed to predominate, rather than so much white as with the present English-French."*

In America today, we now refer to what Mr. Smith called dark blanket as the solid red color (the color classification as the Dachshund breeds use). Considering its northern route, the basset that came from Russia might have picked up its reddish colored dark blanket from its distant Dachshund cousins in Germany, namely the Basset Allemande.

The Smith brothers also used imports from the Walhampton Pack and from other sources, such as "Baillet's Trompete II" and "Fr. Ch. Baillet's Corvette" from France. Many other imports were brought over to the US, some registered with the AKC and some with the UKC. To most Basset Hound lovers, the basset to beagle crosses done by the early English breeders, such as Sir Everett Millais, are the only ones to be concerned with. But to those of today who are aware of Carl Smith's influence on bassets, there are more modern reminders. Mr. Smith took his "Russian" ancestry bassets and bred them to what he referred to as "Real English Beagles" or "Old English Beagles." It is possible that Mr. Smith might have confused these Russian ancestry hounds, of which he and his brother had acquired two, with what was becoming known as the Basset Hound breed. There is no recorded history on the hounds named "Old Deck" and "Dolly M." They just appeared on the scene in American pedigrees with the explanation given by Mr. Smith that they were of Russian basset ancestry.

## PEDIGREE OF SMITH'S BROWNIE S

Sailor Boy (Beagle)

Scott's Jack (Beagle)

Gipsey Queen (Beagle)

Smith's Brownie S (crossbred)

Smith's Major D (Russian Basset)

Smith's Spotty N (crossbred)

Nellie (Beagle)

*Smith's Brownie S.*

To further complicate things, the Smith brothers bred the "Smith's Major D" to some of the Beagles to produce the type of hunter they felt they needed. You will recall that "Major" was the result of the "Old Deck" ex "Dolly M" breeding. A favorite bitch pictured in Mr. Smith's book was "Smith's Brownie S."

She was small, sniped nosed, predominately "red" in color and light-boned. "Nellie" was what Smith called an "Old English Beagle" ("Oliver" ex "Beulah Girl"). "Brownie S" is the great granddam of the brothers' "Smith's Red Pathfinder" and "Ch. Smith's Red Powder" ("Smith's Red Bear Tongue" ex "Walhampton Passion"). Either of these studs can be found behind almost all lines of today's American Basset Hounds and, through them, many other countries bassets.

In the Smith brothers' later breedings, they bred their hounds to their imported French and English bassets. The Smiths were hunters and bred for utility, what they considered to be the right thing to do at the time. Until they actually acquired French and English basset bloodlines of the day, breeding "Russian" bassets to Beagles seemed sensible. In today's Basset Hound history there are 20th century Beagles, Bloodhounds and, most likely, some rather large 19th century Dachshund-type (Basset Allemande) blood too!

In 1921, Gerald Livingston started the Kilsyth pack in Long Island. It was the first known organized Basset Hound pack in America. Mr. Livingston and Mr. Erastus Tefft (Staridge Pack) drafted heavily from the Walhampton Pack in England and imported from France. Eng/Am. Ch. Walhampton Ferryman was a fifth-generation descendant of Ada, one of the Nicholas ex Inoculation offspring (the original Basset to Bloodhound breeding of Sir Everett Millais). It was Mr. Livingston who first brought the "modern" bassets, both French and English, to America.

It was not until around 1925 that the "Basset Hound" was accepted for registration with the United Kennel Club (Kalamazoo, Michigan). Registrations and interest flourished through the early 1950s. Although there was keen interest in the Basset Hound among those persons whose hounds were UKC-registered, the probable lack of a national breed organization within the perimeters of the UKC took its toll until there were almost no UKC Basset Hounds to be found.

A study of the four-generation pedigree of the hound "Upland Blair's Game Boy," an American hound bred by Samuel Blair and registered by Mrs. A. W. Porter (Upland) and eventually owned by Charles R. Rogers (Timber Ridge Bassets) reads like a "Who's Who" of the Basset Hound world. Included are: Ch. Smith's Red Powder (Carl Smith), Walhampton Passion (George Smith), Eng/Am. Ch. Walhampton Andrew (Gerald

Livingston), Nottke's Venus (Carl Nottke) who was bred from the Dalby Hall pack hounds from England, Al's Chief of Genesco (L. Thompson) bred from Eng. Ch. Amir of Reynalton ex Walhampton Nicety, and Eng. Ch. Lavenham Pippin (Erastus Tefft).

Around 1926 Mr. G. W. King (Maple Drive Bassets) started breeding Basset Hounds in Gobles, Michigan. The hounds he bred were from stock gathered from both Erastus Tefft (Staridge) and Gerald Livingston (Kilsyth). Mr. King owned the dog Staridge Pol, who sired Maple Drive Marlin, who would figure quite significantly in American pedigrees as the sire of Ch. Mon Phillipe of Greenly Hall. Phillipe was out of the bitch hound, Coquette of Greenly Hall, and was bred by Mr. and Mrs. Fogleson.

## CONTINUING ENGLISH INFLUENCE

The most famous breeder of the 1930s involved in crossbreeding the basset was Mrs. Nina Elms (Reynalton kennels), who owned Bloodhounds, Beagles, and Basset Hounds. Mrs. Elms showed and won with all three breeds of hounds. On May 19, 1933, shortly after Maj. Godfrey Heseltine's death, Mrs. Elms acquired several of the Walhampton Pack's best show hounds. They included Ch. Walhampton Lynnewood and Ch. Walhampton Nightshade. Mrs. Elms bred the pair to produce a litter of which four out of five completed their championship titles. Ch. Orpheus of Reynalton was one of this litter, who would later be bred to the Bloodhound bitch Sheba of Reynalton.

The resulting litter from this Basset to Bloodhound mating contained a crossbred bitch named Suzanne of Reynalton. Later, Suzanne was bred to a basset Nightshades's Majesty of Reynalton (Loyal of Reynalton ex Ch. Walhampton Nightshade). This mating produced the crossbred bitch Reynalton Symbol who was subsequently bred to the basset Grims Worship (Westerby Marquis ex Wick Welcome). This resulted in the dog Grims Sermon, sire of Grims Garrulous out of Garble.

Grims Garrulous was registered as a cross-bred Basset Hound by the Kennel Club in England. When she was bred to the Basset Hound Ch. Grims Wideawake, she became the dam of Ch. Grims Gracious, who was owned by Mrs. M. Rawle (Barspark kennels), and found her way into the pedigrees of many British Basset Hounds. Through Mrs. Rawle and the Barnspark prefix, this 20th-century pedigree tie to the Bloodhound has been delivered to many parts of the world. When Gracious was judged by the Earl of Northesk, at the Crufts dog show in 1958, he said of her:

*"A nice-headed bitch with deep-set eyes showing haw; good neckline running into a long well-ribbed body. Very good front; well-placed hocks and good tail carriage. Nice free mover."*

While most of the basset breeds may have had their beginnings in France, the Basset Hound, as it is known and loved all over the world today, is mostly of British and North American influences. There seems to be ample evidence that there were hounds of a "low-set" stature in England many hundreds of years before the first "bassets" were sent to Lord Galway. However, the modern British Basset Hound breed is made up of the influences of the original French Couteulx and Lane strains, Beagle crosses, Bloodhound crosses, and later American Basset Hound imports. It was Miss Peggy Keevil, of the famous Grims Bassets kennel, that virtually saved the breed from extinction in England during World War II. Miss Keevil would travel for miles during all types of weather to find whatever food was available to feed the hounds.

The Grims Bassets kennel was established by Miss Keevil of Inkpen, near Newbury in England, with the purchase of a bitch named Dulcamara of Reynalton in 1935. This bitch was joined shortly by Walhampton Medway (also known as "Merman"), "Marquis" and "Labram" from the Westerby Pack, and "Wick Welcome." The Grims name came from Grim's Ditch, near where Miss Keevil lived in Surrey, where she had already established herself in Scotties around 1931. Miss Keevil's hounds were to go on to influence the Basset Hound breed all over the world.

During those difficult years it was through the work of Miss Keevil, Mrs. Edith Grew with Maybush Basset Hounds, and Mrs. Elm's Reynalton Hounds that the Basset Hound as a breed was in any condition, after the war, to continue its growth and development. Mrs. Keevil imported the Basset Artesian-Normand hounds: Ulema de Barly, Aigion des Marriettes, and Corenemuse de Blendocques. Ulema was a prepotent sire and he had a great influence on bassets the world over. Aigion was the brother of Azur, France's top sire, and he also sired some good hounds. Corenemuse did her share, but the studs would have more opportunity to influence more bassets than she.

The Basset Hound Club of England re-formed in 1954 after having been disbanded in 1921 due mainly to the differences between the hunting and the show enthusiasts. Mrs. Angela Hodson, Rossingham Bassets, is reported to have expended great effort at bringing about the new Basset Hound Club. It was later, with the help of John Evans, that Miss Keevil, who also hunted her Grims hounds, succeeded in getting the Basset Hound Club to form, in 1969, the Basset Hound Club Pack. In 1975 the name was changed to Albany Pack. The name was derived from Albion, which is the Old English word for Britain. The club hopes to ensure the Basset Hound's true hunting instinct and abilities by actively supporting this aspect of the sport. To this day the club pack supporters hold hunt days, run booths at shows, etc. The pack, known as the Working Branch, is still a large part of the Basset Hound Club's agenda throughout the year.

The Rossingham Bassets became a major influence in the world of Basset Hounds through the bitch Ch. Grims Willow. She, in turn, produced hounds that became known to both North American and British pedigrees: Eng. Ch. Rossingham Amber, Badger, Am. Ch. Barrister of the Notrenom Bassets, Blessing, Ind. Ch. Brocade and Cosy.

**Walhampton Granby**

**Walhampton Lightheart**

**Walhampton Liquor**

**Walhampton Medway (Merman'32)**

**Walhampton Lymington**

**Walhampton Meanwell**

**Walhampton Mermaid**

**GRIMS DAISY**

**Walhampton Musket**

**Walhampton Lynnewood**

**Walhampton Lyric**

**Dulcamera of Reynalton**

**Walhampton Grazier**

**Walhampton Nightshade**

**Walhampton Nicknack**

Another of the influential new club members was Mr. George Johnston and his Sykemoor Bassets. He and his son, George Jr., started their kennel with Rossingham Amber and showed her to championship. After his father's death in 1958, George Jr. continued his interest in Basset Hounds, raising many Sykemoor champions and authoring two books, *The Basset Hound* and *The Hounds of France*.

Nothing much has been said, thus far, regarding coats. Since the current American standard lists as one of the three disqualifications for the breed, "A distinctly long coat," perhaps it is well to theorize concerning the reasons for such occurrence. To some degree, there is a suspicion of some spaniel blood, possibly blamed on either accidental or intentional breeding at the Royal kennels at Sandringham, England. This suspicion is recorded both in Basset Hound history and Clumber Spaniel history. The Field Spaniel might have also used the British Basset as a cross to get its long back and/or low stance. There have been cases of soft, long, and silky coats in Basset litters. The coat was one of the reported concerns Miss Keevil had about the breed just after World War II. In 1969 a litter was whelped by Mrs. Margot MacDougall in Australia, and she reported that four out of six turned up with long hair.

Randy and Penny Frederiksen, while on a trip to Japan in 1984, report having observed the same problem of coat on a purebred Basset Hound of British Basset lines. They also report that while living in England during 1990, they observed a few Basset Hounds with distinctly long, silky coat hairs.

There is even more confusion generated when the term "rough coat" is used in describing Basset Hounds. Let us now put aside the notion that there were ever two official coat types for the Basset Hound. The early English writers were mistaken about the Basset " with the coat like the Otterhound." Mr. J. C. Macdona, in 1875, was the first to show a "Basset Griffon Vendéen" and since it was called a "basset" by the French, it was considered to be of the same "breed" as the other bassets newly arrived in England. As mentioned previously, in the 1890s Mrs. Mable Tottie is reported to have tried crosses between the "rough-coated" bassets, but with no great results. The fact that, after World War I, there were no longer any Basset Griffon Vendéen being shown in England only added to the myth of the "rough-coated" Basset Hound. By breeding closely into certain Basset Hound strains, hounds can be produced with distinctly long-haired coats. They are neither of the Griffon type nor of the spaniel type, just longer than desired.

*Grims Daisy.*

Possibly they are a throwback to the original large French hound breeds. During an interview with Mr. Frederiksen, Mr. Leslie Kelly (Belbay Bassets) made mention of a hound that he lovingly nicknamed "Elvis" who had such a coat. Some of the coarse hairs on the underside of the tails on these hounds were up to six or more inches long. It was Kelly's contention that these longer-haired hounds came from breedings done at the Dalby Hall Basset Pack in England, but very near the Scottish border. These hounds, Kelly says, were rugged and a bit rougher in coat and physique. Hounds from the Dalby Hall kennels figured predominately in early Staridge, Maple Drive, and Nottke Basset pedigrees. These hounds were extremely good hunters as testifed to by his interviews with both Kelly and Mrs. Elizabeth Streeter (Skycastle), who started pack hunting with AKC Basset Hounds. She remembered that breeders would ask her if she would like to have their "long-haired" hounds since they did not meet the show standard. Mrs. Streeter described these hounds by saying, "They were great hunters!" She preferred these hounds and wanted a whole pack of long hairs, however, they would not breed true. Later, Mrs. Streeter changed her Skycastle French Hounds pack by being the first to import the Petit Basset Griffon Vendeen into America. While they hunted more like Beagles or Terriers, they were enjoyable to both Mrs. Streeter and the pack's supporters. It was sad to see Mrs. Streeter pass away just as her beloved Petit Basset Griffon Vendéen was becoming popular in the US.

In summary, the Basset Hound's line of descent can be traced in a general sense by starting with the Saint Hubert Hounds in France around 700 AD to the large French hounds developed by the 15th century (Griffon Vendéen, Artois Hound, Normand Hound, Bleu de Gascogne, Fauve de Bretange). From there, and by the end of the 16th century, the basset-sized counterparts to the large hounds had been formed. Those were Basset Griffon Vendéen and Petit Basset Griffon Vendéen, Basset Artois, Basset Normand, Basset Bleu de Gascogne, and Basset Fauve de Bretange. By the 19th century, the Basset Artois together with Basset Normands had been used to develop the two dominant French basset kennel strains of Mons. Lane and the Comte le Couteulx.

These two major French basset strains formed the basis for the modern Basset Hound that was to be further developed by English and North American breeders. Beagles were crossbred to the Couteulx strain first and then the Lane basset strain was put into the mix because the exiting English lines were too inbred and needed an outcross. Even that was not to provide enough help as the English later decided to breed the Bloodhound into the basset lineage. With a possible interlude within a spaniel breed to help in the development of the Clumber Spaniel, the Basset Hound's next link would come from the introduction of the "Russian" basset-sized hound previously mixed to the Beagle breed.

The Basset Artesien-Normand hound (developed in its own right by breeders in France through combinations of the Couteulx and Lane basset strains) was to influence the still forming Basset Hound in England as well as in America. In England, the Bloodhound was again put to the Basset Hound and also would later need help from the Basset Artesien-Normand breed. The modern Basset Hound had been fully developed as a breed by the 1950s, since which time there hopefully have been no other outside influences on the breed's development.

The modern Basset Hound breed in America is a mixture of the early French and British breeding, including those of the Beagle/Basset crosses and the Bloodhound/Basset crosses, the "Russian" basset ancestry (through the Beagle crosses), and later imports of the Basset Artesien-Normand. There is a lack of documented proof concerning any Bloodhound crosses in America, but it is highly suspect. However, after the imports made during the past 44 years of American Basset Hound strains into England and Europe, and vice-versa, they each now have the same recessive traits in their gene pools.

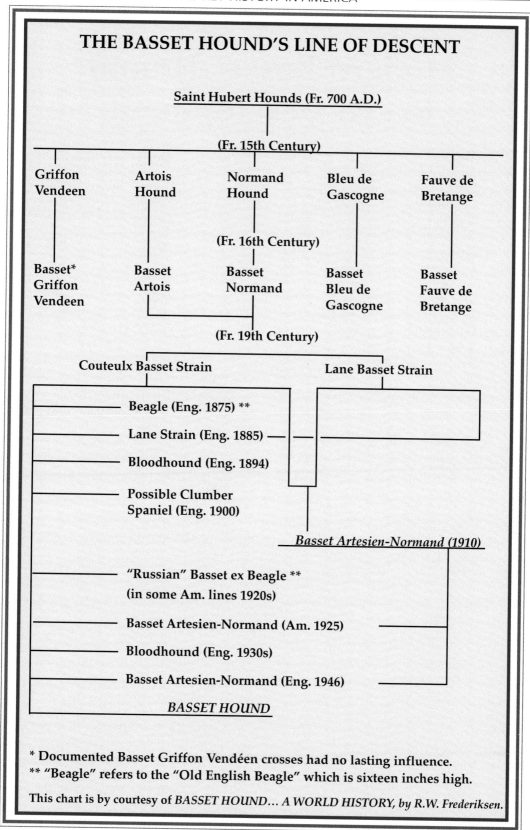

# THE BASSET HOUND'S LINE OF DESCENT

**Saint Hubert Hounds (Fr. 700 A.D.)**

**(Fr. 15th Century)**

| Griffon Vendeen | Artois Hound | Normand Hound | Bleu de Gascogne | Fauve de Bretange |

**(Fr. 16th Century)**

| Basset* Griffon Vendeen | Basset Artois | Basset Normand | Basset Bleu de Gascogne | Basset Fauve de Bretange |

**(Fr. 19th Century)**

**Couteulx Basset Strain**          **Lane Basset Strain**

Beagle (Eng. 1875) **

Lane Strain (Eng. 1885)

Bloodhound (Eng. 1894)

Possible Clumber Spaniel (Eng. 1900)

*Basset Artesien-Normand (1910)*

"Russian" Basset ex Beagle ** (in some Am. lines 1920s)

Basset Artesien-Normand (Am. 1925)

Bloodhound (Eng. 1930s)

Basset Artesien-Normand (Eng. 1946)

*BASSET HOUND*

\* Documented Basset Griffon Vendéen crosses had no lasting influence.
\*\* "Beagle" refers to the "Old English Beagle" which is sixteen inches high.

This chart is by courtesy of *BASSET HOUND... A WORLD HISTORY, by R.W. Frederiksen.*

# Modern Basset Hound Breed Development

Unfortunately, it seems that those initially searching for a Basset Hound as a family pet often perceive it as a rather small character suitable to lie around in front of a fireplace, or to clown around for cute photographs in the most ridiculous of settings. Uneducated in the breed, they become easy prey for the local "backyard breeder" who also has little, if any, knowledge of the breed. The modern Basset Hound, to the breed's enthusiasts, however, is known as a rather large, majestic dog on short legs with a slight crook in the front legs to support the hound's massive chest and a strong, well muscled rear end, ensuring drive. It exhibits a specific type (referring to length of ear, loose skin, heavy bone and a sad, soulful expression, etc.) that distinguishes it from any other hound. There is a definite difference from the 35- to 45-pound hounds that were developed with the Beagle crosses. Unfortunately, some of that undesirable type is still seen today due to the unscrupulous breedings practiced by those exploiting many breeds for the almighty dollar!

Though the original French hound ancestors were large, they were not so large as to be in the 80- to 90-pound range as seen in some kennels around the world today. Those who really know the breed respect it as a formidable hunter as well as a great companion. In the early history of the different basset-sized breeds, the sportsmen of the time knew of the basset's all-around usefulness. Originally for the driving of deer, boar, and roebuck, the Basset Hound soon became known as a good hound to have when shooting after small game such as hare, pheasants and rabbits. When used in small packs for the individual hunter, they are marvelous to see and hear. Hounds with melodic voices is how they are described by those who have known them as hunters, but those who only know the breed as a companion or show hound will attest: Basset Hounds have deep voices that, when made use of, seem to come from a deep, hollow cavity and, in groups, are known to make a room vibrate with their neighbor-loving music!

The increasing popularity of the Basset Hound in the 1950s was to be accompanied by its own problems: exaggerations of type, unsoundness of front and rear assemblies, as well as shyness, to name but a few. Some of these problems were a result of enthusiasts not realizing that a scanty glance of a few pages on Mendel's theories did not make them "qualified" breeders. The complications in breeding the Basset Hound are broad, to say the least.....the hound is a man-made dwarf, plain and simple! We see this creature of man's own selective breeding as a beautiful work of living art while Mother Nature sees the Basset Hound as a combination of very complicated genes with some disastrous consequences!

The new Basset Hound enthusiasts that came on the scene in this time period were more interested in pet life and the show rings than hunting and field trials. It is not essentially different today, some 40 years later, although a handful of very dedicated field-trial devotees have kept that discipline alive and well in the Basset Hound Club of America. BHCA is, at present, the only parent breed club that hosts all of the disciplines at their annual National Specialty. At any rate, on both sides of the Atlantic, the great hunting packs dropped out of sight, and the show dog became the beginning and end for most of the world's Basset Hound enthusiasts.

Within the Basset Hound breed there are, and have been, numerous kennels who have been able to, favorably or unfavorably, influence the breed's destiny by the strength of their qualities or inherited problems. As these dogs are shown and used for breeding, their influences on the breed, as a whole, can be seen throughout any country. In the US, England, and Canada during the 1950s, most Basset Hounds fell into only a few particularly known kennel "strains." All had Basset Hound type, however, certain kennels sported a distinct look that immediately gave the "breed-educated" spectator a clue as to the general parentage of the hound. Some of these "looks" or "styles" came from strong early kennel strains such as Belbay, Grims, Lyn Mar Acres, Rossingham, Sykemoor, Notrenom, and Santana-Mandeville. It is important to note that the terms "look," "style" and "strain" are being used all within the context of Basset Hound type. A kennel "strain" references a certain line of animals possessing common attributes and/or an identifiable look that stands them apart from the rest. This is what most people hope that they are saying when they use the words "my line." While the terms can be confusing, it must be said that others may have the same "style" of hounds as your kennel but yet not be from the same "strain," or, have not yet come so far as to claim their own. A modern example of this is the Stoneybluff Bassets "strain" of hounds which would be classified as in the Lyn Mar Acres "style" of Basset Hound. Certain prepotent studs have, in fact, developed styles by being so strong as to cross more than successfully with other kennels' hounds and thereby over-shadowing the kennel's particular look or style. Not wanting to give all of the credit to certain studs, there are many kennels whose particular looks came directly from their bitches rather than the studs they used. Craigwood

comes immediately to mind when considering the strength of a kennel's bitches. Other major kennels of the '50s time period were Hess', Belleau, Millvan, Le Chenil, Look's, Lime Tree, En-Hu, Hubertus, Norman's, Siefenjagenheim, Blue Hill, Hartshead, Nancy Evan's, Sherlitt's, Braun, Long View Acres, The Ring's, Barnspark, and Double B's.

In the 1960s, more kennels added their names to the list of "strains": Kazoo, Houndsville, Wingjay's, Het's, Manor Hill, Crutchfield, Topohil, Nancy Evans, Westacre, Jagersven, Ren-Lo, Northwoods, Musicland, Slippery Hill, Hardacre, Oranpark, Rollinhills, Verwood, Fredwell, Richardson's, Margem Hills, Abbot Run Valley, Tason, Supai, Hiflite, Reepa, Talleyrand, Galway, Chevalier, Mel-Ann Acres, Akerwood, Courtside, Bar-Wick, Solitude Creek, Clowverleaf, Ballymaconnel, Windamohr, Coralwood, Bridi, Glenhaven, Fochno, Cotton Hill, Sand-Dell, Forestbay, Eleandon, Le Clair, Sykemoor, Merribea, and Chantinghall.

The Abbot Run Valley Hounds of Walter and Marjorie Brandt had a particular strong strain of mostly red and white hounds. Students of Basset Hound pedigrees would give most of the credit to the hound, Ch. Abbot Run Valley Brassy; however, "Brassy" was from a Lyn Mar Acres hound and a bitch named Ch. Ro-Fre La Reine de la Belle. The particular look of the "Brassy" hound was

*Ch. Abbot Run Valley Brassy, sire of 48 champion get, shown here by owner Walter Brandt.*

from his sire, Ch. Lyn Mar Acres Top Brass. This was an interesting turn of events because this hound started a whole new divisional look or style to the hounds that were, still yet, closely related to the Lyn Mar Acres stock. Most would tend not to think of the "Brassy" style of hounds when picturing modern Lyn Mar Acres hounds in their mind's eye.

*Am/Bda. Ch. Sir Tomo of Glenhaven, one of the few truly prepotent Basset Hound stud dogs.*

Another hound of the '60s was Am/Bda. Ch. Sir Tomo of Glenhaven, owned by John and Margretta Patterson and Emily Kultchar of Margem Hills. This "Tomo" hound, and the "Brassy" hound were not too unlike the original Morgan horse (a thoroughbred horse who continually produced the same style of horse until it became recognized as its own breed). What might be even more interesting is that for all of the dark tri hounds produced by Tomo, the red and white Brassy hound was his maternal uncle. Tomo was, in most cases, able to reproduce his own style with nearly every bitch hound. A well-bred hound, Tomo comes down from what is basically half to full Lyn Mar Acres stock, but bred by Eleanor Bliss' Eleandon Basset Hound kennels. It is an interesting pedigree because it brings two hounds on the paternal side, which are half-brother/half-sister, together in the sire, and then, the sire's maternal granddam *is* the dam, and she also is the product of a half-brother/half -sister breeding. Tomo was one of the great sires, producing 32 champions, and one of the most influential hounds in North American Basset Hound history. This hound had style of carriage, elegance in head, and very strong genes. So marked was the power of this hound's pedigree, that in parts of the US, the brownish or tan eyebrows on a predominately black blanket tri hound is looked at as the "Tomo" style of hound, whether or not the hound has "Tomo" in his or her pedigree. If the hound did have Tomo in its pedigree, you would be able to tell it in some physical manner. One of Tomo's most prolific sons was Am/Can. Ch. Margem Hills Mr. Brown, and he too would continue to produce his sire's qualities in most of his litters.

Another famous hound of the tan and white coloration was the Eng. Ch. Breightmet Chimer, although he was registered as a tri-colored hound. A reported sound, compact hound with very good front, bred by Mrs. Baynes, out of Grims Vanish ex Grims Charlie, "Chimer"was the pick puppy for Grims Bassets. He is famous to this day for providing his get, and generations of their descendants, with tight, rounded "Chimer" feet.

As we moved into the 1970s, even more specifically recognized strains had developed and others continued on. These kennels had not just taken over from where another left off, or even just started breeding, but they became known, or continued to be known, by their hounds' general appearances. The following are some of the main kennels that fall into this category: Shoefly, Beauregarde, Langpool, Homelyope, De-Alo, Bar-B, MacKimm's,

*Ch. His Lordship of Lyn Mar Acres*

Eleandon's Butcher Boy

*Ch. Bliss Haven's Hanford Jewel*

Eleandon's Black Magic

*Ch. His Lordship of Lyn Mar Acres*

Eleandon's Daisy Mae

*Ch. Lyn Mar Acres Fyre Ball*

AM/BDA. CH. SIR TOMO OF GLENHAVEN

Kilsyth Lucky

Ch. Lyn Mar's Clown

Ch. Maitri of Lyn Mar

*Ch. Lyn Mar Acres Fyre Ball*

Basso of Banbury

Ch. Headline of Lyn Mar Acres

Ch. Maitri of Lyn Mar

Lochopt, Harper's, Stoneybluff, Laguna, Custusha, Bayroc, Topohil, Rebelglen, Beaujangle, Marshills, Houndsville, Rebownd, Bluvali, Redbird, Kinslow, Silver Bow, Pinedell, Coran, Ren-Lo-Run, Bantrybeigh, Poverty Knob, Ro-Barb, Cloverhill, Balleroy, Hunting Horn, Strathalbyn, Birchcroft, Craigwood, Beacontree, Jagersven, Von Skauton, Ran-Su, BevLee, Thompson's, Bugle Bay's, Rome-ing, Russtan, Olde Fashion, Switchbark, Beartooth, Windmaker, Sagaces, Hushanda, Dixie's, Mi-Lin, My Lu, Smith Farm, Brackenacre, Tailgate, Desiree Acres, Charford, Valhala, Von Hollandheim, Halcyon, Redemption Rock, Sadiron, Jercat, Delmas, Bow-Ridge, and Tal-E-Ho. This does not mean that these kennels, or the kennels before them, were either right or wrong in their particular style of hounds. It simply means that the hounds could be reasonably recognized as to their probable breeding kennel.

There are many Basset Hound enthusi-asts who have been breeding for years upon years and who have come up with lots of top-winning hounds, but whose kennels have only recently (*historically speaking*) achieved the goal of a distinct strain for their hounds. While some began their kennels

much earlier (some in the '60s and '70s), their distinct strains were only becoming apparent by the '80s. In fact, several of these kennels had strong beginnings and then, for whatever reasons, decided to change breeding direction until finally hitting on what they really liked, or what would work for them. Some of these kennels are: Briarcrest, Scotts-Moore, Castlehill, Wilburdan, Ambrican, Heathrow, Fort Merrill, Sanchu, Branscombe, Sanlyn, Black-jack, First Class, Verulum, Bone-A-Part, Dusan, Brevis, Stonewall, Chasan, Glad-some, Delorblanc, and Woodhaven.

Establishing a line usually takes about three to four generations of concentrated effort. A particular kennel's look or style can also be lost. In fact, it can be lost much easier than it can be acquired. Because dis-tinct lines may bring along particular prob-lems or "genetic baggage" that had not yet been erased, the idea of just breeding one distinct line to another and coming up with a completely new one is not an easy thing to do. You must be willing to go back to one or the other of the two lines and concentrate on that line's qualities that were, hopefully, introduced by the initial breeding process. Even if the breeding kennel is not large, it is best to actually have two different "lines" of hounds from the same basic genetic background within the kennel. This can easily be done by concentrating on the attributes of two or more prepotent dog or bitch hounds. There are many, many Basset Hound kennels that have had big winners in the past and that have had very good hounds, but there are not many, historically speaking, that have really made a lasting impression on the breed.

In modern times, it is likely the general consensus that the most influential modern Basset Hound lines in the world would have to be these two kennels: Lyn Mar Acres and Santana-Mandeville. From these, many more very strong Basset Hound kennels sprang, but these two stood out among their peers and, in fact, throughout the years. While quite different, in both beginnings and in style, each produced some extremely memorable hounds. To this day, in America, when inquiring of Basset Hounds, enthusiasts tend to ask the question, "Are they Santana or Lyn Mar background?"

## THE LYN MAR ACRES INFLUENCE

The Lyn Mar Acres kennel has been written about in numerous books and is, in fact, still a current breeding kennel, although a closed one. The late Mr. M. Lynwood (Woody) Walton and his wife, Margaret (Peg) Walton, started with hounds of the Kilsyth Bassets and the Greenly Hall Bassets. Hounds with such names as Ch. Lyn Mar Acres Top Brass, Ch. His Lordship of Lyn Mar Acres, Ch. Lyn Mar's Clown, Am/Itl. Ch. Lyn Mar Acres M'Lord Batuff, Ch. Lyn Mar Acres Endman, and Ch. Lyn Mar Acres Extra Man were to become known the world over.

The Lyn Mar Acres hounds were sought after for many reasons, but primarily for their overall structure. They usually possessed well-laid-back shoulders, good length of body, excellent head type, and strong pedigrees. Some of the kennel's early critics complained of the lack of bone size and flat feet in some of the early generations

of Lyn Mar hounds. Mrs. Walton would still take exception to these criticisms since she feels that their first Basset, Duchess, had an excellent front and feet with good, thick pads, which she passed to her get. Her first breedings were to Promise, and her last litter was by her grandson, both of whom had good fronts and feet. With respect to bone size, the Waltons considered what they were breeding to be adequate for a functional hound in the field. The Lyn Mar Bassets can be traced back to the Walhampton hounds directly through the Kilsyth and Westerby hounds they used. Lyn Mar also used Mrs. Consuelo Ford's Bijou of Banbury pack's stallion hound, Basso of Banbury. He became the sire of Ch. Headline of Lyn Mar Acres out of Ch. Maitri of Lyn Mar. Through the hounds, Roughwood Elmer by Ch. Lyn Mar's Clown out of Grims Unity, and "Domino," ("Grims Ulema de Barly" ex "Westerby Dorcas"), the Lyn Mar Basset hounds made use of the great French Artois-Normand Basset sire, Ulema de Barly. The early Smith brothers' Bassets out of Ohio also influenced nearly all American breeders through the Lyn Mar pedigrees. In Lyn Mar Acres' case it was Ch. Smith's Red Powder in the pedigree of Ch. Maitri of Lyn Mar. Her sire, Ch. Promise of Greenly Hall, had Red Powder as a maternal grandsire, and her dam, Ch. Duchess of Greenly Hall, had him as a paternal great-grandsire.

*Ch. Lyn Mar Acres Press Agent, a multiple Group and BIS winner.*

```
                              Kilsyth Baronet
                Kilsyth Lucky
                              Kilsyth Mitzi
          Ch. Lyn Mar's Clown
                              Ch. Promise of Greenly Hall
                Ch. Maitri of Lyn Mar
                              Ch. Duchess of Greenly Hall
  ROUGHWOOD ELMER
                              Sans Souci de Bourceville
                Grims Ulema de Barly, Fr. Imp.
                              Querelle de Barly
          Grims Unity, Eng. Imp.
                              Grims Worship
                Grims Wallflower
                              Grims Waspish
```

During the late 1950s, when there were too many closely related hounds in England, the Basset Hound Club decided to import a hound. They negotiated with Lyn Mar Acres kennel and finally imported Lyn Mar Acres Dauntless (Lyn Mar Acres deMarch ex Lyn Mar Acres Black Magic). He was owned by the Club, but was kenneled at Miss Keevil's Grims Basset Hound kennel. Mrs. Walton had hoped that the English would show Dauntless to an English bench championship, however, this was never to be. They tried, but the judges of the time did nothing for him. Miss Keevil, recognizing his true potential as a stud, bought him from the club and kept him. He was used at stud, but only sparingly. Due to the quarantine limitations in England, many had to use offspring of Dauntless when they bred. By the late 1960s Dauntless was somewhere in most English pedigrees.

```
                              Ch. Lyn Mars Clown
                Ch. Lyn Mar Acres Top Brass
                              Ch. Headline of Lyn Mar Acres
          Lyn Mar Acres deMarch
                              Ch. Lyn Mars Clown
                Ch. Debbie's Gift
                              Lyn Mar Acres Merrie Mischief
  LYN MAR ACRES DAUNTLESS
                              Lyn Mar's Actor
                Ch. His Lordship of Lyn Mar Acres
                              Ch. Duchess of Greenly Hall
          Lyn Mar Acres Black Magic
                              Kilsyth Lucky
                Lyn Mar Acres Charm
                              Ch. Maitri of Lyn Mar
```

*Ch. Debbie's Gift, taking a Group first at Perkiomen Valley K.C. to finish her championship in 1955.*

During 1967 the Lyn Mar Acres kennel imported an English-bred bitch, Flareout Aria. She was bred by Mrs. Fae Morgan from Eng. Ch. Wingjay's Ptolemy ex Wingjay's Vanilla. Aria ("Teema") was registered as a lemon and white bitch in England when she was born in September, 1966. That she became a brilliant red and white is attributed by Mrs. Walton to the Lyn Mar feeding program. She was bred to three studs at Lyn Mar: Bats, Am/It. Ch. Lyn Mar Acres M'Lord Batuff (who was exported to Italy), and to Lyn Mar Acres Lord Hyssop. One of the kennel's later famed hounds was Ch. Lyn Mar Acres Extra Man, a son of Ch. Lyn Mar Acres End Man (who was exported to England) and a Batuff grandson.

*Ch. Lyn Mar Acres Debutante, a Debbie daughter by Ch. Lyn Mar Acres Top Brass in 1959.*

# THE SANTANA-MANDEVILLE INFLUENCE

The Santana-Mandeville hounds of Mr. and Mrs. Paul and Helen Nelson is an interesting study. They started as two separate kennels, Santana (Paul Nelson) and Mandeville (Helen Parkinson). The joining of the kennels only succeeded in helping them to become one of the most widely known kennels around the world. Hounds such as Ch. Santana-Mandeville, Tarzan, Ch. Santana-Mandeville Olivia, Ch. Santana-Mandeville Egghead, Ch. Santana-Mandeville Gigolo, Ch. Santana-Mandeville Rodney, Ch. Gladstone of Mandeville, and Ch. Santana's Count Dracula helped to spread their fame.

In beginning her Mandeville Basset kennel, Helen traveled to many kennels and finally was fortunate enough to acquire Hamlin's Missie, a daughter of Ch. His Lordship of Lyn Mar. "Missie" was bred by Ida Mae Hamlin, a dear and close friend of Peg Walton. Mrs. Hamlin's husband, Sam, who was interested in gunning, had purchased a dog hound from a private pack on Peg Walton's recommendation. It became his first Field Champion, a Lordship son. It was also through Mrs. Walton's help that "Missie" went home with Helen. Later, Helen acquired Huey of Cypress through her friendship with Dorothy Hicks in California. It was the combination of Huey and Missie that clicked to produce such hounds as Ch. Gladstone of Mandeville, Ch. Gwendolyn of Mandeville, Gustav, Dewey, and others. Ch. Santana-Mandeville Phoebe and Mandeville's Pretty Penelope were also produced by the same combination, but from another breeding.

The Santana side of the union took its heritage from the famous Belleau Bassets of Cordellia Jensen Skapinsky and later through the hound, Ch. Belbay Chevalier, acquired by Mrs. Skapinsky from the Belbay kennels of Leslie Kelly. It would take the overall show success and the luck of the particular time in history to allow the Santana-Mandeville hounds to spread their influence. The fact that the two kennels, Santana-Mandeville in California and Lyn

Ch. Belbay Design
Ch. Belbay Chevalier
Ch. Belbay Treasure
Ch. Santana's Count Dracula
Ch. Mon Phillipe of Greenly Hall
Ch. Beautiful Minnetonkie
Beautiful Minnehaha
CH. SANTANA-MANDEVILLE TARZAN
Ch. Mon Phillipe of Greenly Hall
Ch. Huey of Cypress
Ch. Miss Bess CD
Ch. Santana-Mandeville's Phoebe
Ch. His Lordship of Lyn Mar Acres
Ch. Hamlin's Missie
Hamilin's Lady

Mar Acres in New Jersey, were on opposite ends of the continental US was also a great factor in their relative importance to the breed! One of the best known of the Santana-Mandeville line was Ch. Santana Mandeville Tarzan.

To complete our Santana-Mandeville discussion, it is necessary to backtrack a bit in history and further discuss the influence of the Belbay Basset Hound line in the Santana pedigree. Mr. Leslie Kelly obtained his first Basset Hound from Mr. Carl Smith and from Mr. Carl Nottke. Mr. Kelly bred and showed his hounds under the Kelly prefix and then later adopted the name of Belbay for his kennel. Both he and his wife, Grace, decided that a "...Basset's bay should sound like a bell's tone...Belbay." It has been reported that Mr. Kelly also used the Neliegh prefix. This is not true. Mr. Kelly has said that he only bred to a couple of bitches that belonged to a person who used Neliegh as his kennel name. He took a couple as stud picks and later used one of them in his breeding program.

Mr. Kelly used his hounds for hunting under the gun, as did Carl Smith. He enjoyed hunting rabbit and pheasant. Later, in 1941, Mr. Kelly began to show his hounds and met with great success. Belbay Bassets were the first to be selectively bred for coloration. He had both tri and red-colored hounds. However, after a suggestion made by Mrs. Consuelo Ford that an all-red pack would look really nice, Mr.

Kelly came to the same conclusion. The Belbay "red" Bassets became an important influence on the breed in America. According to Mr. Kelly, the deep red blanket color came from Carl Smith's hounds with their Russian Basset ancestry. Mr. Kelly's Belbay Bassets developed not only a color identification but also some physical qualities that would have long-lasting influences on the breed. The Belbay Bassets were usually shorter coupled in body, but had smooth, well-sprung rib cages. They also sported good bone, tight

Ch. Santana-Mandeville Tarzan, an outstanding sire of his time.

feet, shorter sterns, and happy dispositions. Additionally, they seemed to have a coat that would stay cleaner than most other Basset Hounds.

It is important to note that the Belbay hounds formed the major influence of the Santana Basset kennel of Paul Nelson before he and Helen's Mandeville Bassets joined forces. Helen's hounds claimed heritage closer to the Lyn Mar style and the combination of the two produced some rather nice hounds. They did, however, tend to get away from Santana's old Belbay look as the years went on.

# Kennel Influence After the Mid-1960s

The reader should be aware that all 875+ members of the Basset Hound Club of America were invited to contribute information on their activities for use in this section. Some did, others did not. The author's writing in this section was limited by the membership's response and the opinions expressed herein are solely that of the author. The kennels that did participate are addressed alphabetically and, while the length of their narrative varies for specific purpose, the overall length of individual kennel narratives is not necessarily indicative of importance, or influence, during this period. Overwhelmingly, the discipline interest of the majority of the membership is the conformation ring. As a result, this section deals with the kennel influence that affected the conformation of the Basset Hound during this time period. Other disciplines, trialing, tracking, obedience, etc., are covered in their respective sections.

*Ch. Acorn Hill's Brandy with owner/handler Dennis Fitch.*

## ACORN HILL

Very new to the breed, Sandy Lee and Dennis Fitch and their Acorn Hill Bassets have gotten off to a good start with their bitch, Ch. Acorn Hill's Brandy. Co-bred by Sandy Lee and Dennis with Brian Kinnear, Brandy appears to be a very nice bitch with a pedigree that affords a number of ways to go in future breeding. I know the sire well and the dam's side of the pedigree has a number of excellent producers also. With any luck, we can expect some future winners from this bitch.

## ALLENHILL

The Allenhill kennel of Sally and Kevin Allen, located in Carmel, Indiana, began in April, 1983 with the purchase of Homestead's Ka-Ka-Katie. "Pie" was a result of the breeding of the bitch, Ch. Homestead's Tin Lizzy to the excellent producer, Ch. Lochopt Halcyon Collegian. She finished at 11 months of age and enjoyed a bit of specialing before being bred to Ch. Halcyon Crackerjack. This breeding produced another fine hound, Ch. Allenhill Piecracker, a BIS winner.

Pie's littermate, Homestead Carousel also came to live with the Allens and was bred to Ch. Beartooth Sidney CD. This breeding produced Ch. Allenhill Bea Sweet, WB at the 1987 National Specialty. This writer is proud to have been the judge that selected this excellent bitch at that show.

The foregoing dogs were the foundation of Allenhill's limited breeding program. They consider themselves to be very fortunate to have had such nice hounds with which to begin, and have worked hard to breed only to improve their dogs. One of their favorite accomplishments is having bred Ch.

*Ch. Allenhill Platform Rocker, going WD, BW from the Bred by Exhibitor class at the 1994 Kentuckiana BHC Specialty. Handled by Kevin Allen under breeder-judge Bill Russell.*

Allenhill Platform Rocker who attained his title being shown only at specialties, finishing with all majors from the Bred by Exhibitor class.

## AMBRICAN

The Ambrican Basset Hound kennel makes for an unusual and interesting story. Basically it is a show-oriented kennel that had its beginnings in three different countries before it eventually came together in America. Penny Frederiksen began her career in Bassets by following her mother's lead in England, owning her foundation bitch in 1970, and later taking her hounds with her to Canada. Penny's kennel prefix at the time was Charford. In America, Randy Frederiksen was using the Coran prefix and had began breeding and showing in 1972, after having owned a Basset since 1968. The current kennel name of Ambrican was first used in 1982 and came from the combination of the three countries involved: America, Britain, and Canada, as well as the fact that Penny is British, Randy is American, and they met in Canada.

Mrs. Bert Salyers was already a part of the Coran exhibiting program in Texas, so she was invited to become a named partner in Ambrican after the new prefix was established. Since beginning the use of the Ambrican prefix, the kennel has completed

30 titles on 20 hounds. Including the previous Charford and Coran prefixes their hounds have completed 47 bench championship titles, 10 obedience titles and 4 tracking titles. The obedience and tracking titles were acquired through the patient work of Mike Salyers, Nancy Chapman, and Kay and Craig Green. Four of the hounds are now listed in the Register of Merit.

Already having had foundation bitches for each of their own previous kennels, it must be said that the following hounds were significant contributors to the nearly immediate success of the Ambrican Bassets: Am/Can. Ch. Charford Gretchen, Charford Foxglove, and Coran Country Elvira. The following studs added some winning power in the making of some fine hounds: Am/Can. Ch. Coran Country Chaz, Ch. Windmaker's Summer Thunder, and Ch. Strathalbyn War Paint.

During the first few years of breeding, the kennel sought to produce hounds that it could continue to build on. This did not, of course, always pan out. Ch. Ambrican Ariana's (Chaz ex Coran Country Cilver) first and only litter was sired by Summer Thunder and was one such dead-end street. A breeding of Chaz to Strathalbyn Fan Dancer produced Ch. Ambrican Barrabus, a large red and white hound who has gone on to

Am/Can. Ch. Sand-Dell's Rasput                  ion Black

Am/Can. Ch. Longbay's Black Diamond

Can. Ch. Sand-Dell's Cherry Blossom

Am/Can. Ch. Coran Country Chaz ROM

Am/Can. Ch. Margem Hills Mr. Brown ROM

Sadiron's Painted Lady (Coran)

Ch. Coran's Penelope O'George ROM

AM/CAN. CH. AMBRICAN IVAN

Am/Can. Ch. Chantinghall Dominic

Am/Can. Ch. Chantinghall Zachary

Can. Ch. Chantinghall Cousin Maud

Charford Foxglove, Can. ptd.

Am/Can. Ch. Chantinghall Dominic

Can. Ch. Charford Esmerelda

Charford Celina, Eng. Imp.

*Am/Can. Ch. Ambrican Ivan.*

produce no fewer than five champions. The breeding of Coran Country Elvira to Summer Thunder produced Ch. Ambrican Charmaine (Foxglen) who became an ROM producer and was named BHCA Top Brood Bitch in 1990. One of Charmaines's sons, sired by Ch. Ambrican Barrabus, Ch. Foxglen Ambrican Albert CD TD (Chapman) was shown for a while in the Texas area and he had two champion littersisters. Charmaine's dam, Elvira, was also used with Ch. Strathalbyn War Paint and she produced Ch. Ambrican Folklore. Am/Can. Ch. Charford Gretchen was bred to Chaz and produced Ch. Ambrican Jeremy CD, and Ch. Ambrican Josephine CD TD (Green). The use of Gretchen's half-sister, Charford Foxglove, bred to Chaz produced Am/Can. Ch. Ambrican Ivan.

Later, Can./Am. Ch. Charford Gretchen, bred to War Paint, produced Am/Can. Ch. Ambrican Lipizzan, Ambrican Limosine CD TD (Chapman), Ambrican Lupin, mj. ptd. (Sadiron), Ambrican Lipstick, and Ambrican Lapwing (Heathrow).

For the second-generation program Ambrican continued the Strathalbyn connection because it was working very well. The breeding of Ivan to Ch. Strathalbyn Livinthion produced a lone surviving pup called Ambrican Nicolette (Beard). This bitch currently lacks only one point to finish. Two new hounds were acquired, eight-month-old (Ch.) Strathalbyn Lugano and his sister Strathalbyn Lisa. Lisa was eventually bred to Ch. Ambrican Barrabus, but died during whelping. She literally "dropped" dead of a heart attack in the whelping box before presenting any puppies. With a cool head and

Ch. Tantivy Dunkirk

Strathalbyn Hathaway, mj. ptd.

Strathalbyn Biscuit

Ch. Strathalbyn War Paint

Ch. Lyn Mar Acres Extra Man

Strathalbyn Coldstream Gina

Tantivy Blond Sidonia

Am/Can. CH. AMBRICAN LIPIZZAN

Am/Can. Ch. Halcyon Crackerjack

Am/Can. Ch. Sleepyhollow Riveredge Sam

Ch. Tal-E-Ho's Red Pepper

Can./Am. Ch. Charford Gretchen

Can./Am. Ch. Chantinghall Dominic

Can. Ch. Charford Esmerelda

Charford Celina, Eng. Imp.

*Am/Can. Ch. Ambrican Lipizzan.*

fast reaction, they were able to save six of the eight puppies inside of her. One of the survivors was Can. Ch. Ambrican Myrtle CD (Dalfen), who has produced champions for her Canadian owner. Others that survived are Ambrican Merlin CD TD (Chapman), Ambrican Foxglen Magical (Foxglen), a champion producer, and Ambrican Mysterious (Topsfield), who has pointed get in the ring.

With the arrival of Lugano and Lisa in 1986, the ties to that side of the pedigrees were strengthened. Strathalbyn and Tantivy breeding strains were both important parts of the two Ambrican previous prefix backgrounds, Charford and Coran. Lugano also allowed the kennel to become involved in pack activities. He was drafted into the Timber Ridge Basset Hound Pack in Maryland after having earned most of his bench points

as a puppy. He became one of the lead hounds for two hunting seasons, taking time out only to complete his bench championship with a Specialty win. Lugano won the BHCA Jr. Sweepstakes in 1968 and nearly stole the show with his vocal antics in the ring.

When the Ambrican kennel was moved to England for a little over a year's time (April '90—July '91), Lugano stayed behind with the Ft. Merrill Bassets to produce two champion daughters from his first litter. After Lugano reached England, it was decided that he would stay there for stud use after Randy and Penny returned to the States. Lugano sired several litters before catching up with his kennelmates again. His puppies' wins earned him the title of Top Stud Dog in England for 1992. The kennel was at its maximum of 26 hounds prior to moving to

England. The expense of shipping and quarantine required a dramatic reduction in number of hounds. Only six bitches were taken over. Ivan, Lipizzan, and Ariana stayed with Bert Salyers, as did two young puppies that eventually wound up in Canadian homes. Most others were homed out or arrangements were made with other show kennels that wished to use them.

The bitch hounds, having spent half of their time in the dreaded six-month quarantine of the British Isles, left little time to do any breeding as some were still very young. There was one lost opportunity when a freak snowstorm shut down all modes of transportation so the selected bitch could not be mated. The bitch was Lipizzan's sister, Ambrican Lipstick, who was eventually bred to Lugano when he

arrived back in the US from England. This produced Ch. Ambrican Quadrille (Kinslow/Barringer) and Ch. Ambrican Quest For Fame, both of which completed their title requirements within a month of each other at just over a year of age. Both now have puppies in the ring.

The success of the Lipstick to Lugano breeding gave encouragement for a repeat breeding for the first time. The result was two promising young hounds named Ambrican Sportsman's Park and Ambrican Saratoga. Not yet having what they considered the right bitch ready, they've not yet used Lipizzan within their own kennel. He has, however, still managed to produce five champions, including Ch. Ft. Merrill Lipz Stick (Urban), America's Number One Basset Hound in 1994.

*Ch. Strathalbyn Lugano.*

|  |  | Ch. Lyn Mar Acres Sir Michelob |
|---|---|---|
|  | Ch. Lyn Mar Acres P.B.R |  |
|  |  | Ch. Lyn Mar Acres Lovage |
|  | Ch. Strathalbyn Limited Edition |  |
|  |  | Lyn Mar Acres P.T Bimbo |
|  | Strathalbyn A Touch Of class |  |
|  |  | Am/Can. Ch. Strathalbyn Panic |
| CH. STRATHALBYN LUGANO |  |  |
|  |  | Ch. Tantivy Dunkirk |
|  | Strathalbyn Hathaway, mj. ptd. |  |
|  |  | Strathalbyn Biscuit |
|  | Strathalbyn Wideawake |  |
|  |  | Ch. Tantivy Ferdinand |
|  | Ch. Tantivy Trickster |  |
|  |  | Tantivy Diable |

Am/Can. Ch. Longbay's Black Diamond

Am/Can. Ch. Coran Country Chaz ROM

Sadiron's Painted Lady (Coran)

Ch. Ambrican Barrabus

Ch. Strathalbyn Hit and Run

Strathalbyn Fan Dancer

Strathalbyn Coldstream Gina

THE "T" LITTER

Am/Can. Ch. Coran Country Chaz ROM

Am/Can. Ch. Ambrican Ivan

Charford Foxglove, Can. ptd.

Ambrican Patience

Dk. Ch. Johlibas Jago

Johlibas Nitouche, Dk. Imp.

Dk. Ch. WSF Johlibas Kathleen of Master

While in Europe they found a bitch in Denmark that was actually owned by Elisabeth Knap of Norway, (her pick puppy), who had originally imported a Lyn-Mar Acres hound (Nor. Ch. Lyn-Mar Acres Brass Top) many years before. The pedigree was tight and they were fortunate to be able to arrange for her importation. Johlibas Nitouche was subsequently bred to Ivan and produced a litter that includes Ch. Ambrican Highlander Pearl, (Green); Ambrican Foxglen Penelope, pointed, (Foxglen); Ambrican Ft. Merrill Promise, major pointed, (Ft. Merrill), and Ambrican Patience.

The third-generation breeding of Ambrican hounds has begun with the breeding of Ch. Ambrican Barrabus ex Ambrican Patience. The resulting "T" litter is currently in the whelping box, so only time will tell. They also look forward to incorporating Lipizzan and Quest into the program. The "T" litter was represented at the 1996 BHCA Nationals by the WD/BW, Ch. Ambrican Trademark, under judges Jerry Rush and Bob Booth, respectively.

Having had many Specialty-winning hounds, they have tended to keep the kennel's show ring action steered toward the Specialty shows. There have been some 36 Best in Specialty show awards to date. Bert's interest, however, has always been in the all-breed ring, so with the help of handlers such as Tracy Potts (Texas) and Nancy and Bryan Martin (Illinois), the hounds have also done well on the all-breed circuits. The kennel was also able to produce the 1990 BHCA National Specialty winner, Am/Can. Ch. Ambrican Lipizzan, (handled to that win by Nancy Martin). Lipizzan took the number two spot overall in 1991 (handled by Bryan Martin) and also won the BHC of Canada National Specialty. In 1992, Lipizzan was awarded the Number One Basset Hound in America recognition. His cousin, Am/Can. Ch. Ambrican Ivan (originally trained and handled by Tracy Potts) marked his career by achieving the number two spot in 1989 and 1990 as well as an all-breed BIS award (handled by the Martins). Ch. Stoneybluff Seigfreid (handled by Bryan Martin) was co-owned for a short while and he was also shown to an all-breed BIS award.

Breeding usually only once a year, Ambrican has strived to produce balanced hounds that are able to successfully compete in the ring and be structurally sound enough to accomplish the breed's task in the field. Endurance through sound structure, including tight feet and long rib cages, started to take on even more importance to the kennel's ideals after becoming involved with an active pack of hunting Bassets.

Ambrican's objective of having and maintaining two distinct, yet related, styles within the kennel has been upheld. From the original Ambrican mating of Charford Foxglove to Coran Country Chaz, the son Ivan and their granddaughter Patience look like peas in a pod. This produces the white-blazed, regular tri-colored hounds. The breeding of Charford Gretchen to Strathalbyn War Paint, and their daughter Lipstick, bred to Lugano,

them in terms of fronts, rib length, and good feet. These same attributes were also evident in Penny's original English-bred hounds. From the use of the Strathalbyn hounds, War Paint, Fan Dancer, Livinthion, Lugano, and Lisa, they feel that they have gained in the dark and/or speckled tri-colored look, head, bone, and drive.

Penny Frederiksen is a listed judge of the breed in England and has judged several sweepstakes in the US, and Canada. Randy has judged nearly 20 matches and sweepstakes over the years in the same three countries. Their efforts are geared toward the

*Ambrican Trademark. Breeder: R. & P. Frederiksen. Owner: Mrs. Bert Salyers.*

continues to produce the predominately black and white (sometimes speckled) hounds, the other style they were hoping to attain. Every now and then, especially with their more recent litters, they do pop up with some red and whites as the color is in the pedigrees. Do not get the impression that they specifically breed for color because it represents the very last variance considered.

Giving credit to those kennel strains from which they have immediately profited, they recognize that the Chantinghall backgrounds of Foxglove, Chaz (including the Margem Hills strain through Am/Can. Ch. Margem Hills Mr. Brown) and Gretchen has benefited

breeding and exhibiting areas, as well as raising their young daughter, Rachel; consequently they've not yet sought to become AKC judges. Randy also wrote a privately published book *Basset Hound....A World History* in 1987, which met with breed enthusiasts' overall approval. He is a current first-term director of the Basset Hound Club of America. Currently residing in northern Ohio, their Ambrican Basset Hounds are slowly making their mark in that part of the country. Mrs. Bert Salyers is still located in Texas and is in constant contact with the main kennel as she orchestrates the showing of Ambrican Basset Hounds in the Southwest.

## BANDIT

Shirley Hiatt's Bandit's Bassets of Havelock, North Carolina, began with the purchase of Anubis Sancho Bandit from Judi and Brian Kinnear, (**Bridi**), from their very first litter. Meeting with little eventual success in the show ring with that particular pup, he was Obedience trained and achieved his CD. He was a Bandit resident for thirteen and one-half years before he succumbed to cancer.

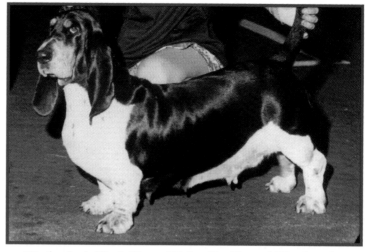

*Windmaker's Black Storm CD, bred by Jim and Wanda White and owned and handled by Shirley Hiatt.*

Shirley then purchased a bitch, Windmaker's Black Storm, "Beauty," from Jim and Wanda White. The day this bitch finished her CD, she was also Best of Breed over Specials and went on to a Group 3rd. Unfortunately, six months later she died of cancer. Even though she had other dogs to show, this discouraging event held Shirley out of the show ring for several years. A son of this bitch, Bandit's Texas Ranger, was RWD form the 6-9 Puppy Class at Shirley's first Nationals in Lexington, Kentucky, under breeder judge Len Skolnick.

Another favorite at the Bandit kennel is Ch. Craigwood's Feliz CD ROM, sired by Ch. Windamohr's Gamble and out of Craigwood's Charisma. She did well in the show ring, obedience ring, and in the whelping box. This bitch was a Group placer in the show ring and produced seven champions: Ch. Bandit's Winter Harvest CD; Ch. Bandit's Good Time Girl CD; Ch. Bandit's Texas Renegade CD; Ch. Bandit's Brandi of Jones CD; Ch. Zack Pack; Ch. Bandit's Scarlet Fever; Ch. Cleopatra Marckowski, and Bandit's Kirbie, who was major pointed.

A BHCA member since 1971, Shirley has been active and successful in both the show and obedience rings. She has also been extremely active with her bassets in Therapy Dogs International, working with them in that capacity in her local area.

*Ch. Craigwood's Feliz CD, ROM, going BW under judge Michele Billings.*

*Ch. Vahhala's Special Issue CD, CGC, ROM, winning BOB under breeder-judge Don Martin.*

## BANTRYBEIGH

Chris George's Bantrybeigh Bassets got its start with the purchase of her first show prospect from the Northwood kennel of Don and Barb Martin. Unfortunately "Windy" did not make it in the ring, but she did give Chris her first champion, Ch. George's Little Blarney. The breeding of Blarney produced Ch. Bantrybeigh's Fianna, Ch. Bantrybeigh's Clancy, and Ch. Bantrybeigh's Broughshane. Most of Chris's breeding stock today can be traced back to her original bitch.

In 1986, Ch. Vahhala's Special Issue CD CGC ROM, came to Bantrybeigh. Call named "Linc," he has had a significant impact on the kennel's breeding program. Chris continues to show in conformation and dabble in obedience, "Thanks to Linc," she says.

*Ch. George's Little Blarney, with Chris George handling under breeder-judge Ann Thain.*

## BAR-B

Barbara Dunning of Riverside, California purchased her first Basset in 1954. After a little research, she decided that she wanted her dog to be different; the type of dog that no one else in the area had. Bassets were relatively scarce at the time and the search was not an easy one. She found and purchased a dog named Gordon's Boy Socrates, sired by Ch. Belbay Chevalier (known then as the "Chevy" dog), who was owned by Nancy Evans of Scottsdale, Arizona.

Reading her local paper one day, Barbara noticed an ad for a "Basset Hound Picnic" and decided that this would be a great place to take her dog and to meet other Basset fanciers. At the picnic she met Mr. Ben Harris, then the President of the Basset Hound Club of Southern California. She recalls that Ben had such a passion for Basset Hounds and judging that before she knew it, he had her signed up as a member and soon thereafter she entered her dog in the club's upcoming Specialty. In those days, the Southern Cal entries ran around 200, so you can imagine her excitement when her dog took a third in his class.

Barbara's kennel name, "Bar-B," was made up from the first three letters of her name and the other B stands for the first letter of the name of her daughter, Beverly. Her first show-quality bitch, Wilhelmina of Salt Box Farms, came from breeder Marge Adams and she finished from the 6-9 Puppy class! She didn't show many of her own dogs at the time since she was working for and traveling with professional handler Ben Brown. She spent two years as his assistant, showing all-breeds and Bassets for other breeders.

It was after her stint as a handler's assistant that Barbara went back to showing her own breeding and started hosting all-breed handling classes for the next 25 years. It was during this period that Barbara had twin girls, both of whom became active junior handlers, one taking a BIS junior handler at the age of twelve. During this same time period she also ran her own all-breed board-

*Shown here with Barbara Dunning in 1965 is Ch. Bar-B Patrick O'Toole.*

ing and grooming kennel for ten years and currently has her own one-and-one-half-acre kennel for Bassets only in Riverside.

One of Barbara's dogs, Ch. Bar-B Honest Abe, had won the Sweepstakes and also BW at a BHCSC Specialty, but she claims that nothing can compare to the thrill of having this same dog win BOB at a Southern Cal Specialty, from the Veteran Dog class

*Ch. Bar-B Honest Abe, taking a Group first in 1972, handled by Barbara Dunning under judge Robert Waters.*

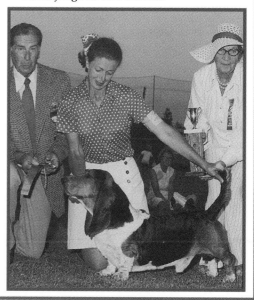

*Ch. Bar-B Tailor Made, in 1972 going BW and BOB under breeder-judge Margretta Patterson.*

some years later! Barbara has taught several Basset Hound seminars for aspiring AKC judges and has judged numerous Specialty Sweepstakes nationwide. She is very proud, in her early 70s, to be still actively breeding and showing her own dogs. She is equally proud to have served on the Board of Directors for the Basset Hound Club of America.

Barbara Dunning has certainly produced consistency in breed type over these many years. It is plain to see that her dogs of yesteryear would still be competitive in today's environment, as are the ones that she currently shows.

## B'S

Barbara Langlois from Chalmette, Louisiana started her kennel in 1975 under the BobBar prefix, but after divorcing, the Bob was dropped and the Bar was changed to B's. Breeding and showing were a new adventure to Barbara and soon became the major focus in her life. She claims that the many dogs that have passed through her life have brought her incredible joy.

Her goal, as with most other serious breeders, was to produce that "great Basset" who would, in turn, produce more of the same! As a result, much time was spent studying and learning; applying the knowledge gained and much praying that it "would all come out right."

The first "right one" for Barbara was Ch. BobBar's Southern Wonder. "Won-Won" was sired by Ch. Windamohr's Gamble and was out of Hooper-Knoll's Fantasy of BobBar. From the moment of her whelping on April 20, 1980, she was the center of the universe for Barbara. The second "right one" was Am/Can. Ch. BobBar's Gumbo File. Whelped in 1981, and handled to his championship by his owner Matt Mathews, he was specialed by Pat Willer. He was also out of Fantasy and sired by Ch. Romansway

*Ch. Bar-B Handsome Floyd Patrick at 16 months, taking BOS in 1994.*

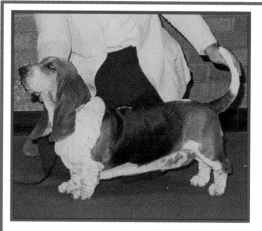

*Ch. BobBar's Southern Wonder, in show pose in an informal setting.*

Gilt Edged Bond. "Gumbo" finished at one year of age, was the winner of numerous Specialties and Group placements, and won an all-breed BIS in 1983.

Barbara's philosophy was to never breed just for a litter. The breeding had to be extremely selective in terms of quality of those mated. With this limited breeding practice, she still was able to finish some 19 champions. No longer active in breeding or exhibiting, Barbara keeps her finger on the pulse of the breed through judging and continued membership in the Basset Hound Club of Greater New Orleans.

## BEAUJANGLES

Beginning in the early 1970s, the Beaujangles Bassets, originally co-owned by Diane Malenfant and Claudia Lane of Glendale, Arizona, was able to define a particular style to their hounds and successfully export it to developing Basset Hound kennels. Their foundation stud, Ch. Blue Billy Bojangles ROM, was largely responsible, as a review of his inbred pedigree will show.

The Beaujangle style of hound can easily be pointed out at any show in the country. This particular style, which was portrayed in most, but not all, Beaujangle hounds was very low to the ground, usually long, with adequate bone, and they were "go-getters" in the ring! To the student of the breed, this style was able to develop as a result of the Belbay/Santana-Mandeville influence obvious in Billy's pedigree. He was given to Diane and Claudia by Judy Ryan, a member of the local Valle Del Sol Basset Hound Club, when she saw how enthusiastic they were about their newfound hobby of showing dogs. Little did they know that he would turn out to be such a consistent and prolific sire that he became the Top Producing Sire in the history of the breed, a record he still holds with a total of 59 AKC champion get to his credit.

*Ch. BobBar's Gumbo File' in 1983, winning one of his numerous Group placements.*

From his very first litter, which produced his first champion out of Mary Jane and Bob Booth's Hiflite's Joanna, it was apparent that Billy possessed something special as a sire. Evidently many other prominent breeders felt the same way, as many very fine bitches from outstanding kennels were sent to him for stud service. A roster of his offspring follows. Note that it includes his most famous son, Am/Can. Ch. Belyn's Roustabout ROM, ("J.R."), three-time BHCA National Specialty BOB winner!

*Ch. Blue Billy Bojangles ROM (1972—1984), shown by Claudia Lane in the early 1970s.*

|  |  |  |
|---|---|---|
|  | Santana's Miltie The Burglar | Ch. Santana-Mandeville Tarzan ROM |
|  |  | Miss Jenny Magoo ROM |
|  | Ch. Nancy Evans Double Cross ROM | Ch. Gladstone of Mandeville |
|  | Tyburn's Rose of Albany | Ch. Santana-Mandeville Rachel |
| Lindsay's Supersport |  | Jagara's Ringo Ace |
|  | Ch. Nancy Evans Sir Galahad | Ch. Nancy Evans Twinkle De Barry |
|  | Ch. Lindsay's Blissful Bridget | Ch. Dunn's Chief Thunderfoot |
|  | Ch. Dunn's Miss Hazel | Dunn's Lady Tinkerbell |
| CH. BLUE BILLY BOJANGLES ROM |  |  |
|  | Clowverleaf's Agamemnon II | Agamemnon Of Clowverleaf |
|  | Ch. Musicland's Bill Bailey ROM | Ch. Millvan's Blondie |
|  | Ch. Musicland's Demure Danseuse | Ch. Look's Musical of Musicland |
|  |  | Ch. Bassett's Eloise ROM |
| Lindsay's Classy Cassy |  | Jagara's Ringo Ace |
|  | Ch. Nancy Evans Sir Galahad | Ch. Nancy Evans Twinkle De Barry |
|  | Ch. Lindsay's Blissful Bridget | Ch. Dunn's Chief Thunderfoot |
|  | Ch. Dunn's Miss Hazel | Dunn's Lady Tinkerbell |

Bred on some of the top old names in the breed, such as Ch. Santana-Mandeville's Tarzan, Ch. Santana's Count Dracula, Ch. Bassett's Barry de Belleau, Ch. Look's Musical of Musicland, Ch. Look's Choice, Ch. Abbott Run Valley Asa, and Ch. Lyn Mar Acres Clown, Billy is likely to stand for years as the breed's top sire.

A half decade later, another hound, one of Billy's grandsons, was to apply additional luster to the Beaujangles kennel name. From a very young age, "Robbie," Ch. Beaujangle's Ten ROM, (1979–1993), appeared to be destined for greatness. Few dogs deserve or earn the adjective great, but his owners knew that Robbie really was. He did it all!

As a young puppy, he finished with four Specialty majors and exceeded all of Beaujangles' hopes and aspirations. As an inbred grandson of the top-producing sire in the breed history, he too became a top producer with 49 AKC champions to his credit, ranking him second only to Billy on the all-time Top-Producing list. But he was also a top-winning show dog with many, many Specialty Bests of Breed over all the top-winning dogs of his day. Always breeder-owner-handled, he also won an all-breed BIS. Bred by Claudia and Diane, he was owned by Claudia and Vickie McMackin. His owners knew him as a gentle, sweet, noble hound who enriched the history of the breed.

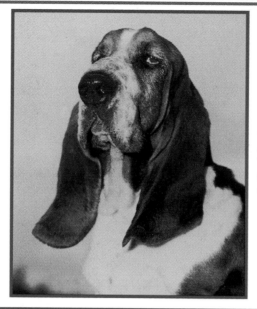

*Ch. Blue Billy Bojangles ROM, all-time top producer, sire of 59 champion get listed below.*

1. Ch. Beaujangle's Kachina Doll
2. Ch. Beaujangle's Jason Belyn
3. Ch. Beaujangle's Furoshus Otis
4. Ch. Beaujangle's Cameo Blue
5. Ch. Beaujangle's Blue Chip
6. Ch. Beaujangles's Rythm N' Blues
7. Ch. Supai's Wonder Woman
8. Ch. Musicland's Billy Bayou
9. Ch. Sylvia Jane P. Beaureguarde
10. Ch. Beaujangle's Mean Mr. Mustard
11. Ch. Belyn's Roustabout ROM *
12. Ch. Sydney P. Beaureguarde ROM
13. Ch. Beaujangle's Bacissa Melissa
14. Ch Beaujangle's Furoshus Martha
15. Ch. Belyn's Phoebe Star
16. Ch.Tumbleweed's Hudson Han' Me Down
17. Ch. Tumbleweed's Easy Rider
18. Ch. Blue Lick Astoria (BIS winner)
19. Ch. Studington P. Beaureguarde
20. Ch. Sara Jane P. Beaureguarde
21. Ch. Blue Lick Aardvark (BIS winner)
22. Ch. Boomerang's Windchimes
23. Ch. Stephie Jane P. Beaureguarde
24. Ch. Blue Lick Abelard
25. Ch. Sandy Hill's Kid Natural
26. Ch. Beaujangle's Wild Card
27. Ch. Boomerang's Magic Morgan
28. Ch. Beaujangle's Think Blue ROM
29. Ch. Blue Lick Aeolian
30. Ch. Bugle Bay Blue Cheese
31. Ch. Hi Ranch Mr. Surrey
32. Ch. Barrister's Prima Facie
33. Ch. Boomerang's Show Off
34. Ch Boomerang's Mor-A-Dees Please
35. Ch. Blue Lick Adonis
36. Ch. Hi Ranch Nena De Amor VIP
37. Ch. Heritage Color Me Blue
38. Ch. Blue Lick Aaron
39. Ch. Hi Ranch Baby Julieann
40. Ch. Hi Ranch Willie Nelson
41. Ch. Barrister's Hung Jury
42. Ch. Beaujangle's Jas'n O'Belforrest
43. Ch. Barrister's Hostile Witness
44. Ch. Beaujangle's Stormy of Viclee
45. Ch. Beaujangle's Out Of The Blue
46. Ch. Barrister's Yankee Clipper
47. Ch. Beaujangle's Hot Stuff
48. Ch. Beaujangle's Patch Of Blue
49. Ch. Beaujangle's Elvira
50. Ch. Jolly Times Bet On Roger
51. Ch. Blue Lick Anthem
52. Ch. Jolly Times Ruff N Ready
53. Ch. Sandy Hill's Hillary Kramer
54. Ch. Hi Ranch Piccolo Pete
55. Ch. Blue Lick Anenome
56. Ch. Boomerang's Come On Back
57. Ch. Viclee's Son Of Billy
58. Ch. Pinewood's Miss Candy
59. Ch. Beaujangle's Boz Skaggs

*Ch. Beaujangle's J. P. Beaureguarde ROM (1981–1992), winning an all-breed BIS, owner-handled by Claudia Lane.*

Some three years after the arrival of "the ten dog," Ch. Beaujangles J.P. Beaureguarde ROM, known as "Jeep," came on the scene. Jeep, sired by "Ten" out of Ch. Stephie Jane P. Beaureguarde, was owned by Claudia Lane, Vickie McMackin, and Sandi Baldwin. Fran Gray and Mary Bastable were the breeders. Jeep also ranks among the Top Ten producers in the breed's history with 43 AKC champions to his credit. As a show dog his career was short but spectacular. He finished from the puppy classes with three five-point major wins and Group placings. He accumulated five all-breed Bests in Show and several Specialty Bests, always owner-handled.

No kennel can survive without good bitches and Beaujangles was not without them. Some of the more notable were Belyn's Jezabel of Beaujangle ROM (1975–1985), who was a full-sister to Ch. Belyn's Roustabout ROM, otherwise known as "J.R." Jezabel was the dam of the "Ten Dog" and four other champion get. Ch. Beaujangles Think Blue ROM (1980–1994) was the dam of eight champions, five with the Beaujangle prefix and three with the Stonewall kennel name.

It should be obvious to all that Beaujangles has made a major impact in the breed over the past 25 years and that their impact will continue for the next 25 years through the tightly bred offspring that have departed their kennel.

*Ch. Beaujangle's Ten ROM, sired by Ch. Beaujangle's Mean Mr. Mustard ex Belyn's Jezabel of Beaujangle ROM.*

*Ch. Humphey Jo CD, TD, going BW in 1961.*

*Ch. Party Doll's Geraldine TD taking a Specialty BOS in 1970.*

## BEELEE

The BeeLee Bassets of Lena and Billy Wray go back to at least 1960 when Lena, currently a Life Member of BHCA, initially became a member of the club. Billy became a member in 1965. One of Lena's first dogs to attain "star" status was Ch. Humphey Jo CD TD, who became one of the first triple-titleholders in the breed. The Wrays were heavily into both showing and tracking. One of their bitches, Ch. Party Doll's Geraldine TD, earned her "T" at the first Nationals to offer tracking in 1970.

Although the Wrays have almost continually shown dogs in conformation over these many years, far and away, their most successful has been their recent dog, Ch. Bugle Bay's Kolache. A showy dog, and well presented by his handler Fred Rosson, Kolache was able to garner a number of all-breed Bests in Show.

*Ch. Bugle Bay's Kolache, taking the first of his several Bests in Show in 1994.*

## BEVLEE

The BevLee kennel began, as so many do, with the gift of a homeless Basset Hound to Beverly and Lee Stockfelt and their children in 1961 in Birmingham, Alabama. Pretty Girl quickly became a member of the family, and moved with the Stockfelts to Huntsville, Alabama, in 1962, where she was joined by another pet, an AKC-registered Basset, Miss Humphrey. In 1964 an effort was made to form a Basset Hound Club in Huntsville by Bill Cline, who had bred and shown Bassets in the Seattle area before moving to Huntsville. Unfortunately, there was not enough interest among the eight or ten Basset owners for the club to succeed, but the Stockfelts' interest in Bassets grew, and they actually showed Miss Humphrey at several all-breed fun matches in Huntsville and Birmingham. She was bred in 1966, and when the time came to register the pups, Beverly and Lee selected BevLee as their kennel name, for obvious reasons! Some years later the subtitle, "Literary Hounds" was added, along with the distinctive bookshelf logo, and all subsequent BevLee dogs bore registered names with a literary reference.

*Ch. BevLee's Tom Sawyer, going BOB over Specials, from the classes, in 1975. Handled here by breeder-owner Bev Stockfelt.*

*BevLee's Pooh Bear of Willi-O, en route to his championship in 1967.*

In mid-1966, the family moved to the Dallas/Fort Worth area, with Miss Humphrey and her eight six-week-old puppies. Shortly after the move, Beverly saw a notice for a fun match by the Dal-Tex Basset Hound Club. In a typical novice move, Miss Humphrey was dragged to the match and won a first prize in Novice (the only entry in that class)! Thanks to the kindness and courtesy of the Dal-Tex members, the Stockfelts were taken in hand and their interest cultivated. They were accepted as members of Dal-Tex shortly after the fun match, and, the membership's advice taken to heart, Miss Humphrey was never shown again, and her pups went to good homes!

Bill Cline owned Nancy Evans' A-GoGo and had bred him to one of his bitches, Carroll's D-Debbie, in early 1967. By then, the showbug had bitten the Stockfelts and they were in the market for a show prospect. Bill offered them one of the GoGo/Debbie pups, and he was named BevLee's Pooh Bear of Willi-O (Willi-O was the Cline kennel name). Willie was shown in puppy classes at Dallas area shows in the fall of 1967 and early 1968. He finished at 13 months. His winning record was, in part, due to the fact that he was unique in the Dallas area at that time. Willie was an open red and white, quite short in body, and weighed close to 60 pounds (quite heavy at that time). The vast majority of the dogs being shown in that area at the time was based on Margem Hills breeding and were typically very black with tan eyebrows, long

*Ch. BevLee's Elsinor, going WB and BOS in 1981. Handled by Bev Stockfelt under breeder-judge Frannie Messinger.*

and lean, and relatively lightweight. Whenever Willie went into the ring, he immediately stood out; judges either loved him or hated him!

Inevitably the question of breeding arose. Willie was the obvious choice for the sire, but there was no bitch available. Bill Cline came through again, giving the Stockfelts GoGo's dam, Ch. Abbot Run Valley Debbie, for a linebreeding. However, another dog had caught the BevLee eye, one being shown by Jimmy and Micky Helms: a large, mostly black dog named Ch. Musicland's Bill Bailey. The resulting Bill Bailey ex Abbot Run Valley Debbie litter became the first of a long line of BevLee pups and established the BevLee type, which was primarily open red and white with somewhat cobby bodies and a head somewhat more coarse and chunky than was widely popular at the time. Willie was later linebred and

outcrossed to several bitches and proved to be consistent in producing his type.

In 1968, the Helms offered the Stockfelts a nice young Wirehaired Dachshund, and she became the foundation of BevLee's second breed. Over the years, BevLee Dachshunds went to several other Basset breeders who established their own second breed lines. Between 1966 and 1993, BevLee produced 53 Basset Hound and Dachshund champions. Several BevLee dogs became the foundation of other successful kennels, and the BevLee name appears in many pedigrees.

In addition to breeding and showing, Beverly and Lee were active in dog club affairs. They joined the Dal-Tex Basset Hound Club in 1966 and the Basset Hound Club of America in 1967. They were charter members of the Basset Hound Club of Greater Fort Worth and the Trinity Valley Kennel Club. Both served their clubs as officers as well as in other capacities. Beverly was an editor of BHCA's *Tally-Ho*, was the BHCA Secretary for several years, and was named a BHCA Life Member in 1991. Beverly was approved as an AKC judge of Basset Hounds and Dachshunds in 1981, and as her judging assignments increased, breeding and showing decreased. The kennel became virtually inactive after 1990, and Beverly died of cancer in 1993, marking the end of more than a quarter century of dog activity. Her husband Lee has established the BevLee Memorial Fund with a cash do-

*Ch. BevLee Davy Jones ROM.*

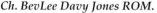

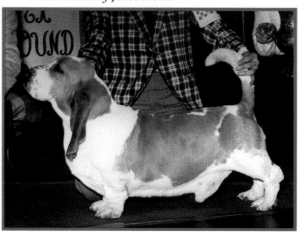

nation to BHCA. The fund honors Beverly's memory and anyone may make donations to it in memory of any person or dog to be so honored in the catalog at the National Specialty. The interest earned by this fund is to be used each year for the purchase of a Trophy to be awarded at the Nationals to the breeder of the BOB winner, the breeder having always been considered by Beverly to be the key link in the breeding/exhibiting/winning cycle. Beverly was a knowledgeable and successful breeder, a dedicated BHCA worker, and a devoted dog enthusiast who is missed by her peers.

*Ch. Craigwood-Seabreeze Chloe with owner-handler Norm Wiginton, after having won WB at the 1990 Nationals.*

## BIRNAM

New to the scene, historically speaking, are the Bassets of Birnam dogs, bred, owned, and shown by Norman and Mary Ann Wiginton. Establishing their kennel in 1987 with the purchase of their first show-quality Basset, Milldonn's Sir Basil of Birnam, they were fortunate to have been able to come up with a winner right from the start. "Basil" was purchased from Donna and Millard Howard and had been bred from Craigwood stock. He started a winning tradition for Norm and Mary Ann by going Best in Sweepstakes at the 1987 New Orleans BHC Specialty and finished his championship quickly by going Breed from the classes at all but one show.

In 1988 the Wigintons were invited by Sandra Campbell to visit her Craigwood kennels in Greenville, South Carolina. It was during that trip that they purchased Craigwood-Seabreeze Chloe who went on to become WB at the 1990 BHCA Nationals in Holland, Michigan.

During the time that Chloe was being shown, an agreement to co-own a bitch with Craigwood was struck. This bitch, Sleepyeye Butterscotch Drop, was to be bred to Basil, the Wiginton's original dog. Of the nine puppies that were whelped in that litter, five went on to finish their championships, earning Butterscotch the distinction of ROM. One of the produce finishing from this litter was Ch. Birnam's Magnolia of Craigwood, who went Best in Junior Sweepstakes at the 1990 Nationals and finished with two BW awards at the Suncoast and Greater San Antonio BHC shows. The other littermates, themselves Specialty show and Sweepstakes winners were Ch. Craigwood's Heart of Gold, Ch. Craigwood's Chandler of Birnam, Ch. Craigwood's Oliver of Birnam, and Ch. Craigwood Heartbeat of Birnam.

Thoroughly enjoying their newfound hobby and understandably encouraged with their success to date, Norman and Mary Ann set about the task of finding new property which would be more suitable for their purpose of breeding and showing the Bassets. They were fortunate, in 1991, to find 18 beautiful acres in the countryside of Milton, Florida where they have established a fine kennel with approximately 12 runs and several exercise areas, one of which is a fenced five-acre area in which the dogs can run.

Their next breeding was that of Ch. Craigwood-Seabreeze Chloe to Ch. Craigwood's Solow Hobby Knox, producing

*Ch. Birnam's Magnolia of Craigwood, winning a Best in Sweepstakes at nine months of age. Handled by owner Norm Wiginton under breeder-judge Virginia Kovalic.*

Ch. Birnam's Sage of Craigwood. Chloe's second breeding was to Ch. Craigwood's Oliver of Birnam, "Bob," producing Ch. Birnam's Ollie Bobba and Birnam's Song on the Breeze, "Zoe." Ollie finished his championship with three Specialty show wins and Zoe is currently being shown.

Ch. Milldonn's Sir Basil of Birnam, their original foundation stud, was then bred to Ch. Craigwood's Chelsea of Birnam and produced Ch. Birnam's Rising Son Alfie. He was also bred to Ch. Milldonn's Dreamy Dancer and produced Ch. Baywind's Autumn of Birnam. Out of the 15 puppies that Basil has sired, 7 have attained their championships, earning him the ROM.

Their Ch. Birnam's Magnolia of Craigwood was bred to Ch. Birnam's Rising Son Alfie and produced Birnam's Baby Huey and Birnam's Summer Blaze. "Maggie's" second breeding, to Ch. Hiflite Briarcrest Extra Man ROM, in the spring of 1996 resulted in five very promising youngsters.

In their relatively short time in the breed, the Wigintons have owner-handled over a dozen of their Bassets to their championships, of which two have attained their ROM status. They modestly attribute their early success to the Craigwood breeding program with which they started and the advice and friendship of Sandra Campbell over the past years. Having known this dedicated couple since their first Nationals win, I can further attest that their interest, training, and dedication continue to play a major part in whatever success they enjoy. There are always those that will attribute such early success to just plain good luck, but I must say that I've always found that the harder I've worked at anything, the luckier I've gotten with it! I suspect that such is the case here.

*Ch. Musicland's Ravishing Ruby, Bluvali foundation bitch.*

## BLUVALI

The Bluvali Bassets of Paul and Margie Wikerd started with the purchase of Wikerd's Lady Amanda in 1972. An incorrigible pup, she would eventually, through Margie's persistence, become Wikerd's Lady Amanda CDX. In 1973, the Wikerds relocated to St. Paul, Minnesota, joined the Twin Cities BHC and met new and knowledgeable friends, the Hills, the Jacquarts, and the Arbs. By 1974 they were ready for another dog and were lucky enough to be able to get "Daphy," Musicland's Baby Doll CD. Daphy attended her first trial at Duluth in

*Ch. Bluvali Double Or Nothin, a Ruby son.*

July of that year and Paul, at the last moment, decided that he wanted to handle her in conformation, thus ending Margie's handling career before it ever got started! Unfortunately, Daphy was lost at the tender age of two and a search for a replacement was started.

For the next 18 months, the Wikerds would continue their Basset Hound education by attending shows and trials, and through their membership in the local BHC and BHCA as well. In 1976 they were able to obtain Ch. Musicland's Ravishing Ruby, who was to become their foundation bitch and a super mother.

In 1977, and now located in Dryden, New York, the Wikerds searched for a suitable stud for Ruby. On the advice of Jeanne Hills, Paul and Margie visited the kennel of Gary and Dawn Towne to have a look at their stud force. One look at Ch. Heine Von Skauton and they knew that they had found what they wanted. In August of that year, Ruby delivered ten healthy pups by Heine. From this litter they kept and finished Ch. Bluvali Double Delight CD, Ch. Bluvali Double Or Nothin, and Ch. Bluvali Double Dare. In 1979, Ruby was bred again, this time to Ch. Lochopt's Halcyon Collegian,

*Ch. Bluvali Tom Collin, with handler Paul Wikerd in 1981.*

producing Ch. Bluvali Tom Collin and Ch. Bluvali Tammy. Not only did Ruby join the Register of Merit, but four of her five champions had Specialty wins to their credit. One of them, Delight, was BOS at the 1979 and 1980 Nationals.

The Wikerds did a number of breedings over the next few years, but suffered some major setbacks as a result of both parvovirus and rock ingestion, and consequently progress seemed frustratingly slow. In 1981 the Townes took Double Dare (Polly) and bred her to Ch. Belyn's Roustabout, producing Bluvali Bathilda Von Skauton, Arnalda Von Skauton and Klondike Von Skauton. Delight, meanwhile, was determined not to become a mother despite numerous breedings. Finally, after specialist consultation, she was bred to her brother Double Or Nothin, but of the three pups, only one, Manassas Von Skauton would survive to adulthood. This breeding was repeated in late 1982, hoping for a daughter, and produced Bluvali Thank Heavens and Bluvali Thornbird who was lost following surgery.

One of the Wikerds' favorites was Ch. Bluvali Ethan, whelped in November 1985, by Ch. Bluvali Tom Collin out of Bluvali Thank Heavens. Also in this litter

were Chs. Bluvali Eden and Erin. Ethan is a fourth-generation grandson of Delight. He was retired from the ring at under two years of age, but was already a Specialty BOB winner and a multiple Group placer.

Ch. Bluvali Alexandra's daughter, Chantilly, was bred to Ethan and in 1988 she whelped Ch. Bluvali Francis Micah, Argentine Ch. Bluvali Frances Margaret and Bluvali Sweet Jezabel UDT CGC. Also in 1988, Erin was bred to Ch. Lochopt Saxony Stile, producing Ch. Bluvali Slumber Thyme, Ch. Slumber Leila, Koka Treat, and Mocha Java. Bred to Bluvali Jeremiah in 1990, she produced Ch. Slumber Cody. In addition to the Chantilly litter, Ethan also was bred to Ch. Lochopt Debenture, producing Ch. Lochopt Phil Sheridan, (MacBride), and bred to Jacquart's Volya, she whelped Bluvali Poppin Fresh TD and Bluvali Pipin Hot.

Both Margie and Paul have served BHCA in numerous capacities over the years and Paul was president of the club when he passed away from cancer in 1993. Margie still maintains the kennel in Homer, New York, and has been approved to judge the breed.

*Ch. Bluvali Ethan, taking a Group first, Paul Wikerd handling, in 1987.*

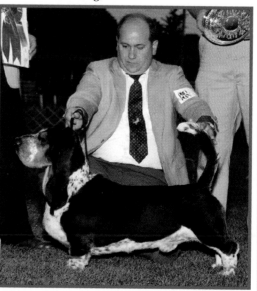

# BONE-A-PART

When Ted and Pat Ellis were looking at the house they were contemplating buying, Ted's first comment was, "Look dear, it has a fenced-in backyard. Now we can get a Basset Hound." Pat vaguely remembered promising something like that before they were married and thought no more about it. Shortly after buying the house, they purchased a Basset puppy. They named her Priscilla and wanted something French to go with that name. Pat suggested Bonaparte and asked how to spell it properly. Their son piped up "BONEAPART" ! They added the hyphens and that started the next 30 years of Bone-A-Part Basset Hounds.

An old-time breeder advised them early on that if they could combine the temperament, bone, and skin of the Santana Kennel and the sound conformation of the Lyn Mar line, they would really have something! They did, and they achieved their goal. Their first show Basset was Bridi's O. Keta and she was eventually bred to Ch. Ramblebriars

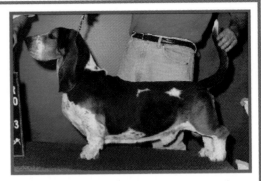

*Am/Can/SoAm. Ch. Bone-A-Parts Jacks Or Better, shown in South America.*

Local Broker ROM. This litter produced Ch. Bone-A-Parts Brass Buttons and Bone-A-Parts Black Velvet ROM. These four Bassets are behind everything in their kennel today.

By linebreeding and outcrossing carefully, they were able to produce quality and consistency. They brought in Ch. Chmar's Dixie Drifter to tighten up the Santana line. He was bred to Bone-A-Part's Romeing Kizzy ROM, and six of the litter of seven finished their championships. These exceptional littermates were: Am/Can/Bda. Ch. Bone-A-Parts State Of The Art, Am/Can/Bda. CD., Am/Can. TTI, Am/Can. CGC; Am/Can. Ch. Bone-A-Parts Agony N' Ecstasy; Ch. Bone-A-Parts Class Act; Ch. Bone-A-Parts Major Motion; Ch. Bone-A-Parts High Performance and Ch. Bone-A-Parts P.R. Man TD.

Movement, temperament and overall quality of conformation have been the Ellis' goal. They have finished no fewer than 68 AKC champions and there are several more still out there with points and waiting to finish. There are additional dogs of their breeding winning in numerous other parts of the world as well.

One hound that they are especially proud of is Am/Can/Bda. Ch. Bone-A-Parts Ms. Trixie Delite TTI CGC. She was one of four in her litter to finish. She started her show career at the BHCA Nationals, going Best in Senior Sweepstakes in 1986. Finishing in America in nine

*Am/Can/Bda. Ch. Bone-A-Parts Ms. Trixie Delite, en route to her American championship in 1987 with Ted Ellis handling.*

shows, she went to Canada with Davida Scott, Scots-Moore Bassets, and was WB, BW at the Canadian National Specialty, finishing her titles in Canada and also in Bermuda.

After returning home to Florida, Trixie was BOB at the Kentuckiana Specialty, BOS at the Suncoast Specialty in 1989, and BOS at the Pilgrim Specialty in 1994, achieving that distinction from the Veteran Bitch class. She went on to garner an AOM, again from

Bred by Exhibitor class at the 1989 BHCA Nationals. Four out of that litter of six went on to become champions. The remaining two were major pointed.

Another fine dog from this kennel is Am/Can/SoAm. Ch. Bone-A-Parts Jacks Or Better, who was BOB at the South Florida Specialty, BW at the Suncoast Specialty in 1990 and finished his championship at the Suncoast Specialty in 1991. After siring several nice champions, he went to Ben Canna

*Buster, Mo, and Salud, three champions typical of those residing at Bone-A-Part.*

the Veteran Bitch class, at the 1992 BHCA National Specialty and won BISS at the Suncoast Specialty in 1993, also from the Veteran class. In 1995 she obtained her Therapy Dog certification so that she could visit Ted in the nursing home, and she was a hit with everyone. (For those who may not be aware, Ted Ellis was involved in a serious auto accident and never fully recovered from its effects. He passed away on August 2, 1995.)

Ms Trixie is now happily retired. Her son, Am/Can/Bda. Ch. Bone-A-Parts David Copperfield, was the top-winning show dog, all-breed in Canada for 1993. His littersister, Ch. Bone-A-Parts Witchey Woman, won the

Bassets in Brazil in 1993 and is producing nicely there as well.

Bone-A-Part dogs have always done well at the BHCA National Specialty shows over the years. Three of their dogs have won the Open class: Bone-A-Parts White Tie & Tails CD; Bone-A-Parts Romeing Buffalo, who also went RWD; and Am/SoAm. Ch. Bone-A-Parts Bentley, now in Argentina at Scared Rabbit Bassets. Ch. Bone-A-Parts Seminole Wind was RWD from the 12–18 Month class in 1994 and went on to finish in four shows with three Specialty wins. Pat and Ted made many lasting friendships and always had fun. Ted believed, and Pat continues to believe, when it ceases to be fun, it's time to quit!

*Am/Can. Ch. Bow-Ridge's Charleston, going BIS. Breeder-owner-handler Roxanne Bowman under judge Ellsworth Gamble.*

## BOW-RIDGE KENNELS, REG.

Although relatively new members of BHCA, our Canadian neighbors, Roxanna and Lou Bowman purchased their first Basset Hound back in 1964 and have been long

*Am/Can. Ch. Bow-Ridge's Peter Frampton, Canada's Number One Producer, winning BHCC Specialty from the Veterans class under Mildred Heald.*

time competitors at our National Specialties. Their two excellent foundation bitches were Ch. Jarry's Taluhla, strong in Belbay background, and Ch. Sand-Dell's Anastasia, of Santana-Mandeville bloodlines. In fact, she was a Santana-Mandeville J.P. Morgan granddaughter. Their first litter in 1966 was by Ch. Westacres Black Haskell and out of Taluhla, producing their first homebred champion, Ch. Bow-Ridge's Absalom. Taluhla's first win was a five-point Specialty (BHCC) under breeder-judge Mercedes Braun.

Anastasia was a note-worthy specimen in her own right. She was the Bowman's third champion and she went on to become the Top Basset in Canada in 1971 (first time for a bitch). In 1973 she was BW at the BHCA Nationals under breeder-judge Owen Derryberry. Anastasia can be seen in the Gallery of Nationals Winners.

Making the greatest impact and moving the Bow-Ridge bloodline forward were Ch. Bow-Ridge's Georgette and Ch. Bow-Ridge's Scintillation. Georgette, bred to a young male that the Bowmans were attracted to at the 1973 Nationals, Am/Can. Ch. Harper's Jim Beam, produced the first Bow-Ridge BIS dog, Ch. Bow-Ridge's Charleston. His littersister, Ch. Bow-Ridge's Amanda, had the strongest influence on the breed since she was to become the dam of Canada's number-one producing Basset Hound, Am/Can. Ch. Bow-Ridge's Peter Frampton and the number two producer as well, Am/Can. Ch. Bow-Ridge's Designer Genes. When planning current breedings, the Bowmans still try and match pedigrees that will concentrate Amanda's influence to the fullest genetic potential.

Frampton was able to produce not only more champions than any other Basset in Canada, but nearly every one of them had Group placings to their credit. He is the sire of Can. Ch. Kendorba's Boston Blackie, Canada's number-one Basset for 1983 and 1984, and Am/Can. Ch. Bow-Ridge's Chauvinist, number three in the US in 1980 and number two in Canada in 1983. Chauvinist amassed a career total of over 100 US Group placings.

Chauvinist sired many champions, the most notable of which were Am/Can. Ch. Bow Ridge's Designer Genes, Can Ch. Bow-Ridge's Limited Edition, and Can Ch. Tavyecho's A.J., Canada's number-one Basset Hound for 1985, 1986, and 1987.

Some of the more recent breeding plans revolve around the Designer Genes offspring, Am/Can. Ch. Bow-Ridge's Gregor Mendel and Can. Ch. Bow-Ridge's Hot Dam, as well as the Specialty winner (BHCC) Am/Can. Ch. Best Lena Horne, a very typey Frampton daughter. From a breeding of Lena to Designer Genes, four have finished their Canadian championships, including Am/

*Am/Can. Ch. Bow-Ridge's Chauvinist, taking one of his numerous Group firsts, handled by Bobby Barlow.*

*Am/Can. Ch. Bow-Ridge's Macho, shown here going BW, handled by Jerry Rigden under judge Tip Tipton.*

Can. Ch. Bow-Ridge's Varley, who distinguished himself by winning Best in Junior Sweepstakes at the BHCA in 1992 followed by WD in 1993. He has further distinguished himself in Canada by winning the Basset Hound Club of Canada Specialty three consecutive years; 1994, 1995, and 1996. His photo is in the Gallery of Nationals Winners section.

While occasional planned breeding continues, their exhibiting has become somewhat curtailed due to the addition of Lou's name to the list of hound judges in Canada. There are approximately 60 Bow-Ridge Canadian champions, 12 American, 1 Mexican and 1 Italian. The Bowmans continue to enjoy the fellowship experienced through the fancy and continue to serve the breed in many activities, committees, and positions through the CKC, Seaway K.C. and the Basset Hound Club of Canada.

*Dual Ch. Branscombe Dulcinea CD, TD, VC, ROM.*

# BRANSCOMBE

Back in the early 1970s the media liked to present the Basset Hound as a lovable, lazy clown with no ambition in life beyond securing the best seat on the couch. It was then that Francis and Ruth Paule set a goal for themselves. They were disturbed by this popularized image of a breed that had been developed to hunt rabbit with great accuracy and endurance. And they knew that they wanted to enjoy activities with the Branscombe Basset Hounds they bred. They decided to participate in any and all of the AKC performance events then in existence (field trials, tracking, and obedience) according to each dog's capabilities. Also, believing that the breed standard of conformation was essential to performance, they showed their Bassets in conformation as well. One of only a handful of members who do so!

First came their show-bred foundation bitch, FCh. La Z Dee J's Bonny Bell, bred by Alfred Harris, who early on demonstrated her determination to hunt rabbit. From her has come a line of Branscombe Bassets, first in Illinois and later in North Carolina, who have come to be counted on for their versatility in performance. For many Bassets, given the opportunity, their love of hunting precludes all other possible activity. There is no "couch-potato" evident in the Basset working in the field.

*Dual Ch. Branscombe's Man of La Mancha CD, TD, VC.*

*Dual Ch. Branscombe Trumpeter, shown going BW in 1993, with breeder-owner-handler, Ruth Paule.*

Beginning with "Bonny's" son, Dual Ch. Branscombe Troilus TD, sired by Ch. Slippery Hill Rudyard, there have come eight Dual Champions in Bonny's direct line. Two of these, littermates Dual Ch. Branscombe's Man of La Mancha and Dual Ch. Baranscombe Dulcinea, became the first and second Bassets in history to achieve titles in all four AKC title events then recognized.

Next to hunting, the Paules found that their Bassets enjoy tracking people. As a breed they have a natural ability for this and, as quite young puppies, take eagerly to the training and being out in the field with their

owners. Some 15 of the Paules' Bassets have earned TD titles. Branscombe Aldonza TDX, owned by Bill Lindsay and Branscombe Albert Alexander, Am/Can. CDX TDX, owned by Margaret Haselden, have distinguished themselves at the advanced level.

Fewer Branscombe Bassets have ventured into the obedience ring, with four obtaining CDs. This likely has been because the Paules themselves were hesitant about obedience and much preferred being outdoors with their dogs. Certainly there are a number of Branscombe offspring enjoying and achieving in obedience with their owners, reflecting the increase nationally in the number of Bassets working in obedience.

The Paules have limited their breeding program to one or two litters a year. In planning, they focus on passing on, through line-breeding, those qualities of mind and spirit that make for great performance, while improving conformation through careful outcrosses. Several Branscombe bitches, Dulcinea, Bugle Ann and Ch. Branscombe Bianca TD and Ch. Branscombe Portia TD are listed on the ROM. "Doc" Paule served on the Board of Directors of BHCA, was president from 1985—1987 and was instrumental in the making of the tracking and field trial films. Since the death of Francis Paule, Ruth has had to limit activities, but is aiming to maintain their line that is strong in performance and sound in conformation.

*Dual Ch. Branscombe Bugle Ann TD, VC, ROM.*

*Dual Ch. Branscombe Troubadour TD,*
*VC, owned by Melody Fair and Fritz Hager.*

*Dual Ch. Branscombe Good Intentions,*
*owned by Leslie Hager.*

*Dual Ch. Branscombe Kachina, BHCA 1992 Futurity Stakes Winner, owned by Melody Fair*
*and Fritz Hager.*

# BRIARCREST

Knox and Bette Williams' Briarcrest kennel was started in the Corpus Christi area and had its roots in the Margem Hills line through Am/Bda. Ch. Sir Tomo of Glenhaven. Of course, Tomo had a high percentage of the Lyn Mar bloodline. In 1966 they acquired, from Margretta Patterson and Emily Kultcher, Margem Hills Brag-A-Bout, ("Molly Molly"). She was a very sound, refined, black tri bitch with an outstanding front, sired by Tomo. Also purchased at the same time, but from Jean Wills, was her littersister, Margem Hills Dragon Lady. Dragon Lady was a red bitch

of the Margem Hills hounds were eventually acquired. Rasputin of Margem Hills, a fine young male, unfortunately was to die suddenly of cancer while in the kennel of Frank and Dorothy Hardy, needing but one point to finish his championship. Ch. Knox's Hope of Margem Hills (a Tomo grand–daughter) was easily finished, as well as Margem Hills Top Deck and a young red and white pup, from Jean Wills, Margem Hills Mr. Brown. After finishing Mr. Brown, he was shipped to Michigan and co-owned with Finn and Mary Louise Bergishagen. He was bred quite extensively, and among his numerous winners was one National Specialty winner. Brownie lived a good life for many years at Jagersven. When he was bred to Randy Frederiksen's bitch, Ch. Coran's Pene–lope O'George, he produced an excel-lent black tri bitch, Ch. Briarcrest Double Bubble as well as Am/Can. Ch. Coran Country Cojac, Ch. Coran Country Cache, and Ch. Coran Country Copyl. Bubbles did some very nice winning in the late 1970s, including taking several Specialty BOBs. She

*Ch. Margem Hills Brag-A-Bout, in 1967, handled by Bette Williams, under breeder-judge Peg Walton.*

with very little white on her. Both these bitches were about 25 percent Santana-Mandeville, as their dam was a Ch. Nancy Evans Double Cross daughter.

Dragon Lady was bred to Ch. Oranpark Dexter, producing the flashy, dark mahogany Ch. Knox's Kash McCall, who was sold to Bob Vickers. After completing her championship, Brag-A-Bout was bred to Ch. Lyn Mar Acres End Man, producing an excellent black tri bitch, Knox's Imogene of Briarcrest. Four more

was later bred to Jagersven Amos (a Ch. Lyn Mar Acres End Man son) and produced a very nice black tri male, Ch. Briarcrest Lee N' Perrin ("Wooster").

In 1976, Frank and Virginia Kovalic gave the Williams the bitch Stoneybluff Caroline. She was five years old at the time and was out of that "super" litter sired by Ch. Jagersven Monarch II and out of Ch. Lyn Mar Acres Michelle. Not shown until the age of seven, she still was able to attain her championship.

One of their highlights was when she won the Veteran Bitch class at the 1980 Nationals. Pleased with many of the Stoneybluff dogs, they used Stoneybluff Basil on their bitch Strathalbyn Bernadette, whom they had gotten from Eric and Erica George. This breeding produced a nice bitch for them, Briarcrest Stoneybluff Whiz. Whiz, bred to Ch. Stoneybluff Silvester, produced a big open tri male, Ch. Briarcrest Stoneybluff Bevo, which they kept, and the Kovalics took Ch. Briarcrest Stoneybluff Beth.

*Ch. Lochopt Fantasy ROM, dam of Ch. Hiflite Briarcrest Extra Man.*

At the 1981 Nationals in Lebanon, Pennsylvania, Knox noticed a puppy bitch standing in last place in the 6–9 Month Puppy Bitch class that took his eye. Eventually she was moved to the front and won her class. This was Lochopt Fantasy, a Ch. Lochopt Halcyon Collegian daughter out of Ch. Lochopt Risk of Rebownd. Never slow to make a decision, Knox purchased her from Rick Cromley on the spot. (What Knox did not know was that this writer was on the opposite side of the ring trying to decide between Fantasy and another bitch that Barbara Cromley had brought to that show for me to choose between the two of them! I had wanted a Lochopt bitch to breed to our recently acquired Switchbark's Ashmore. I was disappointed, but since it was Knox that had gotten her, I figured something could eventually be worked out to accomplish the breeding.) Knox and Bette finished her in six shows, losing only once. A couple of years later, Knox gave Fantasy to the author, with the understanding that she would be bred to Ch. Switchbark's Ashmore, who by then had won the breed at the 1984 Nationals. Callnamed "Fancy," she was bred three times to "Moe," all with good results.

*Ch. Briarcrest Double Bubble, handled to a BOB by Knox Williams, under breeder-judge Jim White.*

*Ch. Hiflite Briarcrest Extra Man ROM, foundation stud of Briarcrest since 1987.*

In late July 1987, my wife, Mary Jane, called Knox and Bette and told them that we had bred Fancy for the last time and that this three-month-old litter had a tri male that was the best thing that Hiflite had ever produced and that we wanted them to have him. Not only did we feel that they at least had a dog coming, since they had given us Fancy, but we were afraid that they were about "burned out" with the dog game. Not wanting to lose them from the breed, we thought it well to praise the attributes of the pup to a considerable extent. It worked! Knox said, "If he's that good, we'll come down right now!" and they did!

Knox likes to tell the story that he has only had his "breath taken away" two times. One was the first time he saw Bette, and the second was the first time he saw "Butch." Knox was convinced that the 12-

*Ch. Lil Creek U-Haul O' Briarcrest, a Kicker son and current Briarcrest Special.*

week-old male was the best puppy that he had ever seen and felt that he had all of the old Lyn Mar breed type. It was agreed that the name would be Hiflite Briarcrest Extra Man, and he went to Austin that day and, bypassing the Briarcrest kennels, moved directly into the house, where he still rules!

Butch won his first points, a four-point major, going BW at the BHC of Greater San Antonio Specialty under breeder-judge Jean Sheehy at the age of six months. Knox finished him at the Houston K.C. show, under breeder-judge Margretta Patterson, the day after he had gone BOB from the classes at the BHC of Houston Specialty, under

*Ch. Briarcrest Kicker O' Lil Creek, taking a 1993 Group placement.*

breeder-judge, the late Appie Myers. When he was two years old, he was handled as a Special by Pat Willer, amassing 50 BOBs, 12 Group placements and 8 Specialty Bests.

Since 1987, the Briarcrest breeding program has been built around this hound's bloodline and his sons and daughters. At the encouragement of Pat Willer, Knox agreed to breed him to Ch. Lil Creek Additional Premium (a bitch with some Santana blood as a result of Sandie Roush's Chasan line), owned by Dottie Christiansen. Having produced two champions, Ch. Lil Creek Christine and Ch. Lil Creek Raisa the Red, this breeding was repeated. This second breeding produced Ch. Briarcrest Kicker O' Lil Creek. Bred again, for the third time, they produced Ch. Lil Creek Fast Track and Ch. Briarcrest Gypsy O' Lil Creek. Bred to a daughter of Additional Premium, Ch. Lil

Creek Uffda, he produced Ch. Lil Creek Carrie and Ch. Lil Creek Briarcrest Top Gun. "Gunner" was sold to Danny and Julie Jones and was campaigned by Danny in the early '90s. He was BW at the 1990 BHCA Nationals and went on to win the Group at the prestigious Westminster K.C. in 1992.

Ch. Briarcrest Kicker O' Lil Creek was shown with success as a Special in 1993, winning Groups and Specialties. He was a large, long, very heavy boned black tri, with considerable ticking. He had a head piece and breed type that would "take your breath away!" (Third time for Knox!) Unfortunately, he was lost to cancer, in his prime, at four years of age. A month before he died, he was bred to his granddaughter, Ch. Briarcrest Extra E-Z O'Chasan, a Butch daughter. From this breeding came two of the newest Briarcrest champions, Ch. Briarcrest Walks At Night and his sister, Ch. Briarcrest Shawnee. Kicker, the sire of Briarcrest special Ch. Lil Creek U Haul O' Briarcrest, is listed in the ROM, having sired no fewer than 12 champion get.

Butch was bred to Stoneybluff Cottonhil Winger, co-owned by the Williams and Virginia Kovalic. From this breeding they produced Ch. Briarcrest Stoneybluff Pecos, an up-and-coming Briarcrest stud dog heavy in Lyn Mar bloodlines. Knowing that there was a "niche" in the genes between Butch and the big typey Santana bitches of Chasan, the Williams agreed with Sandie Roush to breed Butch to Ch. Marguerita O' Thompson. This litter produced four champions, one taken by the Williams to become Ch. Chasan Briarcrest Extra Dot. Marguerita's littersister was bred to Butch, producing Ch. Briarcrest Chasan Cover Girl and Ch. Shalazar's Lover Boy O' Chasan, co-owned with Debbie Eskew. A repeat of this breeding produced Ch. Briarcrest Extra E-Z O' Chasan, who has become a good producer for the kennel. The Cover Girl bitch was specialed and handled by Pat Willer, finishing the year as the number-two Basset in the breed in 1995.

Butch was bred back to his granddaughter, Chasan's Devil or Angel, a Kicker daughter, who is co-owned with Sandie Roush. This breeding resulted in an excellent red and white bitch, Ch. Briarcrest Chasan Xtra Fancy. She is a large, long bitch, with what is probably the best front and shoulder layback that Briarcrest has yet produced. Knox and Bette feel that in the breedings to those bitches with Santana-Mandeville heritage, Butch is able to refine the progeny, giving them lots of neck, style, temperament, and a very high percentage of good forequarters.

*Ch. Briarcrest Chasan Xtra Fancy, going WB for a five-point major at the 1995 Kentuciana Specialty under breeder-judge Carla LaFave.*

Butch has been used extensively at stud by a number of kennels and has produced no fewer than 47 titleholders with numerous additional pointed get still being shown. Knox and Bette are especially appreciative of the support of Sharon and Steve Calhoun (By-U-Cal) and Barbra and David Keene (Morningwood). Without their quality bitches, Butch's super production record would not have been possible.

## BRIERWOOD

*The author graciously acknowledges the Launey family to tell the story of its involvement in Bassets.*

With intercom Christmas carols cajoling shoppers into impulse purchases, the career mother steered her child-in-tow away from the mall pet shop window explaining that Christmas time was not the time to buy daddy a kitten. "Besides," she discouraged, "your daddy grew up with dogs." The child did not forget. Nor did the directive to work on a set of criteria for compatibility to the household deter the child's study of library resources. A few months later four breeds were selected in secret and mother and child conned Daddy into attending a local dog show. The Basset Hound was on the list and it brought a smile to Daddy's face! The letter writing campaign began. In June Daddy received a surprise puppy for his birthday.

This good quality pet introduced the entire family to the dog fancy. We had a lot to learn. She was not show quality; tracking does not involve laying a trail of yuppy puppy Jelly Bellies through the woods in the fashion of Hansel and Gretel; lagging behind five paces does not earn a qualifying score in obedience; and we should have found out how good she was in the field before she was spayed. She did honor us with the first AKC title our family ever earned. Carsie Marie and the birthday puppy earned a CD.

Father had great interest in performance events. He readied his own favorite Basset Hounds for obedience, tracking, and field competition. In the developmental years of the agility, Chris Launey announced US Dog Agility Association trials throughout the US He felt quite privileged to announce the very first AKC agility trial. Chris was known as "The Voice of Astro World Series of Dog Shows Performance Events," presiding as master of ceremonies from inception. Thou-

*Ch. Brierwoods Brigand CD, after having won Best Jr. in Sweeps, WD and BW at the 1987 BHCA Nationals at the age of seven months, two days.*

sands of the general public were helped to understand and enjoy flyball, scent hurdle racing and agility. Chris died unexpectedly at the age of 49. News of his death traveled the Internet among the agility fanciers before many Basset Hound fanciers knew or read about it in *Dog News* and *Tally-Ho*.

Mother found dog show trips a delightful respite from the annoying weekend vegetative state in which she often found father and child watching TV kung-fu movies. Applying what she had learned, Mother set about purchasing the very best line bred show-quality foundation bitch available. Fourth pick from the first breeding of a very successful pairing at Musicland would become Ch. Musiclands Southern Comfort CD TD ROM, dam of 1987 BHCA Nationals Best Junior Sweepstakes, WD and BW, 1987 BHCA Nationals tracking qualifier, 1989 Nationals Best Brace in Show and multi all-breed Best Brace in Show, BHCA 1989 Nationals Tracking qualifier. "Sophie" was devoted to Chris Launey. No other being was first in her heart. She died 12 days after Chris Launey.

Basset Hounds that have been produced by or earned titles while at Brierwood include: Moonbeams Lunar Apogee CD, who excelled at tracking down Jelly Bellies in the woods; Ch. Musiclands Southern Comfort

CD TD ROM; Ch. Brierwoods The Red Douglas, the puppy that stayed when the child asked, "Can I keep him, Mother?"; Brierwoods Musical Schooze TDX, who earned her TD at the Colorado Nationals while her owner watched from the gallery with a newly broken leg; Ch. Brierwoods Brigand CD, winner of 1987 Nationals Best Junior, WD and BW at the age of seven months and two days old; Ch. Brierwoods Zoe TD, a dog who intensely loved, lived and died too young; Ch. Brierwoods Lou Ann Hampton CD, who, braced with Zoe, won the 1989 BHCA Nationals Best Brace and numerous all-breed Best Brace in Show; Musiclands Lily TD, tracked by Judith Bowers in quest of tracking a dog from each of the seven groups before applying to AKC for a tracking judge license; Brierwoods Mavourneen TD, who cemented our friendship with a lovely family in Colorado; Ch. Musiclands Pink Panther 1989 BHCA Nationals Best Junior; Ch. Brierwoods Precious Sue; Ch. Brierwood Winter Shadow TD, my devoted companion through the grieving process; Ch. Brierwoods Mary Katherine, a puzzle to this day; Thai Ch. Brierwoods Mary Jo, her owner a puzzle to this day; Ch. Brierwoods Stella G, a lovely bitch and companion; Brierwoods Miles From Home TD, a handsome fellow who tracks well in deep snow; Dual Ch. Branscombes Troubadour TD VC, the most talented, engaging, yet naughty hound you will ever meet; and Ch. Moonbeams Astronomer, a special gift from my dear friend Linda Beam, who finished his championship at a BHCA Regional then went on to become a multiple Group and Specialty Show winner in 1996. "Astro" was transferred to Dr. Malisa Martinez of Buenos Aires. The return of two bitches to Brierwood, bred by her, includes the pedigrees of Ch. Raspor's Tiger Black, his littermate, and bloodlines that include Ed Smizer's Riveredge pedigrees.

Brierwood-bred or affiliated dogs have titled and participated in obedience, tracking, conformation, futurity, and field trials.

*Ch. Brierwood Winter Shadow (Ch. Musiclands Spike Jones ROM ex Ch. Brierwoods Zoe) with handler Ed Smizer.*

*Ch. Moonbeams Astronomer, being awarded a Group placement, handled by Bryan Martin under judge Barbara Alderman.*

Yet, for all that Brierwood has accomplished, contributed and enjoyed as a family involved in the Basset Hound fancy, there is a significant debt to the friendship and tutelage of Bob and Mary Jane Booth, Jeanne Hills, Randy Frederiksen, Linda Beam, Judith Bowers, Cindy Horvath, Ruth Paule, Fritz Hager, Jim and Marge Cook, and Nancy and Bryan Martin. We have felt an obligation to support and participate when and wherever inspired or asked. With every opportunity to participate, support and serve, you benefit from an opportunity to learn. And by reinvesting your time and knowledge, you honor those who have invested in you.

Sanda has served as an officer of BHCA and on various committees including Education, Futurity and Audit. She currently chairs the Research Committee. She has also authored numerous articles that have been published in *Tally-Ho*. In 1996 she presided as Chairman-Secretary of BHCA's first combined TD TDX VST Tracking Test, which earned the club a letter of commendation by AKC Field Rep John Barnard. The regional committee of Texans that she chaired in 1996 pursued and earned BHCA the privilege of offering this advanced tracking test to the membership.

## BRISTLECONE

Thad and Carol Makowski of Boulder, Colorado began their interest in Basset Hounds in 1979 when they acquired their first Basset, Ch. Gentle Julius Too CD, "Juluis," who was out of a dog owned by Bill and Libby Sallada. (Bill and Libby Sallada have done yeoman's service for the breed in the rescue of Bassets nationwide.) They joined BHCA at that time and began breeding in 1985 when they acquired their foundation bitch, Halcyon-Beartooth Po of Mi-Lin, from Doc and Vicki Steedle, through Byron and Carol Wisner's Beartooth kennels in Billings, Montana. This important bitch was bred to Ch. Jagersven Huckleberry Finn and produced Ch. Bristlecone's Angelfire, Bristlecones's Sophie, and Bristlecone's Snow Queen. Snow Queen, "Loretta," was bred to Ch. Chrislane's Entertainer and produced Ch. Bristlecone's Stars N' Stripes and Ch. Bristlecone's Skyhi Den Cherie. The quantity of dogs bred by the Makowski's thus far has been very limited, however, they have been pleased with the quality, good health, and absence of whelping problems. More litters with these same goals are planned for the future.

*Ch. Bristlecone's Stars N' Stripes shown by Carol Makowski, taking BW en route to her championship.*

## BUGLE BAY

Basset Hounds have been a part of the lives of Jim and Marge Cook since 1965 when they purchased their first puppy while living in Tucson, Arizona. Pandy became their companion and, when she was six months old, they enrolled her in an obedience class. Jim says that when Pandy graduated fourth in her class, Marge was hooked! Pandy eventually became Nancy Evans Pandora UDT and was their start in this breed.

Their first conformation dog was a bitch from California of Santana-Mandeville breeding. Bred by Harvey and Dorothy Fullerton, Ch. Le Clair's Merry Madelyn UD is credited with the development of an outgoing, merry temperament in the Bugle Bay line, something for which it is well known. When bred, she provided the kennel with some good genetic material in the form of two very special bitches, Ch. Bugle Bay's Ado Annie CD and Ch. Bugle Bay's Soufflé UD.

By this time, the Cooks had already started field trialing, and even though both of these girls had some age on them, they still were able to accumulate some field points. Although their dogs were from show

*Ch. Bugle Bay's Meatball, sire of ten champions, two of which are dual champions.*

lines, they had some talent in the rabbit department, probably through Merry Madelyn's dam, Hartshead Magnolia.

In recent years Jim and Marge have finished two dual champions, sisters who were sired by Ch. Bugle Bay's Meatball. Both of these bitches were also gems in the whelping box. Between them, Dual Champion Bugle Bay's Anise O'Stillhouse TD ROM and Dual Champion Stillhouse Abagail CD TDX ROM, have produced 16 titled offspring. Abby is the first Basset Hound to achieve

*Dual Champion Bugle Bay's Anise O'Stillhouse TD, dam of six champions.*

all the titles of Dual Champion CD and TDX. She earned her last title of CD at nine and a half years of age.

The Cooks finished their first tracking dog in 1971. In those years no one was tracking in Texas, so they held the line in one hand and the book in the other! They claim to have made many mistakes, but say that their dog was a good one and made up for their errors!

Currently Marge teaches tracking classes and is the tracking chairman for Texas Tri-City Obedience Club. She also taught obedience classes for 15 years at the same club. In addition to having finished three UDs and many CDs and CDXs, she is also the training director of handling classes for the Fort Worth Kennel Club, for which Jim is the current show chairman.

In all, the Cooks have produced no fewer than 44 bench and field champions as well as numerous tracking and obedience title-holders. In addition, they have had many HIT (High in Trial) and BIS wins. Jim and Marge Cook and their Bugle Bay Bassets are one of a handful of fanciers who have "done it all" in the breed and are truly deserving of much recognition for their dedication and effort in promoting the Basset Hound as an all 'round hound!

*Ch. Bugle Bay's Firecracker CDX, TDX, being shown by his owner, Evelyn Gregory. Both Anise and Firecracker were sired by Ch. Southlake Wailin Willie CD.*

*Above: Ch. Bugle Bay's Sukiyaki ROM, owned by David and Barbara Keene, (Morningwood).*

*Ch. Bugle Bay's Snow Cone CD, TD, going Best in Sweeps in 1990. Handled by Marge Cook under judge Judy Webb.*

73

## BY-U-CAL

Sharon and Steve Calhoun, of Bell City, Louisiana, acquired their first Basset Hound while Steve was in the Navy and stationed in Norfolk, Virginia. The time was 1972, and at a local veterinarian office, they met a Basset Hound fancier who had some Oranpark Bassets that he had gotten from California. They were invited to a Basset match and have been hooked ever since.

Upon completion of Steve's active duty with the Navy, they returned to Lake Charles, Louisiana. Shortly thereafter, they met Janet (Bergendal) Champagne, who loved Basset Hounds and was active in the Texas Basset Hound Club, located in Corpus Christi, Texas. Learning from Janet and many others along the way, as well as through their memberships in BHCA and numerous Basset Hound Clubs in Texas and Louisiana, they pursued their study of genetics and good Basset Hound structure.

Their first champion, Ch. Geronimos Big Daddy, was acquired through the help of Pat Willer. Sharon finished *big* at the BHC of Greater Houston Specialty when she was eight-and-a-half-months pregnant with their first son in 1976. Wanting to advertise this milestone, they thought it necessary to establish a kennel name. While designing the ad, they came up with "By-U" to symbolize their local area and the "Cal" from their last name.

In time, they began to acquire better show and breeding stock and found that much of what they wanted was to be found in the Hiflite and Glenhi kennel stock. Hiflite, however, was not breeding at that time, so the Calhouns tried to breed and acquire dogs that tied back into the Hiflite gene pool. To establish their current bloodline, their first Group-winning bitch, Ch. Macklands Queen Anne's Lace, sired by Ch. Glenhi's Downrite Spade King and acquired for them by Pat Willer, was flown to Michigan to be bred to Ch. Margem Hills Mr. Brown.

Through the years, they have bred strictly for their own use in the show ring. In doing so, they have not produced a large number of dogs, but their quality has been excellent with the percentage of champion offspring continually increasing. The breeding of Ch. By-U-Cals Freckles to Ch. Hiflite Briarcrest Extra Man has produced four champions thus far, with three other pointed get currently in the ring. Of these, Ch. By-U-Cals Razzle Dazzle took an AOM at the prestigious 1996 Westminster K.C. show, has won BOB and BOS at BHCA regional Specialties, and has won BOB at six other Specialty club

*By-U-Cal's foundation bitch, Ch. Macklands Queen Anne's Lace, shown by owner, Sharon Calhoun. On the right is Annie's sire, Ch. Glenhi's Downrite Spade King, shown by owner Don Heronimus, under judge Thelma Brown.*

*Ch. By-U-Cals Razzle Dazzle, receiving an AOM at the 1996 Westminster K.C. show. Handler, Pat Willer and judge, Betty Stenmark.*

## CAPRIOLE

Kathy Bova of Highland, Michigan, is no newcomer to Bassets, having gotten her first one in 1965. Making the usual mistake that most of us do, she saw one in a local pet store and just had to have it. Luckier than most, this one was only one generation removed from show stock. Enrolling in obedience training, she was encouraged by the instructor to pursue the dog's CD. This accomplished, and having watched conformation at these same shows, she decided to give the show ring a try also. The most that she was able to accomplish with this dog in conformation events were two Reserve Winners ribbons, but as she says, "I sure learned a lot!"

In 1968 Kathy was asked to join the BHC of Greater Detroit. This was back in the days when well-known breeders Chris Teeter (Long View Acres) and Queenie Wickstrom were active members of that club. Kathy is still a member, having held every office and served on every committee over the years. A BHCA member since 1970, she has participated in obedience, tracking, and conformation events. Her Capriole Muddy Brown Sneaker TDX was the first Basset bitch in Michigan to achieve her TDX title.

shows. In addition, Razzle Dazzle has won numerous Groups and Group placements at all-breed shows. Another very nice bitch of this breeding was Best in Jr. Sweepstakes at the 1995 BHCA Nationals. A third bitch went to Mexico to be specialed in quest of achieving the title of Top Basset in that country.

Steve and Sharon say that it doesn't seem like they've been involved in the sport all that long, until they look back at all that has happened since that first pet in Norfolk to their first now having one in the National Rankings. They recall that someone told them right after they got started in the breed, "If you are still in dogs after seven years, you will be there the rest of your life!" They're pretty sure that he was right! This writer can attest that this couple has enjoyed significant success in the Beagle breed as well. Razzle Dazzle was selected BOB at the 1996 National Specialty.

*Right: Capriole Ruffian, Am/Can. TD. Bred to Margem Hills Mr. Brown, she produced Capriole Muddy Brown Sneaker TDX, the first Basset to achieve that title in Michigan.*

## CASTLEHILL

A kennel that's "not been around that long," historically speaking, is the Castlehill kennels of Jim and Sharon Dok. Established in 1978, the Doks have made their mark on the breed. There aren't many places on their ten acres in Gilroy, California, that you won't see a Basset Hound. Something under 20 of them share their living space, frolicking in the fenced yard, sleeping next to the kitchen, playing in the garage, or sunning on the deck.

From what I've seen in recent years, there seems that there has been considerable recognition of the quality of the Castlehill hounds since there is usually one in serious competition at Specialty shows nationwide. Primarily, the Doks are in Bassets for the love of the breed (and English Setters as well!) as Jim explains, "for themselves" and for the satisfaction of matching one of their dogs to the right person. They realize that not every dog can be a show dog, but they place each of their pet-quality Bassets in the same way that they place a potential champion—with care and thought. They recognize, as we all should, that "Bassets are not the dog for everybody."

How did they get their start? Sharon laughs, "Jim got the Basset Hounds when he married me." Sharon grew up with Bassets because her parents, like many others of that generation, became enchanted with Cleo, the Basset star of the TV show, "The People's Choice." When Sharon and Jim married, they bought their first Basset for a pet. Their next several Bassets were show dogs. After a few litters, they had four champions and then, as Sharon puts it, "we were on."

The Dok's first nationally noted dog was Am/Can. Ch. JerCat's Kirby of Aikane. "Animal," as he was known, was sired by Ch. Hallmark Malcolm and out of Ch. Tal-E-Ho's Lotus. He was bred by Cathie and Jerry Spencer, JerCat Bassets. Animal was the number-one Basset Hound for 1982, 1983, and 1984. During that period he amassed a record of 135 Group placements with 46 Group firsts and 7 all-breed BIS.

*Am-Can. Ch. JerCat's Kirby of Aikane, in 1982 winning one of his numerous Group firsts with handler Ric Byrd, under breeder-judge Margretta Patterson.*

*Am/Can. Ch. Castlehill's Top Spot, winning the Group in 1990 with handler Ric Byrd.*

Some of the Doks' notable Bassets are: Am/Can. Ch. Castlehill's Top Spot, sired by Ch. Dan D's Gimli of Sanchu and out of Ch. Rebelglen's A Minor Calamity ROM; Ch. Castlehill's Ava Gardener, sired by Ch. Craigwood's Reese and out of Ch. Castlehill's Hot Cinders; and Ch. Castlehill's Totally Fur Sure, sired by their Top Spot and out of Ch. Sanchu's Cream de Mocha. "Topper's" show record includes an all-breed BIS, multiple Specialty BIS and he was the number-one Basset Hound for 1990. Ava Gardener was the 1993 BHCA Nationals BW at the 1993 Specialty in San Diego. Her photo is featured in the Gallery of Nationals Winners section. "Shurl" is the most current competitor of the three and is still being shown. She is also a Specialty show winner and has multiple Group placements to her credit.

Jim and Sharon still make a fair number of dog shows each year as they continue to enjoy breeding and showing their own dogs. Both have recently started their judging careers as well. Sharon has already had the honor of being selected to judge the Regular Dog classes at the 1995 BHCA National Specialty and Jim was selected by his peers

*Ch. Castlehill's Totally Fur Sure, a specialty winner and multiple Group placer.*

to judge the 1995 BHCA Futurity. The future of the breed will remain in good hands with experienced younger members of the national breed club like the Doks.

## CHANTINGHALL

The Chantinghall Basset Hound kennels were started in 1959 by Mr. and Mrs. Jim and Rosemary McKnight. The kennel originally hailed from Lanarkshire in the United Kingdom. They were very successful breeders on both sides of the pond. After moving to Canada in 1968, they bred their UK-bred bitch Can. Ch. Chantinghall Amethyst to the Am/Can. Ch. Solitude Creek Sophocles. This dog, purchased by the McKnights, was from a Lyn-Mar Acres hound, Am/Itl. Ch. Lyn-Mar Acres M'Lord Batuff out of Ch. Solitude Creek How 'Bout That. The union produced a dog called Am/Can.Ch. Chantinghall Dominic, who became a major influence on Canadian Bassets, as well as American dogs for many years. One of the most successful Chantinghall Bassets was Am/Can. Ch. Chantinghall Aire 'n Graces. She was sired by Dominic out of Am/Can. Ch. Eve-Ning's Over the Rainbow who, incidentally, was sired by one of our early dogs, Ch. Hiflite's Top of the Mark. She became Canada's top-winning Basset bitch for 1975–77 and Top Canadian Hound for 1975 and 1976. While the McKnights are no longer breeding Basset Hounds, the Chantinghall name begets visions of magnificently structured front assemblies and long, well-balanced bodies. Even though they typically could have used a bit more bone for most Basset breeders' tastes, the Chantinghall hounds could not help but be recognized for their ease of gait and proper movement.

Late in their breeding program they began breeding to the Strathalbyn and Stoneybluff lines, but this came too late, just before they closed their kennel breeding operation, so nothing from any of these combinations ever made big success in the show ring. Ambrican Bassets' heritage claim an allegiance to the Chantinghall Bassets and credit them for helping to support good ribs, great feet and fronts, while at the same time understanding that they also had some problems with show-dog dispositions.

## CLOVERHILL

Judy Tuck's interest in Bassets had a rather dubious start, resulting from the purchase of a pet bitch, "Snoopy," by Judy's husband Doug. It is safe to say that she thought this young pup to be something less than good looking! Though as Bassets do, she "grew on her." In retrospect, she blames the start of her current-day obsession with the breed on Doug.

In the early 1970s, in Limestone, Maine, Judy's interest in breeding and showing dogs grew as well. She started selectively breeding Snoopy's daughter and granddaughter and showing in Canada in 1973 and 1974. In 1976 Doug got out of the Air Force and they moved down to Bowdoinham, Maine, where her Cloverhill Kennel was established and where they still reside. By this time Judy had finished three of her dogs in Canada and had begun to seriously show in this country, starting with

*Am/Can. Ch. Corkery's Abercrombie, ("Socks"), shows off his great expression.*

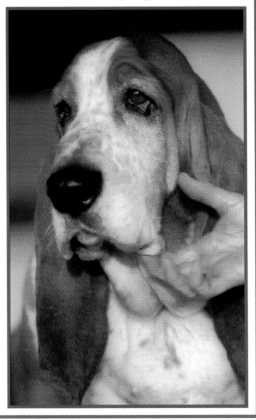

her Can. Ch. Corkery's Solemn Melody, whom she had obtained from Deirdre Fisher McKinnon. Melody finished her American championship in 1980 and became the foundation bitch for Cloverhill. One has only to look at this bitch's pedigree to conclude that, if all went right, Judy would have a leg up on early success in the breed.

At this point Judy had only four dogs. One of them was Corkery's Sweet Charity ("Katie"), who was given to Judy by Deirdre for finishing Am/Can. Ch. Corkery's Kadidja, ("Marta"). Her pedigree is the same as Melody's. Judy also co-owned with Deirdre, Am/Can. Ch. Corkery's Abercrombie ROM ("Socks"), who became Cloverhill's premier stud dog. His pedigree is the same as Melody and Katie on the dam's side, but he was sired by Can. Ch. Chantinghall Simon Templar, a Gin Dic's Bit O' Brass ex Chantinghall Melody son.

The first homebred to bear the Cloverhill name was Am/Can. Ch. Cloverhill's Copper Penny, out of her foundation bitch Melody and sired by Bob Bubb's Ch. Forestbay Cock-O-The-Walk. Penny was then bred to Socks to produce Ch. Cloverhill's Windsong and Am/Can. Ch. Cloverhill's Coppertone ("Toni"). Toni, bred to another well-known Cloverhill dog, Am/Can. Ch. Cloverhill's Littlest Hobo, produced Ch. Cloverhill's Cover Girl ("Sally") and Cloverhill's La Gitana, who is owned by Celeste Gonzales. In 1987 Judy acquired Ch. Silver Bow's Cloverhill Tramp (a big dog, callnamed "Fridge" for his size!). Fridge was a Socks son out of Ch. Silver Bow's Sarah Bernhardt, bred by Madelyn Smith of Silver

*Am/Can. Ch. Corkery's Solemn Melody, foundation bitch of Cloverhill kennels.*

Bow Bassets in New Hampshire. Fridge was bred, in 1988, to Sally and produced Am/Can. Ch. Jolly Time G Q of Cloverhill, ("Jake"), co-owned by Judy and Celeste Gonzalez.

This writer first saw Jake in the specials class at the 1990 Nationals in Holland, Michigan, and was more than suitably impressed. I had brought along a bitch, in season, looking for a stud at the Nationals that might be compatible in pedigree and could give me some help in rear improvement. Jake was to be that dog and Judy bred her for me one time before we left. That breed-

Ch. Forestbay Montgomery

Ch. Manor Hill Father James ROM

Manor Hill Moon Bonnet

**CAN/AM. CH. CORKERY'S SOLEMN MELODY**

Am/Can. Ch. Tal-E-Ho's Prancer

Can. Ch. Manor Hill Sweet Tooth

Ch. Manor Hill Tooth Fairy

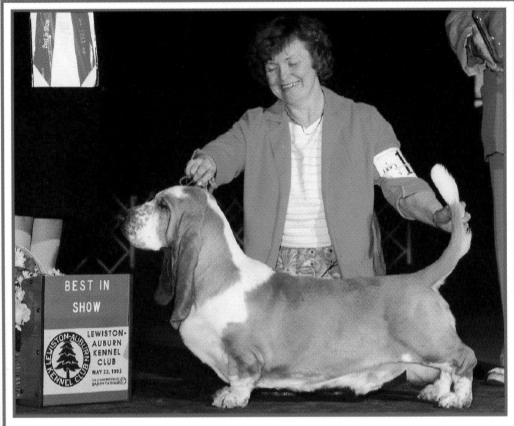

*Am/Can. Ch. Jolly Time G Q of Cloverhill, winning a coveted all-breed BIS in 1993 with Judy Tuck, handling.*

ing of Jake to our Courtyard's Piaget of Hiflite produced Ch. Hiflite's Rags to Riches, who finished by going WD at the 1992 Nationals. Jake produced well for Cloverhill, siring at least a dozen other champions, both within his bloodline and as an outcross stud as well. Many of his progeny were Specialty winners. Socks also did the kennel proud, having produced in excess of 15 champion get when bred mostly within his bloodline. I saw Jake win the Veteran Dog class at the Pilgrim Specialty in June '96 and could still see why we used this dog as a stud.

*Am/Can. Ch. Corkery's Abercrombie ROM.*

*Ch. Silver Bow's Cloverhill Tramp.*

## CORALWOOD

Bill Barton's involvement with Bassets may have had a rather auspicious start, given the manner in which he became acquainted with his first one. It started in 1960 with a commitment "to take care of him for awhile!" Bill's cousin, Jean Williams Watts, an Air Force nurse stationed in California, had purchased a beautiful tri bitch from Helen and Paul Nelson (Santana-Mandeville) named Miss Clancy of Canoga Park. She was sired by Ch. Huey of Cypress and out of Ch. Darwins Blondie II. Becoming very interested in the breed, she later bred this bitch to the Duane Newton's solid red Ch. Newton's Imperial, sired by Ch. Long View Acres Uncle Ed and out of Newton's Tina Marie. As luck would have it, when the pups were about eight weeks old, Jean received orders to transfer overseas. Not being able to take the dogs, she left the bitch with her parents and prevailed upon Bill to take her favorite little red male pup.

This pup was named Mister Tandy of Coralwood, with the Coralwood prefix coming from the particular section of town in which he lived. One day, while walking Mister Tandy, he was stopped by someone who encouraged him to enter this pup in an upcoming dog show. Completing the preliminaries, Bill entered his first show in 1960 at the Monmouth County K.C., where he placed second in a puppy class of two! He was to learn later that his competition that day was a pretty young handler named Chrissy Boutell, daughter of the late Clip and Helen Boutell of the Double B kennels in Connecticut. After the judging, it was explained to Bill that his dog had great potential, but that he needed a

little education in the art of presentation. Bill was encouraged and "bitten by the dog show bug!" The enthusiasm rapidly spread to the rest of the family, especially his daughter Sally, to whom he attributes much of his success in the breed. She became an excellent junior handler and did much of the training and showing of the Coralwood Bassets. She is still actively involved today, albeit in another breed.

Ten months after their start, the Bartons returned to the ring and finished Mister Tandy. Anxious to continue in their newfound hobby, in 1963 they contacted Walter and Marge Brandt (Abbot Run Valley) and purchased a seven-month-old red-and-white male, Abbot Run Valley Crackerjack, sired by Ch. Abbot Run Valley Prankster and out of Abbot Run Valley Sassy. Also, in that same year, they purchased a one-year-old tri bitch, Abbot Run Valley Anita. She was sired by Ch. Abbot Run Valley Brassy and out of Ch. Abbot Run Valley Gem. After finishing, Crackerjack was bred to Anita, producing five very nice puppies. From this breeding they kept a lovely red-and-white bitch, Pearl. It was their intention

*Ch. Coralwood's Kadiddlehopper, winning BOB in 1970. Handled by Bill Barton under breeder-judge Dr. Leonard Skolnick.*

to use this breeding and their other stock as the foundation upon which they would base their breeding program. As it turned out, Pearl, after finishing her championship, was unable to conceive and Anita had other internal complications.

Not to be discouraged, Bill purchased a red-and-white bitch from Nancy Lindsay of Lime Tree fame. This bitch was named Richardson's Ann of Lime Tree and was sired by Ch. Lime Tree Micawber and out of Ch. Richardson's Autumn Fire. Breeding Ann (callnamed Dottie) to Ch. Mister Tandy of Coralwood produced Miss Mandelene of Coralwood. "Mandy" was bred to Crackerjack and produced what Bill considered then, and now, to be one of the most elegant and finest moving bitches to be shown in the late 1960s and early 1970s. This bitch was Ch. Coralwoods Kadiddle-hopper (Kattie), and she established one of the best show records of any of Bill's Bassets. She was BOS at both the 1970 and 1972 National Specialty and, in 1971, was the number-one Basset bitch (Phillips System) and the tenth-ranked Basset overall.

No longer breeding Bassets, Bill is now an approved judge of all Hounds. He continues to be proud of the mark that his kennel has left on future generations of the breed and sincerely credits Walter and Marge Brandt for their conscientious breeding program that contributed so much to his.

## CRAIGWOOD

Sandra Campbell's Craigwood Bassets got their start with the purchase of a pet bitch, Pongi Fongi, in 1960. She was bred once to a dog named Clinch River Hercules and produced Ch. Campbell's Shoo Fly, the dog that began Sandra's interest in breeding and showing Bassets. In 1966 she purchased a show-quality dog from Paul Saucier, Geronimo of Rockin-Pas. "Mo" was sired by Ch. Maverick of Rockin-Pas, BW at the 1965 National, and was out of Ch. Tomo's Hells-A-Poppin. Ch. Geronimo of Rockin-Pas went on to have a great show career guided by the able hand of Carroll James, PHA, winning 2 all-breed Bests in Show, 16 Group firsts and numerous Specialty wins. Not widely used as a stud, he produced seven champion get. Mo came

*Ch. Coralwood's Copper Peg, going BW in 1969 under breeder-judge Doug Knight.*

*Ch. Geronimo of Rockin-Pas, foundation stud of Craigwood Bassets at the age of five years.*

out of retirement to show in the Veterans class at the 1972 Nationals, again, guided to this win by his old friend, Carroll James. Sandra handled him in the specials class, her first and last time to show the dog herself, and went on to win the Breed under Joe Braun. The Craigwood dogs that followed Mo have had ten other major Nationals wins since 1972, a real tribute to those dogs and their breeder.

In 1971 Sandra was able to acquire the dog, Ch. Field's Lancer, from Lee Field of Paul's Valley, Oklahoma, for her breeding program. Lancer was quite closely bred, having been sired by Ch. Forestbay John Mathais and out of Ch. Hiflite's Terrianna,

doubling up on the Abbot Run Valley Brassy portion of the Lyn Mar lines in the Manor Hill breedings. Lancer was campaigned throughout the South for several years, winning 91 BOBs, 1 major Specialty, and 47 Group placements, again, under the able hand of Carroll James. Lancer was initially bred to Ch. Pretty Penny of Craigwood, producing two bitches that went on to acquire their championships and become foundation bitches for the kennel, Ch. Amazing Grace of Craigwood and Ch. Blackader's Kate of Craigwood. He was equally successful in other breedings and easily earned his ROM status.

Around 1973, a close friendship with Nancy Taylor, also of Greenville, South Carolina, developed into sort of a "partnership" with the Bassets. Sandra and Nancy co-owned a number of the dogs and worked together very closely in showing and breeding, while sharing the Craigwood prefix. It was during this period that Sandra and Nancy acquired two more studs for the kennel. The first was Ch. Hiflite's Kentucky Wonder ROM, bred by Carol O'Bryant and Mary Jane Booth, sired by Ch. Hiflite's Brumeister and out of Hiflite's Caroline. This dog was also closely bred on the Manor Hill bloodlines and produced well for the

*Ch. Field's Lancer ROM, winning one of his many BOBs. Shown here by Carroll James under breeder-judge Vance Evans.*

BEST OF
BREED-VARIETY

*Ch. Hiflite's Kentucky Wonder ROM, in 1975 being handled by co-breeder Carol O'Bryant under judge Ed Kaufmann.*

Switchbark Craigwood Amen, she produced Switchbark's Chastity who went on to produce two National Specialty winners when bred to another stud dog purchased during this same time frame, Ch. Windamohr's Gamble ROM, affectionately known as "Bones." Bones added an additional avenue to maintain the Manor Hill and Coralwood influence in the kennel. Sired by Ch. Manor Hill Father James and out of Coralwood's Cousin Kate, he finished his championship in nine shows. Among his notable wins were: Best in Junior Sweepstakes at the Kentuckiana BHC Specialty, a five-point major from the puppy class at the Potomac BHC Specialty, a BOB at a regional Specialty along with many other BOBs, Group placements and several BIS.

kennel, contributing much to today's size, level toplines, and strong rears, for which the Craigwood name is well known. Among some of Wonder's more notable champion get were Ch. Bonamie Bella of Craigwood (the author's all-time favorite Basset bitch), Ch. Sherra's Darling Betsy, Ch. Switchbark Craigwood Amen, and Ch. Solow-Switchbark I'm A Wonder.

During this same period, Sandra acquired Wonder's littersister, Ch. Hiflite's Cher of Switchbark, from Carol and Jerry O'Bryant. Wonder and Cher were both obtained at the start of a long-standing friendship and Basset breeding relationship between Sandra, Nancy and the O'Bryants (Switchbark). The friendship endures to this day, but Nancy ceased her involvement in the dog sport in the late 1970s. Cher was a lovely bitch that had but one litter. Bred to Ch.

*Ch. Bonamie Bella of Craigwood, a Wonder daughter and Craigwood brood bitch, shown here by Nancy Taylor under breeder-judge Eileen Schroder.*

Bones was responsible for adding additional "type" to what were already large, long, heavy-boned dogs and bitches with good toplines and strong rears. The combination of bitches sired by Wonder, bred to Bones, created another excellent line of show stock and brood bitches for the kennel. Bones proved to be a very productive stud for Craigwood also, producing among many other notable hounds, two National Specialty winners: Ch. Craigwood's Going In Style, 1981 BW, co-owned by Sandra Campbell and Joanna Reynolds, and Ch. Switchbark Ashmore ROM, owned by Bob and Mary Jane Booth.

purchased from Addie Birdwell. Bart was sired by Ch. Oranpark Gladstone and was out of Woodstock Beulah. He was used sparingly but was able to produce some bitches that would pass on those attributes for which he had been selected.

The next "outside" stud to be purchased was Ch. Windamohr's Prodigal Son ROM, "Harold." He was sired by Windamohr's Anthem and his dam was Windamohr's Golden Nugget. Harold finished his championship, but it would be fair to say that he was not the handsomest of Bassets! As is often the case, however, success in the show ring and success as a producer do not

*Ch. Windamohr's Gamble ROM, and his son, Ch. Look Out-Craigwood Top Rock, shown going BOB and BW, respectively, in 1980. Handled here by Sandra Campbell and Steve Atwood.*

The bitches that had been sired by Lancer were bred to both Wonder and Bones and began to establish the "look" that Sandra was after, reinforcing more of the same type and establishing a Craigwood "line." It was at this juncture that Sandra felt the need to outcross in an effort to maintain bone size, shorten leg length, improve arch of neck, refine the heads, and, hopefully, increase pigmentation. To aid in these areas, she selected Ch. Santana's Bart, whom she

always go hand in hand! Ch. Abbot Run Valley Brassy may well be the best example of this axiom! In terms of sheer numbers, Harold became Craigwood's top-producing stud to date.

Ch. Belyn's Face Value, sired by Bones, out of Am/Can. Ch. Belyn's Irish Cream, also produced several stud dogs that have since added to Craigwood's continuing success in the whelping box and the show ring. Among these dogs was Ch. Craigwood's

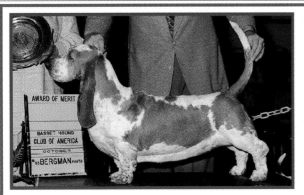

*Ch. Craigwood's Shimmer, shown winning a BHCA AOM in 1993.*

Cash Flow of Belyn, out of Windamohr's Fiesta. Cash had a fantastic show career handled by Doug Holloway to eight BIS and many Specialty BIS. He was the top-winning Basset Hound for three years. He sired a number of champion get, including 1992 Nationals BOS winner, Ch. Craigwood Kelsey, Ch. Craigwood Chelsea, and Ch. Craigwood's Cash Rebate, not to mention one litter out of Ch. Craigwood's Sparkle where six of the seven pups became champions, some from the puppy classes. From this breeding came Ch. Craigwood's Shimmer, a Specialty-winning bitch and two-time Nationals AOM winner; Ch. Craigwood's Pocket Change, top-winning Basset Hound for 1995; Ch. Craigwood's COD; Ch. Craigwood's Cashback of Birnam; Ch. Craigwood's Glitz and Glitter; and Ch. Craigwood's All That Sparkles, most all of whom have had exciting show careers.

Always seeking to improve and refine, Sandra, in 1993, brought in another outcross through the leasing of Ch. Tailgate Hoot Gibson for a one-year period. While at Craigwood he finished his championship and attained his ROM status. It was felt that the infusion of some additional Santana-Mandeville blood would be beneficial. Some of these get include: Ch. Craigwood's Promise of Spring, Ch. Craigwood's Kiss Me At The Gate, Ch. Switchbark-Craigwood Marilyn, and Ch. Craigwood's Impressive Illusion,

that latter of which has several Group wins and an all-breed BIS to her credit.

In addition to these promising Craigwood dogs, those hoping to continue the tradition are: Ch. Craigwood-Solow Hobby Knox, a multiple BIS winner, who currently resides in Italy; his son, Ch. Craigwood's Higgins of Switchbark, himself a multiple-BIS winner, BISS winner and the 1996 Westminster BOB winner; Ch. Craigwood's Pocket Change, top-winning Basset Hound for 1995 and the 1995 Westminster BOB winner; Ch. Craigwood's Shimmer, two-time Nationals AOM winner; Ch. Craigwood's Lasting Impression; Ch. Craigwood's Kelsey; Ch. Craigwood's Chelsea; Ch. Craigwood's Dream Keeper; and Ch. Craigwood's Geo Splendor along with a number of hopefuls still in the whelping box.

To date, there have been in excess of 100 dogs and bitches with the Craigwood prefix that have attained their conformation championships. Although this writer has attributed much of the Craigwood success to their outstanding production of bitches over the years, the kennel owner, however, prefers to cite the benefits of the excellent stud dogs that she has been able to use in her breeding program over the years. Of course, these dogs have sired many wonderful bitches for Craigwood, and without the bitches there could not have been more great dogs! It is obvious that the future is secure at Craigwood.

*Ch. Craigwood's Cash Flow of Belyn ROM, shown winning BOB at the Valley Forge Specialty in 1992.*

# ELYSIAN

The Elysian kennels of Mary Lou and Don Graves is located in Cleveland, Tennessee, just a few miles east of Chattanooga. Mary Lou's introduction to Bassets came by way of a mixed-breed puppy. While living in Florida in 1973, Don brought home, as a gift for Mary Lou, a half-Basset—half-German Shepherd pup that came to be known as the "Bas-erd!" Named Daisy, she became a treasured pet.

Mary Lou had spent her adult life as a professional horseperson, having been trained in Europe and the United States in classical dressage. She had been showing horses since the age of 12, but the thought of showing dogs had never occurred to her. In 1974, when they moved to Tennessee, they bought the farm on which they still live, naming it "Elysian," after a horse that she owned. Another year passed and they decided that even though their bas-erd Daisy was great, they really should own "the real thing." Answering an ad in the Atlanta news-paper, they returned home with a female Basset Hound. They had been told that even though she was out of a pet-quality bitch, her sire was Ch. Ramblebriar's Local Broker, a fine Basset of that day, and that she was "really too good to be a pet!" The "Ch." before the name of the sire made them inquisitive enough to ask questions and visit some dog shows. At the Chattanooga show that year, they met Sandra Campbell (Craigwood), showing Ch. Hiflite's Kentucky Wonder. Both Sandra and the dog, unknown to them at the time, were responsible for starting the Graves into "Bassetdom."

Mary Lou rapidly envisioned the possibility of having her own litter of "black" puppies sired by that "black dog" of Sandra's and her own bitch, now named Lily Lightfoot. After some discussion, Sandra recommended breeding Lily to a different stud dog, one that she had that would be more of a linebreeding. That particular dog happened to be red and white, so Mary Lou wanted to know if the puppies would still

*Ch. Elysian Sweet William ROM, by breeder-owner-handler Mary Lou Graves, winning the Breed under breeder-judge Pat Hirsch.*

be "black like Kentucky Wonder!" The answer, of course, was probably not. Consequently, Lily was bred to Wonder! She delivered only one puppy, but it was "black!" This pup was named Wonder's Never Cease and went on to attain her CD.

During the late 1970s, two more bitches were acquired from Craigwood: Ch. Craigwood's Terrific Tulip and Craigwood's Vicious Violet. Violet was bred to Ch. Santana's Bart, another "red" dog from Craigwood, and the resulting litter contained one that would go on to become Ch. Elysian

sire a litter out of Petunia, resulting in the dog, Ch. Elysian Sweet William ROM, who became the BOB winner of the 1986 Eastern Regional. The next breeding of Petunia was to be to another fine hound, Ch. Birchcroft's Juan 'N Only, belonging to Ellen Crofford's Birchcroft kennel. This breeding produced Elysian Myrtle ROM. Myrtle, bred back to her half-brother Sweet William produced Ch. Elysian Winterberry, another excellent Elysian hound.

Another bitch, Switchbark's Bar-K-Bobblee, was acquired that contributed sig-

*Ch. Elysian Winterberry, a Sweet William son, after having gone BW at the 1990 Kentuckiana Specialty, under breeder-judge Bob Booth.*

Buster Larkspur ROM. It was at this point that Elysian Bassets truly came into existence and Mary Lou forgot all about the color of the dogs!

Buster was eventually bred to the original "black" puppy, Wonder's Never Cease CD, by now call named "Poppy." This breeding produced Elysian Precocous Petunia, who never finished her championship, due to the loss of an eye, but became the cornerstone of the Elysian line nonetheless.

During this same time period, Ch. Craigwood's Terrific Tulip was bred to Ch. Windamohr's Gamble, producing Elysian Bachelor Button. Button was then used to

nificantly to the Elysian breeding program over the years. Bobblee was bred to Buster Larkspur and a daughter from that breeding went on to produce Ch. Ladiga Tombigbee of Elysian. Tommy, in turn, was bred to a Sweet William daughter, producing an excellent litter that included four bitches that placed 1, 2, 3, and 4 in their Futurity class at the 1992 Nationals. Another male littermate, Ch. Elysian Forget-Me-Not, went on to be awarded BOS at the 1996 National Specialty. There are presently a total of 20 Bassets residing at Elysian, 9 of which are champions. Others are on their way!

*Ch. Elysian Forget-Me-Not, winning one of his numerous BOBs with handler-friend, Gwen McCullagh.*

## FIRST CLASS

Jacquelyn Fogel received her first Basset Hound as a Christmas present in 1969 while she was attending the University of Arizona. This small, but pretty bitch, Dennis & Jacquelyn's Salome, was predominantly of Nancy Evans and Santana-Mandeville bloodlines. She was bred three times, once to Ch. Kinslow's Rueben Russel, producing Phorever Phoebe. Phoebe's daughter, Always Abigail, was a littersister to Jackie's first champion, Ch. My-T Manfred, and in 1982 she was bred to Ch. Tal-E-Ho's Eager Beaver to produce Fogel-Rich's Great Pumpkin. This petite, but very sound red and white bitch was shown by Bryan Martin at the 1983 National Specialty, placing first in the 9–12 Month Puppy Bitch class. She had been awarded Best in Sweepstakes the previous weekend at the Pilgrim Specialty.

Though she never completed her championship, she became the foundation bitch for the type of Basset Hound that Jackie has become known to produce.

In 1984 it was decided to include more of the Tal-E-Ho bloodline into the kennel's breeding program. To accomplish this, Ch. Tal-E-Ho's Max-A-Million was purchased from Henry and Ann Jerman. Max earned his championship quickly and was bred to Fogel-Rich's Great Pumpkin, producing Ch. Fogel-Rich's Valuable Asset. Valuable Asset was the dam of Ch. Fogel-Rich's Sophia and Ch. Fogel-Rich's Baby Swiss. Max-A-Million went on to be campaigned as a Special for a short time, but his show and breeding careers were cut short by misdiagnosed hypothyroidism.

In 1989 Jackie acquired B's Creole Pearlymae from Barbara Langlois.

*Ch. Tal-E-Ho's Max-A-Million, winning a BOB, handled by Jackie Fogel under judge Lee Canalizo.*

*Ch. Fogel-Rich's B's Hot Stuffing, with handler Jackie Fogel, receiving an AOM at the 1994 Westminster K.C. show under judge Pat Laurans.*

Pearlymae, a beautiful tri-color bitch, finished her championship in just eight shows and was bred to Ch. Tal-E-Ho's Max-A-Million, her

*Ch. First Class Andromeda, going BOS from the classes. Handled by Jackie Fogel under judge Bill Bergum.*

grand-uncle. This breeding produced Ch. Fogel-Rich B's Hot Stuffing, "Murphy," who was ranked in the Top Ten Bassets for three years, earning the Number Two spot in 1993.

With the Tal-E-Ho bloodline at an end, Jackie looked for an outcross to help lock in the soundness that she had been regularly producing. In 1989 she leased Ch. Fogel-Rich's Sophia, already bred to Ch. Stoneybluff Winter Storm, to Canadian breeder Glenoria Molnar. An agreement had been reached that the first-pick puppy from the litter would come back to First Class Bassets (the kennel name was changed in 1990 from Fogel-Rich to First Class). Am/Can. Ch. Blackjack First Class Mystery, one of two bitches that came back, finished quickly. She was then bred to Ch. Fogel-Rich's Wall Street (littermate to Valuable Asset) to produce Ch. Blackjack First Class Rusty Nail, ranked Number Five Basset in the late '90s.

First Class Basset's 15th champion is Ch. First Class Andromeda (Ch. First Class Charles Jourdan out of Ch. Fogel-Rich's Baby Swiss). When Andromeda is bred to Ch. Blackjack First Class Rusty Nail, she should pull together all of the outstanding foundation kennels (Tal-E-Ho, Stoneybluff and B's) in the First Class line.

## FORT MERRILL

In 1959, Gene and Joan Urban purchased a Basset Hound puppy as a family pet for their three sons. The dog was a good, sound red and white dog sired by Ch. Felix of Le Chenil who was by Ch. Mr. Smee of Hopedale and out of Ch. Santana's Comtessa Dior. His pedigree was a mixture of Santana, Lyn Mar, and Belbay bloodlines. As time passed, Monsieur Pierre La Rue began to become more Joan's dog than her sons'. So much so, in fact, that he caused her to become interested in dog shows and she showed him to his Mexican and American championships. He was shown as a Special very sparingly and was a consistent Group placer in the early '60s in what was then known as the Texas Circuit. There were very few Basset Hounds in southern Texas at that time and Joan was very anxious to breed and show Pierre's offspring. His first litter was out of a half-sister, Crutchfield's Desdemona, who was also sired by Ch. Felix of Le Chenil. Desdemona belonged to Carol and Bob Williamson, for whom Joan showed and finished two of the males out of the litter, Ch. Williamson's Handsome Hamlet and Ch. Williamson's Julius Caesar.

In 1964, Joan acquired and finished Ch. Sisu's Cherie Amie, a Ch. Sherlitt's Lemon Drop Kid daughter. "Lemmie" was a typey lemon and white dog that had done quite a bit of winning in the late '50s and early '60s. In 1966 she purchased a large red and white

*Ch. Fort Merrill Lipz Stick, shown here handled by Bryan Martin, winning one of her 31 Group Firsts under judge Judy Doniere.*

dog named Ch. Nancy Evans Sir Galahad from Mr. and Mrs. Carl Furhman of San Antonio. The Furhmans had campaigned this dog to 16 Group firsts and an all-breed BIS, quite a feat for a Basset at that time.

It was during the summer of 1966 that something happened that would change Joan's whole outlook on Basset Hounds. A newcomer to the breed appeared at a puppy match in Corpus Christi with a puppy that he had bought from Margaretta Patterson (Margem Hills). That puppy was Margem Hills Tish The Dish, and Joan remembers her as the "most gorgeous thing that she had ever seen!" The "newcomer" was Alan Turner of Kingsville, Texas, who was to later purchase Ch. Glenhaven's Butcher Boy and, with Glen Smith's permission, began using Glen's prefix, Glenhaven. Alan made quite a name for Glenhaven in the late '60s. It was in February 1967 when he purchased a bitch named Little Tear Drops and brought her to Joan to be bred to Sir Galahad. This bitch was a littersister to Ch. Nancy Evans Fair Exchange (a Tomo daughter ex Eleandon's Happy Times). That breeding produced Ch. Glenhaven's Lord Jack, who was purchased by Hettie Page Garwood of Austin. Walt Shellenbarger handled Jack to numerous major wins and he won the coveted Top Hound for 1971. Ch. Sisu's Cherie Amie was the second bitch to be bred to Galahad, and in June, 1966, that breeding produced Ch. Joan Urban's Peter Gunn, owned by Knox Williams III and Ch. Joan Urban's Honey West, owned by Micky and Jimmy Helms.

After having observed the type and quality of Margem Hills Tish The Dish and Ch. Glenhaven's Butcher Boy, Joan began to place many of her younger Bassets in good homes and contacted Peg Walton (Lyn Mar Acres) in an effort to secure a good bitch of those bloodlines. In October 1967 she was able to purchase a three-month-old bitch, Lyn Mar Acres Plane Fare, callnamed "Wendy." Wendy was sired by Ch. M'Lord Batuff and out of Ch. Lyn Mar Acres Quick Trip, and was intended to become the foundation bitch of her "new" Bassets. Having planned to breed this bitch back to her grandsire, Ch. Lyn Mar Acres Press Agent, she was shipped back East to Mt. Holly twice for the breeding, but to no avail. Consequently, she was bred to a local dog with compatible bloodlines in 1970. This dog was Ch. Margem Hills Mr. Brown, a red and white sired by the Tomo dog and out of Ch. Margem Hills Madame Queen, owned at that time by Knox Williams. This breeding produced Ch. Joan Urban's Top Flight, who was co-owned with Glenys Wells and was first in the Bred by Exhibitor class at the 1972 BHCA Nationals. Also from that litter was Ch. Joan Urban's Etc. of Tantivy, "Happy," who was sent to hunt with Jane Luce in the Tantivy Basset Pack, and later yet, sent to the Strathalbyn Pack of Eric and Erica George.

Joan was never able to get Wendy in whelp again. This unfortunate turn of events, plus two others, a move to a neighborhood inappropriate to raising dogs and the approval to judge Bassets, served to keep Joan out of the breeding arena for the next ten years. The purchase of a Corpus Christi area ranch, part of which had been the site of the old Fort Merrill originally established in 1850, allowed her to get back to a long postponed breeding program. They named the ranch Fort Merrill Ranch and registered their cattle brand with the State of Texas, thus the Fort Merrill prefix on all of their cattle and canines. Wendy's only litter would be her last Basset litter to carry the "Joan Urban" prefix.

During this time period, however, and at Joan's request, the "Happy" bitch was bred twice by Eric George. The first of these breedings was to the George's Ch. Lyn Mar Acres PBR, a Ch. Lyn Mar Acres Sir Michelob son and out of Ch. Lyn Mar Acres Lovage. This produced a dog named Strathalbyn Spokesman and a bitch named Strathalbyn Spotless. Spotless eventually came to live at Fort Merrill. It was through these littermates that, in 1981, Joan began putting her breeding program back together. Over the next ten years she did a lot of breeding with the George's Strathalbyn bloodlines that were in some way related to the original bitch she had given them. Other breedings within this line were done with dogs relating back to the Plane Fare bitch. The Fort Merrill prefix was used in registering these offspring. The second "Happy" breeding was to Ch. Strathalbyn Shoot To Kill, and it was a bitch from this litter that came to be shown and finished by Joan. This was Ch. Joan Urban's Strathalbyn Et Al, "Electra." Electra was bred to her paternal half-brother, Strathalbyn Sidhiron, a Shoot To Kill son out of Ch. Strathalbyn Bobbie. She used this stud on a number of her bitches. Many people

Hound Show in May, 1987. Several additional Fort Merrill hounds were sent to hunt with the Timber Ridge Pack.

The Georges had bred Spokesman to Am/Can. Ch. Strathalbyn Panic and produced Ch. Strathalbyn Rival. This was a Wendy grandson and he was generously given to Joan to show and use in her breeding program. Spokesman was also bred to Strathalbyn Divadhata, a Ch. Lyn Mar Acres Extra Man daughter out of Tantivy Blond Sidonia ROM. This breeding produced

*Ch. Fort Merrill Snowflake, winning the Brood Bitch class at the 1995 Nationals, with her produce, Ch, Fort Merrill Lipz Stick and Ch. Fort Merrill Mae West.*

thought that Sidhiron was a look-alike for Ch. Lyn Mar Acres Journeyman. The Electra breeding to this dog produced Ch. Fort Merrill Marilyn, WB at the 1985 BHCA Nationals, Ch. Fort Merrill Lightnin', and Ch. Fort Merrill High Trump. Also bred to Sidhiron was her Strathalbyn Bethshebae which produced Fort Merrill Recruit, Ch. Fort Merrill Lieutenant, (Salyers/Frederiksen), and Ch. Fort Merrill Serendipity. "Seri" went to hunt with the Timber Ridge Pack of Meena Rogers and was chosen Grand Champion Basset Hound at the Bryn Mawr

Strathalbyn Dhaktivadhanta, "Dee Dee." She was also sent to Fort Merrill and another half-brother—half-sister breeding was done, producing a very nice lemon and white bitch, Ch. Fort Merrill Nearly Vanilla. Vanilla was bred to Fort Merrill Recruit to produce Fort Merrill Aunt Teedo. This bitch in turn became the dam of the littermates Ch. Fort Merrill Holly, WB at the 1989 BHCA Nationals, and Ch. Fort Merrill Noel, RWD at the same National.

Spotless was also acquired and bred to Sidhiron. This mating produced Fort Merrill

Daisy, who was then bred to Fort Merrill George West, a Recruit ex Vanilla son. This breeding was to give her Ch. Fort Merrill Snowflake, the Brood Bitch class winner at the 1995 Nationals. While Daisy went on to hunt with the Wayne Dupage Pack of Ted Kjellstrom, Snowflake stayed at Fort Merrill and was one of the very few bitches that Joan bred more than once. She produced two litters, the first by Ch. Strathalbyn Lugano (Frederiksen), which produced Ch. Fort Merrill Mae West, "Godzilla," who was Best in Jr. Sweepstakes at the '91 Nationals. The second breeding of this bitch was to the Frederiksen/Salyers dog, Am/Can. Ch. Ambrican Lippizan, which produced Ch. Fort Merrill Hot Lipz, (Maggie), Ch. Fort Merrill Snow Job, and Ch. Fort Merrill Lipz Stick. "Stix" was handled by Bryan Martin to a very impressive show record of 3 all-breed BIS, 23 Specialty BIS and 31 Group firsts. She also won an AOM at the '93 Nationals and was BOS at the '94 Nationals after having gone Breed at Westminster that same year as well.

While Stix was out being famous, her littersister, Maggie was at home producing the seventh generation of get from the original Ch. Lyn Mar Acres Plane Fare. Maggie soon became known as "Fast Maggie" since she made her own arrangements to breed herself to her brother which produced Fort Merrill Straight Man, Fort Merrill Straight Laced, and Fort Merrill Anchor Man. Following in his mother's footsteps, Anchor Man, at seven months of age, was able to sneak in and breed himself back to his dam, Fast Maggie! From this unexpected litter came Ch. Fort Merrill Kissing Bandit and Fort Merrill Don Juan. When Joan finally gained the opportunity to select the stud for Maggie, she selected the Kintner's Ch. Deer Hill's Great Gatsby because of the tie back into Strathalbyn and, of course, because she very much liked the dog. This breeding was also a success, producing a very nice litter of two dogs and three bitches. Most noteworthy from this litter are Ch. Fort Merrill's Great

Gatsby, "Bomber," and Ch. Fort Merrill Fatl Attraction, "Lottie," who was RWB at the '96 Nationals at the tender age of ten months!

It remains to be seen what the future will bring with the offspring of Stix and Godzilla and Maggie. Joan plans to continue to breed hounds that "she likes to look at," but that "can follow a trail over and through difficult terrain without tiring."

In 1998, Joan's Basset breed primer was published by T.F.H. Publications. It is entitled *A New Owner's Guide to Basset Hounds* and is a colorful and handy guide.

*Ch. Bowler's Greta Garbo CD, winning BOS with owner-handler Kristen Eskew.*

## FOUR OAKS

The Four Oaks Bassets kennel of Kristen and Don Eskew was established in Barboursville, West Virginia in the early to mid-'70s with the acquisition of Bowler's Greta Garbo. A lovely bitch for her time, Greta went on to attain her bench championship and her CD as well. Sired by Ch. Musicland's Casey Jones and out of Am/Can. Ch. Musicland's Morning Glory, she was whelped in December, 1973.

Another very worthy bitch in the Four Oaks kennel was Ch. Switchbark Craigwood Lola, sired by Ch. Switchbark Craigwood Amen ROM out of Strathalbyn Bydora. In trying to decide how she might best breed this quality bitch, an agreement was reached between Kristen, Carol O'Bryant and the author to co-own the bitch and eventually breed her to Ch. Switchbark's Ashmore ROM. It is humorous to note that when Kristen brought the resulting litter over to Switchbark for the rest of the co-breeders to "have a look" and, per-haps, take our pick, there weren't any takers! I recall thinking that I couldn't remember when I'd seen an uglier bunch of pups! Anyhow, we all eventually agreed that if we were of a mind to keep any of them, it would be the big long black one! Kristen did decide to keep him and he became Ch. Four Oaks Little Syndicate, call-named "Syd." Among many notable wins over the next few years, Syd became the Number Two Basset Hound for 1989. I guess the moral to this story, if any, is that sometimes "you just gotta grow 'em out!" Unfort-unately for the Basset community, Kris' interest in recent years has, in large part, gone to Chihuahuas, a long-time favorite of husband Don. It is noted that she has been very successful in that breed as well.

*Above: Ch. Switchbark Craigwood Lola, in 1985 going BW. Handled here by Kristen Eskew under judge Chuck Herendeen.*

*Right: Ch. Four Oaks Little Syndicate winning the Group by breeder-owner-handler Kristen Eskew under breeder-judge Bill Russell.*

## HALCYON

The Halcyon kennels of Lamont "Doc" and Vicki Steedle was established in 1971 when they obtained their foundation bitch, Ch. Tess Von Skauton CD ROM, as a puppy, from the Townes. Watching the breed from ringside while showing Tess, they noticed many Lyn Mar dogs with the movement, type, and elegance that they admired. When it became time to breed, they took Tess to Ch. Lyn Mar Acres Extra Man. That first Halcyon litter included one Canadian and four American champions. One of the get, Ch. Halcyon Lumberjack, was Best in Senior Sweepstakes, WD

*Ch. Halcyon Firecracker, in 1984 handled by Mike Sosne.*

and BW at the 1975 BHCA National. Additionally, he became an all-breed Group winner and won several other Specialties. Another, Ch. Halcyon Suffragette CD, finished with five majors, three of which were earned at Specialty shows, and was High in Trial in the 1979 National Specialty Obedience competition.

Lumberjack sired the multiple Group-winning Ch. Halcyon Crackerjack, among the

*Ch. Halcyon Lumberjack, winning a Group Third in 1977. Handled by Vicki Steedle under breeder-judge Margretta Patterson.*

breed's top producers and an all-time leading winner of Specialty shows. Notable among Crackerjack's many wins was his BOB at the 1983 BHCA National Specialty.

Suffragette produced, among other champions, Ch. Halcyon Tattletale. Tattletale was WB and BW at the 1980 American and Canadian National Specialties and repeated the same wins again at the 1981 Canadian Nationals! Suffragette also produced Ch. Halcyon Schoolmarm, Best in Sweepstakes at the 1978 Nationals and she was RWB at the same event in 1979. When bred to Ch. Halcyon Crackerjack, Tattletale became the dam of the Group-winning 1982 National Specialty WD, Ch. Halcyon Firecracker.

Tess' second litter was sired by Lyn Mar Acres Radar and produced Ch. Lochopt Halcyon Collegian, a top producer in the breed. He was the sire of several influential producers, including Ch. Halcyon Lochopt Letterman who sired two National Specialty BOB winners and Ch. Lochopt Fantasy, who produced a leading top producer in Ch. Hiflite Briarcrest Extra Man, along with many other champions. Letterman finished his championship with three consecutive Specialty five-point wins. Among his get was Ch. Halcyon Tailgater (out of Tattletale), an all-breed BIS and a multiple Group and Specialty breed winner. Tailgater won BOB at the 1991 National Specialty from the Veterans class. Another Letterman son, Ch. Brasstax Robin O'Locksley (out of Halcyon Soothsayer, a repeat of Crackerjack), was BOB at the 1987 National Specialty.

Tailgater was another qualifier for the breed Register of Merit as a producer. His son, Halcyon Sergeant, out of Ch. Hiflite Halcyon Buttercup, a Fantasy daughter, produced several champions including Ch. Halcyon Hat Trick, Ch. Halcyon Triple Play, and Ch. Halcyon Show Me D'Way To Go Home, among a very limited number of get. Sergeant's son out of a Letterman daughter, Halcyon Showoff, was a most recent National Specialty winner for the Halcyon kennel, taking Best in Futurity in 1994. A Collegian double-great-grand-daughter, Ch. Hiflite Ultrabrite, was WB and BW at the 1995 National Specialty and is owned by the Halcyon kennel. In summary, the Halcyon kennel has produced among its champions 3 National Specialty breed winners, 3 National Specialty point winners, and 5 Group winners in more than 25 years of breeding and in less than 20 total litters. All are down from the initial unions of their foundation bitch and two Lyn Mar Acres sires, with every subsequent breeding carefully planned to selected sires or dams with pedigrees nearly duplicating those of the best ancestors from those first pedigrees.

Doc and Vicki take special pride in the fact that most of these Halcyon wins were owner-handled under breeder-judges and that many of today's top-producing and top-

*Ch. Halcyon Tailgater ROM, going BOB from the Veteran Dog class at the 1991 Nationals. Handled by breeder-owner Vicki Steedle under breeder-judge Mary Jane Booth.*

winning Bassets are down from Ch. Halcyon Crackerjack, Ch. Lochopt's Halcyon Collegian and/or Collegian's son, Ch. Halcyon Lochopt Letterman. The Halcyon foundation bitch, Tess, was a heavily ticked tricolor and that ticking is characteristic of a great many of the progeny of the Halcyon kennel, be they black, standard tris, or red and white. The Steedles have served BHCA over a long period in a wide variety of capacities ranging from Doc's terms as president, treasurer, and nationals coordinator to Vicki's service as a board member and long terms as *AKC Gazette* columnist and *Tally-Ho* editor. Their record is truly one of distinction.

*Ch. Halcyon Tattletale, going BW at the Rock Creek Kennel Club show in 1980. Breeder-owner handled here by Vicki Steedle under breeder-judge Alice Lane.*

*Ch. Harper's Rhett Butler, winning one of his numerous Bests of Breed, handled by his breeder-owner Medora Harper.*

## HEARTLAND

Cathy Willey's Heartland Bassets got started in 1987 with the purchase of a Basset from a pet store. (Doesn't everyone?) She took him to obedience classes and fell in love with the challenge of the sport. "Gus" eventually obtained his CD.

When her daughter wanted to try Junior Showmanship, Cathy purchased a quality hound from Chris George (Bantrybeigh). As a result of this purchase of Bantrybeigh's Merlin, Chris George became Cathy's mentor and best friend. While Cathy's daughter did not meet with success in the Junior's ring, she did take "Merlin" through eight weeks of beginners obedience classes, and at the age of 12, and in 3 shows over 8 days, put a CD on Merlin!

A foundation bitch, Daffy Blackberry Brandy, was purchased and bred to Merlin with good results. From a litter of six, three were titled. Ch. Heartland's New Generation, "Pepsi," Heartland's Spittin' Image, CD, CGC, "Shilo," and Heartland's TNT, CD, CGC, "Mikey." Brandy was bred one more time, to Merlin's sire, Ch. Valhala's Special Issue, CD ROM CGC. From this litter Cathy kept Heartland's Something In Red, "Morgan," a lovely red and white male with the movement she liked. Morgan is proving to be a great obedience dog as well as a sound conformation hound, but his true love seems to be hunting! Through Merlin and Morgan, Cathy has taken up Pheasant and Rabbit hunting, just so she can enjoy watching her hounds do what they were bred to do.

Although she breeds and shows her own dogs, Cathy feels that her heart will always be in obedience. She considers it a challenge, not only to take a fine working Basset Hound into the obedience ring, but to breed one who is sound enough to withstand the rigors of training and that has the proper temperament and attitude for obedience and the field.

## HARPER

Tom and Medora Harper started in Bassets around 1960, according to one of their first interviews in *The Hound Crier*, a publication of the then forming BHC of Greater Corpus Christi. Their foundation bitch was Moore's Prissy Sissy. Her owners had suggested breeding her back to her father, Ch. Millvan's Deacon, but the Harpers thought this a bit close and selected Tyburn's Indian Emperor instead. Tyburn was tight Santana-Mandelville breeding from the kennel of Carolyn Babson of the Chicago area. From that breeding they kept a male, (Ch.) Hugo Von Haus Harper, and finished him. His dam died, unfortunately, at an early age, so the Harpers now found themselves with a foundation stud rather than a bitch! One of their well-known dogs was Ch. Harper's Rhett Butler, a nice linebred dog who gained several Group wins, a Specialty win, and produced some nice champion offspring by the time he was three years old. He can be found, not too far back, in a number of relatively current pedigrees.

*Ch. Harper's Slippery Hill Lefty, a Butler son, and a Group winner as well.*

*Bantrybeigh's Merlin CD and Heartland's Spittin Image CD, CGC.*

*Heartland's Something In Red with breeder-owner-handler Cathy Willey.*

## HEATHROW—PYPERWYND

In the early 1960s Dick and Pat Waterhouse started to fly the Basset flag. The kennel is located on beautiful acreage in the rich farmlands of Sumas Prairie, District of Abbotsford, Province of British Columbia. Their first Basset was just a pet, but they became so enchanted with the breed that they decided to find another female as a companion for the one they already had. In their quest, they spotted an advertisement in the newspaper for a female Basset puppy that was, on inquiry, a show prospect. At that time, showing dogs was not on the agenda. However, on taking puppy home, they decided to work with the breeder and take the puppy to some matches. Needless to say, that was the beginning of showing for all the family. Meeting with a very small measure of success in the show ring, and even less in the whelping box, a decision was made to purchase new stock. Importing hounds from the well-known Forestbay kennels brought them some further merit. Experience is a good teacher and lessons had been learned.

In 1973 fate took a hand and presented Dick and Pat with the opportunity to purchase a young red and white male puppy named Bevlees Injun Joe. Joe turned out to be a super showman who loved every minute of show business. He and his handler, Jim Campbell, made a name for themselves in record time. Joe also finished his American championship under the expert handling of the late Marvin Cates. Joe's descendants have inherited his love of the show ring.

At about this time, it was decided that what was needed was a linebred quality bitch, if one could be found. Eventually, Mrs. Margaret L. Walton (Lyn Mar Acres) sent a beautiful tri five-month-old bitch, Lyn Mar Acres Tosca. She had a gorgeous head, arch of neck, absolutely sound front and rear, and even as a puppy, moved like a well-oiled machine.

Thus began a success story far beyond their expectations. This success was achieved with very few litters over those early years. Due to a very busy working lifestyle, the whelping box only came out occasionally, so the breedings had to be well chosen. The name "Heathrow" gradually started to cover itself with glory. American and Canadian Specialty winners came from

*Shown here in an early photo (L. to R.) is Bevlee's Injun Joe with two of his get, who went on to become Ch. Heathrow's A Touch of Class and Am/Can. Ch. Heathrow's Touch of Minx.*

the first Tosca litter in 1976. From the second litter in 1978 came their first Best-in-Show bitch, Am/Can. Ch. Heathrow's Classic Image. One of Heathrow's most treasured wins came with Am/Can. Ch. Heathrow's A Touch of Minx: Best in Specialty under noted breeder-judge Guiseppe Benelli.

In 1981, their daughter, Susan, and husband, Harold Pybus, who already bred and showed Irish Setters, decided to breed Basset Hounds under the Pyperwynd prefix, planning, of course, to work within the Heathrow bloodlines. They also started out with their own bitch, Am/Can. Ch. Jubilation First Class, out of Ch. Heathrow's Class 'n Brass ex Chantinghalls Honey Chile. This bitch was taken to Am/Can. Ch. Heathrow's A Touch of Class, resulting in the litter born in 1984, which produced Am/Can/Bda. Ch. Pyperwynd IM Reddie Freddie.

Lyn Mar Acres Tosca was lost to cancer at a relatively early age, but she left those at Heathrow and Pyperwynd a tremendous legacy to continue breeding and showing. The multiple Best-in Show winner, Am/Can. Ch. Bevlees Injun Joe, was lost in 1982. He did an excellent job of piloting Pat to a Best in Show on one occasion when there was no one else available to do the honors. Class and charisma were Joey's trademarks.

Hard work does pay off and sorrow tends to fade into

*Am/Can. Ch. Heathrow's Classic Image, handled by Jeri Cates, winning BOB under noted judge, James Edward Clark.*

the mists of time when you consider the successful hounds and their individual accomplishments. With limited space, only a few are mentioned here, but these, and all the others, were and are important. They were the guides and measurements of the breeding program.

*Am/Can/Bda. Ch. Pyperwynd's IM Reddie Freddie, as a younger dog in 1987. Handled by Hal Pybus.*

| | |
|---|---|
| Am/Can. Ch. Heathrow's A Touch of Class | Sire of Freddie |
| Am/Can. Ch. Heathrow's A Touch of Minx | Multiple Specialty BIS & all-breed BIS |
| Am/Can. Ch. Heathrow's Classic Image | Multiple BIS & Specialty BIS BOS, 1983 BHCA National |
| Am/Can. Ch. Heathrow's Classic Maggie Minx | Multiple Specialty BIS |
| Am/Can/Bda. Ch. Pyperwynd IM Reddie Freddie | Sire of Mikey |
| Am/Can. Ch. Pyperwynd IM Brassy and Classy | Multiple Specialty BIS |
| Am/Can. Ch. Heathrow's Carry on Class Act | Sire of Basil and Abbot |
| Am/Can/Bda. Ch. Sir Ethans Basil of Heathrow | BOB, 1992 BHCA National |
| Am/Can. Ch. Sir Ethans Abbot of Pyperwynd | Multiple BIS |
| Am/Can. Ch. Pyperwynd IM Hope and Glory | Multiple Specialty BIS |
| Am/Can. Ch. Pyperwind IM Millie | Multiple Specialty BIS |

During his show career, IM Reddie Freddie garnered many trophies and ribbons. He was shown a total of 219 times with the following results: 210 BOBs, 136 Group firsts, 57 other Group placings, 34 all-breed Bests in Show and 10 Specialty BOBs. In 1988 in Canada, Freddie was Number One Basset Hound, Number One Hound overall, and Number Three all breeds. In 1989 he was Number One Basset Hound, Number Two Hound, and Number Nine all breeds.

While Freddie was making a track record in Canada, his son, Mikey, Am/Can. Ch. Heathrow's Carry on Class Act, owned by John Hackley of Tacoma, Washington, was excelling on the United States show scene. He became the Number One Basset Hound and the Number Five Hound in the US in 1989. It is believed that this was the first time in the breed that a father-son combination were Number One at the same time. In 1992, Mikey's son, Am/Can/Bda Ch. Sir Ethans Basil of Heathrow went on to become the only Canadian dog to win BOB at the BHCA National Specialty.

The Heathrow-Pyperwynd breeding program is small, but with dedication, a strong foundation, and successful legacy, the tradition of class and quality can be expected to continue.

*Am/Can. Ch. Sir Ethans Abbot of Pyperwynd, by Hal Pybus going BIS under judge Donna Cole.*

*Am/Can. Ch. Pyperwynd IM Millie, by Hal Pybus going BOS at the BHC of Greater Seattle under breeder-judge Sharon Dok.*

## HET'S

Het Garwood was born into a family of Fox Terrier lovers. Her grandfather owned a littermate of Ch. Sabine Rarebit, winner of the third Westminster show. As a child, she had Fox Terriers as well as other terrier breeds, Spitz, Beagles, and an English Cocker Spaniel from hunting stock. She acquired her first Basset Hound in 1960 from Robert Mattes, a former professional handler, then later a Hound Group judge, who was also a charter member of the Basset Hound Club of Greater San Antonio (formerly the BHC of Greater Corpus Christi). That Basset helped to establish an interest in exhibiting and breeding in the mid-'60s. She purchased and finished her first Basset championship on her (Am/Mex. Ch.) Hiflite's Jodi. Soon thereafter, she acquired (Ch.) Het's Hiflite Charlotte and finished her as well. Both Jodi ("Skunk," for the stripe down her back) and Charlotte were bred by the author and Mary Jane Booth, sired by Ch. Glenhaven's Butcher Boy ROM, and out

*Above: (Ch.) Hiflite's Jodi, shown going WB, BW and BOS for a three point major at Houston in March of 1968. Handled by Roy Murray, PHA, under judge Maurice Baker.*

*Below: Int. Ch. Concho's Don Juan, Top-Winning Dog, all-breeds, in Venezuela 1971–72.*

MEJOR EJEMPLAR DEL GRUPO CAZADORES

SOCIEDAD CANOFILA DE CARACAS

*Ch. Glenhaven's Lord Jack ROM, shown taking an all-breed BIS in 1971 at Yuba City, CA, under judge Forrest Hall.*

of their Ch. Kazoo's Question Mark ROM. As an aside, I recall Het asking me to show Skunk for her at Oklahoma City one weekend when I had Roy Murray showing our "pick" from that same litter, (Ch.) Hiflite's Sherrie Ann, at the same show. I agreed and off we went. To make a long story short, Skunk won the five-point major with me handling. Talk about watching your mother-in-law going over a cliff in your brand new Cadillac!

He acquired (Ch.) Glenhaven's Lord Jack and a littermate, Glenhaven's Fireball. They were sired by Ch. Nancy Evans Sir Galahad (Urban) and out of Little Tear Drops, a littermate of Ch. Sir Tomo of Glenhaven (Patterson). Lord Jack went on to become the top-winning Hound, all-breeds, in 1971, under the able hand of Walt Shellenbarger, PHA. Sparingly bred, Jack produced some 20 title-holders in conformation, obedience, and field.

Het also owned Am/Can/Dom/Col/Ven. Ch. Concho's Don Juan who was shown to his American championship at about the same time as Jack was being campaigned on the West coast. He was also sired by Ch. Glenhaven's Butcher Boy, but was out of Ch.

Manor Hill Greta. He was sent to Sra. Carmen Benitez of Caracas and was handled by Richard Guevara. Don Juan was bred by Carol Friend of San Angelo, Texas.

In addition to having had the 1980 BHCA Nationals WD and the 1984 Nationals WB, Het also produced a number of top-placing Cairn Terriers and got her first PBGV in the mid 1980s. Over the years she has been editor of *The Hound Crier* and *Saber Tails,* magazines of the BHC of Greater Corpus Christi and the Petit Basset Griffon Vendeen Club of America, respectively. She has also written numerous articles and stories for publications such as *Dog World, Dog News, Tally-Ho, Cairn Courier, Saber Tails* and others. She is a Life Member of BHCA and is particularly well known for the lavish productions she wrote and directed for entertainment at numerous BHCA annual banquets. After 33 years, she closed her kennels in 1993. She kept two Bassets and two PBGVs to live in retirement as "house dogs."

*Ch. Glenhaven's Lord Jack ROM, shown going BOS at nine years of age at the Dal-Tex BHC Specialty in 1976. Owner-handled by Het Garwood under judge Anne Rogers Clark.*

Eleandon's Black Magic

Ch. Sir Tomo of Glenhaven

Ch. Lyn Mar Acres Fyre Ball

Gh. Glenhaven's Butcher Boy

Brigadier

Eleandon's Happy Times

Ch. Eleandon's Gypsy

PEDIGREE OF THE FIRST TWO QUESTY BREEDINGS

Ch. Abbot Run Valley Brassy

Ch. Manor Hill Top Spot

Ch. Bonnie Ridge Fire Bird

Ch. Kazoo's Question Mark

Kazoo's Black Sambo

Ch. Kazoo's Frances

Long View Acres Gold Nugget

## HIFLITE KENNELS, REG.

*Those readers having read the "About the Author" section of this book will be already familiar with the usual false starts that the Booths, like most others, had in getting started in this breed. There was also an article in the December, 1984 Bugler in which Hiflite was featured in an "In the Spotlight" article that pretty much covered the author's kennel from its inception through 1980. For those who have never read the Bugler article, I will, briefly as possible, cover those years here.*

After a number of false starts, we were quite fortunate to purchase Kazoo's Question Mark, in June 1964, from Mary Jo Shields (Kazoo) at six months of age. Known as "Questy," she started her show career in the spring of 1965. She was handled by Roy Murray and finished at the Dal-Tex Specialty with a five-point major on November 21, 1965.

The airline strike in 1966 prevented us from using our choice of stud dogs, Marg Patterson's Ch. Sir Tomo of Glenhaven, but we were able to locate a Tomo Son within driving distance, Ch. Glenhaven's Butcher Boy, owned by Alan and Dorothy Turner of Kingsville, Texas. Questy whelped a litter of eight on October 30, 1966, of which four went on to finish their championships: Ch. Hiflite's Tomfoolery, owned by Tom and Penny Bloomer; Ch. Hiflite's Sherrie Ann, kept by us; Ch. Hiflite's Jodi, owned by Het Garwood; and Ch. Hiflite's Trudy, owned by Mary Jo Shields. Two others in that litter went to Mexico, with one of them finishing there, and the other two were purchased by Alan Turner. We certainly owe Tom and Penny a debt of gratitude for putting Hiflite "on the map" with the showing of Tomfoolery.

*Ch. Hiflite's Sherrie Ann and Ch. Hiflite's Tomfoolery, shown each winning a major from the Puppy classes, and "Tommy" going on to one of his many Group firsts that day.*

*Ch. Kazoo's Question Mark ROM, Hiflite foundation bitch.*

"Tommy" is typical of what that breeding produced, even when repeated. All had nice type, good bone, refinement, and decent rears, but left much to be desired in toplines. Looking to improve both topline and rears, we selected Questy's half-brother, Ch. Manor Hill Fringe Benefit, as the stud. Considering his pedigree and his appearance, we believed that we would soon have what we were looking for! Mother Nature, however, had other ideas. This breeding produced a litter of seven in May, 1967. Of the three males, only one finished: Ch. Hiflite's Top of the Mark. This hound's only further contribution, of which I am aware, comes by way of being the sire of the bitch, Ch. Eve-Ning's Over the Rainbow, a bitch that produced well for the Chantinghall kennels of Jim and Rosemary McKnight. It seemed strange that he was able to contribute, having only an improved rear, but still severely lacking in topline. Of the four bitches, Hiflite's Georgy Girl was the only one shown and she had only one major when we ceased showing her. Georgy Girl was sound as the dollar used to be, but "less than flashy" in the show ring!

As the time to serve in Vietnam approached, we had to thin out a little, so we kept Sherrie Ann and Georgy Girl, and Questy was placed in co-ownership with the Bloomers.

Bred once again to Butcher Boy, she whelped in the spring of 1968. Six of that litter went on to finish their championships: Ch. Hiflite's Penny Bee (kept by us); Ch. Het's Hiflite Charlotte; Ch. Hiflite's Pow Wow; Ch. Hiflite's Brumeister; Ch. Hiflite's Sock It To Me Tommy; and Ch. Hiflite's Big John TD. Penny Bee was pretty much what we wanted to continue to produce. She was a lovely bitch and finished with three majors in only four shows. Improvement-wise, she needed the shoulder blades placed a little more rearward, and perhaps a slightly increased length of upper arm.

The genes of the Basset Hound are unpredictable at best, and while Penny Bee was highly successful in the conformation show ring, she was as equally a major disaster in the whelping box! Bred three times, once to each side of her line and once outcrossed, she produced only one champion, Ch. Hiflite's Sancho Panza. The overall quality of her pups' fronts was very poor; consequently she was placed in a pet home and lived out a happy life.

During this same time frame, Sherrie Ann was bred to Ch. Forestbay Orvil of Manor Hill, (a full-brother to her mother's sire, Ch. Manor Hill Top Spot). Once again, our aim was to straighten out the toplines and improve rears, while changing little else. Orvil

*Hiflite's Penny Bee shown finishing in 1969.*

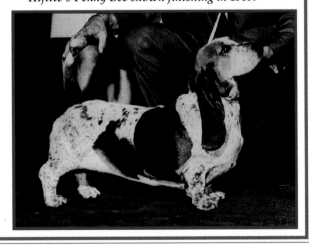

had as good a rear as we'd ever seen. Of the four surviving bitches from that litter, two finished. Ch. Hiflite's Julianna did extremely well, being novice owner-handled to her championship very quickly. Her littermate, Ch. Hiflite's Terrianna, breezed through also. Terri was owned by Lee Fields of Paul's Valley, Oklahoma. Lee was new and short-lived "in the game," and when he sought breeding advice, we recommended that his bitch be bred to Ch. Forestbay John Mathias. This was a nice linebreeding and produced Ch. Field's Lancer, later acquired by Sandra Campbell (Craigwood).

In 1969 we purchased a dog from Joan Scholz, primarily for breeding. Manor Hill Lawyer Calhoun went on to finish his championship and he was bred to both Sherrie Ann and Georgy Girl. One of Sherrie Ann's litter of four finished, Ch. Hiflite's Broadway Joe. Joe was owned and shown by Alice Lucas and her mother of Louisville, Kentucky. We kept nothing from that breeding. Georgy Girl, bred to Calhoun twice, produced two very small litters, but two of her daughters made very significant contributions: Hiflite's Caroline and Ch. Hiflite's Cher of Switchbark. Caroline was co-owned with Carol and Jerry O'Bryant, (Switchbark), and was eventually bred to their Ch. Hiflite's Brumeister, from the second Questy ex Butcher Boy litter. This breeding produced one of the major Hiflite contributors to the breed, Ch. Hiflite's Kentucky Wonder. He proved to be an excellent producer for Sandra Campbell, and we attribute much of the predictability of good toplines and rears within our line today to this dog. Also kept by us from the Georgy Girl breeding was another bitch very similar in type to both Georgy Girl and Caroline, Hiflite's Cecilia, known as "Cissy." These produce were all quite sound and embodied the topline and rear improvements that we had been seeking. The major problems now

*Hiflite's Cecilia, going BW and BOS in 1972 for a three-point major. Handled here by Bob Booth under judge Fred Hunt. She was a bitch that was typical of what we were producing when our breeding program temporarily ceased in 1973.*

were "blah" coloring and, to some degree, a lack of the previous elegance of the Butcher Boy ex Questy breedings. We accepted that we had to endure several generations of the "uglies" to garner the soundness that we knew we could achieve in the breed. Unfortunately, all of this occurred at a time when career commitments forced us to disband the kennel and we were unable to do any further breeding for a period of nearly ten years. Fortunately, others were using some of our bloodline in their breeding programs, consequently what we had started with was not entirely lost.

In March, 1981, we went to the airport to pick up two hounds, given us by Carol and Jerry O'Bryant, to "get us back in the breed!" We had never seen either of them until they came out of their crates that day, but we couldn't have been more pleased. These were Switchbark's Ashmore (Moe) and Switchbark Promise 'T Hiflite (Missy), both descended from the breedings of Questy and Butcher Boy, by way of Georgy Girl, Caroline, Wonder, Cher, Bru, etc. Missy finished her championship, as did Moe, who went on to take the Breed at the 1984 Nationals and won many other Specialties as well. These hounds, Moe in particular, rep-

*Ch. Switchbark's Ashmore ROM, in 1984, owner handled by Bob Booth under breeder-judge Don Martin.*

resented all of the qualities that we would have wanted to achieve and maintain in our own breeding program had we been able to continue it. At that point, we felt that we hadn't missed a beat! We offer many thanks to Carol and Jerry, and also to Sandra Campbell, who became the owner of Kentucky Wonder.

From 1981, to the present, we worked mostly within the Manor Hill bloodlines that we started with. Our early 1980 breedings were limited, with Moe being used sparingly. We purchased a Redemption Rock bitch and dog, "Joni" and "Sam," who were the remnants of the Manor Hill type that we liked. It was not until we were able to acquire Ch. Lochopt Fantasy, from Knox and Bette Williams, that we were able to further improve on what we wanted our kennel to consistently produce. This was accomplished through the breedings of the offspring of the Moe ex Fancy breedings and the Moe ex Joni breedings. Our breed-

ing program was relatively limited, generally producing only what we needed to keep us in the ring. Typical of our dogs at this time are Ch. Hiflite's Dynamoe, co-owned with Doris Courtney (Courtyard) and Ch. Hiflite's Black Gamin.

Redemption Rock Samaritan, "Sam," was bred to a Moe ex Fantasy daughter, Hiflite's Ashlynne, producing Courtyard's Kismet of Hiflite ROM, owned by Doris Courtney. "Kizzy," a magnificently fronted bitch with outstanding breed type, was not shown due to a poor topline, but went on, as evidenced by her ROM, to become an outstanding producer for Courtyard. Doris Courtney only kept bitches with perfectly pure front structure, and she had a number of them. We did a breeding of the Dynamoe dog to Kizzy and took Ch. Courtyard's Kreggo of Hiflite as our pick from that litter. He was clearly one of the soundest dogs we ever owned or showed, and was typical of the structure we wanted to produce. We also took another bitch from Kreggo's litter, Courtyard's Piaget of Hiflite and bred her back to the Manor Hill side of the pedigree by using Ch. Jolly Time GQ of Cloverhill, as the stud. This breeding produced our 1992 Nationals WD, Ch. Hiflite's Rags to Riches.

Far and away, the most famous of the Hiflite dogs has to be Ch. Hiflite Briarcrest Extra Man, our pick of the litter from the last of the three Moe ex Fantasy breedings. Many people, over the years, have asked why we didn't keep that dog. The answer, of course, you have read in the Briarcrest story. Surely "Butch" has contributed more to the breed than any other Hiflite dog by virtue of his record as a stud dog at Briarcrest. His record of titleholders is in the middle 40s, with many more pointed get being shown and more breedings still being done. He was the top stud dog for 1994 and 1995, and his daughter, Ch. By-U-Cal's Razzle Dazzle was BOB at the 1996 National Specialty.

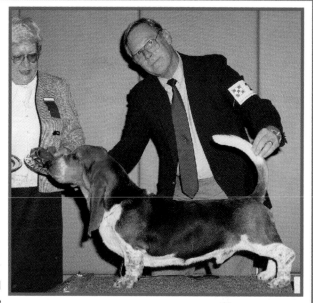

*Ch. Hiflite's Black Gamin, a Moe ex Fantasy son, taking his first five-point major from the Puppy class.*

Our breeding of Ch. Hiflite's Quick Trick, a very tightly bred Butch daughter, to Doug Taylor's Ch. Dragon Thunder Von Skauton, also produced very nicely for us. Ch. Hiflite's Ultrabrite was BW at the regional preceding the 1995 Nationals and was BW at the Nationals as well, completing her championship at that show. She is now owned by Doc and Vicki Steedle, with Vicki having handled her to all of her wins. Her brother, Ch. Hiflites's Ultra Motion, has also finished with several Specialty wins, and is owned by Carol and Jerry O'Bryant (Switchbark).

Most of all, Mary Jane and I are really thankful for the friends whom we have made in this sport and who have truly enriched our lives. In addition, our Basset peers have accorded us the honor of judging your hounds at the National Specialty twice, distinct honors for which we shall always be grateful.

*Ch. Hiflite's Dynamoe, a Moe ex Hiflite Redemption Rock Joni son.*

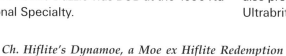

*Ch. Courtyard's Kreggo of Hiflite, winning BISS at the San Antonio Specialty under breeder-judge Carla LaFave.*

## HYDE-E-HO

Though Tim Hyde has only been a member of BHCA since 1994, he has owned Bassets for about 20 years. He has just done his first breeding ever, and it was a successful one! His dog, Ch. Hyde-E-Ho's Banana Pudding was sired by Ch. Fogel Rich's Wall Street out of Tim's bitch, First Class Ashley Hyde. "Trent" completed his championship at only 18 months of age. His breeding can easily be traced back to the Tal-E-Ho bloodlines, consequently he is named after his great-great-grandsire, Ch. Tal-E-Ho's Top Banana. Judging from the first litter, if Tim continues to breed like this, he will attract much attention in the breed.

*Ch. Hyde-E-Ho's Banana Pudding, handled by Kelly McCoy Davis for owner Tim Hyde under judge Ed Gilbert Jr.*

# JAGERSVEN

The Jagersven kennels of Mary Louise and Finn Bergishagen started in 1961 with the purchase of Jagersven Samantha from Chris Teeter of Long View Acres kennels. *The Complete Basset Hound* by Braun has already detailed the major contributions of Chris Teeter's Long View Acres dogs. After being shown to her championship, Samantha was bred to Ch. Siefenjagenheim Dominoe, a breeding that produced Ch. Jagersven Gigi. Gigi was whelped on February 24, 1965 and in October, 1966 was selected as WB, BW, and BOS at the BHCA National Specialty.

Gigi was later bred to Ch. Lyn-Mar Acres Press Agent. From that breeding she produced Ch. Jagersven Mariner (a Group winner), Ch. Jagersven Mimi, and Ch. Jagersven Monarch II, the latter of which was sold as a puppy to the Kovalics. Bred to two of the Kovalic's bitches, Monarch produced six champions. Mimi was also bred to Ch. Lyn Mar Acres End Man and produced Jagersven Amos, the sire of Ch. Jagersven Huckleberry Finn ROM, as well as the sire of champions for Halcyon and Briarcrest kennels.

In 1969, Shadows' Snow White was purchased, at the age of 18 months, from Jim and Carol Schadt. She became the foundation bitch which would take the kennel in a different direction. Snow completed her title in just a few shows, all under breeder judges. She went on to be awarded BOS at two BHCA National Specialty shows, first at the spring 1970 show, and later, from the Veteran Bitch class in the fall 1975 Nationals. We were looking for a stud for her and, while at the 1970 Nationals, we found Ch. Margem Hills Mr. Brown, owned by Knox and Bette Williams (Briarcrest kennels).

The combination of "Brownie" bred to Snow produced six champions: Ch.

*Ch. Jagersven Gigi, shown being awarded BOS from the classes at the 1966 Nationals under breeder-judge Nancy Lindsay with Finn Bergishagen handling.*

Jagersven Blue Banner, Ch. Jagersven Blue Ribbon, Ch. Jagersven Blueberry Muffin, Ch. Jagersven Blue Tango, Ch. Jagersven Blue Jeans, and Ch. Jagersven Blue Bonnet. Mr. Brown had been shipped to Michigan for his breeding to Snow. After going home to Texas for a short time, he returned to Jagersven where he and Snow shared the

*Am/Can. Ch. Shadows' Snow White as a class bitch. Handled here by Mary Louise Bergishagen under breeder-judge Alice Lane.*

*Am/Can. Ch. Margem Hills Mr. Brown ROM, as a class dog being awarded BW at the Dal-Tex BHC Specialty in September, 1970. Handled here by Roy Murray, PHA, under breeder-judge Joe Braun.*

couch until they both died at the age of 14. In addition to this litter, Brownie also produced over 15 champions for other kennels, with a CD, several TDs, and a TDX titleholder as well.

Blue Ribbon, when bred to Ch. Stoneybluff Freckles (a Snow grandson), produced Ch. Jagersven Benchmark. Bred to Ch. Stoneybluff Napoleon (a Jagersven Monarch II son), she produced Chs. Jagersven Pot O'Gold and Jagersven Golddigger. Benchmark produced six American, one Danish, and seven Canadian champions before he died at an early age. He was also the grandsire of Ch. Halcyon Crackerjack, BOB at the 1983 National Specialty.

Ch. Jagersven Blue Banner, not to be outdone by her other kennelmates, won BOB at the 1978 Nationals. She was the first Veteran Bitch to do so, and the first bitch to win a National Specialty in 13 years. When bred to Ch. Jagersven Benchmark, she produced Ch. Jagersven Snow Capped, who was first in the Veteran Dog class at the 1984 Nationals. The combination of Gigi, Snow, Brown and the Lyn Mar breedings are behind nearly every one of the 50 some champions finished by Jagersven through 1991 when they ceased showing.

*Ch. Jagersven Blue Banner.*

*Ch. Jagersven Blue Ribbon.*

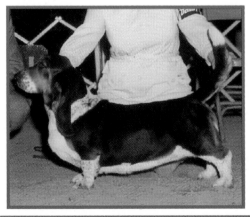

*Ch. Stoneybluff Freckles (a Shadows' Snow White grandson).*

*Ch. Jagersven Benchmark, (Freckles ex Blue Ribbon).*

*Ch. Jagersven Snow Capped, (Benchmark X Blue Banner), shown winning the Veteran Dog class at the 1984 BHCA Nationals. Handled here by Mary Louise Bergishagen under breeder-judge Al Tiedemann.*

## JERCAT

Since the December, 1981 *Bugler* article on JerCat Bassets, Cathie and Jerry Spencer have moved their home to a larger property, but still remain in Southern California and are still very much dedicated to Basset Hounds. The number of Bassets that were a part of their breeding program over the years was numerous, but primarily reflected the Tal-E-Ho bloodlines, and to a large degree, that style of dog. The Tal-E-Ho and the early JerCat lines mixed well. Tal-E-Ho's Hot Diggity was bred to JerCat's Megan and produced one of the top-winning dogs on the East Coast, Ch. JerCat's Talk Of The Town, owned by Doug and Diane Fuerst.

An eventual father/daughter breeding produced Ch. JerCat's Ballou. Ballou was able to produce the style for which Cathie was looking. Among those produce were: Ch. JerCat's Jellybean Dream, Ch. JerCat's Queen'sborn, Ch. JerCat's Run For The Roses and JerCat's Tribute To Jesse, owned by Bob and Elaine Cortner, to name a few.

Still remaining as their all-time favorite and one of the highlights of the JerCat kennel was Ch. JerCat's Kirby of Aikane. "Animal" was a product of one of the Spencer's earliest Bassets, Ch. Hallmark Malcom, (Tailgate), being bred to Ch. Tal-E-Ho's Lotus, a Prancer ex Bubbles daughter. Animal was owned by, and lived with, Jim and Sharon Dok. He was handled by his friend, Ric Byrd. Animal was the Number One Basset Hound in the country for three years in a row and had seven all-breed BIS to his credit.

The JerCat breeding program slowed down considerably in the '90s, but they have recently acquired a beautiful bitch from the Woodhaven kennels and they have breeding plans for her. Cathie has been judging for a number of years now and has been fortunate to even have judged in Europe several times. They say that the JerCat story is one of many struggles like most breeders have, but that there has been enough achievements to make it all worthwhile.

*Ch. JerCat's Kirby of Aikane, bred by JerCat, owned by Jim and Sharon Dok, winning one of his numerous all-breed Bests in Show with his handler, Ric Byrd.*

# LOCHOPT

The Lochopt kennel was founded by Rick and Barb Cromley in 1967 in the Northern Virginia area. Since then they have moved numerous times over the years. Currently they are in Flagstaff, Arizona, and no longer very active in breeding or exhibiting their Bassets, though they still maintain a small kennel of their older dogs and Rick has a new Harrier that he shows from time to time.

Shortly after their initial start up in the breed, the Cromleys were wiped out with distemper during the period prior to the multi-strain vaccines. It was at that point that they started over with Rebownd's Cha-rade, a Ch. Lyn Mar Acres End Man daughter out of Ch. Gorham's Go Holly Go of Rebownd and a Windamohr bitch, Windamohr's Daffodil, who was sired by Ch. Kazoo's Galloping Gitch and was out of Ch. Manor Hill Lemon Twist. Although Daffy was never successfully bred, they continued to admire much that her bloodlines repre-sented.

I recall meeting Barbara for the first time at a Virginia show while I was stationed at Langley AFB and living in Poquoson, Virginia. The Basset judging that day was "wild," with Barbara having what I thought was clearly the best entry, and she barely got a look! She looked totally dejected and, not knowing her, Mary Jane and I went and introduced ourselves and told her what a fine bitch she had and that she should not give up. I think the bitch may have been Charade. At any rate, we soon became close and traveled to quite a number of shows together over the next couple of years until job transfers separated us. We both admired many of the same things about certain bloodlines and as a result, the Cromleys became the owners of Hiflite's Liza Jane,

who along with Charade, became two of their early champions in the breed. Liza Jane became the dam of their first homebred champion, Ch. Lochopt Escapade and Mary Ann and David Clark's Saxony foundation bitch, Lochopt Pollyanna.

Charade was bred to their Lyn Mar Acres Journeyman, producing four lovely bitches for them: Ch. Lochopt Risk of Rebownd, Ch. Rebownd's Jeopardy of Lochopt, Ch. Rebownd's Encounter of Lochopt, and Lochopt Monopoly of Rebownd. Keeping

*Ch. Lochopt Tripoli, going BOS at the 1981 Kentuckiana Specialty, handled by Rick Cromley under breeder-judge John Hackley.*

both Risk and Monopoly, they were bred to both Ch. Ran-Su's Lochopt JD and Ch. Lochopt Halcyon Collegian, producing mul-tiple champions and Specialty winners. One of those, Ch. Lochopt Tripoli, a Collegian daughter out of Monopoly, finished her championship in three consecutive days with three five-point majors.

Risk, bred to their Ch. Lochopt Halcyon Collegian, a product of Doc and Vicki Steedle's Halcyon kennel, produced Ch. Halcyon Lochopt Letterman, sire of the 1991 National Specialty BOB, Ch. Halcyon Tailgater. He was also the sire of Ch. Brasstax Robin of Locksley, himself a top-winning Hound and the 1987 National Specialty BOB winner, as well.

*Ch. Lochopt Saxony Stile, going BW at the 1990 Westminster KC show, handled by Ed Smizer under judge Gayle Bontecou.*

breeding program. Some of their outstanding bitches that have contributed to the Lochopt pedigrees, and some of which have helped other kennels as well, are: Ch. Lochopt Classic, Ch. Saxony Lochopt Sprite (Clark and Fair), Ch. Lochopt Fantasy (Williams and Booth), and Ch. Lochopt Venture. Over these many years I have found that Lochopt produced exceptional fronts on their bitches and have primarily bred very tightly within the Lyn Mar bloodlines. They have found their nearly 30 years in the breed to have been a joy, as well as having provided a bridge to friendships across the US and in Europe. Barbara is currently approved to judge Bassets and PBGVs and has already had the honor of judging our National Specialty in 1992.

Their National Specialty winning Ch. Lochopt Rum Rikki, a Ch. Sanchu Bacardi son out of Lochopt Little Lick, was WD and BW in 1984 and went on to win BOS at the 1985 Nationals. He is an ROM recipient, having himself produced National Specialty-winning bitches. Ch. Lochopt Saxony Stile, sired by Ch. Ran-Su's Lochopt J.D. out of Ch. Saxony Lochopt Sprite, was the 1991 BHCA Top-Producing Stud Dog.

The Cromleys have always felt that their bitches were the strength of their

*Ch. Lochopt Something In Stile, "Tyler," shown winning BOB in 1990.*

*Ch. Lochopt Venture, shown here winning an Award of Merit at the 1991 Nationals, handled by Rick Cromley under breeder judge Mary Jane Booth.*

# MANOR HILL

Starting in the mid-1950s, Ron and Joan Scholz's Manor Hill Bassets developed into another of the main strains of American Basset Hounds. Their first hounds proved to be unsuccessful in winning the top show awards or championship points. Success came later, after finally acquiring (Ch.) Bonnie Ridge Fire-Bird. This bitch was the real beginning of the Manor Hill breeding program. Fire-Bird was from the breeding of Ch. Lyn Mar Acres Barrister ex Bonnie Ridge Best Tip who were both of Lyn Mar Acres backgrounds. She was bred to Ch. Abbott Run Valley Brassy, that new top stud with the Lyn Mar background, but that was producing a very different look. It was at that point that history began for the Manor Hill Bassets.

The Manor Hill kennel went on to produce numerous top dogs and bitches that became Specialty and all-breed winners. Larger than life names among their winning hounds were: Ch. Manor Hill Fringe Benefit, Ch. Forget-Me-Not of Manor Hill, Ch. Manor Hill Top Spot, Ch. Manor Hill Greta, Ch. Forestbay Orvil of Manor Hill,

*Ch. Manor Hill Father James ROM (Ch. Forestbay Montgomery ROM ex Manor Hill Moon Bonnet).*

Ch. Manor Hill Tooth Fairy, and Ch. Manor Hill Father James. On the whole, the Manor Hill hounds were good fronted, with good length of body and driving rears. Their coloration was mainly red/lemon and whites and some brownish (washed out) tris.

Two of their most well-known stud dogs were Ch. Manor Hill Top Spot ROM, and Ch. Manor Hill Father James ROM.

Joan is a BHCA Life Member, has served as BHCA vice-president and is AKC approved as a multi-Group judge. Manor Hill is no longer an active kennel, but they certainly have left their mark on the breed. Some kennels, namely, Switchbark, Craigwood, Courtyard, Redemption Rock, Len-Jo, Corkery, Cloverhill, Hiflite, and even Kazoo, have profited heavily from the Manor Hill line.

*Ch. Manor Hill Top Spot ROM (Ch. Abbot Run Valley Brassy ex Ch. Bonnie Ridge Fire-Bird).*

## MUSICLAND

Surely one of the notable modern-day kennels still producing dogs for the show ring is Musicland. Jeanne Hills, formerly Mrs. Jeanne Dudley, began her Basset Hound kennel after being involved in Dachshunds. She purchased her first Basset Hound from Mr. and Mrs. Richard and Evelyn Bassett (Bassett's Bassets, later known as Notrenom Bassets, were profiled in *The Complete Basset Hound* by Braun). This bitch hound was (Ch.) Bassett's Eloise. Jeanne next acquired (Ch.) Look's Musical of Musicland from Mrs. Jean Look, (also included in *The Complete Basset Hound* by Braun). From these two hounds she established, in 1957, her Musicland kennels. The Musicland Bassets seemed to have the "look" that the general public and many

*Ch. Musicland's Casey Jones ROM.*

breeders alike were after. In 1968 Jeanne bred a bitch to Ch. Orangepark Dexter, (particularly for his shoulders, but what she got was his head style passed on to many generations of her hounds), which only added to the Musicland success and popularity.

> Ch. Santana-Mandeville Tarzan
> Ch. Orangepark Dexter ROM
> Hartshead Maybelline
> CH. MUSICLAND'S CASEY JONES ROM
> Ch. Musicland's Mountain Music
> Ch. Musicland's Mame ROM
> Ch. Musicland's Tico Tico

*Ch. Musicland's Mountain Music at six years of age.*

Certainly a significant contributor to Musicland's continuing success story was the homebred bitch, Ch. Musicland's Jolene ROM. Jolene was whelped on January 1, 1979, sired by Ch. Musicland's Casey Jones out of Ch. Musicland's Rosemarie. Jolene was the dam of 16 champions, and I believe, established a record unequaled to this day. The mating of Ch. Musicland's Houdini and Ch. Musicland's Snow White in 1979 resulted in yet another super producer for Musicland, Ch. Musicland's Valentino ROM. Living up to his well-known, amorous name,

of Ch. Musicland's Demure Dansuese to the stud dog, Clowverleaf's Agamemnon II, bred and owned by Claire Clowe's Clowverleaf's Bassets.

Since whelping her first litter, Jeanne's kennel has produced no fewer than 128 champions, of which at least 26 have attained ROM status in the BHCA Register of Merit. Since 1960 her dogs have won the following awards at the (fall) BHCA National Specialty shows: One BOB, Three Best Of Opposite Sex, One WD and BW, One WB and Four Bests In Sweepstakes. Musicland

*Ch. Musicland's Pool Shark ROM, whelped Nov. 2, 1969, sired by Ch. Musicland's Casey Jones ex Lu How's Winnipesaukee. A sire of 24 champions, he is shown here winning BOB at the 1973 BHCA National Specialty under breeder judge Owen Derryberry.*

Valentino went on to sire 37 champion get. A 1986 mating of Valentino and Jolene produced another renowned Musicland dog, Ch. Musicland's Spike Jones ROM. Following in the footsteps of his predecessors, Spike Jones has gone on to sire 20 champions while also winning Specialty BOBs, Group Firsts and an all-breed BIS. Many of the Musicland hounds picked up a predominately black coloration from the breeding

hounds to this day have a style of their own, an almost "classic Basset Hound." As with any kennel that has lasted a long time, they go through ups and downs in their breeding program. Nonetheless, Musicland is still going strong and has emerged to become a distinctively known Basset Hound style. A Life Member of BHCA, Jean has served as *Tally-Ho* editor, and as awards chairman.

*Ch. Musicland's Spike Jones ROM, going BIS at the Duluth Kennel Club, November 12, 1989.*

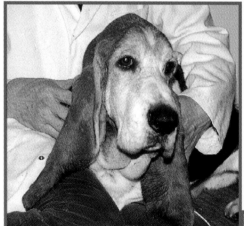

*Middle Left: Ch. Musicland's Valentino ROM, at the age of 11 years. This could be a classic Basset Hound head study. Note the "soft" expression.*

*Middle Right: Ch. Musicland's Jolene, dam of 16 champion get.*

*Lower Right: Ch. Musicland's Spike Jones ROM, shown winning BOB at the Fort Worth BHC Specialty show.*

## MY LU

Louisa A. "Appie" Myers began showing Bassets in the early 1960s. She participated in all disciplines of the breed: conformation, obedience, tracking, and field. Her Ch. Hiflite's Big John TD, sired by Ch. Glenhaven's Butcher Boy out of Ch. Kazoo's Question Mark, just missed being the first triple titleholder in the breed by narrowly losing a first place at the Nationals Field Trial in Sacramento. Unfortunately, Big John succumbed to a respiratory ailment before he could attain his field title.

Big John's daughter, Ch. My Lu's Blossom produced a number of champion offspring by both Ch. Glenhaven's Lord Jack and Ch. Tal-E-Ho's Top Banana. Blossom was also field pointed. Big John produced Ch. My Lu's Leah of Mibersham CD, (Salyers), a back-to-back High in Trial winner. A real favorite of Appie's was My Lu's Sunshine Shirley CD. "Sunny" and Het's Here Comes the General CD, co-owned by Het Garwood, won first and second places (respectively) in Veterans Obedience at the 1980 National Specialty. Both were well past the age of ten. Some other quality hounds from My

*My Lu's Sunshine Shirley CD and Het's Here Comes the General CD, shown with their owner/handler, Appie Myers, at the 1980 BHCA Nationals.*

Lu were: Ch. My Lu's Brunhilde, finished from the Bred by Exhibitor class, and Ch. My Lu's Boo Too.

Appie judged the Regular Dog classes at the 1990 Nationals, selecting as her WD, Lil' Creek Briarcrest Top Gun. "Gunner" went on to become the first Basset Hound ever to win the Group at Westminster. She was also a PBGV fancier, being a charter member of that national club, and acquired her initial PBGVs from Gilbert Pene of France. Her death in 1991 was a great loss to the dog sport.

*Ch. Hiflite's Big John TD, relaxing in front of the fire.*

*Ch. My Lu's Boo Too, shown finishing under breeder-judge Kitty Steidel at the Dal-Tex BHC Specialty in 1985. She was handled to this win by Judy Webb.*

## ORANPARK KENNELS, REG.

Oranpark was the kennel prefix of Mary and Wilton Meyer of California, both breeder-judges and both now deceased. First of all, let me clear up any confusion that may exist concerning the fact that some of their dog's names have the **Orangepark** prefix while other have **Oranpark**. They started out naming them Orangepark after the area in which they lived, but eventually found that they could not register that prefix and subsequently switched to using Oranpark instead. It's just that simple! The Meyers believed that there were two ways to breed good show dogs. One way is to start out with mediocre stock and consistently breed into one outstanding bloodline until the blood of the mediocre stock is so diluted as to have been nearly lost. This method makes the breeder feel that he is getting somewhere because he can see (hopefully) constant improvement. The big temptation, however, is to breed into the outstanding bloodline a time or two and then work within the partly improved line by selecting the best of that. Perhaps this would work if one lived long enough!

The other method, which the Meyers believed to be the better of the two and the one that they tried to use, was to start with outstanding stock and try to keep it outstanding. This, in itself, is much more difficult than is generally realized. The drag

*Orangepark Dexter, shown on his way to his championship. Wilton Meyer is handling under breeder-judge Millie Houchin.*

of the race average tends to pull the bloodline down, and, unless the exceptional parents are closely related, it is very difficult to reproduce their quality and fix the type with any degree of uniformity. So, even this second method is not always successful. Wilton pointed out that a number of years before they started in Bassets, they raised a litter of pups from a mating of Ch. Higgin's Red Coat and Ch. Redwood Rhoda, two of the greatest Irish Setters of their time. None of those get approached the quality of either parent and this he attributed to the fact that the breeding represented a considerable outcross of the bloodlines.

In about 1961, when they got serious about Basset Hounds, they set out to buy a bitch or two of exceptional quality from within the bloodlines that they also considered to be of exceptional quality. The two bitches that they began with were Ch. Santana-Mandeville Minnie and Hartshead Maybelline. Hartshead Maybelline, sired by Ch. Santana-Mandeville Gigolo out of Hartshead Looks Beautiful, was a big, beautiful, glamorous girl with loads of skin and bone. Her expressive eyes were shadowed with black, hence the name Maybelline! She was sweet in dispositon, but stubborn as a mule! The first time she was shown, she went Breed over a large entry. She had a total of nine points and one major when registration difficulties forced the discontinuation of showing her for nearly a year and a half. By the time that was settled, the Myers had decided to breed her.

Their other bitch, Ch. Santana-Mandeville Minnie, was sired by Ch. Santana-Mandeville No-Count out of Miss Jenny Magoo. Described by Wilton as being an elegant, good-moving bitch with an excellent front, she loved to show and was more mercurial in temperament than Maybelline.

At that time, a fair percentage of dogs seen in the show rings in California were sired by Ch. Santana-Mandeville Tarzan. While not a large dog, nor a real eye catcher, he appeared to the Meyers to have a prepotency to pass on a certain stamp of glamour, type with rather exceptional heads, and

*Ch. Oranpark Grover being awarded BIS under judge Dennis Grivas, handled by Jerry Rigden.*

a decent helping of overall quality. Although his stud fee was about double that of most other notable dogs of the time, they decided to dip into his genes and bred both Maybelline and Minnie to him. In the breeding to Maybelline they got Ch. Orangepark Dexter (quite widely used at stud in an attempt to get his head type), and Ch. Orangepark Dotty, as well as two other good pups. From the Tarzan ex Minnie mating, they got Ch. Orangepark Eustace.

These breedings gave them the chance to work back and forth, linebreeding in uncles, aunts and similar combinations without too close inbreeding, so that they could successfully hold onto the qualities that they liked while seeking further improvement. When they bred Minnie's son, Eustace, to the other foundation bitch, Maybelline, they got Ch. Oranpark Roy, who went on to become the Number One Basset Hound (Phillips System) for 1969, and I believe, just nudged out Ch. Glenhaven's Lord Jack by a couple of hundred points for 1970.

For several years the Meyers stayed within what was becoming their "line," with only a few experimental side trips of outcrosses, which proved unsuccessful. These outcrosses gave quite good results in the first generation, but seemed to destroy the chance of continuing the stamp of uniformity and type, which was their objective, in subsequent generations.

The opportunity then presented itself to breed to a hound whose name was legend, but who most had seen only in photos. I am told that Helen Nelson Kellogg considered Ch. Santana-Mandeville Ichabod to be the best Basset that she had ever bred. The Meyers were able to use him twice. His pedigree was close enough (Ch. Santana-Mandeville Tarzan ex Ch. Gwendolyn of Mandeville) to give them just what they thought they needed by way of introducing new blood without mixing up the genes too much. They bred him to old Minnie and to their Ch. Oranpark Sabrina, (Eustace ex Dottie), which gave them two litters to use back and forth in continuing their linebreeding program. They felt that these two litters truly represented an advance along the road to improvement. While never feeling that they significantly improved overall quality over their excellent foundation stock, they did fix the type of their average stock and consistently produced good-quality typey specimens, while hoping for those exceptional individuals to surpass the foundation animals. Another of their well known show dogs was Ch. Oranpark Grover, the top-winning Basset Hound for two years during the 1970s.

## PEPPERTREE

The Peppertree Basset kennels of Ray and Carolyn Young started out in Southern California in 1978 with the purchase of a pet for their youngest son. He wanted to show in junior show–manship, but was too young; it was agreed that mother would train and show the dog until Colin was old enough to take over a few months down the road. Eventually he turned his interest to girls and mom and dad were left with the dogs!

That first Basset turned out to be se- verely affected with thrombopathia. That was their introduction to health problems in the breed. They laughingly refer to themselves as the "Job" of Basset breeders and can think of only two serious health problems in the breed that they *haven't* experienced over the years, thus their interest and involve- ment with the BHCA Research Committee. One of the Young's favorite Bassets came to them from the Sanchu kennels of Chuck and Kitty Steidel. This bitch, Ch. Sanchu's Chablis, came to them as a promising pup in 1987 and is the one that they credit with teaching them how a Basset Hound could move. Carolyn describes the movement as

*Ch. Pinedell's Erik, by Jerry Rush winning a Specialty BOB under breeder-judge Joan Scholz.*

"having a feather on the lead." Her greatest accomplishment, and the Young's biggest thrill, was going WB, BW, and BOB at the Canadian National Specialty. Chablis now spends her time resting on her laurels and pretending that she is still the queen of the kennel.

Carolyn and Ray, now residing in Wash- ington State, are still active with the breed with Carolyn volunteering as the editor of *Tally-Ho*.

## PINEDELL

Jerry and Joani Rush of Sacramento, California, purchased their first Basset Hound in 1962 and began showing their hounds in 1964 under the kennel prefix of Pinedell. All of their hounds were either owner, or breeder- owner-handled by Joani and Jerry.

They have not shown their dogs since 1990, but they finished 28 of their dogs during that 26-year time span.

*Ch. Sanchu's Chablis, handled here by Carolyn Young, going WB, BW, and BOB at the 1990 Basset Hound Club of Canada Nationals under breeder-judge Louis Bowman.*

Some of their early hounds were: Ch. Pinedell-Rhinelan Gretchen, Ch. North–wood's Society Max, Ch. Coralwood's Broadway Taffy, Ch. McKimm's Sonja Solomon, Ch. Kazoo's Bic Banana, Ch. Pinedell's Erik, Ch. Pinedell's Claude, Ch. Pinedell's Bandit, Ch. Pinedell's Tough Guy, Ch. Pinedell's Tangerine Dream, and Ch. Pinedell's Gwendolyn. They have had four of their hounds listed in the Register of Merit.

Jerry Rush is approved to judge Basset Hounds and Beagles, served as a BHCA Director from the Western Region for over four years and was appointed to the office of second vice-president at the 1996 annual meeting of the BHCA. He also judged the Regular Dog classes at

*Ch. Pinedell's Tough Guy, winning the Northern California BHC Specialty in 1988. Joani Rush handling, under breeder-judge Mary Jane Booth.*

the 1996 BHCA Nationals. Joani also plans to pursue judging Basset Hounds in the future.

## REBELGLEN

The Rebelglen kennel of Mary J. (Jo) and John NewMyer, Jr. is located just east of Los Angeles in Duarte. After having fallen in love with the temperament of a neighbor's Basset, they bought their first one, Soupie's Rebel Abigail, as a Christmas gift for their children in 1965. In April, 1966, having heard there was to be a Basset Hound Specialty in their town, Jo was curious enough to attend. That show turned out to be the first independent BHC of Southern California Specialty, with an entry of 116! This experience hooked her on showing and she came away determined to get a Basset to show. Because the local breeders of the time were keeping the best of their litters, she found it necessary to enter into a co-ownership. An agreement was struck, for breeding purposes, on a major pointed bitch from Grace Flory's kennel named Jungfrau Fred, with co-owner Jim Slayman, then the president of the BHCSC.

*Ch. Pinedell's The Bandit, handled by Joani Rush, winning BOB under judge Dorothy Nickles.*

Jim was the NewMyers' first real teacher about the conformation show ring. He was a strong advocate of showing and finishing your own dogs at a time when many of the exhibitors were using professional handlers. It wasn't unusual to see eight or ten professional handlers in the Open and Specials classes at the Southern California shows of the time. (The point schedule for California in 1967 was 22 dogs/17 bitches for 3 points.)

Jo selected Bill Kelly's Am-Mex. Ch. Kelly's Major Topic ("Big Boy," the foundation stud for the Houndsville dogs) to breed to Jungfrau Fred. This choice was based on the quality of his get that were in the ring at the time. He also had, and was producing, the improvements that Fred (and the Flory line) needed: heads, bone, and toplines. The Flory dogs excelled in movement and rears. This breeding was technically an outcross of two heavily linebred complimentary animals. Each was typical of its line, but not repeating the faults of either. (This method became the standard for any future Rebelglen selection of outside studs.) In actuality, there was a nick in the pedigrees of this breeding. Fred was heavily Flory linebred, a line based on Gallio of Belbay. Gallio was a California import, produced by a father-daughter breeding on Ch. Mr. Cyclops of Belbay and a Jet Foret bitch. "Big Boy" was heavily linebred on the old Belleau line of Cordelia Jensen, which included Ch. Belbay Chevalier, a litterbrother to Mr. Cyclops. (The Belleau line was also much of the basis for the Santana-Mandeville line, the Houndsville dogs, and many of the Nancy Evans dogs, as proudly proclaimed by Cordelia in her later years. Cordelia is reported to have told Jo that the only reason she bred out to Notrenom and imported an Abbot Run Valley bitch was solely to improve rears, a constant problem with her line.)

One difficulty remained to be solved before this breeding could take place. After years of competing against each other in the ring and within the local Basset club Grace Flory and Bill Kelly greatly disliked each other. Fortunately, Bill Kelly decided to allow the breeding (handled by Bunny

Witowski, at Houndsville, where Big Boy was standing at stud) because he thought that the NewMyers would be responsible breeders. I'm told that Grace Flory was livid when she found out, and that it cost Jo and John her friendship. (Grace expected all Flory dogs to be bred back to their own line and that is one reason why this combination had never been done before.) This controversy in combining the two lines was the basis for their selection of "Rebel" as their original kennel name, but on later discovering it was unregistrable with AKC due to frequent use by others, they changed their kennel name/prefix to "Rebelglen." Unfortunately, this name had also been used by others so it could not be registered as a kennel name either. By this time, however, so many of their dogs were registered with that name that they decided to just continue its use.

The Jungfrau Fred litter was whelped in January, 1968, by C-section, followed by spaying, and Fred was lost to surgical shock. One whelp was dead in utero, but the orphaned litter of three, two tri females and one light red male, survived. Jo's pick of litter at eight weeks was the tri bitch, "Velvet," (Ch. Rebel's Major Calamity CD), because she was concerned with the loose shoulders on the male, although he was her favorite because of his personality. Jim, the co-owner, chose the male, but sold him back when asked. That male puppy, Ch. Rebel's Frosty Topic, became their first champion. He finished entirely breeder-owner-handled, reportedly the only one in California to do so in 1970. He enjoyed a BOB win from the Open class over nine professionally handled specials. Fortunately they had bred him to Cinnamon Cinder Finale, an Abigail daughter, before he finished. He was found to be sterile shortly thereafter due to testicular cancer, but he lived to be eight years old. From the breeding of this Abigail daughter, they co-owned Midnight Cowboy of Rebelglen with his breeder, Margy Cowans.

Frosty's littermate, Ch. Rebel's Major Calamity CD, was also breeder-owner-handled to her championship, except for one major. Two attempts had been made to

*Ch. Rebelglen's Frosty Too CD, finishing at 16 months. Handled by breeder-owner Jo NewMeyer, under breeder-judge Mary Meyer.*

breed this bitch to Ch. Orangepark Dexter in an effort to improve her head refinement, but she missed twice, despite FSH shots (Follicle Stimulating Hormone) the second time. Just after finishing, and with repeated FSH shots, she conceived and whelped a litter of five in August, 1972. This litter produced Ch. Rebelglen's Ruffles of Sohigh, (co-owned with Mary Beth Hossler, and Rebelglen's Damon), who was major pointed from the Bred-by Exhibitor Dog classes. Ruffles finished at just two years of age, with all points coming from the Bred-by-Exhibitor Bitch classes, breeder-owner-handled by Jo, their second hound to accomplish this. It was during this time that the NewMyers became good friends with Mary and Wilton Meyer.

During their travels to the Northern California and Sacramento Specialties, the NewMyers met and became good friends with Bud and Diane Rinderneck (Rhinelan). They admired and tried to lease the Rinderneck's bitch, Ch. Rhinelan's Pic-A-Dilly

("Polly"). Unable to do so, they entered into a co-ownership of her dam, Kinslow's Windy of Rhinelan, and bred her to the Frosty son, Midnight Cowboy. From that litter of three, whelped in February, 1972, they kept Ch. Rebelglen's Missy of Rhinelan, who finished at 16 months of age. She took her first five-point major by going WB, BOS over Specials at the Valle Del Sol BHC Specialty at seven months of age under breeder-judge Joe Kulper.

Midnight Cowboy was also bred to a Flory bitch, Pompey's Julia. This litter produced Ch. Priscilla of Rebelglen. Bred by Cynthia Curran and co-owned by Jo and Norma Curran, Cynthia's mother, Priscilla, was shown exclusively in the Puppy and Open classes by Jo. Missy and Priscilla, were both bred to Ch. Oranpark Grover (Ch. Santana-Mandeville's Ichabod ex Ch. Santana-Mandeville's Minnie) to improve heads and rears. Because both of these bitches had outstanding shoulder layback, fronts, rib cages, and movement, it was hoped they could overcome Grover's shorter rib cage and straighter shoulders. From these breedings, Priscilla produced Ch. Rebelglen's Frosty Too CD. Pick of his litter, he was owned by John and Jo, and was their third champion to finish solely from the Bred-by Exhibitor classes. Shown as a Special only occasionally, he won several BOBs including the Valle Del Sol Specialty under breeder-judge Sylvia Silk. He finished his CD trained and handled by John. Missy produced a large litter of all light red and whites, like their parents. Included were Ch. Rebelglen's Maude, owned by John and Jo, and Rebelglen's Mandy of Sohigh, also co-owned with Mary Beth Hossler. Maude and Mandy were campaigned at the same time by Jo.

Their co-owned Ruffles bitch was bred several times, but kept missing. After isolating and correcting the problem, she finally conceived, bred to Ch. Rebelglen's Frosty Too. This litter proved disappointing and Ruffles died of a heart attack at five years of age, before she was bred again. Unfortunately, this cost them their only Dexter daughter.

Taking their vet's advice that all bitches should have a litter by age two years to preserve their later fertility, Maude was bred to her grandfather, Midnight Cowboy, to progeny test that side of the line. The resulting litter was very sound and beautiful moving, but a little plain and soft in temperament, so all were sold. The next year she was bred to Frosty Too, her half-brother on Grover. This litter, all red and white, produced Rebelglen's Beauty, Rebelglen's Sugar and Spice, co-owned with Gary and Bev Wallich, and Rebelglen's Trooper, the pick of the litter and co-owned with Mary Beth Hossler. When Trooper died at five months of age, due to gross veterinary incompetence in treating a case of gastroenteritis (administration of high doses of cortisone), the breeding was repeated at Maude's next season.

This repeated litter was their most successful, producing Ch. Rebelglen's So Handsome, Ch. Rebelglen's Sydney, co-owned with Peggy Dorrence, Ch. Rebelglen's Sean

O'Casey, owned by Jack and Peggy Dorrence, and Rebelglen's Sitting Pretty ("Totie"). So Handsome and Sydney were campaigned at the same time, So Handsome in Bred-by classes and Sydney in Open Dog classes. They took turns winning until So Handsome finished at 20 months with all of his points. Sydney finished one month later and was specialed occasionally, winning BOB at the Valle Del Sol BHC Specialty in 1981 under breeder-judge Jim White, duplicating his sire's win there in 1976. He was also BOS at the BHCSC Specialty in 1983 under breeder-judge Wilton Meyer.

For her second litter, Missy was bred to Frosty Too, doubling Midnight Cowboy, Missy's sire and Frosty Too's grandsire on his dam's side. This produced Rebelglen's Frosty Miss ("Trucker"), co-owned with Terry Burian. Trucker was exhibited by Terry and won 11 points, including both majors, before being retired. She whelped her first litter, sired by Ch. Hallmark Malcolm (Ch. Musicland's Hey Jude ex Dixie's Sho Nuff Good Nuff), who was owned by Cathie Spencer (Jercat) and campaigned by handler Ric Byrd. Terry had worked for Ric and admired Malcolm, who was linebred on Dexter and also had Ch. Santana-Mandeville Minnie, dam of Grover, on his dam's side. The resulting litter of three, a mahogany male and bitch and a tri bitch, became Rebelglen's Mister Willing, Ch. Rebelglen's A Minor Calamity ROM, and Rebelglen's Rejoice. Calamity was sold as a puppy on a breeding contract to Jim and Sharon Dok (Castlehill). Mister was co-owned by Terry and Jo, and Jo exhibited him. Rejoice was kept by Terry and later given to Cathie Spencer when Terry could no longer keep her. After producing a litter for Cathie, Rejoice was sold to an eastern breeder. Mister had points and a BOB from the Bred-by classes and was later co-owned with Elizabeth and Bailey Marks, but was retired when he was tested and found to be a carrier of hereditary familial thrombopathia (HFT). Upon finding this, all of their other dogs were tested and found to be clear of HFT and VWD.

Before she finished, although she was pointed and had been campaigned by the Doks, Calamity was bred to Ch. Rebelglen's So Handsome to try to improve on her head and type. The resulting litter was divided by the NewMyers and the Doks, with the pick, a

*Ch. Rebelglen's Maude, shown going BOS en route to her championship.*

tri bitch who became Ch. Rebelglen's Pure Velvet, going to the NewMyers. The Doks then became full owners of Calamity and, after finishing, she became the foundation bitch for their Castelhill Bassets, producing their first seven Castlehill bench champions, bred to various studs, and producing champions in every litter.

Pure Velvet finished at two-and-a-half in November, 1983 with some very nice wins. She once went BOS at the BHCSC Specialty under breeder-judge Lucille Barton over a bitch entry of 29.

Rebelglen's Frosty Miss was bred again, this time to Ch. Tal-E-Ho's Hot Diggity (Ch. Tal-E-Ho's Prancer ex Tal-E-Ho's Bubbles), who had been sold to Cathie Spencer. This litter of seven produced Ch. Rebelglen's Frost-N On The Cake ("Sis"), who was co-owned by her breeders, Jo and Terry Burian. All but two of this litter had overshot bites. Jo campaigned Sis to her championship in the Bred-by classes, solely, including WB at the BHCSC Specialty under breeder-judge Jim White, and her last major under breeder-judge Jerry Rush. Although line-bred back to their line several times, she never produced anything good enough to keep and frequently produced bad bites.

Jo and John had been trying to breed the three Frosty—Maude daughters, Beauty, Sitting Pretty, and Sugar and Spice, to Ch. Blue Billy Beaujangles. After missing twice with Beauty and Sitting Pretty, although Billy was producing litters with no problems, they were finally checked surgically and it was found that Beauty had an infantile uterus and Sitting Pretty's was smaller than normal for her age. Otherwise they were quite normal. After thyroid treatment, Sitting Pretty was bred again, this time to a stud that later proved to have fertility problems, and probably had them at the time of the breedings. So Beauty and Sitting Pretty were sold. After also missing twice, due to a breeding contract dispute, and the subsequent breeding without their permission, the NewMyers were forced by AKC to relinquish their co-ownership on Sugar and Spice, who did produce a litter for the co-owners, the Wallichs. As she was the only Frosty—Maude daughter to ever produce, this was an additional tragedy for the Rebelglen breeding program, which had always previously been based on their bitches. They would now have to rely on the Frosty—Maude sons.

Ch. Rebelglen's Maude had been bred again, to Ch. Desiree Acres Pinball Wizard, a Grover son owned by Kati and Mary Netzley. Unfortunately, a grossly incompetent C-section not only caused an infection that killed the entire litter but also ruined Maude's uterus so that she could no longer be bred.

So Handsome was bred to a Desiree Acres bitch, Desiree Acres Delilah (Ch. Desiree Acres Pinball Wizard ex a Midnight Cowboy daughter), who was co-owned by Jo with Barry Orell. So Handsome and Wizard were both Grover sons. This breeding produced only two male puppies, neither of which particularly impressed Jo when she went to select her pick. She finally decided on the one who "wouldn't leave her alone," and he went on to become Ch. Rebelglen's Bentley, who finished at 15 months, all points under breeder-judges.

Frosty Too was also used at stud by the Netzleys (Desiree Acres) and the Youngs (Peppertree), producing Ch. Desiree Acres Praline N'Cream and Ch. Peppertree's Doctor Watson, owned by Gina Garcia. Watson finished novice owner-handled, except for a BOB under breeder-judge Jerry Rush, handled by Carolyn Young. Frosty Too left five-pointed pups, two with majors. It is a shame one of them did not finish as it would have earned him his ROM.

So Handsome also sired two litters in Montana, including one out of Ch. Beehive's Isis (Ch. Musicland's Rebel Rouser II ex Ch. Musicland's Clinging Vine), bred by Helen Kester and owned by Penny Snavely. This litter produced Ch. Handsome Boy of Pennrich, who won a major at the Valle Del

Sol BHC Specialty under breeder-judge, Mike Sosne.

After finishing and being Specialed for a short while, Bentley was co-owned with and sent to the Rindernecks for field training. They bred him to their Rhinelan's Poppy (FCh. Rhinelan's Mason ex Rhinelan's Jawood-Sweeny) and produced Ch. Rhinelan's Rolls Royce. He also sired a litter out of Linda Deir's FCh. B.J.'s Gilda R. Adner CD (Footsloggers). Also bred to a bitch out of one of the Rhinelan studs, Nichol's Penny Times Five, owned by Denise Nichols, he produced Dual Ch. Tallyhill's Jolly Roger TD, owned by Delores McKinnon. Roger was WD for four points at the BHC of Sacramento Specialty show at 11 months of age, novice owner-handled, under breeder-judge Mary Jo Shields. Bentley was returned to Southern California in mid-1986 so he could be used at stud at Rebelglen. Jo couldn't bear to part with him again for field training, even though he showed great promise. To the day he died, at just shy of 13 years of age, in November, 1995, Bentley was Jo's absolute favorite. They say that they have never had a smarter, gentler, better tempered, or more endearing dog.

Pure Velvet, bred several times, only produced small litters requiring C-sections. Her black and white son, sired by Sydney, swallowed a rock and died during surgery before he was even a year old. The repeat litter produced only two dead puppies after a vet delayed section. Therefore, Sydney left no living progeny. Bred to Bentley, her half-brother (both sired by So Handsome), she produced two tri bitches, the pick becoming Ch. Rebelglen's Mercedes. Although bred several more times, Pure Velvet had no more litters.

Mary Beth Hossler had always wanted to have another red and white male to show, to replace the Maude—Frosty son she lost as a puppy. Several red and white males became available, sired by Doctor Watson, out of Bonnie DeLaCruz's bitch Butterfly's Rainbow. She was a Ch. Tal-E-Ho's Ditto daughter. Mary Beth purchased and named one, and then co-owned him with Jo who was to exhibit him. Until Mary Beth could make arrangements to take him home, he was also to live with Jo temporarily. This puppy became Ch. Butterfly's Showbiz of Sohigh, who went on to be the RWD at six months of age at the BHCSC Specialty under breeder-judge Bill Russell, at his first show. He won his first points from the 6–9 Puppy class at eight months, and his first major, a week later, from the same class. He finished at 17 months, owner-handled by Jo, with three majors, including ones under breeder-judges Bob Booth and Cathie Spencer and a BOB from the classes, over specials. Specialed for a short while, he won several BOBs, including ones under Bill Russell, Cathie Spencer, and Appie Meyers at the BHC of Sacramento Specialty, all owner-handled by Jo. Showbiz never did live with Mary Beth, staying all of his life at Rebelglen, and tragically, he was lost to anaphalactic shock, after swallowing a bee, at eight years of age and after only siring one litter. Showbiz was a very large but well-balanced dog, weighing about 72 pounds when in prime show weight.

Mercedes and Showbiz were campaigned to their championships at the same time. Even though Mercedes had won the 9–12 Puppy class at the BHCA Nationals in 1987, under breeder-judge Bob Booth and had won both of her majors from the Bred-by Exhibitor classes, it was always hard for her to win when Showbiz had already gone WD at the same show, although once she did! This naturally delayed her finishing, so several months after Showbiz finished, they switched her to the Open class. At her next three shows she won five points, including a three-point major. She was only shown four times in the next six months due to a plethora of what they considered poor judges, and/or shows with good judges that were too far away for Jo to travel to alone. She finished with four majors, always breeder-owner-handled. In hindsight, they wish that they had stuck it out in the Bred-by Exhibitor classes, since they didn't breed her for a year after she finished.

Mercedes was bred to Showbiz, and even though there was only one breeding, she produced four puppies. This required an

*Ch. Rebelglen's Bentley, taking a BOB at 17 months of age. Handled by Jo NewMyer under breeder-judge Beverly Stockfelt.*

emergency C-section, after a hair-raising drive through L.A. rush hour traffic on a Friday night! The large red and white male blocking the birth canal was thought to be dead when delivered, but was successfully revived. He was kept, along with his sole red and white sister, and became Ch. Rebelglen's Beamer. Beamer finished with three majors, and all but the last two points from the Bred-by class. When he was young he was not too enthusiastic about being shown, and he seemed to be getting worse. Terry Burian took him and kenneled him between a litter of terriers and her loud, barky Bouviers. This experience, in addition to her socialization of him, seemed to restore his confidence so that she was able to finish him. She then handled him to several BOBs and a BOS win.

Jo was getting older and it seemed it was getting increasingly difficult to raise litters, let alone find a heavily linebred hound with good shoulders, out of good shoulders, to use at stud. Thus Mercedes was never bred again. Her only daughter, Rebelglen's Lexus, was never bred. Beamer was bred to a partially Tal-E-Ho outcrossed Bentley daughter, Rebelglen's Lily, linebreeding on the Tal-E-Ho side. Health problems in part of that litter led the owner, without consulting the NewMyers, to spay and place Lily. This bitch had had an accidental litter by her litterbrother, resulting in a litter with no health problems. Unfortunately, this lost them their only producing Bentley daughter. Beamer was also bred to a Rolls Royce daughter (doubling Bentley) with no problems. If they are unable produce another litter from him, he might be the last of the Rebelglen-named dogs.

Except in rare cases, Jo NewMyer has always shown her own dogs, and usually from the Bred-By Exhibitor classes. This should be the showcase class for all breeders, but, except for Specialty shows, they are usually minimally entered. This leaves the winner of the Bred-By Exhibitor class with the problem of trying to beat the usually large Open class winner for the points, something that, unfortunately, is not easily done, except under the knowledgeable breeder-judges. As a rule of thumb, although there are exceptions, Jo finds that the good breeder-judges are those who were successful breeders themselves and generally exhibited their own hounds in the classes.

Due to the myriad of considerations involved in breeding and showing, Jo often wonders how she enjoyed the success that she has. With limited space for dogs, as well as limited funds, she has always been dependent on co-ownerships to "make it work." For example, in 1982, she co-owned 12 dogs in order to have what she considered necessary to maintain a breeding and showing program. Being aware of the importance of bitches to a breeding program, she always tried to keep the pick of the litter bitch and, if possible, co-own a littersister, if there was one. As you will note, this did not always work out for the best.

*Ch. Manor Hill Molly Molly, foundation bitch for Redemption Rock.*

Jo and John will always be grateful to the many people over the years that taught them about handling, showing, pedigrees, bloodline characteristics, and developmental patterns. These people include Jim Slayman, Barbara Dunning, Cordelia Jensen, Bud and Diane Rinderneck, and Mary and Wilton Meyer. John and Jo have been BHCA members since 1968 and Jo is a Life Member of the BHC of Southern California. She has held every office, except secretary, in that club, including two years as its president. Both of the NewMyers have been members of the Riverside Kennel Club since 1986 and both have been officers and board members of that club. Both are also charter members of the Greater San Diego Basset Hound Club. Jo intends to judge Bassets in the future, and this writer would welcome her, as she will be a very knowledgeable addition to the judging ranks.

## REDEMPTION ROCK

Carla LaFave's involvement with dogs began in 1958 with the purchase of a Saint Bernard puppy. Her interest and involvement grew throughout the years with the showing and breeding of Saints. Shortly after marrying Michael, they started their Redemption Rock kennel in 1973 in Massachusetts. Their goal then, as now, was to produce the best that they could with a limited number of dogs, generally never exceeding 14, including the house dogs. Always keeping their older dogs throughout their life span limited their breeding and showing stock, but they are aware that it is quality, not necessarily numbers, that counts.

Over the past quarter century, they were able to achieve their goals, producing very nice specimens of the breed in terms of type and soundness. They credit much of their

*Ch. Redemption Rock Tangerine.*

*Ch. Redemption Rock Revelation.*

*Am/Can. Ch. Redemption Rock Zapper.*

*Redemption Rock Seranade, dam of Tangerine.*

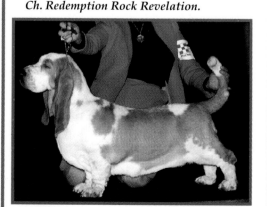

success to purchasing the lovely bitch, Ch. Manor Hill Molly Molly, from Joan and Ron Scholz (Manor Hill kennels). Molly Molly was a littersister to Ch. Manor Hill Father James and Ch. Manor Hill Tooth Fairy, both fine dogs and excellent producers themselves.

Later, they were able to acquire a Tooth Fairy daughter, Manor Hill Ultra Brite. From that point, linebreeding their stock, their kennel grew and they were able to produce several conformation champions. Their Redemption Rock Joshua ROM was out of Manor Hill Ultra Brite, sired by Ch. Coralwood's Roger, and became a good producer for them. One of his daughters, Ch. Rio Vista's Wrong Pajamas was selected as WB at the 1981 National Specialty.

Other notable Bassets from this kennel were: Am/Can. Ch. Redemption Rock Zapper, Am/Braz. Ch. Gurreiero R R Mister Clyde, Ch. Redemption Rock Sit-N-Pretty, (a Joshua littersister), and Redemption Rock Tangerine. Manor Hill Lollipop was also purchased and bred to Zapper to produce Am/Can. Ch. Redemption Rock Cochise, Ch. Redemption Rock Snow Bear, and Ch. Manor Hill Love Unlimited ROM, all from the same litter. He also sired Ch. Redemption Rock Revelation. Some other dogs used in their breeding program were Ch. Topohil Leader of the Pack, Rio Vista Redemption Rocky, Ch. Switchbark's Ashmore, and Ch. Corkery's Abercrombie. Corkery's Candida was bred to Zapper to produce Am/Can. Ch. Cloverhill's Littlest Hobo. Reviewing the pedigrees of these "outside studs," a student of the breed will quickly note their linebreeding potential.

Nearly all of the dogs they have shown were breeder-owner-handled to their championships, providing a great amount of personal satisfaction that accompanies that endeavor. Carla's interest has expanded to judging, consequently they will continue to breed and show their Bassets, but on a limited basis, striving to continue to produce the quality Bassets expected from the Redemption Rock name.

*Ch. Reepa's High Fashion Liz and her littersister, Reepa's Happy Josephine winning Best Brace in Show at Golden Gate in 1966.*

## REEPA

The Reepa prefix is that of Marianne Paulsson of Sebastopol, California. Marianne is a long-time Basset breeder, and more currently a successful PBGV breeder, along with her partner in the latter endeavor, Ruth Balladone. Her knowledge of the Basset Hound, particularly its development on the West Coast, goes back a good 35 years.

Marianne's first Bassets were the two bitches who won Best Brace in Show at the Golden Gate KC show in 1966 under the well-known judge Percy Roberts. These bitches, purchased from Dorothea Fassett in 1960, are Ch. Reepa's High Fashion Liz and Reepa's Happy Josephine. They were sired by Ch. Long View Acres Uncle Ed and out of Sutton's Lucy of Belvedere. Another dog of which she is very proud was Ch. Reepa's High Fashion Spike, sired by Ch. Bell's Rusty Spike out of Sophia De St. Hubert. This dog won the Breed at the 1973 BHCA Spring Specialty show in Dallas, Texas.

*Ch. Reepa's High Fashion Spike, BOB at the BHCA 1973 Spring Specialty show.*

## RIVENDELL

Although experienced in the conformation and obedience rings with Irish Setters and Border Collies since 1973, it wasn't until the summer of 1980 that Chris Wallen acquired her first Basset Hound. It took all of three days to completely fall in love with the breed. The next several months consisted of many hours of research on the breed (something that too many fanciers fail to do!). She eventually contacted Cathie Spencer of JerCat Bassets. After deciding that this was the "look" that she liked best, she asked to reserve a puppy from an upcoming litter sired by Ch. Tal-E-Ho's Hot Diggity ROM, "Hogan," and out of Ch. JerCat's Megan. While awaiting the birth of that litter, Chris purchased two other puppies from JerCat. They became Ch. Gable's Echo of JerCat, who finished at 15 months and a Hogan daughter, Ch. JerCat's Karbon Kopy Kat, "Kitty."

In 1983, the long-awaited puppy was born and soon came home to Rivendell. He eventually became BISS winner Ch. JerCat's Gato Del Sol CD. "Toby" finished his championship in April, 1985. He went back into competition at age seven to gain his obedience title. Although trained in advanced obedience, he was unable to gain his title as his advanced age of nine forced his retirement from jumping.

The first Rivendell litter was produced in 1984 by the breeding of Toby and Kitty. This produced Ch. Rivendell's Miss Kit Kat. Kitty went to live at JerCat in 1984. Eventually, her daughter by Ch. JerCat's Emmit Kelly came back. She grew up to be Ch. JerCat's Cody Jeameau CD, "Cody Jo." Toby was bred twice to Cody Jo, and they produced Specialty winners Ch. Rivendell's Bubba Beuford, Ch. Rivendell's Bijou Rouge ROM, Ch. Rivendell's Knight Magic, and Rivendell's As If By Magic CD.

Ch. Rivendell's Bijou Rouge ROM was bred only twice and produced a total of eight puppies. From her first litter of three by Am-Can. Ch. Pyperwynd's I.M. Reddie Freddie ROM came multi-Specialty winner Ch. Rivendell's Red Storm Rising. Her second litter of five was by Ch. Sanlyn's Classic Ten O'Bayland ROM. This breeding produced Ch. Sanlyn's Rivendell Sweet Enuff, Ch. Rivendell's Sweet N' No Equal, Ch. Rivendell's Nutra Sweet, and Ch. Rivendell's Sweet-N-Lo. This latter, known as "Butter," not only has won multi-Specialty BIS but also achieved an AOM at the 1994 Nationals.

In 1990, Toby was bred to Ch. JerCat's Sin-D-Cated. A daughter, JerCat's Rivendell My-T-Fine CD, was the result. She eventually was bred to Ch. Sanlyn's Classic Ten O'Bayland ROM, and produced multiple-Specialty winner, Ch. Rivendell's Pink Cadillac.

Not a large kennel, Rivendell has continued to produce quality hounds through a limited breeding program. Although concentrating on conformation, Chris also has a great interest in obedience. Her main goal is to produce a versatile hound who can be a competitor in the ring and a companion in the home. Certainly the Rivendell prefix is one that deserves to be watched in the coming years.

*Ch. Rivendell's Sweet-N-Lo, shown by breeder-owner-handler Chris Wallen under breeder-judge Margie Wikerd.*

## SANCHU

The Sanchu Bassets go back to 1967 when Kitty and Chuck Steidel established their kennel with the prefix being derived from a combination of their children's names, Sandra and Chuck. Upwards of 40 Sanchu Bassets have achieved AKC titles, and a few others have garnered titles in tracking and obedience. In the conformation ring, the preponderance of dogs finished their championships from the Bred-by Exhibitor class. A significant goal, they successfully achieved putting one Specialty major-pointed win on each of their dogs, along with the all-breed points, prior to the completion of their championships. The Sanchu foundation includes dogs from very early Tal-E-Ho lines down from their Ch. Tal-E-Ho's Prancer.

Sanchu dogs have gone to a number of different countries, including Germany, Switzerland, Finland, Denmark, and Canada. To Finland and then on to Sweden went Ch. Sanchu's Cottonwood, a Ch. Slippery Hill Hudson ex Ch. Sanchu's Bagatelle son. In the early '80s, Sanchu's Campari went to Denmark, finished a championship in two countries and earned a tracking title. A prominent sire in Germany and the US, bred by Kitty Steidel and Mary Hargett Smizer, was Ch. Sanchu's Sour Mash (Droemont). In the '80s, "Wilbur" sired several lovely bitches for Sanchu; Ch. Sanchu's Cafe au Lait and Ch. Sanchu's Creme de Cocoa (Steidel), and Ch. Sanchu's Margarita (F. Hansen), and Chs. Sanchu's Chardonnay and Chablis (Young). After winning BOS at the 1990 BHCA Nationals, Ch. Sanchu's Kizzy went to Switzerland to live with one of our long-time foreign BHCA members, Ruth Binder-Gresly. Sanchu's Sake achieved his Swiss and German titles in 1994 with Brita Berkel Meier. Ch. Sanchu's Synergist, upon winning the Junior Sweepstakes at the 1993 BHCA Nationals, went to Switzerland to Brita Berkel Meier and Maja Altorfer. In 1993, to continue their linebreeding program, they bought a Ch. Sanchu's Sour Mash ex Sanchu's Cashew daughter, Daphne of Kind Kernel, from Maja Altorfer in Switzerland. Daphne won the Senior Sweepstakes at the 1994 BHCA Nationals.

Sanchu has also had their share of National Specialty wins. Ch. Sanchu's Semolena Pilchard, (Ch. Tal-E-Ho's Prancer ex Ch. Sanchu's Bagatelle), was Best Brood Bitch two years running in the early eighties with different male get at each show. Ch. Sanchu's Baguette of Margett was BOS in 1984. Kizzy was BOS in 1990. A Sanchu Barcardi son, Ch. Lochopt Rum Rikki was BW in 1984 and BOS in 1986. The most prestigious win was that of Ch. Sanchu's Hot Toddy, "Toots," who was BOB at the

1993 National Specialty under judge Judy Webb. She won the Hound Group the next day at the all-breed show under judge Roy Holloway. A multiple Group-winning bitch in '93, she ranked number-one Basset bitch that year. She started out in 1994 with a Group First and Group Third at Palm Springs back to back. While starting the new year out as the number-one Basset through mid-April, and even ranked among the top ten hounds, her career was cut short when a life-threatening emergency spaying became necessary. This unfortunate occurrence, of course, ended her show career until she reaches Veteran class eligibility for the Specialties. She loved the ring and had many admirers.

Today, with Kitty judging and both Kitty and Chuck traveling frequently, Sanchu is winding down. They currently maintain about four Bassets and breed an occasional litter. In an effort to introduce different blood into a small-scale breeding program, a dog from Argentina, Ch. Raspor's Tiger Black, was imported. Kitty saw this dog when she judged at their National and made the arrangement to import him to show him to his American championship and to be used at stud for a short period. He started his American show career in May, 1995 and, with five Group firsts, became the number-three Basset Hound by the end of November, 1995. Eight puppies resulted when he was bred to Ch. Sanchu's Tabasco (Herner & Steidel). They have hopes for a bright future.

*Ch. Sanchu's Hot Toddy, 1993 BHCA National Specialty winner, going BOB at Golden Gate KC in 1994. Shown under breeder-judge Joan Urban, she went on that evening to win the Group under Michele Billings, handled by Mike Stone.*

## SAND-DELL

One of the most influential of Canadian kennels is that of Mr. Ron Sandell's Sand-Dell Basset Hound kennel. Ron Sandell be-gan his kennel in 1965 with a bitch he purchased from the Nancy Evans kennel (another mostly Belbay/Santana style Basset kennel) in the US. The bitch was named Jocamine's Cherry Jubilee. Later Ron acquired Ch. Whistledown Commando and, a little later yet, from the McKnights, Am/Can. Ch. Solitude Creek Sophocles. It was from these hounds, and others in between, that he produced top-quality hounds that easily completed their championships all over Canada and taking some American cham-pionship titles, as well. The Sand-Dell hounds are good-sized hounds with fine temperaments and sound structure. Sand-Dell's Anastasia was BW at the 1973 BHCA Nationals.

## SANLYN

Sanlyn Bassets got its start when Sandi (Baldwin) Anderson bought a six-month-old male Basset puppy through a classified ad for the family as a Christmas present. It did not take long to find out that "Edger" had not been fully paid for by his original owner. Sandi completed payment to Poverty Knob kennels and received Edger's papers. She soon began to enter him at local shows and, in short order, Edger finished his championship.

*Ch. Poverty Knob's Tribute To Maz ROM.*
*"Biddie" was the foundation bitch for Sanlyn.*

Sandi had also become good friends with Jean Severied and Jane Brandt of Poverty Knobs kennels. She would help them with general maintenance of their dogs, help in whelping litters, and kennel sit for them. In appreciation, they gave her "Biddie." Sandi picked her out only because she looked like her mother. Can. Ch. Poverty Knobs Tribute to Maz ROM became the foundation bitch for Sanlyn. Bred to three different studs,

*Ch. Sanlyn's Classic Ten O'Bayland ROM,*
*a Sanlyn multi-Specialty winner and sire of*
*over 20 champion get.*

Biddie produced ten champion get, nine of them by Ch. Beaujangles J. P. Beaureguarde. These included multi-BIS and Group winner Am/Can. Ch. Poverty Knobs Double Stuff, and Group placers Am/Can. Ch. Lil's Fair N Square of Sanlyn, Am/Can. Ch. Sanlyn's Canadian Edition, and Ch. Beaujangles Jazzbeau.

Around this time Sandi began working closely with the Beaujangles kennel. She bought Ch. Beaujangles Brandy of Sanlyn in 1984. Bred to "Jeep," (Am/Can. Ch. Beaujangles J. P. Beaureguarde ROM), she produced multi-Specialty winner Ch. Sanlyn's Forever In Blue Jeans. Bred to Am/Can. Ch. Sanlyn's Logo N Jeepster (a Jeep ex Biddie son), she produced Ch. Sanlyn's Tess N Thunderpaws.

Due to his susceptibility to valley fever, Jeep could no longer live in Arizona, so in 1985 he came to live with Sandi. In 1986, Ch. Beaujangles Silkience, with 13 points on her, moved up to Sanlyn also. She finished in the first show that Sandi entered her in. Bred only once to Ch. Beaujangles Ten, she produced Ch. Sanlyn Dark Crystal and Ch. Beaujangles Peppermint Patti. When Biddie passed away, Claudia Lane sent up Ch. Beaujangles All That Jazz, a granddaughter and a close look-alike. Pebbles was only bred one time to Ch. Sanlyn's Classic Cruiser, producing Ch. Classic Camile.

Jeep was bred to Ch. Blaznsadl's Feilista and Sandi received two puppies back. They were Am/Can. Ch. Bayland's Sanlyn Master Card and Can. Ch. Bayland's Sanlyn Ebony, both co-owned with Doreen Mitchell. Ebony was eventually bred to Am/Can. Ch. Jollytime G. Q. of Cloverhill ROM. This produced four champions, including Ch. Sanlyn Classic Ten O'Bayland ROM ("Stripe").

Stripe finished 13 months, and by the age of four, had won 5 Specialty BIS. Used sparingly as a stud, he produced 24 champions. Some get of note include multi-Specialty and Group placers Ch. Blaznsadl's Sanlyn T-Bone Walker, Ch. Blaznsadl's Ella Fitzgerald, Ch. Tamzil's TCR Bronson of Noslo, Ch. Windy Hill's Romeo, Ch. C.J.'s

*Ch. Blaznsadl's T-Bone Walker, "A.J.," winning BOB from the classes under breeder-judge Diane Malenfant.*

Miss Fortune of Sanlyn, and Ch. Sundance's Phoenix Rising. Specialty BIS winners were Ch. Ashford's William Riker, Ch. Blaznsadl's Sanlyn T-Bone Walker, and Ch. Rivendell's Sweet-N-Lo (also an AOM winner at the 1995 Nationals). Other Specialty winners include: Ch. Classic Zephyr, Ch. Rivendell's Pink Cadillac, Ch. Logo's Eternal Spirit, and Ch. Showtime's Energizer Bunny. Very much a Beaujangles look-alike kennel, we can likely expect continued success in the breed.

## SAXONY

During their search for a Basset Hound puppy in the spring of 1974, David and Mary Ann Clark were referred to Barbara and Rick Cromley (Lochopt) who, at that time, were living in the same city in Virginia. Barbara's inquiry, "Show or Pet?" peaked Mary Ann's curiosity about the sport, and although that first pet was purchased elsewhere, the interest in showing had begun to develop. A short time later, the Clarks acquired Lochopt Pollyanna (Ch. Kingsway Zachariah ex Ch. Hiflite's Liza Jane) from the Cromleys. They began exhibiting that same year, and after attending the BHCA Nationals in October, were hooked. In 1976, they bred the first "Saxony" litter, sired by Peg Walton's Ch. Lyn-Mar Acres Extra Man (Ch. Lyn-Mar Acres End Man ex Tantivy Demon).

David and Mary Ann always have elected to maintain a small private kennel, with the emphasis on quality rather than quantity. They have bred on a limited basis expressly to produce their own show stock, working with and incorporating the pedigrees of other kennels such as Jagersven, Stoneybluff and Lochopt, who shared an interest in similar bloodlines. These selective breedings produced a number of champions over the years, including Am/Can. Ch. Saxony Lipton (Ch. Stoneybluff Silvester ex Ch. Saxony Free Spirit), a Group-placing and multiple-Specialty winner and Ch. Lochopt Saxony Stile ROM (Ch. Ran-Su's Lochopt J.D. ex Ch. Saxony's Lochopt Sprite).

Members of BHCA since 1975, David and Mary Ann have supported the organization in a variety of capacities. In 1984 they jointly coordinated the Club's National Specialty, and Mary Ann has served on committees for several other Nationals as well. Additionally, Mary Ann has served as BHCA secretary, on the board of directors, and as editor-in-chief of *Tally-Ho*. She is also approved by the AKC to judge Basset Hounds and junior showmanship. In addition to their interest in Bassets, David and Mary Ann have bred and exhibited Whippets since 1984. Mary Ann is also a member of the American Whippet Club and served on their 1992 Nationals committee.

*Ch. Saxony Lipton, shown by Mary Ann Clark going BOB in 1985.*

## SCHEEL'S

The Scheels from Denmark seem to have been the most successful of the newer breeders in working with the Tal-E-Ho stock. Birte and Kresten Scheel live in Fredensborg, Denmark, not too far from the Copenhagen area. They have been BHCA members since 1984 and have over the years made it over for a good number of our National Specialty shows. Not only do they make the shows, but they are always competitive and have made at least two major wins. In addition to having some very nice stock, Kresten does an outstanding job of both training and presenting the dogs. One of their earlier dogs, Am/Dk. Ch. Tal-E-Ho's Tiffany was the number-one Basset Hound in Denmark for 1982 and 1983 and was a BIS winner.

They also had the number-one Basset Hound in Denmark for three consecutive years, 1986 through 1988. That dog was Am/Dk. Ch. Scheel's First Edition ROM, one of the leading stud dogs in the breed. He was the sire of nearly 50 champions in Scandinavia, Europe, and the US. "Eddie" was WD and BW at our 1985 Nationals.

I had the pleasure of judging Bassets in Denmark in 1987 at a large Specialty. One of the selections to be made there is BOB 1 through 4, rather like our BOB and Awards of Merit selections.

*Danish Bassetklubben Show, 1987, BOB 1, Am/Dk.Ch. Tal-E-Ho's Zig Zag; BOB 2, Am/Dk. Ch.Tal-E-Ho's Smooth Operator; BOB 3, Am/Dk. Ch. Scheel's Rubber Duck; and BOB 4, Leiflands Madonna of Sanchu.*

*Am/Dk. Ch. Scheel's First Edition ROM, shown going WD, BHCA Nationals, October 3, 1985. Handled by Kresten Scheel under breeder-judge Bev Stockfelt.*

*Am/Dk. Ch. Tal-E-Ho's Tiffany, whelped October 29, 1979.*

Scheel's Riveredge Rubber Duck came over to our 1991 National Specialty and was WD under breeder-judge Cathy Spencer and BW under breeder-judge Mary Jane Booth.

From L to R, Am/Dk. Ch.Scheel's First Edition ROM, Am/Dk. Ch. Tal-E-Ho's Smooth Operator, Am/Dk. Ch.Scheel's Riveredge Rubber Duck, Dk. Ch.Scheel's Clean Sweep, and Am/Dk. Ch.Scheel's Excalibur.

Am/Dk. Ch.Riveredge Rubber Duck in a more recent photo. "Rubberduck" was the # 1 Basset Hound in Denmark in 1989, 1990, 1992, and 1993.

## SCHEILAR

The Scheilar Basset Hounds of Gene, Laraine, and Brenda Scheiblauer were located in West Chicago, Illinois. They got their first Basset in 1964 and attended their first BHCA Nationals in 1966. Although breeding on a very limited basis, this family endeavor managed to produce some 15 champions.

In 1976 their Ch. Scheilar's Miss Priddy was awarded the top-producing dam award from BHCA. They also owned three ROM sires, Ch. Musicland Country Music who was a Group winner, Ch. Scheilar's Rob Roy and his son, Ch. Scheilar's Reagan, both of whom were multiple Group placers. Their Ch. Scheilar's Serena also earned her ROM and was a multiple Group placer.

One of their great thrills in the show ring was when their Ch. Musicland's Angel Eyes was awarded BOS at the BHCA Nationals in 1971. Their Ch. Scheilar's Brandy Alexandra was also a Group winner and a multiple BISS winner. The Scheiblauers whelped their last litter in 1983 and lost their last Basset Hound in 1996. They still maintain their BHCA memberships.

*Ch. Scheilar's Miss Priddy, shown by Brenda Scheiblauer going BOS over Specials to finish her championship under breeder-judge Bill Russell.*

## SCOTTSMORE

Another Canadian member of BHCA, Mrs. Davida Scott of Ottawa, started her Scottsmore Bassets with a Sand-Dell bitch. Her dogs have been consistent winners in the top Canadian Basset positions. The historically recent turn toward the Bone-A-Part Bassets line in Florida has provided Scottsmore with more of what is basically one of the styles contained in the old Santana-Mandeville Bassets.

*Ch. Scheilar's Brandy Alexandra, shown by Brenda Scheiblauer winning the Group under judge Del Glodowski.*

## SHOEFLY

Shoefly Bassets, owned by Andy and Sue Shoemaker and located in the Greater Los Angeles area, began in 1968. The purchase of Ch. Duffy of Hahs-c-enda ROM in 1970 gave Shoefly their first champion, and their first homebred champion, Ch. Heartbreaker's B'Guilin Betsy, finished in 1971.

"Duffy" and "Betsy" were bred, produced three litters, and every Shoefly Basset since has come down from this pairing. Through the years, Andy and Sue have incorporated other bloodlines, most notably Houndsville through the use of Ch. Winchuk So-Sorry Charley ROM, and Tailgate, through the use of Ch. Tailgate Black Bart ROM.

*Ch. Leifland's Iz The Wiz ROM, foundation bitch of Silverado kennels.*

The Shoemakers have always maintained a limited breeding program, usually having one litter a year, never more than two. To date, Shoefly has bred or owned a total of 35 champions, almost all of which have

*Ch. Shoefly's Peter Dawson ROM, in 1990 at two-and-a-half years of age, taking BOB at Rio Hondo KC. Handled by Sue Shoemaker under judge Isabell Stoffers. Peter finished from the Puppy and Bred-By-Exhibitor classes at 17 months of age. He is the sire of no fewer than 15 champion get.*

been shown locally in the Southern California area, owner-handled.

Shoefly has had five BHCA ROM producers over the years, an accomplishment in which they may take considerable pride. Their emphasis in breeding has always been to produce a heavy-boned, low-to-the-ground hound with great substance and type. There is no doubt that they have accomplished that goal as their winning dogs will attest. In addition, they want a Basset that moves with determination and ease and that demonstrates the wonderful, easygoing temperament typical of this breed.

## SILVERADO

One of the newer kennels that has enjoyed significant success is the Silverado Bassets of Mimi (Brandolino) McCabe. Mimi

*Ch. Leifland's Pale Rider, littermate to Iz The Wiz.*

*Ch. Sanchu's Easy Rider, shown in 1993 by handler Ed Smizer under breeder-judge Joan Scholz.*

Izabella, co-owned with Denise McCarrel.

Bred to Ch. Lochopt-Sanchu Applejack twice, she produced Ch. Silverado Sidonia, owned by Joan Urban (Ft. Merrill); Ch. Sanchu's Tabasco, owned by Belen Herner; Ch. Silverado Siouxzie (1992 Nationals WB/BW); and Ch. Fort Merrill Silverado Norm, the number eight Basset in 1994. Norm was previously owned by Joan Urban and is now co-owned by Mimi with Jim Tysseling.

Ch. Leifland's Pale Rider has sired four champion get: Ch. Sanchu's Easy Rider, the number eight Basset in 1993, co-owned with Kitty Steidel; Ch. Sanchu's Creme De Cocoa, owned by Jim and Sharon Dok (Castlehill), and Ch. Sanchu's Hot Toddy, the 1993 National's BOB, owned by Kitty Steidel. This is quite a distinguished record for such a relatively new kennel and we can reasonably look forward to continued outstanding participation by Mimi McCabe and her new partner, Jim Tysseling.

began showing Bassets in 1983. Her foundation bitch was Ch. Leifland's Iz The Wiz ROM, whom she acquired, along with her littermate, Ch. Liefland's Pale Rider, from Kitty Steidel (Sanchu) in 1986. These pups were Danish imports, bred by Fleming and Anette Hansen through their leasing of Ch. Sanchu's Sangaree from Sanchu kennels. The sire of the litter was Ch. Tal-E-Ho's Zig Zag. Both hounds were quite nice and were finished completely owner-handled by Mimi.

Mimi's foundation bitch shared the Top Producing Bitch honors in 1992, a distinction that she would have held individually except for a change in the method of computation. Regardless, it is a distinction that is difficult to achieve and one of which the owner can be justifiably proud, shared or not. All of this bitch's get were Specialty show winners and two of them were National Specialty winners. Bred to Ch. Lochopt Rum Rikki, himself a two-time Nationals winner (1984 BW and 1985 BOS), she produced Ch. Sanchu's Kizzy (1990 Nationals BOS), co-owned with Kitty Steidel, and Ch. Silverado

*Ch. Fort Merrill Silverado Norm, shown in 1995 by Mimi McCabe under judge Monica Canestrini.*

## SILVER BOW

One small kennel that may not be well known but has consistently produced nice quality Bassets is the Silver Bow kennels of Madelyn and Jim Smith, currently residing in New Hampshire. I've known Madelyn for more years than I care to remember and I must say that the only thing that kept her from becoming more well known within the breed is the fact that they were constantly moving all over the place. This plays havoc with one's breeding program, not to mention many other problems. Most of the Silver Bow dogs boast a background that is pretty much the "Brassy" side of the Lyn Mar bloodlines with a tad of Santana-Mandeville blood mixed in. This works well for many that have tried it.

*Right: Ch. Silver Bow's Smoke Ring CD, with his obedience handler, Gerreanne Darnell.*

*Ch. Silver Bow's Smoke Ring CD, going BIS at the Clearwater K.C. show with Ted Ellis handling.*

*Dual Ch. Slippery Hill Cinnamon CD, with her handler, Len Skolnick, winning BOS at the 1967 Baltimore County K.C. show.*

## SLIPPERY HILL

Len and Marge Skolnick owned their first Basset Hound, Boris, in 1956 and bred their first litter in 1961. Nearly all of their show and field champions were descended from that litter. The remainder of their show breeding stock was acquired from the Santana-Mandeville bloodline, these being primarily their first two stud dogs, Ch. Santana-Mandeville Rodney and Ch. Santana-Mandeville Egghead.

Over the years the Skolnicks have bred over 30 show champions, over 30 field champions, 6 grand field champions, and a dual champion. Their dual champion, Dual Ch. Slippery Hill Cinnamon CD, was the first dual champion Basset to hold a Companion Dog title.

An outstanding Basset bred by the Skolnicks was Ch. Slippery Hill Hudson. Hudson,

owned by Mrs. Alan Robson of Glen Moore, Pennsylvania, and handled throughout his career by Bobby Barlow, was one of the top-winning dogs of all time as of the *Kennel Review* statistics of 1992. He was the number one winning Basset Hound for the years 1974—1977, the number one Hound for 1975, and he had a total of 29 Bests in Show, with the next closest Basset having had 17. He was the number ten Hound out of the Top Twenty Hounds for the period 1967—1987, according to a *Kennel Review* article by the respected hound authority, Bo Bengtson. In addition, Hudson was the BOB winner at Westminster for '75, '76, and '77, as well as the 1975 recipient of the coveted Ken-L-Ration show dog award. The highlight of Slippery Hill's breeding years, however, was 1974 when Hudson won the BHCA Nationals BOB and their Field Champion Slippery Hill Sophie won the Field Trial at that same year's BHCA Nationals

The Slippery Hill kennel of the Skolnicks was one of the few to be involved to a significant degree in both conformation and

*Ch. Slippery Hill Hudson, with his handler, Bobby Barlow, winning one of his 29 Bests in Show.*

*Ch. Slippery Hill Paprika, granddam of Hudson, going BW.*

field work. Leonard Skolnick was a popular Basset Hound judge as well as a Hound Group judge for many years. He judged at the Nationals in 1972 and again in 1985 for the 50th anniversary show. He was scheduled to judge the Intersex competition at the 1996 National Specialty, but passed away early in that year. The Basset community will miss "Doc" greatly, on a personal level, as well as for his contributions to the breed and sport. Marge Skolnick still maintains her interest in the breed and remains active in field trialing.

# SOUTHLAKE

Bubba and Freda Burks of Grapevine, Texas are long-time members of the Dal-Tex Basset Hound Club. One of their most competitive and their very favorite Basset was Ch. Southlake Wailin' Willie CD, ROM. Willie was sired in 1979 by Ch. BevLee's Davy Jones out of Ch. Southlake Dolly Pea. One of the things that the Burks were most proud of about Willie was his personality. He loved to entertain people and truly enjoyed life. He thought he was

*Ch. Bugle Bay's Cheesecake TD, a Wailin Willie daughter shown here by Marge Cook, winning the Sweepstakes at the 1991 BHCA Nationals under breeder-judge Mary Louise Bergishagen.*

*Braz/Am. Ch. Slippery Hill Urban Cowboy, a Hudson grandson, owned by Joe and Brenda Tarkas.*

at a Basset social gathering every time he arrived at ringside! He was the only dog that Freda can recall, in 26 years of showing, that she could hear the audience snicker in amusement as he went around the ring.

A number of people had expressed an interest in obtaining Willie because of his "sense of humor," but the Burks knew that he was a special dog and decided to keep him for themselves. He finished easily and also obtained his CD with good scores. Bred only a few times, he produced 14 titlehold-ers with a total of 21 titles.

*Ch. Southlake Wailin' Willie winning the Stud Dog class at the 1991 Dal-Tex Specialty under breeder-judge Peter C.J. Martin. His get are Marge Cook's Snow Cone and Jonelle Bartoli's Cheesecake.*

## SNOWSHOE

Margaret Booth of Palmer, Alaska started her interest in Bassets in the very late 1970s, and her dogs, for the most part, are of Craigwood bloodlines. To this point, Margaret has done considerably more exhibiting than breeding. An active member of BHCA, she is usually seen at every National Specialty show, regardless of its location.

*Ch. Snowshoe Sweet Magnolia, handled by breeder-owner Margaret Booth, taking a Hound Group Second in Alaska in 1980.*

## STONEWALL

As with many dog breeders, Bob Opeka was introduced to the world of dog shows when he was very young. His childhood neighbors in rural Pennsylvania raised and showed dogs and horses and he would occasionally accompany them to shows. When he was 14 years old he showed one of their German Shepherds and was hooked on the sport.

The Stonewall Basset kennels were established in 1975 when Bob and his wife, Nora, purchased an eight-week-old red and white puppy bitch from Holt's kennel in Pennsylvania. They named her Maggie and they tried to show her in conformation and obedience, but she never did finish a title. They also purchased another bitch about two months after buying Maggie. Her name was Greenbury Daisy, bred by Jaci and

*Ch. Craigwood Just In Time, shown here by Margaret Booth winning BOB under judge Clint Harris in Alaska in 1990.*

try. From these numerous competitions, the hounds with the Stonewall prefix were gaining a reputation for their level toplines and a distinctive look that combined elegance with Basset type.

In 1980 it was decided to breed Divine Miss M to Rock of Ages, a half-brother, half-sister breeding. In January, 1981, Stonewall Fantasy was born. Little did they expect that this bitch would go on to become the dam of 11 champions!

It was in October, 1981 that Bob and Nora first had the opportunity to meet Claudia Lane and Diane Malefant of Beaujangles Basset fame. This was their first time to see Ch. Beaujangle's Ten, a dog which they decided must be included in the Stonewall breeding program. In 1982 they had the opportunity to purchase a young male puppy sired by the "Ten Dog," named Top-

Jon Green, in Ohio. Within a year "Daisy" earned her championship and became their foundation bitch.

Since Daisy was heavily linebred on Musicland, when it was her time to be bred she was shipped off to the Musicland kennels of Jeanne Hills. She was bred to Ch. Musicland Rovin Gambler. Two of these get finished their championships, a bitch, Ch. Stonewall Divine Miss M and the dog, Ch. Stonewall Gamblin Man CD.

The end of the '70s and early '80s were a busy time at Stonewall. Many dogs of note were bred: Ch. Stonewall Rock of Ages, Ch. Divine Miss M, and Ch. Stonewall Fantasy, to name a few. It was during this time period that there was considerable Stonewall competition in the show ring all around the coun-

*Ch. Greenbury Daisy (Musicland's Shaft ex Musicland's Proud Mary), foundation bitch of the Stonewall kennels, at 11 months of age.*

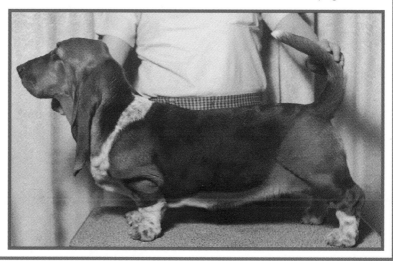

O-Line Stonewall Jackson. Jackson had a great show career with many breed wins and Group placements. More importantly, he went on to become the sire of 17 champions.

During the mid-1980s it was decided to do a combination of breedings, basically using the "Ten Dog" and his son "Jackson" on their Divine Miss M and her daughter Fantasy. Since Fantasy was very tightly

*Ch. Top-O-Line Stonewall Jackson ROM, shown here by Bob Opeka, winning one of his many BOBs under breeder-judge Al Tiedeman.*

linebred, these studs would provide for the needed outcross. This combination of breedings turned out to be very successful as evidenced by the many fine get which were produced, two of which are Ch. Stonewall Roxanne, the 1985 BHCA National Specialty BOB winner, and Ch. Stonewall J.F.K., the number one breeder-owner-handled Basset in 1987 and BOS at the 1988 BHCA National Specialty. Numerous descendants of these dogs are being bred and shown today. All totaled, Stonewall has whelped something over 30 litters and produced more than 50 champions.

Following the divorce of Bob and Nora in 1988, Stonewall Bassets went through a period of a few years where a minimum of dogs from this once very active kennel were shown. In 1990 Stonewall Bassets combined efforts with Kirk Joiner of Ol' South Bassets in Massachusetts. The results of this blending of kennel stock can be seen in the dogs being jointly bred and shown under the current Ol' South and Stonewall prefixes.

*Ch. Stonewall Fantasy, enroute to her championship, under breeder-judge Mary Marischen.*

*Am/Can. Ch. Sanlyn's Classic Cruiser ROM, shown by breeder-owner-handler Kirk Joiner of Ol' South Bassets under judge Tom Conway. "Cruiser" is a multiple Breed, Group, and Specialty winner. He was the Number One breeder-owner-handled Basset for 1992. To date Cruiser has sired 11 champions with many more pointed get still being shown.*

# STONEYBLUFF

It would be difficult to find a better example of a well-thought-out and continuing linebreeding program than that of the Stoneybluff Bassets of Frank and Virginia Kovalic. In Jinny's own words, she takes us from the establishment of their kennel through the seventh generation of dogs carrying the Stoneybluff prefix and the type that has come to be recognized as Stoneybluff Bassets.

Stoneybluff Bassets began in 1965, following the loss of a much-loved 12-year-old Boxer. The house seemed a very empty place after the Boxer's death, so after having read the announcement in the Detroit newspapers, we visited the Detroit Kennel Club Dog Show looking for a replacement. We spent the entire day looking at various breeds, trying to decide what breed we would like to select for purchase. The Bassets touched our hearts and the excitement of the dog show caught our fancy. We decided that a Basset Hound would be our new breed and we wanted a show dog.

We purchased our first Basset from Finn and Mary Louise Bergishagen who had puppies for sale from their first litter. Unfortunately, this purchase did not develop into a show-quality dog, but "Sam" did earn a CD in obedience, and from this a long and lasting friendship developed with the Bergishagens. We went to dog shows together regularly. It was in 1967 when the Bergishagens and the Kovalics made a side visit to Lyn Mar Acres after attending the Nationals in Lebanon that we purchased our foundation bitch, Ch. Lyn Mar Acres Michelle.

Even though "Missy" was only 12 weeks old at the time of purchase, we were already looking for a breeding mate to keep her company. The Bergishagens had bred Ch. Jagersven Gigi to Ch. Lyn Mar Acres Press Agent. Since Press Agent was Missy's grandfather, we decided that this was a good pedigree to begin with.

*Ch. Lyn-Mar Acres Michelle ROM, foundation bitch of Stoneybluff Bassets.*

We purchased Ch. Jagersven Monarch II from that litter at 13 weeks of age. Missy had two litters. She was bred first to Ch. Lyn Mar Acres End Man, which produced Ch. Stoneybluff Ringer, Stoneybluff Madelena and Stoneybluff Penelope. Her second breeding was to Ch. Jagersven Monarch II which produced five champions: Ch. Stoneybluff Napoleon, Ch. Stoneybluff Desiree, Ch. Stoneybluff Antoinette, Ch. Stoneybluff Caroline and Ch. Stoneybluff Jagersven Marie.

*Ch. Stoneybluff Ringer (End Man ex Michelle).*

```
                                    Bats
                    Ch. Lyn-Mar Acres M'Lord Batuff
                           Lyn Mar Acres Sweet Stuff
              Ch. Lyn-Mar Acres End Man
                           Lyn Mar Acres DeMarch
              Lyn-Mar Acres Bur-Lee-Q
                           Ch. Lyn Mar Acres Ballyhoo
Litter # 1
                                    Bats
                    Ch. Lyn Mar Acres M'Lord Batuff
                           Lyn Mar Acres Sweet Stuff
              Ch. Lyn Mar Acres Michelle
                           Ch. Lyn Mar Acres Press Agent
              Ch. Lyn Mar Acres Quick Trip
                           Lenkridge Pollyanna
```

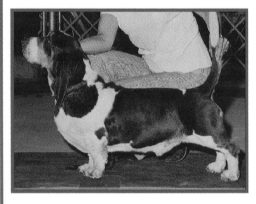

*Ch. Stoneybluff Napoleon (Monarch II ex Michelle).*

```
                           Lyn Mar Acres DeMarch
              Ch. Lyn Mar Acres Press Agent
                           Ch. Lyn Mar Acres Ballyhoo
              Ch. Jagersven Monarch II
                           Ch. Siefenjagenheim Dominoe
              Ch. Jagersven Gigi
                           Ch. Jagersven Samantha
Litter # 2
                                    Bats
                    Ch. Lyn Mar Acres M'Lord Batuff
                           Lyn Mar Acres Sweet Stuff
              Ch. Lyn Mar Acres Michelle
                           Ch. Lyn Mar Acres Press Agent
              Ch. Lyn Mar Acres Quick Trip
                           Lenkridge Pollyana
```

From these two litters, five dogs attained their AKC championship thus earning an ROM for Michelle. We kept all of the puppies mentioned above, along with Stoneybluff Josephine, and they became the core of our breeding program. During this same period we used an outside stud, Jagersven Editor, to breed to Madelena and Penelope.

After becoming familiar with the various kennels, we discovered that Bassets came in a wide variety of types. When we visited Lyn Mar Acres we decided that Peg and Woody Walton were breeding the type of dog we liked best. After many hours of looking at the large picture collection of Bassets and hours of talking about dogs with the Waltons, we realized that we were looking for the long-bodied dog with long smooth ribs, good layback of shoulder, straight front and deep forechest, and a well-angulated rear with smooth movement. The males should have the "Bloodhound" type head, with very deep lip, and the females should have a more refined version of the same. Now, all we had to do was try to breed

|  |  | Lyn Mar Acres DeMarch |
|  | Bats |  |
|  |  | Lyn Mar Acres Kiss Me Kate |
| Jagersven Town Crier |  |  |
|  |  | Ch. Siefenjagenhiem Dominoe |
|  | Ch. Jagersven Gigi |  |
|  |  | Ch. Jagersven Samantha |
| JAGERSVEN EDITOR |  |  |
|  |  | Ch. Abbot Run Valley Brassy |
|  | Ch. Gin Dic's Bit-O-Brass |  |
|  |  | Am/Can. Ch. Nancy Evans Columbine |
| Am-Can. Ch. Shadows Snow White |  |  |
|  |  | Ch. Abbot Run Valley Brassy |
|  | Northwood's Lazy Lizzy |  |
|  |  | Barook's Mata Hari |

the Basset we had pictured in our minds. More easily said than done, as any long-time Basset breeder will tell you!

We have been breeding Bassets for 30 years and about 45 dogs bred at Stoneybluff have received their championship title. However, not all of them have contributed to the ongoing breeding program. On the other hand, there have been others who were never shown who have contributed a great deal to our program. As authorities in genetics recommend, we have held to a program of close linebreeding with the introduction of an outside line when needed. Our outside lines usually include at least one line in the pedigree that has similar blood lines to our dogs. Living by this philosophy of breeding, we feel we have established a consistent type of animal characterized as the Stoneybluff Basset.

In discussing the second-generation breeding, it is difficult to make a long story short. Yet, making sense out of the events that made what we have now requires mention of those who played the major role. I'm going to mention only the dogs that made the most impact on our breeding program. This will leave out many important dogs and breedings that were stepping stones to achieving the results that we know today as a Stoneybluff Basset.

I begin with Ch. Stoneybluff Ringer, a stocky, heavy-boned dog, with a beautiful head. Ringer was RWD at the 1973 Nationals. He was bred to his half-sister, Desiree, from Missy's second litter, producing Stoneybluff Sherlock, who was also a very nice stocky, heavy-boned dog, but one that hated the show ring.

Sherlock was bred to a half-sister, Josephine, and produced Blackjack, who

*Stoneybluff Sherlock, a second-generation stud dog and sire of Stoneybluff Oliver.*

*Ch. Stoneybluff Ferdinand, sire of Ch. Stoneybluff Black Patches.*

of Stoneybluff dogs. Jagersven Editor was also bred to Ch. Stoneybluff Antoinette, which produced Pocohontas. "Pokie" was never shown, but she was a very important influence in our breeding program. Bred to Ch. Stoneybluff Ferdinand, Pokie produced Ch. Stoneybluff Black Patches. Black Patches' conformation and style was exactly the type of dog we were breeding for. Her color and markings made her unforgettable.

From Missy's second litter came Ch. Stoneybluff Napoleon who died at a very early age, a tremendous loss to our breeding program. Bred to Pocohontas he produced Ch. Stoneybluff Monarch ROM and Ch.

was bred to Desiree and produced Ch. Stoneybluff Ferdinand, "Fred." Fred was a typey, long, heavy-boned dog with a magnificent head. Unfortunately, shortly after he earned his championship a disc ruptured in his back. After extensive physical therapy he was again on his feet, but his movement was adversely affected.

The dog that we used as an outside stud, Jagersven Editor, "Eddie," was bred to Madelena (a Ringer littermate), which produced Stoneybluff Late Edition. Late Edition was bred to Ch. Stoneybluff Caroline, from Missy's second litter, producing Stoneybluff Gypsy. Gypsy was then bred to Sherlock and produced Stoneybluff Oliver. Oliver made a great impact on the next (third) generation

*Ch. Stoneybluff Monarch ROM.*

*Ch. Stoneybluff Black Patches, exhibiting the style to which the kennel aspires.*

Stoneybluff Contessa. Bred to Stoneybluff Nicoma, a Ringer ex Pocohontas daughter, he produced Stoneybluff Basil ROM.

Pocohontas was also bred to Stoneybluff Oliver and produced Ch. Stoneybluff Prairie Flower TD, ROM. Her daughter, Ch. Stoneybluff Black Patches, was bred to Stoneybluff Sherlock producing Gabriel, a top producer, and Ch. Stoneybluff Abigail. One other second-generation breeding, Ch. Stoneybluff Ferdinand ex Stoneybluff Jezebelle, produced Ch. Stoneybluff Lady Jane who was to be WB and BW at the 1983 Nationals.

In the third generation of breedings, Stoneybluff Oliver sired some of the nicest dogs in our kennel. Bred to Gabriel, he produced Stoneybluff Jessica, herself a top producer; bred to Ch. Stoneybluff Phoebe, we produced Ch. Hobnail Aldo of Stoneybluff who, in turn, was bred to Prairie Flower, which produced three champion get. Two were males, both of which are used at stud, Ch. Stoneybluff Ginger Beer and Ch. Stoneybluff Ginger Ale, as well as a bitch, Ch. Stoneybluff Ginger Lea. When bred to Nicoma, the Ringer ex Pokie

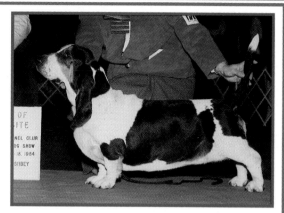

*Ch. Stoneybluff Prairie Flower TD, ROM.*

*Stoneybluff Basil earned his ROM as an outside stud. He died before his owners had the opportunity to use him on any of their own bitches.*

daughter, Oliver produced Ch. Stoneybluff Gertrude, who established a reputation well known in the breed by being the first Basset bitch to win 22 Specialty shows, setting a record, and went on to be selected as BOS at the Nationals in 1989, following up with BOB wins at the Nationals in 1988 and again in 1989. A natural showman, "Gerty" was the dog we considered to be our "ideal" and dream of breeding another one as nice. We considered her movement to be smooth and flawless.

Ch. Stoneybluff Monarch ROM was bred to Abigail and produced Chs. Stoneybluff Alexia and Alecia. They were the winners of the Brace class at the 1984 Nationals.

When bred to Nicoma, the mother of Gertie, he produced Ch. Stoneybluff Tabatha, who won a number of Specialties and Group placements. Bred to Jagersven Ms. Red, Monarch produced Ch. Stoneybluff Count II, and bred to Gabriel, he produced Ch. Stoneybluff Silvester ROM.

Many of the dogs produced by Ch. Stoneybluff Silvester ROM are champions and are now producing today's young show dogs. Silvester was a large red and white dog with a magnificent head. He received his first points, a major, at one year of age. He didn't go back to the ring until he was four years old. He went RWD at the Nationals in 1987. He was bred to Ch. Saxony Free Spirit to produce Ch. Saxony Scentuous and Ch. Saxony Lipton, who won the Sweepstakes at the 1984 Nationals. Scentuous was bred to Ch. Stoneybluff Count II to pro-

*Ch. Stoneybluff Abigail.*

*Ch. Stoneybluff Lady Jane going BW at 1983 National Specialty under breeder-judge Jean Sheehy.*

*Ch. Stoneybluff Gertrude, record setting National Specialty-winning bitch.*

duce Ch. Saxony Stoneybluff Theo, who has produced no fewer than five champions and has some very promising grandchildren getting ready to make their ring debut. Silvester bred to Prairie Flower produced Ch. Stoneybluff Tootsie Roll, who herself has one champion, and a promising bitch in Stoneybluff Seranade. Bred to Black Orchid, he produced Ch. Stoneybluff Winter Storm, who has three champions and is used at stud.

Silvester was also bred to Ch. Brendans Anna Livia, producing Ch. Brendans Stoneybluff Swift and Ch. Brendans Stoneybluff Stella, who were BW and BOS, respectively, at the first BHCA Futurity, as well as Stoneybluff Brendans Sylvia. When bred to Jessica, Silvester produced Ch. Stoneybluff Siegfried, who went RWD at the 1991 Nationals. We feel that he has the nicest layback of shoulder, front and forechest of any male we have ever bred. He was shown by Bryan Martin for six months, winning several Group placements and an all-breed BIS. He has decided that he wants no more of the show ring and enjoys his career as a stud dog. He already has two champion get and some young dogs on their way up the ladder. Last, but not least, is Stoneybluff Charlemagne, sired by Aldo and out of Jessica. He is a very long dog with a beautiful, masculine head. At the age of five, he produced his first litter. We are very pleased with what he is producing.

Ch. Stoneybluff Tabatha.

Ch. Stoneybluff Count II.

Ch. Stoneybluff Silvester ROM.

Ch. Saxony Stoneybluff Theo.

*Ch's. Stoneybluff Alicia & Alexia shown winning the Brace class at the 1984 Nationals.*

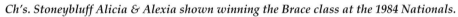

I would like to make a few comments about the help and support that we've received throughout the years. When we first started showing and breeding dogs, we trained and showed them ourselves. We weren't the best in the ring, but we gave it a good try! One day Janie Dozier called and asked if we had a show dog she could purchase. She bought Ch. Stoneybluff Phoebe. At that time we became good friends and after finishing Phoebe, she took three-year-old Gertrude to train and show. They became a good team, but the judges did not see them. At a show in Pennsylvania, Gwen McCullagh saw Janie showing "Gerty" and could not understand why she didn't win. Gwen asked if she could give showing the

have been shown earned their championships due to these two ladies. Janie now lives at Stoneybluff, training and showing the youngsters. Gwen generally shows one or two of our dogs along with the dogs of her own breeding. We are deeply indebted to Janie and Gwen for their friendship and devotion to Stoneybluff Bassets.

Of all the dogs in our kennel, Prairie Flower was the hunter. One day, when visiting the kennel, Kathy Bova watched "Flower" at work and decided this dog would be great in tracking. Kathy took on the challenge of training "Flower" and she earned her TD in 1985.

Breeding dogs cannot be done in a vacuum. Maybe that's what makes it such

*Ch. Stoneybluff Tootsie Roll, pictured winning Senior Sweepstakes at the 1989 Nationals under breeder-judge Knox Williams III.*

dog a try. It was a partnership between dog and handler that lasted four years. While showing "Gerty," Gwen visited our home often. She went into the kennel and looked at the dogs, not believing that we hadn't shown many of them. She then began taking one or two home with her to train and show. Janie was also involved showing some of her own dogs that she bred at Stoneybluff. So many dogs that would never

an infectious sport. Many hours of invaluable discussions about dog types, desired conformation and breeding philosophy, along with showing dogs together, have generated a lasting friendship with Knox and Bette Williams. Jim Lenahan also stepped in when we needed help by housing and training dogs for us. His breeding program now includes dogs from Stoneybluff. Without the financial support of Bert Salyers and

*Stoneybluff Serenade.*

Randy and Penny Frederiksen and their confidence in the quality of the dog, Ch. Stoneybluff Siegfried would not have won his BIS.

At about the same time that we became seriously involved in breeding and showing dogs, we purchased a large parcel of land in partnership with the Bergishagens. The land is on a very high hill that consists of gravel and stones. So, when creating a kennel name, we decided to have the name match the future location of our home, Stoneybluff. Our kennel is attached to the garage of our home. We started with six large runs, which easily accommodate three dogs each. There is a fenced one-acre exercise area off the kennel runs. We

soon lost our heated and insulated garage, along with adjacent fenced exercise areas, to much needed kennel space for puppies and young dogs. The whelping area is in the house, in a room originally designed to be a large utility room. The puppies move out to the puppy area in the garage as soon as they are weaned.

Our 30 years in dogs has been a very rewarding experience. We have been, and still are being, challenged

*Stoneybluff Charlemagne, a stud dog active in the late 1990s.*

*Ch. Stoneybluff Winter Storm.*

to breed outstanding Bassets that can make a positive contribution to the breed. We have developed some close and lifelong friendships through our involvement with the dogs. Our participation in the Basset Hound Club of Greater Detroit and the BHCA has kept us busy working with our own breed. As members of the all-breed Detroit Kennel Club, our horizons in the dog world have broadened. It is a good life!

*Ch. Stoneybluff Siegfried, shown winning RWD at the 1991 National Specialty.*

## SWITCHBARK

As is the case with most people, Carol and Jerry O'Bryant, of Louisville, Kentucky, purchased their first Basset as a pet. Publications of the time increased their interest in the breed and their desire to obtain a Basset that they could show. By virtue of an ad in the old *Hound Crier*, a publication of the then fledgling, but not yet recognized, Tejas BHC, they came across an ad by Tom and Penny Bloomer. (As an aside, the Tejas club was never recognized, but did eventually become the BHC of Greater Corpus Christi, and then, by change of venue, became the currently existing BHC of Greater San Antonio. But we digress!) Responding to the ad for show-quality puppies for sale, they were able to finally acquire their first show Basset, Hiflite's Brumeister. "Bru" was from the litter of the second breeding of

Ch. Glenhaven's Butcher Boy ROM, bred to the Booth's Ch. Kazoo's Question Mark ROM. The Bloomers, owners of Ch. Hiflite's Tomfoolery (same breeding, first litter), were whelping this repeat breeding litter for the Booths since Bob was on his way to Vietnam at the time. It was shortly after Bob returned home from Vietnam that they met the O'Bryants and saw Brumeister for the first time as an adult dog. This visit resulted in a lasting friendship and occasional breeding relationship that has endured over the years.

The O'Bryants did relatively little breeding under the Switchbark prefix, primarily because they preferred dogs to bitches and probably because they enjoyed showing more than whelping. They were able to satisfy their desire to show, and also do an occasional breeding, through a close personal friendship and breeding relationship that developed with Sandra Campbell and her Craigwood Bassets. Their bitch, Switchbark's Chastity, produced two National Specialty winners, namely the 1981 BW, Ch. Craig-wood's Going In Style, owned by Sandra Campbell and Joanna Reynolds, and the 1984 Nationals BOB, Ch. Switchbark's Ashmore ROM, owned by Bob and Mary Jane Booth.

The O'Bryants' show dogs in the late '90s include: Ch. Craigwood Higgins of Switchbark, bred by Sandra Campbell and Ch. Hiflite's Ultra Motion. "Higgins" is a multiple-BIS winner, Specialty BIS winner and was the 1996 BOB winner at the prestigious Westminster Kennel Club show. Having finished Ultra Motion, "Motor," they used him at stud for one of the Craigwood bitches as well as for one of their own bitches.

Long-time members of the well-known Kentuckiana BHC, Carol has served as its show chairperson for many years. For those

*Ch. Hiflite's Brumeister, shown winning BOB under judge Ed Bracy, owner-handled by Carol O'Bryant.*

who may never have attended, I believe it to be well worth the trip for the serious Basset exhibitor-breeder-fancier. In this writer's opinion, it is clearly the most competitive Specialty show next to the BHCA Nationals itself. Carol judges Bassets and a few other breeds (and Jerry should!). Consequently she shows on a limited basis and breeds very seldom, but we can be sure that Bassets will continue to be an important part of their lives.

*Ch. Craigwood Higgins of Switchbark, handled by Carol O'Bryant under breeder-judge Bob Booth.*

## SWITCHSTAND

The Taylors, Missy and Doug, have owned Basset Hounds since 1968, but did not begin exhibiting until 1980. Just after their move to Roeland Park, Kansas, they were buying another Basset when breeder, Don LaRue (Bluelick), said the fatal words, "He's not a bad dog, why don't you try to show him?" With no clue as to how to go about this, they set about learning how from Don, his wife Ginny, Mary Smith, and Pat Berger, of the "late" Heart of America Basset Hound Club. As a result, they finished that dog, Ch. Blue Lick Loose Change, "Hero," bought a bitch from Chris Giles of Tantine Bassets, Tantine's Miss Magic, and finished her. They bred these two hounds, and of the six whelps, they finished two of the bitches.

As with many other kennels, initial good luck turns sour. Both of the finished bitches had been rock eaters, and the surgery had left them sterile. "Hero" began stalking their son with deadly intent and had to be put down. This broke their hearts, but they soon realized that even though they had finished four Bassets, there was a definite need to improve their stock, both physically and temperamentally.

Thanks to good co-ownerships, they were able to accomplish that goal. Madelyn Smith (Silver Bow) had noticed the Taylors at the shows and offered them a co-ownership of a nice bitch, Ch. Silver Bow's Guinevere ROM. After finishing Guinevere, she was bred to Ellen Crofford's (Birchcroft) Ch. Birchcroft's Juan 'N Only. Pick of that litter went back to Silver Bow and finished, Ch. Silver Bow's Switchstand Jedi.

Having admired the Bossland dogs of Jerry and Shirley Brown, they decided to breed Guinevere to Ch. Bossland's Brandon, an owner-handled BIS dog. That breeding resulted in Ch. Switchstand's Keystone Express, Ch. Switchstand's Duquesne, owned by Doris Antczak, and their most productive bitch, Ch. Switchstand's Broadway Limited. "B-way" has already produced two champions: Am/Can. Ch. Switchstand's Matchless and Ch. Switchstand's Nightwatch, both sired by the 1994 Nationals winner, Ch. Dealo's Lehi Fyre Dragon ROM.

*Am/Can. Dragon Thunder Von Skauton, winning the Group with owner-handler Doug Taylor.*

*Am/Can. Ch. Switchstand's Matchless, winning a Group third under breeder-judge Bill Russell. Trophy presenter, breeder Medora Harper.*

A co-ownership of Juley Von Skauton, with the Townes, was acquired and her championship completed. Juley did not do as well in passing on her merits to her progeny. She was, however, a very agile bitch, so they began to work with her in NCDA agility. Although she was a strong-willed bitch—all 65 pounds of her—she became the first Basset to get the Agility I title, much to the delight of the cheering crowds at ringside.

A second co-ownership with the Townes resulted in the acquisition of Am/Can. Ch. Dragon Thunder Von Skauton ROM. Arriving at Switchstand at six months of age, he finished at ten months and had attained his Canadian title at just over one year of age. At four years old, he had won several Specialties, numerous BOBs and a Group first. "Thunderdog" has already sired some very nice get, with one of them giving him the 1995 Nationals BW to his credit.

Doug has recently been approved to judge the breed and both he and Missy expect to continue breeding and exhibiting for the foreseeable future.

## TAILGATE

The Tailgate name was established in 1959 with the acquisition of two Basset Hounds, given to Gail Allen by her mother. It was Gail's mother who owned the Tailgate Antique Shop in San Diego, California. By 1968, Gail owned three additional Bassets: Am/Can. Ch. Musicland's Crazy Rhythm, Am/Can. Ch. Musicland's Hey Jude, and Bayroc's Tomasina, sired by Crazy Rhythm.

Meanwhile, in Rhode Island, in 1969, Gillen Tankard, Margil Bassets, was whelping her first litter sired by Forestbay Old Mac–Donald. In 1970, Gill and Marlene Doherty moved to California. When they began showing, they met Gail Allen and eventually bred to her stock. The breeding of Margil's Rebecca to Am/Can. Ch. Musicland's Crazy Rhythm produced Ch. Margil Mr. Ribbons O'Tailgate ROM. This red and white dog, considered to be the Tailgate foundation stud, when bred to Addie Birdwell's beautiful tri bitch, Woodstock Thalia ROM, produced some very important champions for Tailgate.

*Ch. Margil Mr. Ribbons O'Tailgate ROM, going WD in 1974 under breeder-judge Margretta Patterson. Handled by Gail Allen.*

*Ch. Hallmark
Probably
ROM, shown
in 1980 by
Gail Allen
going BOB at
the Pasadena
KC show
under judge
Kenneth
Peck.*

*Ch. Tailgate
Tootsagana
ROM, shown
by handler
Jerri Cates,
going BW
under
breeder-judge
Diane
Malenfant.*

*Ch. Tailgate
Black Bart
ROM, going
BW with
friend and
handler,
Butch Dixon.*

Also in the early 1970s, Ch. Music-land's Hey Jude was bred to Dixie's Sho'nuff Good'nuff, owned by Elaine Hall of Hallmark Bassets. There were two import-ant offspring in this litter that Tailgate kept: Tail-gate Sounder and his brother, Ch. Hall-mark Mal-colm ROM, who went to Cathie Spencer, JerCat Bassets. When Mr. Ribbons was bred to "Nuffy," they pro-duced Am/Mex. Ch. Hallmark Pro-bably ROM, who was also kept by Tailgate. The off-spring from these important breed-ings were also

*Dual Ch. Tailgate Canis Major, going BW with handler Gail Allen under breeder-judge Ruth Balladone.*

retained and linebred, keying heavily on Santana-Mandeville bloodlines. These breedings were most responsible for establishing the "Tailgate look."

In 1988, an outcross stud, Ch. Brendan's Rory O'Connor, was bred to Ch. Tailgate Tootsagana ROM. This breeding gave Tail-gate an earlier maturing front assembly, some deep black coloration, and another crop of champions, which included Dual Ch. Tailgate Canis Major, Ch. Tailgate Rachel, and Ch. Tailgate Silverado.

Another famous contributor to Tailgate's list of champion get is Ch. Tailgate Black Bart ROM. Gail and Gill feel that Bart is doing as much for the breed in the '90s as Mr. Ribbons did in the '70s. In 1990, Gail and Gill were invited to attend a field trial in Sacramento to watch Ch. Tailgate Dreamboat Annie compete. Owned by Norma and Jim Ferris, Annie

won that day and is now Grand Dual Ch. Tailgate Dreamboat Annie. Annie now has a Dual Champion son of her own, Dual Ch. Tailgate Good Time Charlie, also owned by Norma and Jim Ferris. Gail and Gill have not missed a trial with their Bassets since that day! They feel that the hunting instinct was preserved and passed down through the genes of their wonderful "alpha bitch," Ch. Tailgate Tootsagana ROM.

Gail and Gill would like all Basset fan-ciers to know that if you have never hunted with your hounds, you have cheated both yourself and your hounds, as it is a wonderful outlet for man and dogs. They are proud to have helped several dedicated hopefuls start their own kennels by providing them with foundation stock, lessons on show-manship, and advice on breeding.

# TAL-E-HO

No longer active, the Tal-E-Ho Bassets of Henry and Ann Jerman, formerly of Long Island, and now residing in Florida, were one kennel to set a "new" style in the breed. One of the first Tal-E-Ho hounds that I ob-

*Am-Can. Ch. Tal-E-Ho's Prancer, winning BOB at the Susquehanna BHC show in 1973. Handled by breeder-owner Ann Jerman.*

served "in the flesh" was Am/Can. Ch. Tal-E-Ho's Prancer. I recall judging up their way in the early 1970s and Prancer was entered as a special. A very nice dog, he seemed to pretty much float around the ring. Not many ever leave you with that impression, but he was one of them. I remember awarding him BOB. He was a great Specialty winner and sire.

As we have seen, however, it was left up to his progeny to really set the style of the kennel. The main one to do this was Am/Can. Ch. Tal-E-Ho's Top Banana ("Topper"), owned by the brothers Peter C. J. Martin and Bryan Martin of Northwood Bassets. Topper was the one to distribute the "new" style among many kennels. I put "new" in quotes because it really wasn't a new look, but a rediscovered one of the Jerman's predecessors, the Talleyrand Bassets of Mr. and Mrs. Robert and Kay Ellenberger. The Tal-E-Ho Bassets were the recipients of the notoriety of a well-publicized winner, "Topper," and even more success flowed their way.

Continued success, however, depends on consistently producing top-winning hounds. As with many other successful kennels, many others wish to mate their hounds to yours. The Tal-E-Ho hounds, in my opinion, did offer an added something to the kennels that they were bred to, but many who tried to reproduce their success with Tal-E-Ho-purchased hounds could not. One of the last Tal-E-Ho big-time winners was Ch. Tal-E-Ho's Tootsie. I recall trying to buy her, as a puppy at her first show, before she was even shown, but that was not to be. Tootsie usually stole the show when she went in the ring. She was a fairly large hound for a bitch, but most of the Tal-E-Ho hounds were in the moderate-sized range and fairly compact.

The most enduring Tal-E-Ho look-alike kennel is the Scheel's Bassets in Denmark. Some of the other kennels that benefited from their association with this strain were the JerCat, Sanchu, Northwoods, and Von Hollandheim in Holland.

| | | |
|---|---|---|
| | Ch. Abbot Run Valley Brassy | |
| | Ch. Manor Hill Top Spot | |
| | | Ch. Bonnie Ridge Fire Bird |
| Tal-E-Ho's George | | |
| | | Ch. Abbot Run Valley Brassy |
| | Ch. Talleyrand's Lynette | |
| | | Ch. Talleyrand's Relue Annie |
| CH. TAL-E-HO'S PRANCER | | |
| | | Ch Abbot Run Valley Prankster |
| | Ch. Talleyrand's Keene | |
| | | Ch. Talleyrand's Relue Annie |
| Tal-E-Ho's Ka-Ro | | |
| | | Ch. Abbot Run Valley Brassy |
| | Ch. Talleyrand's Lynette | |
| | | Ch. Talleyrand's Relue Annie |

Jean has belonged to many dog-related organizations and has served as officer, director, board member, and/or committee chairperson/member for most of them. She has the honor of being a Life Member of the BHCA, and has served on numerous committees, as a board member, secretary, second vice-president and president. She and her husband are also Life Members of the Pilgrim Basset Hound Club. Jean is an AKC-approved judge and has judged the BHCA National Specialty show three times and also has officiated at many other Specialties and all-breed shows over the years.

*Am-Can. Ch. Tal-E-Ho's Top Banana, a Prancer son, winning the breed under breeder-judge Wilton Meyer (Oranpark), with co-owner Peter C. J. Martin (Northwoods) handling.*

## TOPOHIL

Jean Sheehy has been active in Basset Hounds since 1963, starting in obedience. Her first Basset litter was whelped in 1967 and it was at that point in time when she decided on the kennel name Topohil. Although her husband, Curt, loved and helped with the dogs, he left most of the breeding and show plans to Jean.

After putting a CD on three of her Bassets, Jean decided to concentrate on conformation. Although her breeding was very limited and she never campaigned extensively, she finished many Basset champions and her dogs figured prominently in many breeding programs other than her own. For a time, during the 1970s, Jean also bred, showed, and finished Bichons Frise. Her kennel story has been written about in numerous other books, consequently it need not be repeated here in detail. One of her well-known stud dogs was Ch. Forestbay Montgomery ROM, bred by Joe and Jackie Kulper of the Forestbay kennel in Massachusetts.

*Right: Ch. Forestbay Mongomery ROM, a Topohil stud dog.*

*Above: Ch. Manor Hill Mayday and Ch. Topohil Ovation, shown by Joy Brewster, winning the Brace class at the 1981 Nationals, under breeder-judge Bill Barton.*

*Left: Ch. Topohil's Glory Bea, taking a Group placement. These hounds are typical of the style Topohil sought to produce.*

## TOPSFIELD

The Topsfield kennel of Dom and Claudia Orlandi, situated on 200 acres in northern Vermont, began its involvement with Bassets when it acquired hounds from the now disbanded Timber Ridge pack of Maryland in the late 1980s. Reflecting the influence of Strathalbyn, Tantivy and Lyn Mar Acres breeding, these early hounds and their offspring regularly hunted at Topsfield until the early 1990s when Dom and Claudia began to focus more attention on breeding hounds for the show ring. Although this new direction has left less time for pack hunting, the Topsfield breeding program remains committed to pro– ducing show-quality Bassets in which form follows function. As such, emphasis is placed on balance and movement in an effort to produce champion Basset Hounds that are capable of great endurance in the field, as called for by the AKC breed standard.

The Orlandis acquired the multiple-Group placing Ch. Bone-A-Parts Cuervo Gold in 1993 (bred by Pat and Ted Ellis and Kelly McCoy Davis), who was bred to their pack hound bitch, Timber Ridge Tatiana, herself linebred on Tantivy Blond Sidonia ROM. This breeding marked the start of the Topsfield show line. In addition to receiving an AOM, Cuervo Gold, with his two get, Ch. Topsfield Swan Lake and Ch. Topsfield Hollyhocks, later went on to win the Stud Dog class at the 1994 BHCA Nationals in Rhode Island. He also won the Stud Dog class at the 1994 Pilgrim BHC Specialty.

Structured on linebreeding, the extensive, but carefully designed, Topsfield breeding program maintains five foundation bloodlines; Ambrican, Strathalbyn, Bone-A-Part, Stoneybluff, and Castlehill, from which

it is breeding its future stock. In addition to Ch. Bone-A-Parts Cuervo Gold, Topsfield's foundation sires include: Ch. Ambrican Quest For Fame, Ch. Stoneybluff Ginger Beer, and Ch. Topsfield Hyssop. Ch. Topsfield

*Ch. Bone-A-Parts Cuervo Gold (Am/Can. Ch. David Copperfield ex Chmar's Lili Marlene), a relatively recent show and stud dog acquisition of Topsfield, with Claudia Orlandi.*

Giselle, Bone-A-Part Topfield Tiz Tops, Ch. Topsfield Hollyhocks, and Ch. Castlehill's Naughtia, (a SBIS winner at seven months), comprise the kennel's brood-bitch base.

Since turning its attention to breeding hounds for the show ring, in four years Topsfield has finished no fewer than a dozen champions with many more youngsters currently pointed. Future champion Circus Circus clearly represents the style and bal- ance that the kennel is hoping to consis- tently achieve. With such accomplishment, this writer looks forward to significant fu- ture success for Topsfield.

*Ch. Topsfield Hollyhocks, (Ch. Bone-A-Parts Cuervo Gold ex Salmon Brook Top Field BMW), Best Jr. Sweeps at the 1994 Pilgrim BHC Specialty. Shown here winning BOB under judge Norton Moore, handled by breeder-owner Claudia Orlandi.*

## VON SKAUTON

Dawn and Garry Towne of Weedsport, New York, acquired their first Basset in 1962, their first champion and foundation stud for the Von Skauton kennel. They named him Schnaps for no good reason and he went on to become Am/Can. Ch. Schnaps Von Skauton and the litterbrother of a field champion.

Though initially the Townes' had an interest in both field and conformation, they soon realized that working both disciplines involved more time than they could handle. Conformation, reluctantly, became their choice.

Their search for their foundation bitch was not to be so easy. Their first purchase died at eight months. For their second try they knowingly purchased one that had a "soft coat" (euphemistic for long hair!). In Dawn's own words, "Her conformation was lovely; she was sound and muscular. We thought we could easily breed away from that unwanted longhair trait. (At the time, long hair was not a disqualification in the Basset standard). We had seen a handsome champion stud with a very tight coat, and after seeing several of his offspring, all carrying that same short, sleek coat, we decided to drive the seven hours involved to breed to him. Six of eight fluffy puppies later we realized our thinking had been simplistic. For several years following, there were people in our area that proudly walked and heaped loads of love on our fluffy mistakes. It was a constant reminder of the necessity for caution and constant study." In the meantime, they continued their search for the elusive foundation bitch. Finally, they found an open-marked, ticked tricolor with excellent type and a tight coat. Unfortunately, the bad luck tagged along. With nine show points, an injury ended her show career. Over the years her breeders, Jack and Ruby Patterson, were able to spot her descendants by their Jacq-Scott's Willie Towne elegant heads. Their second male, Am/Can. Ch. Seneca Sambo Leeno, although specialed on a limited basis, was ranked number nine in the Phillips System in 1970, as well as becoming a significant stud for the kennel.

*Topsfield Circus Circus, (Ch. Stoneybluff Ginger Beer ex Bone-A-Part Topfield Tiz Tops), at eight months and nearly having completed his championship.*

In one of their earliest breedings, Schnaps to a linebred Westgate bitch, they were able to capture a significant piece of the Lyn-Mar Acres bloodline. Combining Siefenjagenheim Lazy Bones and, through him, Ch. Lyn-Mar Acres Clown four times (three times in the pedigree of the bitch and once in Schnaps' family tree), he was aptly call named "Solo," as *he was the litter!* Registered as Napoleon Solo of Schnaps, he went on to gain both his American and Canadian championships. He was specialed in Canada where he achieved a national ranking of number three in 1968.

Bernisci's Princess, a red and white bitch shown and pointed by Bernisci kennels, would prove to be a significant part of the Von Skauton breeding program. Owned by Malcolm and Vivian Plummer, Princess was bred to Schnaps to produce Lynrod's Saba of Schnaps, a very dark black-blanket bitch with a dark face. Saba was bred to "Sam" (Sambo Leeno), which produced Am/Can. Sacata Von Skauton, and Can. Ch. Roquepene Von Skauton. Sacata was bred just once to Blackie's Bleemer, owned by Blackie and Howard Nygood. Bleemer was the son of a top winner of his time, Ch. Manor Hill Fringe Benefit. From this breeding she produced Ch. Warlock Von Skauton, Ch. Tess Von Skauton and major-pointed Lucinda Von Skauton. Roquepene, also bred only once, produced Can. Ch. Kriegen Von Skauton, a multiple-Group winner for his owner, Olive Klevorick of Kevelo kennels. Tragically, Sacata was lost on the vet's table while in labor, due to an overdose of pituitrin, and Roquepene was lost to a virus.

A review of the pedigree of the Schnaps ex Princess litter shows that this breeding also doubles up on the Lyn Mar background (Clown). Schnaps was bred to yet another Clown descendant, their own foundation bitch, "Willie." This mating produced Hilda Helms Von Skauton, who appears in some pedigrees under that name, but it was not

| | |
|---|---|
| | Ch. Lyn Mar Acres Clown |
| Ch. Siefenjagenheim Lazy Bones | |
| | Ch. Webb's Black Amanda |
| Long View Acres Ed Too | |
| | Ch. Slow Poke Hubertus |
| Ch. Long View Acres Frannie | |
| | Ch. Fanny of En-Hu |
| AM/CAN. CH. SCHNAPS VON SKAUTON | |
| | Engle's Black Duke II |
| Hornbrook's Barney Boy | |
| | June's Virginia Girl |
| Nab-A-Line Sorrowful Ruth | |
| | Ferge's Samuel |
| Green's Mary Ann | |
| | Ferge's Wellsville Lucy |

her AKC registered name. Bred to Sambo Leeno, "Hilda" produced Can. Ch. Rommel Von Skauton, who was lost at an early age, and Am/Can. Ch. Vanessa Vamp Von Skauton.

Like Sacata, Vamp would make her greatest mark through her offspring, having produced Am/Can. Ch. Heine Von Skauton ROM and Ch. Von Skauton's Camillus Clyde, when bred to Ch. Willstone Harvey. Vamp's total output, two puppies, was even less than Sacata's. However, if we consider their effect on future generations, these two bitches, while not prolific, must still be considered two significant producers in the breed.

*Ch. Dealo's March Hare Von Skauton winning BOB at the 1977 BHCA National Specialty. Handled by Dawn Towne, under breeder-judge Carlton Redmond, the dog was bred by Ola DeGroat and co-owned by her with Garry Towne.*

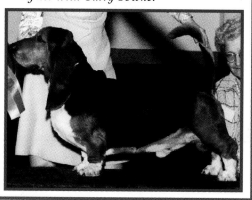

*Am-Can. Ch. Heine Von Skauton ROM, and Dawn Towne. Bred by Mrs. J. W. Heinekamp of Camillus Bassets and owned by Garry Towne.*

From Sacata, the Townes kept "Warlock," a black blanket tri male. "Lucinda," of similar color, went to the Haddle's kennels of James William Haddle, and Tess, another black blanket, went to Doc and Vicki Steedle to become the foundation bitch of their Halcyon Bassets. She produced significantly for the Halcyon kennels. Lucinda came back to be bred to Heine Von Skauton and produced Ch. Haddle's Oliver Von Skauton, a Group placer. Returned again to be bred to Sambo Leeno, she produced Haddle's Tuff Stuff Von Skauton, foundation stud for Joan Deibler's Misty Meadows dogs.

Ch. Von Skauton's Camillus Clyde was the sire of Musicland's Snow White and Musicland's Snobird of Von Skauton. Snow White produced the well-known sire, Ch. Musicland's Valentino. A Valentino son, Ch. Musicland's Diablo, was purchased and made an important contribution to the kennel through Ch. Elwil Abraham Von Skauton. Their Am/Can. Ch. Heine Von Skauton ROM became the 1979 BHCA National Specialty BOB winner. He is also the sire of several Specialty-winning offspring. When bred to Ola and Al DeGroat's bitch, Dealo's Jo Jo Pakwat, he produced Ch. Dealos March Hare Von Skauton. Co-owned with Ola DeGroat, he was the winner of the 1977 BHCA National Specialty. When bred to Ch. Musicland's Ravishing Ruby, owned by Paul and Margie Wikerd, Heine produced Ch. Bluvali Double Delight (twice BOS at the BHCA Nationals), Ch. Bluvali Double or Nothin' (an important stud for the Wikerds), and Ch. Bluvali Double Dare, who came to the Townes. Bred to Dealo's Dimples of Belroute, Heine produced Ch. Dealo Frosty Von Skauton, who is behind several of the MRM Bassets of Olga Doi.

At first glance it would appear that the Von Skauton dogs' influence on the breed is regional in nature. The knowledgeable breeder, however, will recognize the in-depth contribution of this kennel through the success of their dogs in other kennels breeding programs, essentially nationwide. In summary, to date they have produced over 50 American conformation champions and a dozen or more Canadian champions. They have had several nationally ranked dogs in the US and Canada and produced the number one Hound in Thailand. One of their dogs, co-owned and shown by Doug Taylor, was the first Basset agility titleholder. In addition, they had the top obedience Basset one year, sired one that gained a field champion title, and either owned or co-owned two National Specialty winners. As an aside, Dawn was the handler of the 1994 National Specialty winner, Ch. Dealo's Lehi Fyre Dragon, bred by Ola DeGroat and owned by Carol Ceneviva. The Townes recently introduced this dog into their breeding program. Thus far he has produced Ch. Dragon Thunder Von Skauton, co-owned and handled by Doug Taylor. The Dragon Thunder dog has already distinguished himself by having produced two Hiflite champions. One of them, Ch. Hiflite Ultrabrite, was BW at the 1995 BHCA National Specialty.

*Ch. Wagtail's Mischief Maker ROM, going BOS at the 1979 Westminster K.C. show, handled by Sue Whaley.*

## WAGTAIL

The Chipmans, Harry and Mary Louise, have been in the breed for some 20 years and have used the Wagtail prefix for their Bassets. They are longtime, hard-working members of the Potomac Basset Hound Club as well the BHCA. One of their favorites over the years was Ch. Wagtail's Mischief Maker ROM, whelped in 1976, sired by Am/Can. Ch. Tal-E-Ho's Prancer out of Redbird's Merry Miss Muffin. Mischief finished her championship at 14 months of age, going Breed over specials on her way. She earned three of her majors from the Puppy class, and before her second birthday was the top-winning Basset bitch on the East Coast and made the top ten list that year. Another honor for this lovely bitch

was sharing of the BHCA Top Producing Bitch award for 1982. She was listed in the ROM in 1987, having been bred only twice.

## WESTACRES

About the same time as the Chantinghall line was originating in Scotland, the Westacres Bassets were starting in Canada. Mr. and Mrs. Fred Carter began showing a Basset Hound named Schauffleins Logy, but it was when they obtained a bitch named Hartshead Fanfare from the Seitzes (Effie and Emil Seitz, charter members of BHCA), that their career began. The most decorated under the Westacre banner was the BIS-winning Ch. Westacres Hugo the Red. The Carters were among the first to brave the Basset Hound breed in Canadian shows.

# The Basset Hound Club of America, Inc.

The Basset Hound Club of America was started in 1933, at the home of William Fritz, in Detroit, Michigan. The charter members listed were: Mr. and Mrs. Alfred Bissell, B. F. Chaney, Harold R. Frazee, William Fritz, George C. Gregg, Carmon Klink, Alfred E. Kannowski, W. P. Klapp, Jr., James E. Lee, Ann Levy, Gerald Livingston, Carl Nottke, Effie Seitz, and Lewis Thompson.

The constitution and by-laws were drawn up in 1934 and they were adopted in 1935 during the club's first annual meeting. The rules for field trials were drafted in 1936 and the club became an American Kennel Club member club in 1937. The constitution and by-laws were revised and the incorporation of the club was approved at a special meeting. The incorporation, at Racine, Wisconsin, was accomplished through the efforts of Cathryn A. Burton, James Fornary, and George R. Simanek.

According to Mercedes Braun, in her book *The New Complete Basset Hound,* Fourth Edition, 1979, and now out of print, the original standard for the American Basset Hound was written by Will Judy, publisher of the well-known *Dog World* magazine. A well-known dog man in his day, Mr. Judy did the initial work on a number of new breed standards. This attempt at approving a standard was rejected by the membership at its 1940 annual meeting with 40 members in attendance voting. Available records indicate no further action was taken concerning the standard until 1953. A six-member committee composed of Loren Free, Dorothy Hardy, Jean Look, Helen Nelson, Effie Seitz, and Chris Teeter presented a proposed standard at the annual meeting in 1955 and it was accepted by majority vote. Restlessness concerning

the standard seemed to prevail, and in 1961 the membership decided that it should be revised. Braun states: "A committee was appointed headed by Peg Walton. Others on the committee were Dick Bassett, Effie Seitz, and Walter Brandt. The final draft was sent to the Board in 1962. However, this was rejected by AKC. The Board took over the work and it was again presented to the membership in October, 1963. The present standard was accepted by the AKC in 1964."

Peg Walton, in her book *The New Basset Hound,* 1993, recalls the events pertaining to the standard over the years somewhat differently. She states, in part: "When the Basset Hound Club of America was founded in 1933, most of the members' packs consisted of Walhampton hounds and thus the above standard was used with very few changes." The "above standard" to which she refers is the one taken directly from *The Basset Hound Club Rules and Stud Book,* compiled by the late Sir Everett Millais, corrected and made up to March, 1900 by Mrs. Mabel Tottie. She goes on to write: "In the American Kennel Club's purebred dogs book of standards (copyright 1935), we find Heseltine's standard for the Basset Hound 'by courtesy of the Basset Hound Club of America.'" Walton further states, "The few changes between these two standards consist of the word 'perceptibly' instead of 'sensibly' under Head; the elimination of 'i.e., pot-hooked' under Tail and, under Forelegs, the Basset Hound Club of America used 'crook'd knee' rather than 'crooked knee'. Perhaps this is where the English and American language differ, as Webster describes 'crook'd' as having a crook and 'crooked' as being askew. From time to time other words were added or deleted, but nothing that changed the original standard and the points of the smooth Basset Hound remained the same until the new standard went into effect nearly 30 years later. Ch. Walhampton Andrew stood as the breed's ideal for all this time and was pictured in every edition until replaced with a photo of Ch. Siefenjagenheim Lazy Bones." In discussing the revision and approval of the current standard, Mrs. Walton writes: "At a board of directors meeting of the Basset Hound Club of America, held at the home of President Paul Kulp, a new committee was formed to look into revamping the standard. It consisted of: Margaret S. Walton, chairperson; Richard Basset(t), West Coast; Effie Seitz, Midwest; Walter Brandt, East Coast. This group worked together extremely well and the present standard was the outcome, with a few changes proposed by the American Kennel Club. They had asked for certain additions, such as dewclaws may be removed, tail is not to be docked, etc. The membership of the Basset Hound Club of America had already voted to accept the standard, and with the additions in place, it went into effect in 1964 and has stood unchanged since that time."

In researching this portion of the book, this author finds it curious that the reference is made in the Walton book regarding the Webster definition of "crook'd" and "crooked." In rereading that portion of Mrs. Walton's book dealing with the standard, I note that she states: "The standard at the turn of the century is as applicable today as it was in 1900." The standard from *The Basset Hound Club Rules and Stud Book* (March, 1900) is then printed out and paragraph four of that standard reads: "Forelegs short, about four inches, and close-fitting to the chest till the crooked knee, from where the wrinkled ankle ends in a massive paw, each toe standing out distinctly." Sounds like a reasonable description to this writer, and I would tend to agree that it is as "applicable today as it was in 1900!" It would seem to beg the question; Why, then, was the reference to the "crook'd knee" removed during the 1964 revision?

As the club grew, it was determined that the by-laws needed revision and work was started to accomplish such in 1964 under the chairmanship of Col. Julian Dexter. The 1965 annual meeting was conducted under those new by-laws with one major change being in the method of the election of the officers and directors. Previous elec-

*Chief ring steward, Pat Gellerman, calling a class at a National Specialty.*

tions had been by nomination from the floor and limited to those members who were present at the annual meeting. Another major change was reflected in the appointment, by the board of directors, of individual members to fill certain positions within the club. The by-laws were revised again in the mid-1970s and in the mid-1990s. The 1970 effort was chaired by Finn Bergishagen, who withdrew after being elected president, and

conjunction with the Chicago International K.C. all-breed show through 1959, and after 1960, came to be known as the spring Nationals. The first fall annual National Specialty was held in Lebanon, Pennsylvania on October 7, 1960. While there is now only one National Specialty each year, the club did continue to host a spring Nationals at Chicago through 1962. In June, 1963, the California clubs hosted a spring Specialty

*Camaraderie at a typical National Specialty.*

the work was finalized under the guidance of Bob Swanson. The proposed revisions were not finally approved by the membership until 1980. The 1990s' effort in this area was again chaired by Finn Bergishagen and approved by the membership in 1995. This latest change was major in that it changed the composition of the officers and board of directors by the addition of a second vice-president and a corresponding secretary.

The first annual Specialty show was held in Chicago in 1955 with an entry of 40 Basset Hounds. The annual Specialties continued to be held in Chicago, in the spring, in

at Long Beach and after that, the spring show moved to different areas by invitation of a local club. This has since changed to having the local clubs authorized to host a BHCA Regional Specialty show each year, but being limited to two shows per region per year. The annual National Specialty now runs four full days during the week of the first full weekend in the month of October each year. The location moves each year, limited only by the availability of a local host club and the availability of field trial and tracking grounds, and the entries are, of course, significantly higher, numbering several hundred.

Judges for the conformation events are nominated and elected by the membership and must come from among the members who are AKC approved judges.

By about 1963 there was considerable interest in obedience and an obedience committee was appointed. Benjamin Harris was its chairman and other members were Mercedes Braun, Bob Noerr, and Lena Wray. Initially, the Basset Hound was required to jump one and one-half times its height for the high-jump exercise. It took quite some time for the committee to have AKC include the Basset among the other breeds that were required only to jump their height, rather than the one and one-half times their height, but they were eventually successful. Virginia Jones and Joan Thurlow were on the committee at that time and worked very hard for this change. The club offered Obedience classes for the first time at the 1968 Nationals. Tracking was added to the list of events at the Nationals in 1970 with Lena and Billy Wray being among the early leaders of this discipline.

Until the mid to late 1960s, the club had continued to be guided by those having a major interest in the field trialing discipline. This was, and still is, considered by many to have been a normal progression of leadership because the field trialers have historically been credited with having started the BHCA. As pointed out by Merce Braun in her book, "They could foresee the day when it would be possible that the club would be governed by persons who might be unsympathetic, perhaps even opposed to the sport. Bill Rider proposed that a committee could be formed to look after the interests of the field trialers. The board appointed him chairman of the field trial rules and running order committee. In 1963, the AKC agreed to give Bassets running rules of its own although they are still, largely, run under the same rules as Beagles. By 1969 the committee, as it is known today, came into being. Each trial-giving club has a representative on what is now called the Field Trial Advisory Council. This group reviews proposed changes in regulations,

submits needed proposals, oversees the trial schedules, and is in charge of field activities, subject to board approval. John Eylander succeeded Bill Rider for a short time, and then Kenneth McWilliams became chairman in 1971, serving until 1977 when Leonard Skolnick took over. Dale Fleming followed, with Dick Spurling next, and Ken McWilliams taking over again in 1992 "to keep the hounds running!" followed by Bill TenEyck in 1998.

All disciplines of the breed, conformation, obedience, tracking and field trialing, are held at the Nationals each year. To my knowledge, BHCA is the only parent breed club to do this and it gives interested observers the opportunity to see the hounds perform in whatever area their interest may lie.

In the early days of the club, a newsletter was published, at first by the secretaries and then by elected publicity directors. According to Merce Braun, Ethel Ferge was the last to put it out in newsletter form, but this writer can find no record confirming that. Merce also states that Ruth Turner was elected the first publicity director and changed it to a magazine-type publication. Merce Braun followed Ruth in 1963 and Kay Ellenberger took it over in 1965. After the by-laws change in 1965, the editors position was appointed by the board of directors. Jean Spaulding was the first appointee to this Herculean task, followed over the years by Jeanne (Dudley) Hills, Eileen Schroeder, Pat (Fellman) Gellerman, Beverly Stockfelt, Pat (Fellman) Gellerman again, Vicki Steedle, Sherry Neiberger, Vicki Steedle (temporary), Tonta McHale, Brenda Jubin & Eva Balogh (jointly), Vicki Steedle again, Melody Fair, Francisca Vassy, Marjorie Wikerd, Loraine Russell, Mary Ann Clark, Carolyn Young and our newest appointee, Carol Ann Hunt.

The objectives of the club, according to the amended by-laws of March 31, 1995, are:

* to encourage and promote the breeding of purebred Basset Hounds and to do all possible to bring their natural qualities to perfection;

* to urge members and breeders to accept the standard of the breed as approved

by the American Kennel Club as the only standard of excellence by which Basset Hounds shall be judged;

* to do all in its power to protect the interests of the breed by encouraging sportsmanlike competition at dog shows, field trials, obedience trials, and tracking tests;

* to conduct sanctioned matches and specialty shows, field trials, obedience trials, and tracking tests under the rules of the American Kennel Club;

* to encourage the formation of local Basset Hound clubs and assist them in their activities.

The club offers five types of membership, open to all persons who are in good standing with the American Kennel Club and who subscribe to the purposes of this club. Those memberships are Single, Family (husband and wife who are entitled to one vote), Local Basset Hound Club membership, Junior Membership for persons under 18 years of age, having no voting privileges, and Associate Memberships. Those desiring membership are required to sign that they have read and will abide by the clubs Guidelines of Ethical Conduct. These guidelines are as follows:

## GUIDELINES OF ETHICAL CONDUCT

Each member of the Basset Hound Club of America will consider the welfare of the breed when engaging in any activities involving the breeding, selling, or competition of Basset Hounds. BHCA members, both individuals and member clubs, are urged to comply with the following guidelines.

1. Members of the Basset Hound Club of America will abide by the constitution and by-laws of BHCA and of the American Kennel Club.

2. Members will ensure that all dogs in their care are provided adequate food, water and shelter, opportunity for exercise, veterinary care, and personal attention to monitor their needs.

3. Breedings will be directed toward producing Basset Hounds of exceptional quality in breed temperament, Basset Hound type, and ability to hunt game. Only healthy and mature dogs and bitches free of congenital defects and of characteristic breed type, sound structure, and temperament shall be bred.

4. Members should not undertake the breeding of a bitch unless they are prepared to act responsibly regarding the disposition of the resultant puppies. Members shall be discriminating in the placing of puppies and adult hounds, choosing environments in which the Basset Hound will receive suitable care and affection and will not be misused.

5. Basset Hounds offered for sale or males offered at stud must be presented honestly regarding their pedigrees, their potential as bred and their faults or the fault possibilities that may develop in maturity.

6. Members of the Basset Hound Club of America will follow good business practices and ethics in breeding and sales contracts and will honor all agreements. Written agreements in all dealings regarding Basset Hounds are strongly encouraged.

7. No member of this club shall engage in the wholesaling of litters or the selling of breeding stock to commercial sales operations ("puppy mills"). No member will offer or supply Basset Hounds for prizes, raffles, or lotteries.

*Members in an entertainment mode at a National Specialty.*

8. No member shall engage in false or misleading advertising or misrepresentation of his/her Basset Hounds or of those of competitors.

9. Members will practice the principles of good sportsmanship, considering competition to be a challenge, not a threat.

10. All members of the BHCA shall conduct themselves in all aspects of the sport of dogs in a manner designed to reflect credit upon our breed and our club. (Rev. May 94).

There are currently 41 local specialty clubs that are AKC approved and are member clubs of BHCA. It is impossible to provide a list of current local club contacts that will remain current for more than one year. If the reader wishes to contact a local Basset Hound Club in their geographical area, they should contact the American Kennel Club for the name and address of the BHCA corresponding secretary who can provide the names and phone numbers for local club contacts. For those who are on the Internet, much information is available there as well.

The following are the current local clubs and their approximate geographical areas of influence: BADGERLAND BHC, Wisconsin; BERKSHIRE VALLEY BHC, New Jersey, Pennsylvania, Southern New York; BHC OF BRITISH COLUMBIA, BC, Canada; BHC OF CENTRAL INDIANA, Indiana; BHC OF GREATER DETROIT, Western Michigan, Northern Ohio; BHC GREATER FT. WORTH, North Texas; BHC OF GREATER HOUSTON, Southeast Texas; BHC OF GREATER NEW ORLEANS, Louisiana; BHC OF GREATER SAN ANTONIO, INC., South Texas; BHC OF SAN DIEGO, San Diego, California; BHC OF GREATER SEATTLE, Washington; BHC OF HAWAII, Hawaii; BHC OF MARYLAND, INC., Maryland, Virginia, Delaware; BHC OF PORTLAND, OR., INC., Oregon; BHC OF SACRAMENTO, Central, Northern California; BHC OF SOUTHERN CALIFORNIA, Southern California; BHC OF TULSA, Oklahoma, Kansas; BUCKEYE BHC, Eastern Ohio, Western Pennsylvania; CAPITAL DISTRICT BHC, Upstate New York; DAL-TEX BHC, North Texas; EMERALD EMPIRE BHF, Oregon, Southern Washington, Northern California; FT.

DEARBORN BHC, Illinois, Eastern Michigan, Northern Indiana; GTR. MINNEAPOLIS ST. PAUL BHC, Minnesota, Wisconsin; HIGHLAND LAKES BHA, Central and South Texas; KENTUCKIANA BHC, Kentucky, Southeastern Indiana; LENAPE BHC, Pennsylvania; LINCOLNLAND BHC, Illinois; LOOKING GLASS BHC, Michigan, Ohio; MAUMEE VALLEY BHC, Ohio, Pennsylvania; NORTHERN CALIFORNIA BHC, Central and Northern California; PATROON BHC, New Jersey, New York, Eastern Pennsylvania; PILGRIM BHC, New England; POTOMAC BHC, Virginia, Maryland, Delaware, District of Columbia; RANCOCAS VALLEY BHC, New Jersey; SOUTH FLORIDA BHC, South Florida; SUNCOAST BHC, Florida; SUSQUEHANNA BHC, Pennsylvania, New Jersey; TIMBERLINE BHC, Colorado; VALLE DEL SOL BHC, Arizona; VALLEY FORGE BHC, Pennsylvania; and the WESTERN MICHIGAN BHC, Western Michigan, Northern Ohio.

Histories of the majority of these local clubs can be found in the Braun book *The New Complete Basset Hound.* Though this book is out of print, its rights have recently been transferred to the BHCA by Merce's husband, Joe Braun.

The Basset Hound Club of America also has a Life Membership program that honors, from among their current 850-plus members, those members who have made significant contributions to the club and the breed in their 25 (or more) years of membership. Among the Life Members are: Mona Ball, Ruth Bateman, Finn Bergishagen, Mary Louise Bergishagen, Mary Jane Booth, Robert E. Booth, Joseph Braun, Pat Dohr, Norwood Engle, Andrea Mc.E. Field, Dale Fleming, Hettie Page Garwood, Patricia Gellerman, John Andrew Hackley, Benjamin J. Harris, Jeanne Hills, Doris Hurry, Betty Kinslow, Mary Marischen, Donald C. Martin, John McDowell, Kenneth McWilliams, Ruth Paule, William Rider, Lorraine Russell, William R. Russell, Joan C. Scholz, Jean L. Sheehy, Mary Jo Shields, Majorie Skolnick, Howard E. Smith, Jean Spaulding, Elsie Tagg, Ann Thain, Ruth Turner, Joan Urban, James R. White, Wanda White, Barbara Wicklund, and Lena K. Wray.

## THE BASSET HOUND CLUB OF AMERICA OFFICERS, 1935—1997

| Year | President | Vice-President | Secretary | Treasurer |
|------|-----------|----------------|-----------|-----------|
| 1935—36 | William Fritz | Emil Seitz | Carl Nottke | |
| 1937 | Emil Seitz | Otto Grigsby | Carl Nottke | |
| 1938 | Emil Seitz | Harold Fogelson | Carl Nottke | |
| 1939 | Emil Seitz | Consuelo Ford | Carl Nottke | |
| 1940—44 | Consuelo Ford | | Melvin Freeman | Effie Seitz |
| 1945—50 | Roy Smith | Dr. J. P. Honey | Claude Smith | |
| 1951 | Claude Smith | Harold Fogelson | Roy Smith | |
| 1952—53 | Claude Smith | Johnny Bose | Roy Smith | |
| 1954—55 | Johnny Bose | Norwood Engle | Millie Houchin | |
| 1956 | Leslie Kelly | Chris Teeter | Millie Houchin | |
| 1957—58 | Johnny Bose | Chris Teeter | Effie Seitz | Donald Bateman |
| 1959—60 | Dr. D. Wahl | Norwood Engle | Dorothy Shula | Effie Seitz |
| 1961—62 | Paul Kulp | Norwood Engle | Elizabeth Phillips | Julian Dexter |
| 1963—64 | John Eyelander | Norwood Engle | Darrielyn Oursler | David Feron |
| 1965 | John Eyelander | Norwood Engle | Mercedes Braun | Donald Bateman |
| 1966 | Norwood Engle | William Rider | Mercedes Braun | Donald Bateman |
| 1967 | Norwood Engle | William Rider | Mercedes Braun | Clare Clowe |
| 1969 | Joseph Braun | Clifford Warren | Ruth Bateman | Clare Clowe |
| 1970 | Joseph Braun | Clifford Warren | Ruth Bateman | Jean Spaulding |
| 1971 | Joseph Braun | Norwood Engle | Ruth Bateman | Jean Spaulding |
| 1972 | Donald Martin | Norwood Engle | Ruth Bateman | Jean Spaulding |
| 1973 | Donald Martin | Norwood Engle | Eileen Schroeder | Jean Spaulding |
| 1974 | Dodd McDowell | Jean Spaulding | Eileen Schroeder | William Kelly |
| 1975 | Joseph Braun | Finn Bergishagen | Jean Sheehy | Jean Spaulding |
| 1976 | Finn Bergishagen | William Kelly | Jean Sheehy | John Hackley |
| 1977 | Finn Bergishagen | William Kelly | Jean Sheehy | John Hackley |
| 1978 | William Kelly | Clare Clowe | Beverly Stockfelt | Pete Weaver |
| 1979 | Elsie Tagg | Clare Clowe | Beverly Stockfelt | Robert Bubb |
| 1980 | Elsie Tagg | Clare Clowe | Beverly Stockfelt | Robert Bubb |
| 1980—81 | Elsie Tagg | Robert Arbs | Jean Sheehy | Robert Bubb |
| 1981—82 | Finn Bergishagen | Robert Arbs | Jean Sheehy | Lamont Steedle |
| 1982—83 | Finn Bergishagen | Robert Arbs | Jean Sheehy | Lamont Steedle |
| 1983—84 | Finn Bergishagen | Robert Arbs | Jean Sheehy | Melody Fair |
| 1984—85 | Finn Bergishagen | Joan Scholz | Mary Ann Clark | Melody Fair |
| 1985—86 | Francis Paule | Joan Scholz | Mary Ann Clark | Melody Fair |
| 1986—87 | Francis Paule | Joan Scholz | Andrea McE. Field | Melody Fair |
| 1987—88 | Lamont Steedle | Joan Scholz | Andrea McE. Field | Richard Vlach |
| 1988—89 | Lamont Steedle | John Hackley | Andrea McE. Field | Richard Vlach |
| 1989—90 | Lamont Steedle | John Hackley | Andrea McE. Field | Pam Gingrich |
| 1990—91 | Lamont Steedle | John Hackley | Sanda Launey | Pam Gingrich |
| 1991—92 | Paul Wikerd | John Hackley | Sanda Launey | Pam Gingrich |
| 1992—93 | Paul Wikerd | Robert E. Booth | Andrea McE. Field | Pam Gingrich |
| 1993—94 | Paul Wikerd | Robert E. Booth | Andrea McE. Field | Pam Gingrich |
| 1994—95 | Edward Smizer | Robert E. Booth | Mimi Brandolino | Mary Manning |

**By-laws change adds two Officers**

| Year | President | 1st Vice President / 2nd Vice-President | Recording Secretary / Corresponding Secretary | Treasurer |
|------|-----------|------------------------------------------|-----------------------------------------------|-----------|
| 1995-96 | Edward Smizer | Robert E. Booth / Jean Sheehy | Mimi McCabe / Melody Fair | Peter Bach |
| 1996-97 | Jean Sheehy | Dale K. Fleming / Jerry Rush | Mimi McCabe / Melody Fair | Peter Bach |
| 1997-98 | Jean Sheehy | Dale K. Fleming / Randy Frederiksen | Jerry Rush / Melody Fair | Peter Bach |
| 1998-99 | Jim Dok | Randy Frederiksen / Norman Wiginton | Jerry Rush / Carol Makowski | Belén Herner |

# The Standard

The glossary contained in the AKC's *The Complete Dog Book* defines standard as: "A description of the ideal dog of each recognized breed, to serve as a word pattern by which dogs are judged at shows." While this definition is true in terms of the context of that book's glossary, I prefer to think of the standard as being: A word picture, written by the guardians of the breed, to form in the mind's eye the ideal of the animal that breeders continually strive to produce.

The American standard for the Basset Hound endured, from its initial acceptance, until it was changed by the parent club in 1964. The committee appointed to accomplish this task was composed of chairperson Margaret S. (Peg) Walton, (Lyn Mar Acres); Richard Bassett, (Notrenom), representing the West; Effie Seitz (Hartshead), from the Midwest; and Walter Brandt, (Abbot Run Valley), from the East.

The following is the official standard for the Basset Hound.

## OFFICIAL STANDARD FOR THE BASSET HOUND

**General Appearance**—The Basset Hound possesses in marked degree those characteristics which equip it admirably to follow a trail over and through difficult terrain. It is a short-legged dog, heavier in bone, size considered, than any other breed of dog, and while its movement is deliberate, it is in no sense clumsy. In temperament it is mild, never sharp or timid. It is capable of great endurance in the field and is extreme in its devotion.

**Head**—The head is large and well proportioned. Its length from occiput to muzzle is greater than the width at the brow. In overall appearance the head is of medium width. The skull is well domed, showing a pronounced occipital protuberance. A broad flat skull is a fault. The length from nose to stop is approximately the length from stop to occiput. The sides are flat and free from cheek bumps. Viewed in profile the top lines of the muzzle and skull are straight and lie in parallel planes, with a moderately defined stop. The skin over the whole of the head is loose, falling in distinct wrinkles over the brow when the head is lowered. A dry head and tight skin are faults. The muzzle is deep, heavy, and free from snipiness. The nose is darkly pigmented, preferably black, with large wide-open nostrils. A deep liver-colored nose conforming to the coloring of the head is permissible but not desirable. The teeth are large, sound, and regular, meeting in either a scissors or an even bite. A bite either overshot or undershot is a serious fault. The lips are darkly pigmented and are pendulous, falling squarely in front, and toward the back, in loose hanging flews. The dewlap is very pronounced. The neck is powerful, of good length, and well arched. The eyes are soft, sad, and slightly sunken, showing a prominent haw, and in color are brown, dark brown preferred. A somewhat lighter colored eye conforming to the general coloring of the dog is acceptable but not desirable. Very light or protruding eyes are faults. The ears are extremely long, low set, and when drawn forward, fold well over the end of the nose. They are velvety in texture, hanging in loose folds with the ends curling slightly inward. They are set far back on the head at the base of the skull and, in repose, appear to be set on the neck. A high set or flat ear is a serious fault.

**Forequarters**—The chest is deep and full with prominent sternum showing clearly in front of the legs. The shoulders and elbows are set close against the sides of the chest. The distance from the deepest point of the chest to the ground, while it must be adequate to allow for free movement when working in the field, is not to be more than one-third the total height at the withers of

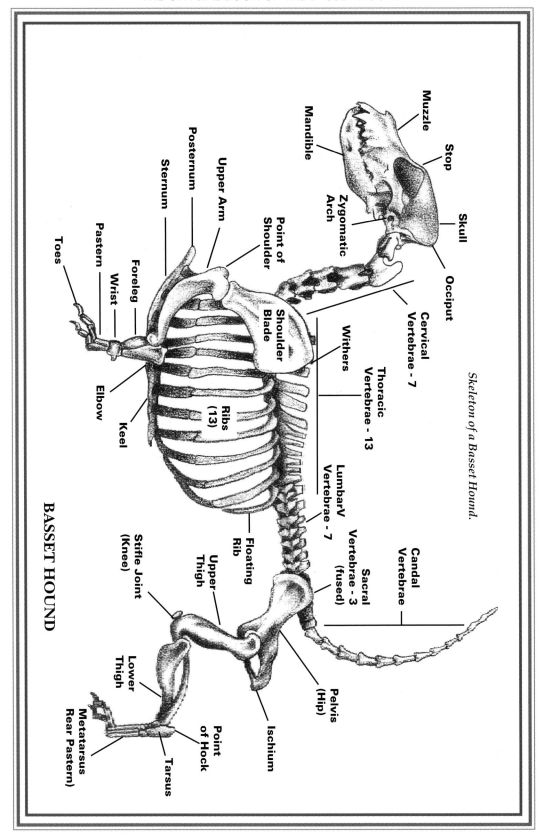

*Skeleton of a Basset Hound.*

Muzzle

Stop

Mandible

Skull

Zygomatic
Arch

Occiput

Posternum

Sternum

Upper Arm

Point of
Shoulder

Cervical
Vertebrae - 7

Toes

Pastern

Wrist

Foreleg

Shoulder
Blade

Withers

Thoracic
Vertebrae - 13

Elbow

Keel

Ribs
(13)

LumbarV
Vertebrae - 7

Candal
Vertebrae

Stifle Joint
(Knee)

Upper
Thigh

Floating
Rib

Sacral
Vertebrae - 3
(fused)

Lower
Thigh

Point
of Hock

Ischium

Pelvis
(Hip)

Metatarsus
Rear Pastern)

Tarsus

**BASSET HOUND**

an adult Basset. The shoulders are well laid back and powerful. Steepness in shoulder, fiddle fronts, and elbows that are out are serious faults. The forelegs are short, powerful, heavy in bone, with wrinkled skin. Knuckling over of the front legs is a disqualification. The paw is massive, very heavy with tough heavy pads, well rounded and with both feet inclined equally a trifle outward, balancing the width of the shoulders. Feet down at the pastern are a serious fault. The toes are neither pinched together nor splayed, with the weight of the forepart of the body borne evenly on each. The declaws may be removed.

**Body**—The rib structure is long, smooth, and extends well back. The ribs are well sprung, allowing adequate room for heart and lungs. Flatsidedness and flanged ribs are faults. The topline is straight, level, and free from and tendency to sag or roach, which are faults.

**Hindquarters**—The hindquarters are very full and well rounded, and are approximately equal to the shoulders in width. They must not appear slack or light in relation to the overall depth of body. The dog stands firmly on its hind legs showing a well-let-down stifle with no tendency toward a crouching stance. Viewed from behind, the hind legs are parallel, with the hocks turning neither in nor out. Cowhocks or bowed legs are serious faults. The hind feet point straight ahead. Steep, poorly angulated hindquarters are a serious fault. The dewclaws, if any, may be removed.

**Tail**—The tail is not to be docked, and is set in continuation of the spine with but slight curvature, and carried gaily in hound fashion. The hair on the underside of the tail is coarse.

**Size**—The height should not exceed 14 inches. Height over 15 inches at the highest point of the shoulder blade is a disqualification.

**Gait**—The Basset Hound moves in a smooth, powerful and effortless manner. Being a scenting dog with short legs, it holds its nose low to the ground. Its gait is absolutely true with perfect co-ordination between the front and hind legs, and it moves in a straight line with hind feet following in line with the front feet, the hocks well bent with no stiffness of action. The front legs do not paddle, weave, or overlap, and the elbows must lie close to the body. Going away, the hind legs are parallel.

**Coat**—The coat is hard, smooth, and short, with sufficient density to be of use in all weather. The skin is loose and elastic. A distinctly long coat is a disqualification.

**Color**—Any recognized hound color is acceptable and distribution of color and markings is of no importance.

## DISQUALIFICATIONS

Height of more than 15 inches at the highest point of the shoulder blade.

Knuckled-over front legs.

Distinctly long coat.

The BHCA completed the development and printing of *The Basset Hound Illustrated Standard*, an endeavor which was in process for well over two years. While this timeframe for accomplishment may seem unduly long, I am aware of numerous parent clubs that have taken eight or ten years to complete the same task! At any rate, this long-awaited document was made available to the membership at the 1996 Nationals. Those responsible for its production deserve a real vote of thanks from the membership as it is a very worthy document that should help the fancier more fully understand the breed. Surely it will be a significant teaching aid for those who will study it in depth as it presents the standard visually, as well as in writing, and utilizes skeletal overlays, which have been needed for a long time.

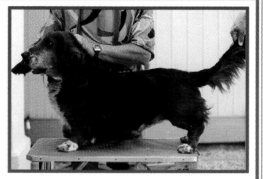

As the standard indicates, "the distribution of color and markings is of no importance." An outstanding Basset bitch, going all the way to BOS, despite her unusual markings.

Basset Hounds with distinctly long coats still exist.

A Basset Hound which is distinctly "knuckled over" on the left front leg.

This Basset Hound is "knuckled over" on both front legs. Knuckling over is a Disqualifying fault.

# Conformation Competition

Far and away, the aspect of the sport that most of the active BHCA members are involved in is the showing of their dogs in the conformation classes at AKC-approved dog shows. These shows run the gamut from AKC sanctioned all-breed club matches through shows held by AKC-licensed clubs at which championship points are awarded. These may be either all-breed dog shows or specialty club shows, such as are hosted by the regional breed clubs and the parent breed clubs, such as BHCA.

The original espoused purpose of holding such shows was to provide a venue where breeders could assemble to view each other's stock and to compare the relative quality of their specimens, and also to assess how well this stock conformed to the standard for their particular breed. Over time these shows have developed into what has become a nationwide competition among the breeds in an effort to achieve the number-one ranking in the country. Of the total exhibitors who enter into the conformation competition, relatively few are in the race for that ultimate rank of number-one, all-breeds. Most are content to merely finish their dog's AKC championship.

To become an AKC champion, a dog must compete and win in a sufficient number of AKC-licensed events to achieve a total of 15 championship points. These points must be won under a minimum of three different AKC-approved judges at a minimum of three separate events, of which two of these events must be classified as "majors" for the breed being shown. A major is an event with a sufficient number of the specific breed entered and shown to make it either a three-, four-, or five-point competition. The points awarded at a given show are determined by the number of dogs in the breed that are exhibited in the particular division in which the show is being held. This number is determined and published by the AKC on an annual basis. It may or may not change yearly, depending on the number of a particular breed exhibited within the division throughout the year.

Entries for each show must be submitted to the show secretary or the show superintendent and must reach that office by the announced closing date in the premium list. These closing dates are generally two-and-one-half weeks prior to the actual show date. You may obtain premium lists for upcoming shows at nearly any show that you might choose to attend. You may also correspond with the superintendents, a complete list of whom are in each issue of *The American Kennel Gazette*, and request to be placed on their mailing lists. This will allow you to automatically receive all premium lists for a given geographical area served by that superintendent.

The AKC publishes pamphlets entitled *Rules Applying to Dog Shows* and *Rules Applying to Registration and Discipline.* They are available from the American Kennel Club by writing to them at 5580 Centerview Drive, Suite 200, Raleigh, NC 27606-3390. These documents, together with the premium list for the specific show, will give the exhibitor what they need to know in order to get entered in the event.

It is required that your hound be at least six months of age on the date of the show that you choose to enter. You will have your choice of six classes (divided by sex) from which you will select one class in which to enter your dog. The class eligibility is covered in *Rules Applying to Dog Shows.* When you have made the appropriate decisions, the entry form and your entry fee is forwarded per the instructions in the premium list. Shortly after the announced closing date you can expect to receive a confirmation of the receipt of your entry and a judging schedule which will tell you where and what time to be present to show your dog.

In order for you to gain championship points toward your dog's championship at any of these shows, it is necessary for you to be selected as the Winners Dog or the Winners Bitch at that event. This selection is made by the judge through the return to the ring of all of the class winners, i.e., Puppy, 12 to 18 Months, Novice, Bred-by Exhibitor, American Bred, and Open classes. From the winners of these classes, the judge then selects the dog that he or she feels best fits the standard for the breed and makes the award of Winners (either dog or bitch), depending on which sex is being shown at the time. The winners of both Winners classes (dog and bitch) are then eligible to continue to compete in that show's Best of Breed competition. The Best of Breed (BOB) class is for those dogs and bitches that have already completed their championship requirements as previously described. From these entries, including the previously selected Winners Dog and Bitch, the judge will select, in the following order, Best of Breed, Best of Winners (BW), and Best of Opposite Sex to BOB. It is in this competition that there may exist the opportunity to gain additional championship points at this particular show. This sometimes occurs if your hound is selected as BW and there were more points available in the sex over which you went BW, i.e., your entry was a dog and the total dog entry was only two dogs (1 point), but you were selected as BW over the WB in which there was a total bitch entry of five bitches (2 points). Your dog would then be awarded two points toward its championship. Additional points at that same show could also be available should your dog be selected over the others in the BOB class. Assuming that there were ten champions entered in the class, irrespective of sex, and your dog was selected as the BOB, your hound would

now be eligible to receive the points available in that particular division for having defeated 15 Basset Hounds. In most cases this would probably be three points, which would qualify as a "major."

Dogs having won BOB are eligible to continue in competition at the Group level. In the case described in the previous paragraph, it is possible that your dog could still win additional points at the same show. By winning first place in the Group, in this case the Hound Group, your dog would be eligible for up to two more points if there were any breeds in the Hound Group that had either a four- or five-point entry in their respective breed. If the largest other Hound entry were only four points, in Afghans for example, and your dog won the Group and went on to Best in Show competition, and won, and there was a five-point entry that day, in any other breed, you dog would now receive that additional point for a total of five points on the day. A five-point "major," one-third of the way toward its championship! Sound exciting? It is! With some breeds, there is so little competition in the breed that this is the only manner in which they are able to achieve a championship. It takes quite an outstanding specimen of the breed, and a lot of good luck as well, to accomplish a championship in this manner.

## WHAT DOES IT TAKE TO WIN?

In a nutshell: a showy, well-trained, and well-presented good-quality Basset Hound. Your hound will be expected to be trained for showing to the degree that he can be posed for examination by the judge. Commonly referred to as "stacked," this means that he will be expected to stand in position while the judge goes over him with his hands, feeling the skeleton of the dog, to determine that the animal has proper structure for its breed. You will then be asked to move your dog individually, generally either in a triangular pattern going away from, around, and back to the judge, or straight out and back to the judge and then around the ring to the end of the line of dogs. During this movement phase, the judge will

*The successful conclusion of the breed judging at a typical outdoor conformation show as Ch. Foxglen Princess Grace poses as BOB at an all-breed show in 1989 under breeder-judge Joan Scholz, handled by breeder-owner Scott Deans. A typically competitive hound, Gracie received a prestigious AOM at the 1992 National Specialty.*

assess how well the hound moves in all three perspectives, in accordance with the guidance furnished in the standard for the breed. Ultimately, in that judge's opinion, the dogs that he selects for the various available awards will have been the best of the competition on that day. Minimally, however, the selected dogs are expected to be deemed to be of championship quality "on the day" or a Winners award is not to be given!

The competition varies, to a considerable degree, from show to show and within particular divisions, and certainly it varies quite widely between some divisions. Showing in conformation should not be undertaken lightly as it is a somewhat costly hobby. In addition to the entry fees, there is the cost of transportation to and from the show. Most shows today are held in conjunction with a second show, so that will usually require at least one overnight stay if you plan to exhibit at both shows. And, unless you plan to lose a lot of weight, remember that eating in restaurants can be expensive.

As a rule of thumb, I've always found that if your dog, on average, doesn't go Winners at one out of three shows, it is probably time to re-evaluate the relative quality of your exhibit! Perhaps it might even be a problem with the manner in which the dog is being presented. Ask another exhibitor for his opinion. Most will be honest with you, but be prepared to hear the truth, which isn't always flattering. There is always the possibility of using a professional handler to finish your dog, but nothing equals the satisfaction of doing it yourself. Probably the ultimate win for most serious breeders and exhibitors is to have one of their dogs win BOB at their parent club National Specialty show. The awards of BOS, WD, or WB at the Nationals certainly would rank as a close second.

## JUNIOR SHOWMANSHIP

Another competition held under the conformation umbrella is Junior Showmanship. This is a competition, judged by AKC-approved judges, which is judged solely on the ability and skill of the juniors in the handling of their dogs as if they were in the breed ring. The conformation qualities of the dogs themselves are not a consideration in the judging of the event. This competition is open to all Junior Handlers from the age of ten years through the last day of their seventeenth year and is divided into classes as follows: Novice, Open, Junior, and Senior. For complete information on these competitions, you can send to the AKC for the booklet: *Junior Showmanship - Regulations, Judging Guidelines and Guidelines for Jun-*

*iors.* This competition encourages family participation in the sport and, in many cases, serves as a starting point for future breeders, exhibitors, professional handlers, and dog show judges. One such BHCA family that came up this route and that remains active in the sport today, is the family of Mr. Donald Martin of Northwood Basset Hounds. Bryan Martin, the oldest son, qualified for the Junior Finals at the Westminster Kennel Club for 14 consecutive years. Today Bryan is a professional handler. His brother, Peter C.J. Martin is an AKC-approved judge of several Hound breeds and Junior Showmanship, as well. Sister Heidi Martin is a most capable dog handler in her own right and did all of the full rendered drawings, design, and layout of *The Basset Hound Illustrated Standard.*

*Heidi B. Martin, placing in the 1980 Junior Showmanship Finals at the Westminster Kennel Club show. Standing, L to R., Judge Edd Bivin, Len Brumby, Jr., Bryan Martin, Peter C. J. Martin and Paul Nigro.*

# GALLERY OF NATIONAL SPECIALTY CONFORMATION WINNERS 1960-1998

*This section is to honor those hounds and their owners who have been selected at the Basset Hound Club of America annual National Specialty shows, as either BOB, BOS to BOB, BW, and/or WD/WB, between 1960 and 1998. This is indeed a significant milestone, for both the hounds and their owners, and is an achievement sought after by every seriously active member of the club. Many aspire, but relatively few achieve.*

## CONGRATULATIONS TO ALL!

# 1960

**Best of Breed:**
## CH. THE RINGS BRUNHILDE

**Breeder-owners:**
**Mary Lees and Robert Noerr**

*Photo Not Available.*

**Best of Opposite Sex:**
## CH. THE RINGS CHOLMONDLEY

**Breeders:**
**Mary Lees and Robert Noerr**

**Owner:**
**Kazoo Kennels**

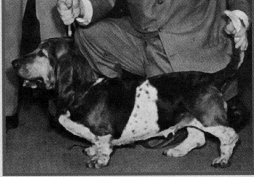

**Best of Winners:**
## HARTSHEAD BELLE DE NANCY

**Breeder-owner:**
**Hartshead Knl., Reg. (Seitz)**

**Winners Dog:**
## HOLLERHOUND FOREVER AMBLE

**Owners:**
**Clifford and Margaret M. Warren**

**Best of Breed:**
CH. LYN MAR ACRES TOP BRASS

**Breeder-owner-handler:**
Lyn Mar Acres Knl., (Walton)

**Best of Opposite Sex:**
ABBOT RUN VALLEY FIONA

**Owners:**
Roger Fredette and
Marjorie M. Brandt

**Best of Winners:**
ABBOT RUN VALLEY FIONA

**Owner:**
Roger Fredette and
Marjorie M. Brandt

**Winners Dog:**
DO-CY-BO'S ESQUIRE

**Breeder:**
Mrs. C. M. Bowers

**Owner:**
Randell Gable

**Best of Breed:**
CH. LYN MAR ACRES BALLYHOO

**Breeder-owner-handler:**
Lyn Mar Acres Knl., (Walton)

**Best of Opposite Sex:**
CH. GLADSTONE OF MANDEVILLE

**Breeder-owner-handlers:**
Mr. and Mrs. Paul Nelson

**Best of Winners:**
TALLEYRAND'S KEENE

**Breeder-owners:**
Robert and Kathryn Ellenberger

**Winners Bitch:**
SANTANA MANDEVILLE'S OLIVIA

**Breeder-owner-handlers:**
Mr. and Mrs. Paul Nelson

# 1963

**Best of Breed:**
CH. JESSE JAMES OF ELEANDON

**Breeder-handler:**
P. Saucier

**Owners:**
N. and M. A. Polizzi

**Best of Opposite Sex:**
CH. DOUBLE B'S VERONICA

**Owner:**
Christine B. Boutell

**Best of Winners:**
KAZOO'S HAPPY HARRIET

**Breeder-owner-handler:**
Kazoo Knl. Reg., (Shields)

**Winners Dog:**
MANOR HILL TOP SPOT

**Breeder-owners:**
Joan and Ronald Scholz

**Best of Breed:**
## CH. HUNTING HORN NOAH #251

**Breeder-owner:**
**Charles and Priscilla Gillespie**

**Best of Opposite Sex:**
## RICHARDSON'S HELLO DOLLY

**Breeder-owner:**
**David B. Richardson**

**Best of Winners:**
## BRIGADIER'S GENERAL MARK

**Breeder-owners:**
**Alvin and Anna Tiedemann**

**Winners Bitch:**
## RICHARDSON'S HELLO DOLLY

**Breeder-owner:**
**David B. Richardson**

# 1965

**Best of Breed:**
## CH. RICHARDSON'S HELLO DOLLY

**Owners:**
**Dr. and Mrs. Lyle H. Cain**

**Best of Opposite Sex:**
## CH. GALWAY'S MESHAK

**Breeder-owner:**
**Elizabeth Dexter**

**Best of Winners:**
## MAVERICK OF ROCKIN-PAS

**Breeder-owner-handler:**
**Paul A. Saucier**

**Winners Bitch:**
## JULIE OF ROCKIN-PAS

**Owners:**
**Tom and Miriam Surles**

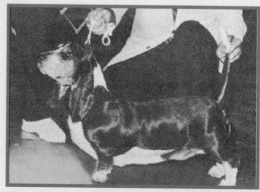

195

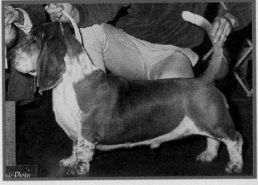

**Best of Breed:**
CH. KAZOO'S GALLOPING GITCH

Breeder-owner-handler:
Kazoo Knl. Reg. (Shields)

**Best of Opposite Sex:**
JAGERSVEN GIGI

Breeder-owner-handlers:
F. and M. L. Bergishagen

**Best of Winners:**
JAGERSVEN GIGI

Breeder-owner-handlers:
F. and M. L. Bergishagen

**Winners Dog:**
MARGEM HILLS SIR TRAMP

Owner-handler:
Margretta Patterson

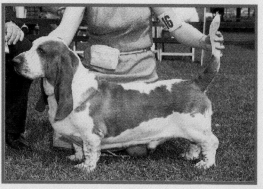

**Best of Breed:**
CH. MANOR HILL
FRINGE BENEFIT

Owner:
James Grinder

**Best of Opposite Sex:**
HOUNDSVILLE DEEJA-DO-IT

Owners:
Emil J. and Bernice D. Witowski

Breeder:
Major W. Kelly

**Best of Winners:**
HOUNDSVILLE DEEJA-DO-IT

Owners:
Emil J. and Bernice D. Witowski

Breeder:
Major W. Kelly

**Winners Dog:**
HUNT'S TOP ACE OF
HIDDEN LODGE

Owner:
James L. Bruet

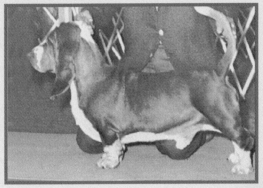

**Best of Breed:**
## CH. GOVERNOR'S CHESTER KLUTCH

**Breeder-owner:**
Jean Kraucunas

**Best of Opposite Sex:**
## CH. MUSICLAND'S PERFIDIA

**Breeder:**
Jeanne (Dudley) Hills

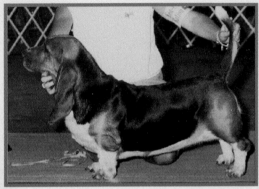

**Best of Winners:**
## GIN DICS BIT O' HONEY

**Breeder-owner:**
Virginia Lemieux

**Winners Dog:**
## FLORY'S MUSIC MAN

**Breeder-owner:**
Grace Flory

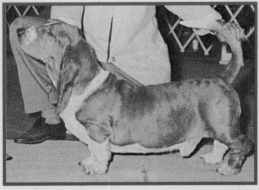

# 1969

**Best of Breed:**
## CH. RICHARDSON'S
## PADRIAC OF CUAS

**Breeder:**
D. Richardson

**Owners:**
Mrs. J. and Joanne Lynch

**Best of Opposite Sex:**
## CH. CORALWOOD'S
## COPPER PEG

**Breeder-owner-handler:**
William Barton

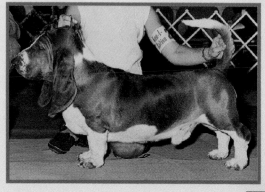

**Best of Winners:**
## MUSICLAND'S CASEY JONES

**Breeder-owner-handler:**
Jeanne (Dudley) Hills

**Winners Bitch:**
## MARGEM HILLS HOB GOBLIN

**Owners:**
John and Margretta Patterson

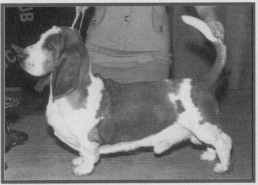

**Best of Breed:**
CH. RICHARDSON'S
PADRIAC OF CUAS

**Breeder:**
D. Richardson

**Owners:**
Mrs. J. and Joanne Lynch

**Best of Opposite Sex:**
CH. CORALWOOD'S
KADIDDLEHOPPER

**Breeder-owner-handler:**
William Barton

**Best of Winners:**
HUNDSWALD'S CINDER

**Owners:**
C. Formuth and Doris Hurry

**Winners Dog:**
SHADOW HILL
NOTORIOUS NORTON

**Owners:**
J. and C. Schadt

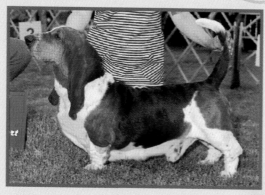

**Best of Breed:**
## CH. TAL-E-HO'S PRANCER

**Breeder-owner-handlers:**
Henry and Ann Jerman

**Best of Opposite Sex:**
## CH. MUSICLAND'S ANGEL EYES

**Breeder:**
Jeanne (Dudley) Hills

**Owner-handlers:**
Gene, Laraine, and Brenda
Scheiblauer

**Best of Winners:**
## DUSAN'S JASON

**Owner:**
Mae Schroeder

**Breeder:**
Paul Mohr

**Winners Bitch:**
## SUPAI'S MOONSHADOW

**Owner:**
James Bruet

**Best of Breed:**
## CH. GERONIMO OF ROCKIN-PAS

**Breeder:**
P. Saucier

**Owner-handler:**
Sandra Campbell

**Best of Opposite Sex:**
## CH. CORALWOOD'S KADDILEHOPPER

**Breeder-owner-handler:**
William Barton

**Best of Winners:**
## SNYDER'S BIG WILHOITE

**Owners:**
Mr. and Mrs. Terrence L. Snyder

**Winners Bitch:**
## MIKOL'S NICOLETTE

**Owners:**
Marcia M. and Richard A. Mikol

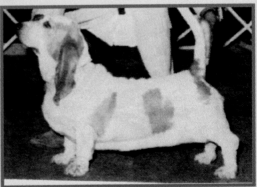

**Best of Breed:**
CH. MUSICLAND'S POOL SHARK

**Breeder-owner-handler:**
Jeanne (Dudley) Hills

**Best of Opposite Sex:**
CH. MARGEM HILLS GINGER FIZZ

**Owner:**
Jean Will

**Best of Winners:**
SANDELL'S ANASTASIA

**Breeder:**
W. Sandell

**Owner:**
BowRidge Knl. Reg'd (Bowman)

**Winners Dog:**
MEL ANN ACRES BIG MAC

**Breeder-owner-handlers:**
Mel and Ann Thain

# 1974

Best of Breed:
## CH. SLIPPERY HILL HUDSON

Breeders:
**L. and M. Skolnick**

Owner:
**Mrs. A. Robson**

Best of Opposite Sex:
## CH. WINDMAKER'S STORM WARNING

Breeder-owner-handlers:
**James and Wanda White**

Best of Winners:
## MARSHILLS WHEELER DEALER

Owner-handlers:
**D. Jones and Tom Underhill**

Winners Bitch:
## TANTIVY DOWNWIND

Breeder-owner-handler:
**Jane Luce**

**Best of Breed:**
CH. TAL-E-HO'S TOP BANANA

**Breeder:**
H. & A. Jerman

**Owner-handler:**
P. Martin

**Best of Opposite Sex:**
CH. SHADOWS SNOW WHITE

**Owner-handlers:**
Finn and Mary Louise Bergishagen

**Best of Winners:**
HALCYON LUMBERJACK

**Breeder-owner-handlers:**
L. & V. Steedle

**Winners Bitch:**
TAL-E-HO'S RED PEPPER

**Owner:**
H. & A. Jerman & Ed Smizer

**Best of Breed:**

## CH. TAL-E-HO'S TOP BANANA

**Breeder:**
H. & A. Jerman

**Owner-handler:**
P. Martin

**Best of Opposite Sex:**

## CH. TAL-E-HO'S RED PEPPER

**Owner:**
H. & A. Jerman & Ed Smizer

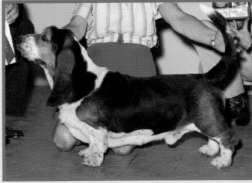

**Best of Winners:**

## SHERLOCK OF BUCKETT'S

**Breeder:**
P. Hirsch

**Owner:**
P. Hirsch & S. & D. Herzog

**Winners Bitch:**

## TAL-E-HO'S POSH

**Breeder-owner-handlers:**
H. & A. Jerman

**Best of Breed:**
## CH. DE ALO'S MARCH HARE
## V. SKAUTON

**Breeder:**
Ola DeGroat

**Owner:**
O. DeGroat & G. Towne

**Best of Opposite Sex:**
## CH. HOOPER-KNOLL'S
## DINAH-MITE

**Breeder-owner-handlers:**
D. Hooper & R. and S. Knollmiller

**Best of Winners:**
## HOOPER-KNOLL'S
## CAPT. FANTASTIC

**Breeder-owner-handler :**
R. & S. Knollmiller and D. Hooper

**Winners Bitch:**
## MUSICLAND'S FANNE FOXE

**Breeder-owner-handler:**
Jeanne (Dudley) Hills

**Best of Breed:**
CH. JAGERSVEN BLUE BANNER

**Breeder-owner-handlers:**
Finn and Mary Louise Bergishagen

**Best of Opposite Sex:**
CH. NORTHWOOD'S
BANANA PEAL

**Breeder-owner-handlers:**
P. C. J. & B. Martin

**Best of Winners:**
BRAUN'S SISTER MI-LIN

**Breeders:**
M. & L. Sosne

**Owners:**
J. & M. Braun

**Winners Dog:**
BUDSANDI'S SHAKE AND BAKE

**Breeders:**
W. & S. Smith

**Owner-handlers:**
S. Smith & E. Krzych

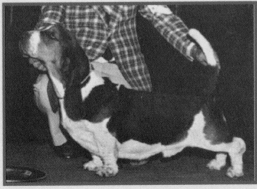

**Best of Breed:**
CH. HEINE VON SKAUTON

**Owner:**
Garry and Dawn Towne

**Best of Opposite Sex:**
CH. BLUVALI DOUBLE DELIGHT

**Owner:**
P. H. & M. Wikerd

**Best of Winners:**
BRUNCH'S CAPTAIN CRUNCH

**Breeder-owner-handler:**
K. Gilbertson & P. Wikerd

**Winners Bitch:**
CRAIGWOOD'S MEGAN

**Breeder:**
S. Campbell

**Owner-handler:**
Windmaker Knl, Reg. (White)

# 1980

**Best of Breed:**
CH. CRESCENDO'S
FOREST O'COCK

**Breeder-owner-handlers:**
R. & P. Bubb

**Best of Opposite Sex:**
CH. BLUVALI DOUBLE DELIGHT

**Owner:**
P. H. & M. Wikerd

**Best of Winners:**
HALCYON TATTLETALE

**Breeder-owner-handler:**
L. & V. Steedle

**Winners Dog:**
HET'S LORD BROWNING

**Breeder:**
R. Douglas

**Owner:**
H. P. Garwood

# 1981

**Best of Breed:**
CH. BELYN'S ROUSTABOUT

Breeders:
B. Bolch & D. Malenfant

Owner:
C. Bolch

**Best of Opposite Sex:**
CH. CRAIGWOOD'S BELLISSIMA

Breeders:
N. Taylor & S. Campbell

Owner:
S. Atwood

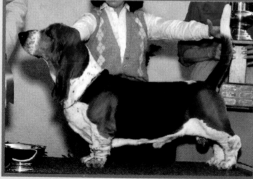

**Best of Winners:**
CRAIGWOOD'S GOING IN STYLE

Breeders:
J. & C. O'Bryant

Owner-handler:
J. Reynolds & S. Campbell

**Winners Bitch:**
RIO VISTA'S WRONG
PAJAMAS

Breeder-owner-handlers:
P. S. & B. A. Christian

**Best of Breed:**
CH. BELYN'S ROUSTABOUT

**Breeder-owner-handlers:**
B. Bolch & D. Malenfant

**Owner:**
C. Bolch

**Best of Opposite Sex:**
CH. JAQUARTS NONIE

**Breeder-owner-handlers:**
J. P. & C. C. Jaquart

**Best of Winners:**
SOLOW'S MAGNA BID
OF CRAIGWOOD

**Breeders:**
S. Campbell & N. Taylor

**Owners:**
L. Thompson & S. Campbell

**Winners Dog:**
HALCYON FIRECRACKER

**Breeder-owner-handlers:**
L. & V. Steedle

# 1983

**Best of Breed:**
## CH. HALCYON CRACKERJACK

**Breeders:**
L. & V. Steedle

**Owner-handlers:**
Ed Smizer & Gwen McCullagh

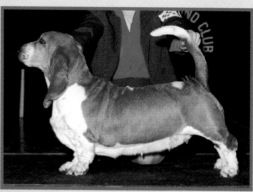

**Best of Opposite Sex:**
## CH. HEATHROW'S CLASSIC IMAGE

**Breeder-owner-handlers:**
R .C. & P. M. Waterhouse

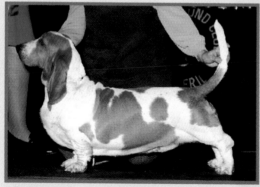

**Winners Bitch:**
## STONEYBLUFF LADY JANE

**Breeder-owner-handlers:**
V. & F. Kovalic

**Winners Dog:**
## BEAUJANGLE'S JAS'N O'BELFORREST

**Breeders:**
J. Williams, D. Malenfant, C. Lane

**Owners:**
P. & B. Belanger

**Handler:**
Pete Weaver

213

**Best of Breed:**
CH. SWITCHBARK'S ASHMORE

**Breeders:**
J. & C. O'Bryant

**Owner-handler:**
Hiflite Knl. Reg.
(Booth)

**Best of Opposite Sex:**
CH. SANCHU'S BAGUETTE
OF MARGETT

**Breeders:**
C. K. & C. A. Steidel

**Owner-handlers:**
M. & M. Hargett & C. K. Steidel

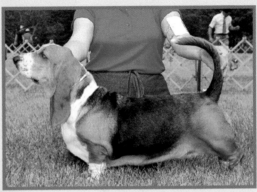

**Best of Winners:**
LOCHOPT RUM RIKKI

**Breeder-owner-handlers:**
R. A. & B. H. Cromley

**Winners Bitch:**
MATILDA BEAU CHEIN

**Breeders:**
J. & J. Fabac

**Owners:**
H. P. Garwood

**Handler:**
J. Webb

**Best of Breed:**
## CH. STONEWALL ROXANNE

**Breeder-owner-handlers:**
R. J. & N. M. Opeka

**Best of Opposite Sex:**
## CH. LOCHOPT RUM RIKKI

**Breeder-owner-handlers:**
R. A. & B. H. Cromley

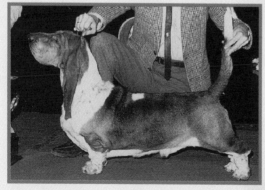

**Best of Winners:**
## SCHEEL'S FIRST EDITION

**Breeder-owner-handlers:**
Birte & Kresten Scheel

**Winners Bitch:**
## FORT MERRILL MARILYN

**Breeder-owner-handler:**
Joan Urban

**Best of Breed:**
CH. BELYN'S ROUSTABOUT

Breeder-owner-handlers:
B. Bolch & D. Malenfant

Owner:
C. Bolch

**Best of Opposite Sex:**
CH. MUSICLAND'S JESSAMINE

Breeder-owner-handler:
Jeanne Hills

**Best of Winners:**
ROME-ING POLKA O'THOMPSON

Breeders:
Mr. & Mrs. L. Thompson

Owner-handler:
M. & J. Manning & D. Whitney

**Winners Dog:**
JAQUART'S WALTER
WONDERFUL

Breeder-owner-handlers:
J. & C. Jaquart

**Best of Breed:**
CH. BRASSTAX ROBIN
OF LOCKSLEY

**Breeders:**
G. Seifman & V. Steedle

**Owner:**
G. Seifman

**Handler:**
B. Martin

**Best of Opposite Sex:**
CH. STONEYBLUFF GERTRUDE

**Breeder-owners:**
V. & F. Kovalic

**Handler:**
G. McCullagh

**Best of Winners:**
BRIERWOOD BRIGAND

**Breeders:**
C. C. & S . J. Launey

**Owners:**
C. C. & S. J. Launey & Cheryl Fisher

**Handler:**
Sanda Launey

**Winners Bitch:**
ALLENHILL'S BEA SWEET

**Breeder-owner-handlers:**
Kevin and Sally Allen

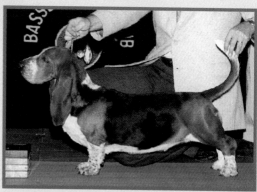

**Best of Breed:**
CH. STONEYBLUFF GERTRUDE

**Breeder-owner-handlers:**
V. & F. Kovalic

**Handler:**
G. McCullagh

**Best of Opposite Sex:**
CH. STONEWALL J.F.K.

**Breeder-owner-handlers:**
R. J. & N. M. Opeka

**Best of Winners:**
MISTY MEADOWS CONLAN

**Breeder-owner-handler:**
Joan M. Diebler

**Winners Dog:**
LONGBAY NIGHT CAP

**Breeders:**
J. & C. Huggins

**Owner-handlers:**
F. & M. L. Bergishagen

**Best of Breed:**
CH. STONEYBLUFF GERTRUDE

**Breeder-owner-handlers:**
V. & F. Kovalic

**Handler:**
G. McCullagh

**Best of Opposite Sex:**
CH. HALCYON TAILGATER

**Breeder-owner-handlers:**
L. & V. Steedle

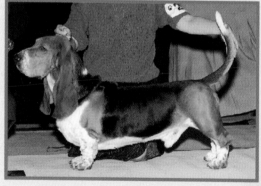

**Best of Winners:**
CANTERBURY'S LORD ELWOOD

**Breeder:**
Diane Bowden

**Owner:**
S. & P. Moffet

**Handler:**
Pat Willer

**Winners Bitch:**
FORT MERRILL HOLLY

**Breeder-owner:**
Joan Urban

**Handler:**
Bryan Martin

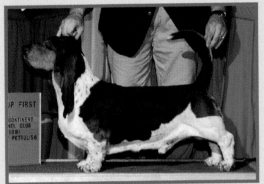

**Best of Breed:**

CH. AMBRICAN LIPIZZAN

**Breeder:**
P.C. Frederiksen

**Owners:**
B. Salyers & P. & R. Frederiksen

**Handler:**
N. Martin

**Best of Opposite Sex:**

CH. SANCHU'S KIZZY

**Breeder-owner-handlers:**
M. Brandolino & K. Steidel

**Best of Winners:**

LIL' CREEK BRIARCREST
TOP GUN

**Breeders:**
D. Christiansen & K. Williams

**Owner-handlers:**
Dan & Julie Jones

**Winners Bitch:**

CRAIGWOOD SEA BREEZE
CHLOE

**Breeders:**
F. Vassy & S. H. Campbell

**Owner-handlers:**
Norman & Mary Ann Wiginton

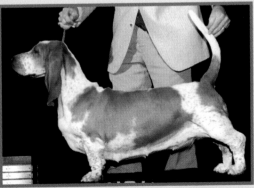

# 1991

**Best of Breed:**
## CH. HALCYON TAILGATER

**Breeder-owner-handlers:**
L. & V. Steedle

**Best of Opposite Sex:**
## CH. CRAIGWOOD FOUR OAKS SPARKLE

**Breeder:**
S. H. Campbell & D. Martin

**Owner:**
S. Campbell

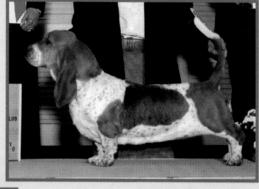

**Best of Winners:**
## SCHEEL'S RIVEREDGE RUBBER DUCK

**Breeders:**
B. & K. Scheel

**Owners:**
H. & S. Scully, E. Smizer,
& B. & K. Scheel

**Winners Bitch:**
## RAN-SU'S DEVON

**Breeder:**
S. Suftin

**Owner-handlers:**
S. Suftin & J. Caito

# 1992

**Best of Breed:**
CH. SIR ETHAN'S
BASIL OF HEATHROW

**Breeders:**
M. & T. Dyde

**Owners:**
R. C. & P. M. Waterhouse & H. J.
Pybus

**Handler:** H. J. Pybus

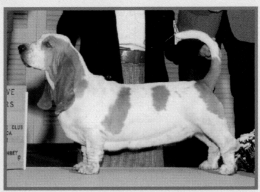

**Best of Opposite Sex:**
CH. CRAIGWOOD'S KELSEY

**Breeder-owner-handler:**
Sandra Campbell

**Best of Winners:**
SILVERADO SIOUXZIE

**Breeders:**
M. Brandolino & K. Steidel

**Owner-handler:**
M. Brandolino

**Winners Dog:**
HIFLITE'S RAGS TO RICHES

**Breeder-owner-handler:**
Hiflite Knl., Reg. (Booth)

**Best of Breed:**
CH. SANCHU'S HOT TODDY

**Breeder-owner:**
Kitty Steidel

**Handler:**
Mike Stone

**Best of Opposite Sex:**
CH. CRAIGWOOD SOLOW
HOBBY KNOX

**Breeder-owners:**
S. Campbell & L. Cain

**Best of Winners:**
CASTLEHILL'S AVA GARDENER

**Breeder-owner-handlers:**
Jim & Sharon Dok

**Winners Dog:**
BOW-RIDGE'S VARLEY

**Breeder-owner-handlers:**
Roxanna & Louis Bowman

# 1994

**Best of Breed:**
## CH. DEALO'S LEHI FYRE DRAGON

**Breeder:**
Ola DeGroat

**Owners:**
C. Ceneviva

**Handler:**
D. Towne

**Best of Opposite Sex:**
## CH. FORT MERRILL LIPZ STICK

**Breeder-owner:**
Joan Urban

**Handler:**
Bryan Martin

**Winners Bitch:**
## FOXGLEN RED HOT WHEELS

**Breeder-owner-handlers:**
Scott Deans & Betsy Batchelder

**Winners Dog:**
## THE EDITOR'S SPAGHETTI

**Breeders:**
S. F. Bouchard & J. R. Tysseling

**Owners:**
Dr. & Mrs. M. Sinkoff
& S. F. Bouchard

**Best of Breed:**
CH. RAN-SU'S DEVON

**Breeder:**
S. Suftin

**Owner-handlers:**
S. Suftin & J. Caito

**Best of Opposite Sex:**
CH. SASQUATCH
THUNDERBOLT N LITEFOOT

**Breeder-owner-handlers:**
Barbara Brandt & Donna Coker

**Best of Winners:**
HIFLITE'S ULTRABRITE

**Breeder-owner:**
Hiflite Knl. Reg. (Booth)

**Handler:**
Vicki Steedle

**Winners Dog:**
INGRAM'S KASPAR

**Breeders:**
Diane & Hayes Ingram

**Owners:**
Dee Duffy & D. & H. Ingram

**Handler:**
Hayes Ingram

**Best of Breed:**
## CH. BY-U-CALS RAZZLE DAZZLE

**Breeder-owner-handlers:**
Sharon & Steve Calhoun

**Co-Owners:**
Alyce & Richard Gilmore

**Best of Opposite Sex:**
## CH. ELYSIAN FORGET-ME-NOT

**Breeders:**
M.L. Graves & Leslie Newman

**Owner:**
Mary Lou Graves

**Handler:**
G. McCullagh

**Best of Winners:**
## AMERICAN TRADEMARK

**Breeder:**
R. & P. Frederiksen

**Owner:**
Mrs. Bert Salyers

**Handlers:**
B. Martin & B. Barringer

**Winners Bitch:**
## STONEYBLUFF KATHERINE

**Breeder-owners:**
Virginia & Frank Kovalic

**Handlers:**
B. Martin & G. McCullagh

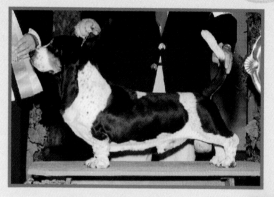

**Best of Breed:**
CH. DEER HILL'S GREAT GATSBY

Breeder-owner:
Archie & Carole Kintner

Handler:
Bryan Martin

**Best of Opposite Sex:**
CH. BY-U-CAL'S RAZZLE DAZZLE

Breeder-owners:
Sharon & Steve Calhoun

Co-Owners:
Alyce & Richard Gilmore

Handler:
Pat Willer

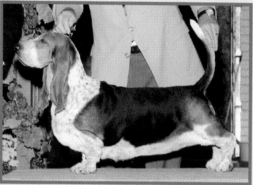

**Best of Winners:**
MISTY MEADOWS ASPIRATION

Breeder-owner-handler:
Joan M. Deibler

**Winners Dog:**
BY-U-CALS EXTRA EXTRA

Breeder-owner-handlers:
Sharon & Steve Calhoun

Co-Owners:
Alyce & Richard Gilmore

**Best of Breed:**
CH. BY-U-CAL'S RAZZLE DAZZLE

**Breeder-owner-handlers:**
Sharon & Steve Calhoun

**Co-owners:**
Alyce & Richard Gilmore

**Best of Opposite Sex:**
CH. DEER HILL'S GREAT GATSBY

**Breeders:**
Archie & Carole Kintner

**Owner:**
Gilbert Kahn

**Handler:**
Bryan Martin

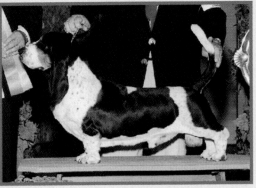

**Best of Winners:**
DEER HILL'S LICORICE

**Breeder-owners:**
Archie & Carole Kintner

**Handler:**
Bryan Martin

**Winners Dog:**
FORT MERRILL FULL MONTY

**Breeder:**
Joan Urban

**Owner-handlers:**
J. Greenland & M. Stover

# Obedience

The Basset Hound has a reputation, to some degree, of not being an intelligent breed. A lack of trainability is one of the often used explanations as to why there are so few Bassets currently competing in obedience trials. This mindset, however, is absolutely false. The truth is that they *are* very intelligent. In fact, they have taught themselves many "tricks" to help them get their way. One well-planned snuggle, a flop on their back asking for a belly rub, or (their ultimate weapon) one sad look from their big brown eyes, and their owners melt away and stop insisting that they do a task that they find of no value. Of course, as humans, we don't want to admit that our Basset Hound can train us better than we can train them, hence their reputation. Despite what you may have believed up to this point, Basset Hounds have had quite a respectful and full history covering over 35 years in the realm of obedience.

## WHAT IS OBEDIENCE?

Obedience is simply a dog following directions or commands from a handler. To test this ability, AKC has devised competitive events called trials where a handler and dog are judged on their performance. There are three levels: Novice, Open, and Utility. Novice is the beginning level. It can be best equated with grammar school. Dogs are tested on their ability to individually perform the basic obedience skills of the heel on and off lead, stand for examination, and the recall. There are also group exercises which include a one-minute long sit and a three-minute long down, with the owners stationed across the ring. Open competition is the equivalent of high school. The exercises are more complex. The dog is required to heel off lead, drop on recall, retrieve on flat, retrieve over a high jump, and perform the broad jump. The group exercises for this level include a three-minute long sit and a

*Margot Fontaine UD, owned by Joy Parker, early in her obedience training days.*

229

five-minute long down, with the handlers out of sight. Although there are no group exercises, Utility is still considered the most difficult level. Exercises include the signal exercise, scent discrimination, the directed retrieve, moving stand for examination, and directed jumping. Utility is very much like "doggy college." As with people, every dog is not cut out for it.

Competitive teams of dog and handler are scored on a point system. Each exer-

three legs, the dog qualifies for its obedience title. At the Novice level, that is a Companion Dog, or CD, title. For Open, it is called Companion Dog Excellent, or CDX. At the Utility level, the dog would receive a Utility Dog title, or UD. These title initials are permanently added to the end of the dog's name and are part of its official AKC record. The more advanced title will supersede the preceding title. Above Utility there are still two obedience titles that can be achieved.

*Three of the five High in Trial winners at the BHCA Nationals: Santana Briget, UDT, mother of Bridlespur Nudger, UDT, HIT Nationals winner, 1968–1972; Buzz Taylor's Hopalong, UDT, HIT winner at the 1974 Nationals; and Buzz Taylor's Autumn UDT, the 1973 Nationals HIT winner. Autumn is still the only Basset Hound to place (7th Place) in a classic for all-breeds.*

cise has a certain point value allotted to it, and all the exercises at each level add up to 200 points. Points are lost through errors made by either the dog or the handler during the exercises. The severity of the deduction depends on the type of error committed. For instance, a crooked sit may be only a half-point deduction, where as a double command by the handler, or lack of response by the dog, would lose all of the points for that exercise.

A perfect score is 200, and a qualifying score is 170 with at least half of the points available earned in each exercise. Dogs that successfully receive a qualifying score achieve what is called a "leg." By achieving

The Utility Dog Excellent, or UDX, title is for dogs that achieve ten additional passing scores in both Open B and Utility classes at the same shows. The UDX was established by the AKC in the 1990s. Although there are several Bassets that are well on their way, there have been no Basset Hound that has achieved this prestigious title.

The ultimate obedience title is that of OTCh., or Obedience Trial Champion. This is also the only obedience title that can be added as a prefix to the dog's name. OTCh. points are awarded to only the first- or second-place dogs competing in Open B and Utility B, and are based on how many dogs are competing in each category. There is a minimum number of dogs required to compete before points are even awarded. To win this title, the dog must already have a UD degree and earn a total of 100 OTCh. points. The dog must also receive a minimum of three first placements, and at least one first place in both Open B and Utility B competition.

## HISTORY

When looking at the history of Basset Hounds in obedience, one has to be aware of a major change regarding competition that came about in the mid-1960s. Prior to this time, Basset Hounds, along with most other breeds, were required to jump one-and-one-half times their height at the withers over the high jump, and twice that distance over the broad jump. Although there were some notable exceptions, due to the low-slung and heavy construction of our breed, many Basset Hound enthusiasts refused to take a chance of their dogs' injuring themselves and opted not to compete beyond the Novice class.

Lulu's Red became the first Basset Hound to achieve a CD degree in 1959. He was soon followed by his brother, Lulu's Patches. These two litter brothers were the first two Basset Hounds purchased by Marge and Walter Brandt. The Brandts would eventually be well known for their conformation dogs under their kennel name Abbot Run Valley. Patches eventually became the first Basset to achieve a CDX title, and in addition, he became a conformation champion.

In 1960, Buzz Taylor purchased his first Basset Hound from the Bridlespur Hunt Club. Bridlespur Nudger UD, became the number-one rated obedience Basset for seven years. For five of those years, the number-two Basset in obedience was Santana Briget UD, also owned and trained by Mr. Taylor. Bred together, they produced three obedience title winners including Buzz Taylor's Hopalong UDT and Buzz Taylor's Autumn UDT. Both of these hounds would eventually win High In Trial awards at the Basset Hound Club of America National

*Buzz Taylor heeling Buzz Taylor's Zibbelene UDT. Note the eye contact. This bitch never lagged, she always kept perfect heel position.*

Specialty. Autumn even placed seventh in the Super Dog class at the first Chicago Gaines Classic (an invitational competition for the top obedience dogs in the country). To date, Autumn is the only Basset hound to have ever placed in the Super Dog class at a Gaines Classic.

The most famous Basset Hound in the obedience world was OTCh. Buzz Taylor's Goober UD. A grandson of Nudger and Briget, and son of Autumn, he was the first, and to date, only Basset to achieve the coveted title of Obedience Trial Champion. Buzz Taylor's Zibbilean CDX, a Goober daughter, was the last Basset to be trained by Mr. Taylor. Cut short due to back problems, her career included three High In Trial awards and multiple first placements. "Zibb" placed fourth in Novice competition at the Gaines Regional in 1984, and third in Open competition at the 1985 Gaines Regional. This makes her the only Basset to have ever placed twice at a Gaines Regional, to date. Both "Goober" and "Zibbi" traveled throughout the country with Buzz giving obedience demonstrations and conducting training seminars.

In 1963, there was a grass roots effort spearheaded by Benjamin Harris of California to revise jump-height requirements for the breed. Through his persistence, a committee was formed by BHCA in 1964. Mr. Harris was appointed chairman, and the committee began to look into many obedience exhibitors' concerns. Through years of hard work, research, and diligence, the goal

*OTCh. Buzz Taylor's Goober UDT. Goober is the only Basset Hound to ever become an Obedience Trial Champion. He is the son and grandson of all the Buzz Taylor Bassets before him.*

of lower jump heights was finally achieved. AKC amended the official obedience regulations in June, 1969 to what they are today. Basset Hounds are currently required to jump the nearest multiple of 2 inches to the height of the dog at the withers over the high jump, and twice that distance over the broad jump.

The 1960s was quite the "golden era" of Bassets in obedience. There was an increased interest in obedience among Basset Hound owners across the country. The banner year was 1966, when prior to the reduction of jump heights, 13 Bassets earned their UD degrees. In 1968, BHCA expanded their National Specialty to include an obedience trial. In the first five trials, from 1968 to 1972, the highest scoring dog at the Nationals trial was Bridlespur Nudger UD.

Other pioneers of obedience include Joan Thurlow of California, Billy and Lena Wray from Florida, Marge Cook of Texas, and Shirley Hiatt of North Carolina. There are many other truly dedicated people from around the country that have contributed in obedience throughout the past and/or are currently competing.

## HOW TO GET STARTED

I am often asked how early one should start training their Basset. My answer is always the same, "You already started when you first brought him home!" Your Basset is learning things from you whether you want him to or not. Thus the positive and negative experiences you instill in your new puppy can influence him for life. If there is one golden rule about Bassets, it is that their brain is directly connected to their stomach. Cookie training works well on both puppies and adults. In addition, there should be no formal training sessions and no strict corrections for young puppies as they do not have an adequate attention span to tolerate this. Even with older dogs, it is best to sprinkle several training sessions throughout the day. This will make your Basset eager to perform these tasks for you, and it will instill a good working attitude throughout his life.

*Ch. Linpet's "A" Is For Abercrobmie CDX. "Abbie" is shown practicing for the Open competition. Note the obvious effort and intensity he displays.*

There are many fine books available that are totally devoted to teaching obedience. Obviously, they are able to give you much more detailed instruction on how to train your dog than just this one chapter. For the person truly interested in becoming involved in obedience, it is strongly recommended that you sign up for training classes. This will give you one-on-one time with a trainer who can answer your questions, as well as present you and your dog with many distractions. Classes will also provide a neutral training environment with a group of strange dogs.

Equipment that you will need is relatively inexpensive and available at any pet-supply outlet. I recommend a small-link-chain slip collar, often referred to as a choke chain, and a six-foot leather or nylon lead. I prefer

a chain collar as your dog will soon learn to respond to the noise of the chain when corrections are made. The collar should not have more than two inches of excess links when tightened around your dog's neck. This way when you reach down close to your dog's collar to make a correction, you will be holding the lead close to the snap instead of the chain. Remember, never leave this collar on the dog when you are not working him. Slip collars, both chain and nylon, are dangerous as the rings can catch under a fence or between the crack of a deck and could strangle your dog in a matter of minutes.

To put the collar on properly, hold it out in front of you. The lead should be attached to one end. Slip the chain through the ring on the other end. The lead end of the collar should be held in your left hand, and the circle part of the collar should be in your right hand. It should form a horizontal "P" with the loop hanging down. Slip the collar over the dog's head. The part of the chain attached to the lead must go over the top of your dog's neck when he is sitting on your left side. This way the chain will release easily after it is jerked tight.

There is, of course, some simple training that you can do at home. Teaching your Basset obedience, or house manners, will only make him easier to live with. Here are a few commands that you can teach your dog in a relatively short time.

**Sit:** This exercise starts with your Basset standing in front of you. Hold a cookie in your right hand above your dog's head *(you will eventually use your right hand for the sit signal)*. Tell your dog to "Sit" as you move the cookie away from you and toward his back. Gravity being what it is, your dog will have to sit to keep his keen little eyes on that cookie. Obviously, with a positive reaction, he gets the cookie (or piece of it). If your dog jumps up in an attempt to grab the cookie, say, "No," and take the cookie away. Wait a few seconds until he calms down and is watching you, and then start over again. Another method starts with your dog on your left side. Tell him to sit and pull up on his lead with your right hand. With your left hand, reach down your dog's back to just in front of his hip bones. Squeeze inward with your thumb and middle finger as you gently apply downward pressure. You are pushing in on nerve pressure points, and the dog will generally sit quickly.

**Stay:** When your dog will sit on command, you can move on to the stay. Have your dog sit on your left side. Tell him, "Stay," and give him a hand signal by placing your right palm in front of your dog's nose. Step out in front of your dog using your right foot. If your dog gets up, correct him by giving short jerks upward on the lead with your right hand directly above his head and telling him to "Sit." When your dog is secure with you standing right in front of him, start backing away until you are at the end of the lead.

When you return to your dog, move directly back to your original position. Eventually you will walk completely around behind your dog so that you again end up with him on your left side. If your dog gets up, or shifts his body as you are moving around him, correct him from where you are, and make sure that he is put back into his original sitting position. Of course, when you are done with this exercise, don't forget to give him plenty of praise.

**Heel:** Start with your Basset sitting on your left side. Give the command, "Heel," and take off walking with your left foot. Walk briskly, and keep encouraging your dog to stay in position, his shoulders aligned with your left leg. When you stop, have your dog sit, again aligned with your left leg. If your dog wanders out of position, give him several sharp jerks on the lead while repeating the heel command until he returns to your left side. If he loses interest and/or starts to sniff the ground, give him a correction with the lead or change direction. You can turn to your right or left, or even totally about (remember to turn to your right so your dog goes around you). Keep a brisk pace and give your dog constant praise to keep up his interest and his attention.

**Down:** Basset owners have a distinct disadvantage with this exercise due to our dog's stubby little legs; but what the heck, what's another challenge! Start with your Basset sitting at your left side. Tell him, "Down!" At the same time, grab the top of the lead closest to the collar with your right hand and give it a sharp pop downward. If there is no response from the dog, take hold of his right front leg at the elbow with your right hand and slide it forward. With your left hand, put pressure on his shoulders and gently push him off balance to his right. If necessary, use your left arm and elbow against the side of his body to help guide him down. When he is lying down *preferably on his right hip*, he gets a cookie. The down is a very defenseless position. Depending on your dog's confidence level, this exercise may take a bit more perseverance than the other exercises.

**Recall:** Before you teach the recall, your dog should already be solid on the sit and stay. There are actually two parts to this exercise. The come and the finish. Start with your dog sitting on your left side. Tell him, "Stay," walk out to the end of the lead, turn and face him. Tell your dog, "Come," and reel in the lead toward you. Your dog should end up sitting straight in front of you. If you need, you can take several steps backward to help encourage him to come to you or correct a crooked sit. The end of this exercise is called the "finish." With your dog sitting in front of you, tell him, "Heel." Your dog should get up and swing his body to your left. He needs to end up sitting in heel position (aligned with your left leg). Some people teach their dogs to walk completely around behind them to end up on their left. This is acceptable also. In fact, it is very useful to teach your dog both ways to finish. Just remember to use a different command for the other version, like "Flip" or "Swing." This way the dog will not get confused.

**Here and Heap:** There are two other commands that most people teach all of their dogs. The "Here" command means simply to "get over here" (the command word used is the option of the trainer). It should be anything but "Come," as this will eventually mean a formal exercise ending with a straight sit in front of the handler. The "Here" should be taught when your dog is on lead. When he becomes interested in something other than you, tell him, "Here," and give him a gentle pop with the lead. When he comes to you, give him lots of praise and a cookie. Continue to repeat the exercise until the pop of the lead is no longer needed.

The "Heap" command is very similar to the down, and taught the same way, but the position is less restrictive. To your dog, it should mean to stay in a lying position, although he can still sniff, shift, roll, lie on his back, or fall asleep. Again, the command word is optional. You will really appreciate your Basset knowing this exercise when company comes to visit or when you are out with your dog and don't want him in your lap.

*U-CD Red Bay Blushing Roxanne CGC, CDX, OA, owned by Arnold and Marcia Krause, is retrieving over the high jump. Roxanne is owned by Marcia and Arnold Krause of Canoga Park, California.*

## AGILITY

One of the newest performance sports to hit the dog world is agility. Basically, it is a competition where dogs are run through an obstacle course. There are several organizations that run trials and give out titles, following their own rules. For the sake of consistency, we will only talk about agility as it is conducted by the American Kennel Club.

division. Dogs 14 inches and under at the withers (which covers most Basset Hounds) are in the 12-inch division. The 16-inch division is for dogs who are 18 inches and under at the withers. Dogs 22 inches and under will compete in the 24-inch division

There are 16 types of obstacles that can be used on a course: a dogwalk, seesaw, A-frame, pause table, open tunnel, closed tunnel, single-bar jumps, other single jumps,

*U-CD Red Bay Blushing Roxanne CGC, CDX, OA, practicing for agility competition.*

Through AKC, there are three levels of competitive agility: Novice, Open, and Excellent. The Novice course has the fewest obstacles, a total of 12 to 13, with 10 mandatory obstacles and no weave poles. The Open course will have 15 to 17 obstacles with 11 mandatory obstacles, and is designed with more complexity and added difficulty. The Excellent courses have 18 to 20 obstacles and are designed with the most difficulty. Each level is separated into five divisions dictated by the required jump heights. Dogs 10 inches and under, at the withers, are in the 8-inch

panel jump, double oxer jump, triple oxer jump, tire (circle) jump, window jump, broad jump, and weave poles. The dogwalk, seesaw, and A-frame are considered contact obstacles. Contact zones are designated areas at both ends of the obstacle and are painted a different color. The dog is required to touch the contact zones on these obstacles to receive a qualifying run. The pause table is usually set in the middle of the course. The dog is required to jump up on it, and lie down or sit (at the discretion of the judge) for five seconds.

The runs are timed and there is a maximum time limit allotted for the dog to run the course. Like obedience, the dog-handler teams start out with a perfect score. In agility, a perfect score is 100 points. Deductions are marked if the dog goes off course, balks at an obstacle, or takes an excessive amount of time to run the course. The dog-handler team is considered to be eliminated if the handler runs the wrong course or touches an obstacle or the dog, if the dog or handler knocks down any obstacle or jump, if the dog refuses the same obstacle more than the maximum limit in the class, misses a contact point, performs three wrong courses in any class, or jumps off the seesaw prior to reaching the end of the board. Faults so severe that they require mandatory excusing include the dog's leaving the course area and discontinuing working, excessive handling and harsh commands or corrections, dog's fouling the ring at any time during the run, failure to per-

*Roxanne acquired her Open agility title in 1996, becoming the first Basset Hound to acquire this AKC title. Roxanne is owned by Marcia and Arnold Krause of Canoga Park, California.*

*Roxanne displays her prowess on an agility teeter-totter.*

*Roxanne was the number-one obedience Basset Hound for 1993 and 1995 under the Delaney System.*

form a contact obstacle, or taking more than the maximum time limit to run the course.

A qualifying score is considered a minimum of 85 points within the time limit. Each qualifying score is awarded a "leg," and three legs qualify the dog for a title. NA, or Novice Agility, is the first title awarded to dogs on the beginning level. OA, or Open Agility, and AX, or Agility Excellent, are the next two advanced titles. The MX, or Master Agility Excellent title, is earned after the dog has acquired the Agility Excellent title and has earned qualifying scores in the Agility Excellent class at ten additional trials. As in obedience, the titles will be added to the end of the dog's name, and the highest title will supersede the preceding title.

Each course is designed by the judge using a variety of the mandatory and additional obstacles. Contestants do not know what the course will look like, or what obstacles will be used on the course until the day of the trial. There is a warm-up period prior to the runs when handlers entered in that class can walk through the course and map out their strategy. In the Novice class, the dogs may be taken on the course at a designated time prior to the start of the class and allowed to go over the contact equipment to become familiar with it.

## HOW TO START

Food! Again, the great motivator is the key to this fun and entertaining sport. It is imperative that before you start, you are sure that your dog is physically able to run the course. Since there is a lot of jumping, it is important that your Basset has a sound front end assembly. When you begin training, set jump heights no higher than 8 inches. Once they learn how to jump reliably, you can raise the jump heights. If you are starting with a puppy, you should not jump them at full height until they are mature and their bones are strong and well developed.

The idea of agility is to teach your dog to take the obstacle to which you direct him. You must first teach your dog to listen to you and to watch the obstacles in front of him. To do this, you use food to target him forward. The best way to start training is with the help of a friend or family member. While you hold your dog on one side of a jump, your helper, on the other side of the jump, excitedly shows your dog a piece of food and gets his attention on it. Have your helper place the food on a target like a plastic lid or wash cloth, and stand back. At this point, you give your dog the command "Wait," and move to the side of the jump. Give the command "Jump" or "Over." If the dog makes the jump, he gets the food! If the dog goes around the jump, it is up to your helper to grab the food before the dog gets to it. It won't take long before your dog makes the connection between jumping the obstacle and getting a treat. Once he can do one jump, have him do two with you giving him the "Jump" or "Over" command before he gets to each obstacle. You can build from there by adding other types of obstacles, like tunnels, and setting them up so your dog is not just running in a straight line.

Contact equipment such as the A-frame, dogwalk, or seesaw is also taught with lots of food. In the beginning, the obstacle is often lowered or stabilized, and baited with many tidbits of food. Basically, it turns into a banquet for your Basset. He eats his way across! As your dog becomes more comfortable with the equipment and gains confidence, the food is reduced.

Of course, this is just a very short overview of basic training techniques. You will also need to learn how to direct your dog verbally as well as how to use your body language. It is always better to find training classes for this sport as they can help you learn handler cues and problem solving. If this is just not possible, there are several quality books that have been written about this subject over the past several years.

*Roxanne conquers the agility bar jump and weave poles.*

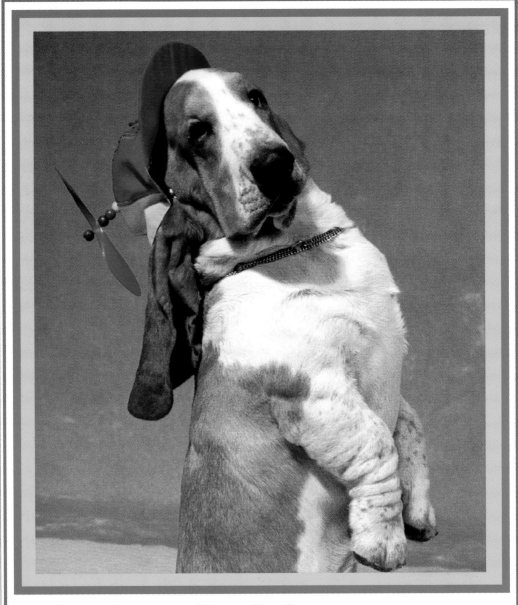

*Charlie, the movie star, in one of his typical beguiling poses.*

## MOVIE STAR CHARLIE

Though not truly an "obedience dog" in the strictest sense of the definition, BHCA member Nancy Mulligan's Tri-M's Airman of Pine Ark certainly qualifies as an exceptionally *obedient* dog. As a result of this talent, Charlie has been quite gainfully employed over the past ten years. He has performed in a movie with Steve Martin, and has done TV ads for the State of Florida and nationally as well. The Golf Channel has spotted him at the golf club with the boys, talking about the "Mulligan" (and not knowing that his name really is Mulligan!) In 1994, he was featured in the Florida Lottery segment as the "Lucky Dog," going in and out of the mansion after his big win. He even has his own agent! Now a senior citizen, Charlie is seriously considering retirement in the near future and looking forward to watching one of his kennelmates picking up where he leaves off.

# THE VERSATILITY CERTIFICATE PROGRAM

During the mid-1980s there was a growing interest in celebrating the efforts and hard work of Basset Hound owners who participate in multiple fields of performance events and to honor those hounds who can successfully compete in several fields of endeavor. To accomplish this purpose the Versatility Certificate Program was established by the Basset Hound Club of America.

The goal of the program is to do everything possible to bring the natural qualities of the Basset Hound to perfection. The program is intended to do everything in its power to protect and advance the interests of the breed and to encourage sportsman-like competition at conformation dog shows, field, obedience, and agility trials and tracking tests. In recognition of their accomplishments, those hounds meeting the eligibility requirements are awarded the Versatility Certificate.

To become eligible for this award, the BHCA member-owned dog must earn a minimum of 11 VC points from at least 3 of designated disciplines. VC points are not cumulative with in a group, therefore, only the points from the highest ranking title in a discipline are counted. For example, a UD entitles a dog to five points, but no additional points are awarded from his CD or CDX titles. Points available for the award of Versatility Certificate are in accordance with the following schedule:

## DISCIPLINE VC POINTS

**A. CONFORMATION**

| | |
|---|---|
| Champion | 5 |
| 10 bench points with one Major | 4 |
| 5 bench points | 2 |

**B. FIELD TRIALING**

| | |
|---|---|
| Field Champion | 5 |
| 30 field points, including one first place | 4 |
| 15 field points, including one second place | 3 |
| 7 1/2 field points, including one second place | 2 |

**C. OBEDIENCE**

| | |
|---|---|
| Obedience Trial Champion | 8 |
| Utility Dog Excellent | 6 |
| Utility Dog | 5 |
| Companion Dog Excellent | 4 |
| Companion Dog | 2 |

**D. TRACKING**

| | |
|---|---|
| Tracking Dog Excellent | 5 |
| Variable Surface Tracking | 5 |
| Tracking Dog | 2 |

**E. AGILITY**

| | |
|---|---|
| Excellent Agility | 5 |
| Open Agility | 3 |
| Novice Agility | 2 |

When a dog fulfills the requirements, an application is made by the dog's owner to the Versatility chairperson. After the information has been verified, the owner will receive an official Versatility Certificate signed by the BHCA president and the Versatility chairperson. The dog's and owner's names will be published in *Tally-Ho*, the club's newsletter, and the owner may then use the initials "VC" after the dog's name in advertising and in publications. It should be noted that this is a BHCA title, so it is not to be used on entry forms for AKC events.

## The following Basset Hounds have qualified for Versatility Certificates since the program began:

| | |
|---|---|
| Ch. Bugle Bay's Bouillion CDX, TD, ROM | Owner: James & Margery Cook |
| Ch. Bugle Bay's Souffle UD | Owner: James & Margery Cook |
| Ch. Winwars Brandywine UD, TDX | Owner: Kay Green |
| Ch. Strathalbyn Last Call CDX, TDX | Owner: Kay Green |
| Ch. Pinebrook's Apollo CDX, TDX | Owner: Kay & Craig Green |
| Ch. Branscombe Dulcinea CD, TD, ROM | Owner: Francis & Ruth Paule |
| Dual Ch. Branscombe Troilus TD | Owner: Francis & Ruth Paule |
| Dual Ch Branscombe's Man of LaMancha CD, TD | Owner: Francis & Ruth Paule |
| Ch. Chez Bonheur Ante-Bellum CD, TDX | Owner: Sue Boyd |
| FC. Tallhils Jolly Roger CD | Owner: Delores McKinnon |
| Ch. Branscombe Bugle Ann TD | Owner: Francis & Ruth Paule |
| Ch. Red Fern Boston Fern CD, TD | Owner: Rhonda Crooks |
| Ch. Branscombe Harry Hotspur CD, TD | Owner: Ruth Paule |
| Ch. Bugle Bay's Fire Cracker CDX, TD | Owner: Evelyn Page Gregory |
| Ch. Brevis Concorde CDX, TD | Owner: Heather Nadelman and Brenda Jubin |
| Dual Ch. Bugle Bay's Anise O'Stillhouse TD | Owner: James & Margery Cook |
| Dual Ch. Branscombe Troubadour TD | Owner: Chris & Sanda Launey and Fritz & Jackie Hager |

## JUST DO IT!

*No matter if it is obedience or agility, the most important point to grasp is that training is fun and enjoyable for both you and your Basset Hound. Training your Basset will not only make him a better companion and family member but it will also bring the two of you closer together. It won't be long before you will be able to "read" your dog and better understand his likes and dislikes. Training can help make a dominant dog more tolerant, or bring a shy dog out of his shell. One thing is guaranteed, you will never regret the extra time you spend with your Basset, or the special bond the two of you will inevitably form.*

# GALLERY OF NATIONAL SPECIALTY OBEDIENCE: HIGH IN TRIAL WINNERS

*We honor those hounds and their owners who have been awarded High In Trial at the Basset Hound Club of America annual National Specialty obedience competition. The reader should know that National's obedience competition did not begin until the 1968 Nationals. This award represents a significant milestone for both the hounds and their owners. It is an achievement sought by all involved in the obedience discipline. Like the other disciplines, many aspire but few achieve. This award is very objective and the owners and their hounds have spent many, many hours in preparation for the competition.*

Bridlespur Nudger and owner, Buzz Taylor, being awarded HIT at the BHCA Nationals in 1968. This was the first year that BHCA held obedience at the Nationals and Nudger and Buzz went on to garner this award for the following four years as well. High In Trial

## 1968–1972: BRIDLESPUR NUDGER, UD
### Owner: Buzz Taylor

## 1973: BUZZ TAYLOR'S AUTUMN UDT
### Owner: Buzz Taylor

## 1974: BUZZ TAYLOR'S HOPALONG UDT
### Owner: Buzz Taylor

*1975: MY COUNTRY BLOSSOM Owner: Patricia Bergh; 1976: IMPERIAL JEM Owner: Lisa & Larry McDowell, and 1977: SHERMAN D-TANK Owner: S. & J. Reynolds: No photographs available.*

1978: CH. BUGLE BAY'S
SOUFFLÉ, UD
**Owners: James & Margery Cook**

1979: CH. HALCYON
SUFFRAGETTE
**Owners: L. F. & V. L. Steedle**

1980: CH. BUGLE BAY'S FONDUE
**Owners: James & Margery Cook**

1981: BUGLE BAY'S MUCH ADO
**Owners: Francis & Ruth Paule**

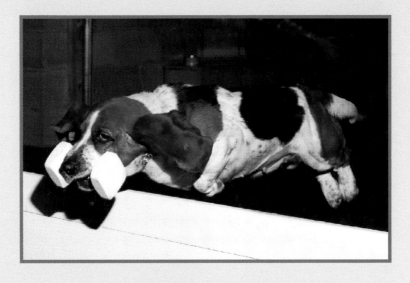

## 1982: CH. BUGLE BAY'S RUTABAGA
**Owners: Pamela Sue Wagerly**

## 1983: BAYROC'S ANDREW
**Owners: E. & C. Hahn & S. & H. Porter**

1984: MISTY MEADOWS
SYLVESTER
Owner: Joan Deibler

1985: LOHRAINE
Owner: Barbara Proctor

1986: TAL-E-HO'S
BAYBERRY SACHET
Owners: MacBride & Lenahan

## 1987: TOBY FRECKLED TOES
**Owner: Nichole Turner**

## 1988: CH. BAYBERRY'S RUM RUNNER
**Owners: James & Barbara MacBride**

1989: CH. BUGLE BAY'S
EGG NOG
**Owners: James
& Margery Cook**

1990: CAN. CH.
LONESTAR'S JESSE
BARFIELD
**Owners: B. Wilson
& J. Greenhalgh**

1991: MISHA DOUCETTE
LAFAYETTE
**Owner: Paulene Malone
No Photo Available**

1992: LIL' CREEK'S ISADORA
DUNCAN CD
**Owners: Joy Parker
& Dotty Christiansen**

1993: CH BUGLE BAY'S
SNOW CONE TD
**Owners: James & Margery Cook**

1994: BH VINCENT VAN GOGH
CD, CGC
**Owners: Mary & Tony Falloretta**

1995: DOLLY'S HOT ROD
BEAU DUDLEY
**Owners: Carol & Ron Asberry**

1996: BLUVALI POPPIN'
FRESH TD
Owners: Coleen Clemett &
Maragie Wikerd

1997: NORTHSTAR'S MELODY
Owners: Elizabet & Kathryn
Wielesworth

1998: REYMAR ENCHILADA
PICANTE
Owners: Margaret Dietrich

# Tracking

The mystery of how an animal tracks has never been solved. If we could only get inside the brain of a dog and compute its reasoning, we could understand the whole phenomenon. Nevertheless, our canine friends do an extraordinary job of stalking the scent, be it minutes, hours, or days old.

Contrary to what the novice might believe, the tracklayer's shaving lotion, perfume, or underarm deodorant is not what the dog tracks, but it may play a part. Many factors figure in the animal's being able to follow the tracklayer. Certainly the vegetation on the ground, the disturbance of the vegetation, and the soil play a great part in it. The wind, humidity, ground moisture, temperature, and odor of the tracklayer influence his scenting powers. A 60-pound tracklayer is harder to track than a 130-pounder. So weight makes a valid statement. The person that smokes or consumes alcohol surely makes a distinctive scent, and certain dogs may turn on or off to these smells. Snow, rain, and fog all deserve special consideration as they affect each dog differently.

In order to prepare yourself for tracking, the right equipment is essential. A snug, but not tight, harness made of nylon or leather is employed. A harness is used so the handler will not be tempted to guide the dog along the track. A six-foot lead can be used at first. Later you can graduate to a 40-foot line. A parachute line, a clothesline rope, or nylon cord will be suitable. Some dogs don't like the drag or pull caused by a heavy line or snap, so you must experiment with the gear. Boots and rain gear are a part of your attire in the field. Articles for the dog to find should include gloves, shoes, socks, neckties, plastic objects, and wooden or metal items. The further along you advance in tracking, the more variety

of items are used. Wooden dowels or metal stakes with bright-colored tape will help you plot the track. Clips and clothespins can be useful for the flag-wise dog.

Teaching the dog to get from point A to point B, using his nose, is the first challenge. The Basset Hound is noted for his love affair with food. With this desire in place, the food method is how most hounds are taught to track. Rubbing food on the tracklayer's shoes or dropping morsels along a given path usually kicks the Basset vacuum cleaner into high gear. Some just like the joy of smelling the food. Certain dogs really couldn't care less about eating. Other methods can be used such as retrieving articles or favorite toys while on the track. Most Bassets think this is a silly process and aren't too turned on with the retrieving. In some cases withholding food and teaching the dog to "sniff for his supper" by tracking his way to the food dish is effective. Some trainers have luck playing hide and seek with the tracklayer and the dog. Occasionally you will find a dog that just isn't interested in tracking. He may dislike the thorny bushes and the hot or cold weather. Some of these dogs just lack the scenting power, or lack the ability to put it together. These hounds prefer to be at home sitting on the sofa or guarding the refrigerator door. Dogs who are on powerful medicines, or who have suffered high fevers, also may not get the sniffer to work properly.

Generally, however, the Basset Hound has a truly remarkable nose. Those who have tracked with Bassets know what gems they are. The physical qualities the Basset possesses make him the right candidate for finding the scent. His long ears enable him to trap and stir up the scent. His dewlap and draping lips can engulf the smell. His wrinkled brow helps to abet the scenting organs. The large nostrils are built to inhale certain aromas. His short legs make him closer to the scent and moderately slow moving, keeping him from overrunning his turns. Tracking is mentally and physically exhausting. Well-sprung ribs give the Basset heart and lung capacity for essential stamina. His stable temperament is another gift, enabling him to meet difficult situations while on the track and to accept them as part of the game.

Once the fanciers start the sport of tracking, they tend to stick with it. It's a great hobby for those who enjoy the outdoors and good exercise for humans and dogs. These sportsmen finish many TDs and TDXs. Even though no Basset has passed the new Variable Surface Tracking (VST) title (started in 1995), it won't be long, as good as these hounds are, before this feat is accomplished.

Some of the early trackers in our sport are still around and some are actively tracking: Ben and Sally Harris in California; Lena and Billy Wray and Buzz Taylor in Florida; and Joan Thurlow in Virginia.

Our ranks have authors among us as well: Sue Boyd is co-author of *Tracking from the Ground Up* and *Tracking Dog Excellent;* Ruth Paule penned *Tracking with a Basset Hound;* Doc and Ruth Paule and Bill and Anne Lindsay were all instrumental in putting together the BHCA video "Tracking With a Basset Hound," a step-by-step guide for beginners.

The Basset community is not devoid of tracking judges. Our ranks include: Buzz Taylor, Sue Boyd, Sally Elkins, Craig Green, Pat Grigg, Flo Voigt, and Lena Wray. All officiate at tests throughout the country. Judges are hard working, often enduring

miserable weather and tough terrain to judge a test. Their work begins by plotting tracks the day before the test. The fruits of their labor are enjoyed when the dogs lead their handlers to the article at the end of the track on test day.

In collecting the material for this section of the book, the tracking fraternity was invited to furnish information about Bassets earning titles since 1985. These handlers are owned by a special breed of dog!

*U-CDX Bluvali Sweet Jezabel UDT, Can CDX, CGC, TT TDI, after a successful retrieve.*

## Colleen Clemett, Renaissance

"Jesse," U-CDX Bluvali Sweet Jezabel, UDT, Can. CDX, CGC, TT, TDI boasts many titles and became Colleen's first tracker. Colleen states that she learned the hard way about trusting your dog, as it took three tries to snare that TD. Jesse knew what she was doing, but it took a little faith by her owner.

Her second tracker was Bluvali Poppin' Fresh TD CGC, better known as Nikki. Nikki began training at 11 weeks and earned her title at the BHCA Nationals in Anderson, Indiana, in 1995. She handled the various distractions beautifully, which included traffic as well as three flocks of birds taking off and landing near her track. Her owner was surprised that she ignored, rather than stalked, those friendly critters.

**Training Note:** Colleen starts turns very early. This is usually within days of beginning training. She originally got the idea while training Jesse. She pointed out that puppies run every which way while tracking. Dogs have trouble with turns because we teach them in the beginning that tracks always go straight.

## Jim and Marge Cook, Bugle Bay

The Cooks were introduced to tracking in 1970. Their Nancy Evans Pandora UDT was the first of her breed to hold a "T" in Texas. Through the years they have bred or owned 15 TDs and 2 TDXs.

Since 1985 they have trained eight hounds. Ch. Bugle Bay's Meringue CD TD, earned her title in Pennsylvania at the 1986 National Specialty and was the only dog to pass that test. Her only puppy, Ch. Bugle Bay's Blackberry Jam (co-owned with Mary Hogan) won his title in Tulsa, Oklahoma, in 1988.

Two sisters earned their "T"s at the Nationals in Michigan in 1988. Dual Ch. Bugle Bay's Anise O'Stillhouse TD was wild about rabbits and went on to her dual championship. Her sister, Dual Ch. Stillhouse Abagail TDX earned her advanced tracking title in Baton Rouge, Louisiana in 1990. The gallery and club members were most excited because she was the first dog to pass a TDX test in that state, and this club had been holding tests for many years.

In 1990, Ch. Bugle Bay's Snow Cone CD TD, earned her reward, also in Louisiana. Her judges were Basset people, Sally Elkins and Lena Wray.

*Dual Ch. Bugle Bay's Anise O'Stillhouse TD; Ch. Bugle Bay's Snow Cone CD, TD; Bugle Bay's Amaretto TD, CGC; Dual Ch. Stillhouse Abagail TDX; Ch. Bugle Bay's Cheesecake TD, (co-owned with Jonelle Bartoli); and Bugle Bay's Quiche Lorraine TD (co-owned with Linda Beam). All are owned by Jim and Margery Cook.*

In 1993, two half-sisters succeeded at the San Diego Nationals. When Marge saw the grounds she thought the team was doomed. There wasn't a hint of green vegetation anywhere. The weeds were five to six feet high. Thankfully, the weeds tended to hold the scent. Bugle Bay's Quiche Lorraine and Ch. Bugle Bay's Cheesecake (co-owned with Jonelle Bartoli) each brought home the cherished "T."

The Rhode Island Nationals in 1994 proved to have the most difficult grounds. At the last moment the scheduled tracking grounds were rejected, and the committee

## Dave and Joan Deibler, Misty Meadows

Misty Meadows Elvira CD, TD, "Elvira," passed her first and Joan's first tracking test with flying colors at the BHCA Nationals in October, 1988, at Transfer, Pennsylvania. Scenting was akin to breathing to Elvira, and she really showed the Deiblers what tracking was all about. She passed her TD in a steady rain, but finished on three *legs.* Her right rear leg was not touching the ground. What they originally thought was a soft tissue injury proved to be arthritis and the start of several immune problems.

*Ch. Misty Meadows Conlan CD, TD, CGC, also known as Shana, poses among her many trophies. She is owned by Dave and Joan Deibler and handled by Joan.*

quickly secured land in a cemetery. Problems evolved as migrating geese were everywhere, and none of the dogs were passing. Bugle Bay's Amaretto TD, CGC, the last tracker of the day, nailed it down and earned the "T." She came off the grounds with goose feathers glued to her ears and nose and a glazed look in her eyes!

**Tracking Note:** In trying to teach dogs to track, Marge often backs up and retrains if a problem arises. Because Bassets love food, she lets the goodies be a big part of their training.

Ch. Misty Meadows Conlan CD, TD, CGC, "Shana," was going BW at the 1988 BHCA Nationals while Elvira earned her TD. Shana passed her TD test at the Mt. Nittany Dog Training Club TD Test held at Furnace, Pennsylvania on April 7, 1991. She started her track easily and after her first turn went off six feet to the right and engorged herself with deer manure. Joan's very firmly enunciated "Track" fell on deaf ears until Shana had her fill. The manure must have been vitaminized as Shana proceeded to run the remainder of her track through pasture land,

*Three handlers and their dogs that all passed their tracking test at the 1989 BHCA Nationals held in Fort Worth, Texas: Ch. Brierwood's Zoe TD, with Sanda Launey; BevLee's Blythe Spirit TD with Cheryl Fischer; and Ch. Bugle Bay's Brunch TD with Cindy Horvath Patrick.*

then into a grape vineyard and between rows of vines to the glove. Two winded judges and one winded handler made it also. One judge commented that she never thought she would have to run behind a Basset!

Ch. Misty Meadows Creamer TD, "Creamer," was another natural tracker who was slow and steady, unlike her mother, Shana. Creamer always gave one a feeling of confidence to be behind her. She required very little training once she connected the track smell with the ultimate goal of the glove. Creamer passed her TD on October 16, 1994 at the Berks County Dog Training Club at Leesport, Pennsylvania. Under difficult conditions, she hit each turn right on and found her glove easily. Creamer had failed the BHCA TD two weeks prior when a huge flock of Canadian geese decided to land between her starting flags. She was never able to get started that day.

Ch. Misty Meadows Paterno CD, TD, CGC, "Joepa," was a personal victory for Joan. Joepa was first certified in 1990. He then proceeded to blow four TD tests, and Joan personally was responsible for two of those because she didn't believe him. After not tracking him for five years, Joan tried again. Joepa had not forgotten his original

training, and this time he kept his mind on the track. He passed his first TD at eight-and-one-half years young at the BHCA National test at Anderson, Indiana on October 7, 1995. Joan almost goofed again, but this time Joepa would not let her fail. He is a true gentleman coach and Joan's proudest TD!

## Cheryl Fischer

Cheryl Fischer, well known in Texas circles for her good obedience dogs, has placed two tracking titles on her dogs. Purchased from Bubba and Freda Burks, Southlake Bassets, Southlake Just a Little Twit UDT was Cheryl's earliest tracker. From Bev and Lee Stockfelt, she purchased BevLee's Blythe Spirit CD, TD. Spirit was one of three Bassets from Houston to earn their titles at the 1989 BHCA Nationals.

## Stephanie and Joe Gonyeau, Oxboro

Stephanie and Joe's first Basset to earn a tracking title was Oxboro's Boughs of Holly TD, who earned her title at the New Jersey Nationals in 1991. The next titleholder was Oxboro's The Great Blue Heron TDX. Harry earned his TD in 1993 and his TDX in 1995. The Gonyeau's next tracking title holder was

Ch. Oxboro's Al You're No Einstein TD. All three of these hounds passed in the tracking test held in 1995 at the Indiana Nationals.

**Training Note:** The Gonyeaus train Bassets year 'round except on days with below-zero temperatures. After the Bassets are actually tracking, they find that the best results come by doing one real track and one motivational track per week. On the days when a Basset is not tracking, the Gonyeaus walk that dog a minimum of one mile at a fast trot. They feel that this regimen produces a dog that is physically capable of tracking and mentally eager to find that lost article.

## Linda Gonzalez

Gin Dic's St. Clothilde CD, Am/Can. TD and Ch. Beacan's St. Bertilia CD, Am/Can. TD are Linda's beloved pals. They are a mother-daughter team. Chloe earned her Canadian TD in Ontario in 1990 and two weeks later her American TD at the BHCA Nationals in Holland, Michigan. A day later she was bred, and from this litter came Linda's first champion, Tillie. Tillie earned her championship in 1992, and her Canadian and American TDs in 1993.

*Ch. Oxboro's Al You're No Einstein TD, zeros in on the glove. Al's owners are Joe and Stephanie Gonyeau.*

## Craig and Kay Green

Craig and Kay have been tracking with Basset Hounds for 20 years. Between them, they have attained 16 TDs and 5 TDXs on their dogs, with most of them on Bassets. Craig has judged about 60 tracking tests in 11 different states since 1985. He has been the tracking correspondent for *Tally-Ho* since 1982 and was author of the tracking chap-

*Ch. Gin Dic's St. Clothilde CD, Am/Can. TD, and her daughter, Ch. Beacan's St. Bertilia CD, Am/Can. TD, owned by Linda Gonzalez.*

ter in Peg Walton's book *The New Basset Hound* (1993). In recent years, Craig and Kay have tracked with the following Hounds:

Ch. Strathalbyn Last Call CDX, TDX, VC. "Striker" passed his TDX in Albuquerque, New Mexico, in 1986 with a solid performance on a test that included an acute turn in the middle of a sandy creekbed.

Ch. Pinebrook's Apollo CDX, TDX, VC. "Bounder" earned his TDX in Denver, Colorado, in 1987 at Chatfield Park. After a slow start, his performance gradually improved throughout the track, including a very difficult turn back across a road he had just crossed.

Ch. Ambrican Josephine TDX. "Feeney" is the best tracking dog the Greens have had. She passed a 980-yard, nine-turn track with a brilliant problem-solving effort at Chatfield Park in 1987. The track included a turn right in the middle of a marsh. She had to work at that turn for some time.

Ch. Pitter Patter's Private Stock CD, TD. "Pookie" was very difficult to train, as he displayed little interest in tracking. However, he passed his TD at Barr Lake Park, north of Denver, in 1987.

Ch. Blue Lick Magic Marker CD, TD. "Fuzzy" obtained his TD at the same test as Pookie. Neither Fuzzy nor Pookie

*Ch. Pinebrook's Apollo CDX, TDX, owned by J. Craig Green.*

displayed the motivation needed for advanced tracking.

**Tracking Note:** Craig has written some excellent articles in *Tally-Ho,* suggesting numerous ideas on how to get a dog motivated to track. His idea for a dog that is having difficulties is to keep the track short

*Ch. Bugle Bay's Firecracker CDX, TDX, CGC tracks in the New Mexico desert. Owned and handled by Evelyn Gregory.*

enough so the dog can experience success. If he is not enjoying the activity, stop tracking until a solution is found. Craig suggests not using blind tracks (tracks with no flags) until the Basset is running consistently and not having major problems. One must be able to tell the difference between tracking behavior and other behavior. The dog's body language may offer clues about this.

## Evelyn Gregory

The unforgiving terrain of New Mexico with cacti, sand, and rocks has been Evelyn's training ground. Happy's Sir Tripsalot UDT was her first. He never passed his X test. He died much too young of lymphoma.

Evelyn's next tracker was purchased as a puppy from the kennel of Jim and Marge Cook. The puppy was tested at eight weeks, and he indicated with his nose that tracking was for him. This was the deciding factor on which puppy Evelyn would choose. Everything was uphill from that point. "Cracker," U-CD Ch. Bugle Bay's Firecracker CDX, TDX, VC, CGC, earned his TDX in six inches of snow in 1995 in Colorado. Evelyn reports that he was in high gear all the way. She was stumbling and sliding on the hilly terrain, but somehow managed to stay upright. When Cracker retrieved the final article it was the thrill of a lifetime.

**Training Note:** Evelyn has tried every tracking method anyone ever suggested and the best one for her has been a variation of Gottfried Dildei's Schutzhund tracking. It is all motivational with food in each footprint to keep the dog focused on what he's doing. The verbal cue is, "Have you got it?" and the dog has to tell that he's "got it" with a strong pull and head down. If he doesn't "have it" his head comes up and he

doesn't pull. Evelyn uses marked tracks for a long time so she knows *exactly* where the track is and stays at the 20-foot knot (or less). She never allows the dog to "shop around" or get off the track more than a couple of feet.

## Margaret Haselden

Can. OTCH, U-UD Tuff Tizzy Samantha, UD, TDX, Can. TDX certainly has accumulated a grand supply of titles for her very

*Can. OTCH, U-UD Tuff Tizzy Samantha, Am UD, TDX, Can. TDX, with owner Margaret Haselden.*

proud owner. Margaret's first tracker, she earned the TD at the Ann Arbor Dog Training Tracking Test in 1989. She soon earned the TDX at Lansing, Michigan.

Margaret's next Basset came to her from the Paules and became U-CDX Branscombe Albert Alexander, CDX, TDX, Can. CDX, TDX—another well-titled fellow. Margaret began training him when he was nine weeks old and had an 'X' in mind for him from the start. He won his TD at six months of age in a field full of scampering mice—very tempting for a hound. Following his feat at the Ann Arbor test, he won his Can. TD at seven months of age in a lush alfalfa field. Al's TDX came at Wickmons Forest, Illinois in 1992. Pulling the last track of the day, Al had the entire gallery following his half-mile route.

**Training Note:** Margaret has good luck shaking a can full of rocks to distract Al from crittering (never throwing or threatening). Running tracks after dark helps to build trust in the dog. She uses meandering plots, instead of straight lines, to help give the hound some variety.

**Training Note:** Karen believes the Basset's nose is second only to that of the Bloodhound, but Bassets are stubborn. She limits her sessions to two, and occasionally three, a week if a problem arises. "Find more" is part of her vocabulary from the start of training. It

*U-CDX Branscombe Albert Alexander, Am. CDX, TDX, Can. CDX, TDX, resting after a tough day on track.*

## Karen Highley, Hokieland

Bassets have been a part of Karen's life since 1970. All of her Bassets have been males, and they have attained some impressive titles: 8 CDs, 6 CDXs, 5 UDTs, 12 TDs, 4 TDXs, and 2 champions. After seeing Joan Thurlow with her UDT Bassets, Karen was inspired to participate in obedience competition. In recent years, however, she has concentrated her efforts on tracking. As she sees it, tracking has no politics and no nit-picking! You and your dog pass or fail, and everyone pulls for everyone else. Karen's hounds travel from Georgia to Massachusetts for tests. Ch. Shadowalk's Bayberry Charlie TDX finished his TDX in November 1996. Bridi's I'm Just Ralph is now a TDX. Bridi's Ike TDX; Bridi's Best Boy Tommy TDX and Bandit's Just Teddy TDX are all candidates for the VST. Needless to say, Karen is a very busy and hard-working lady.

ensures that, if for any reason their tracking is interrupted, a word command is there to restart them. Proofing the dogs for all kinds of weather is a must. Karen also introduces the dogs to horse and cow fields. Throughout training she lays her own tracks.

## Alden and Jo Ann Hilliker, Westwind

The Hillikers have finished six TDs and hope to have a TDX soon. Their first challenge was Cody's Aberle Abagail TD, CD. They drove to Charleston for the test. At the gate of the plantation where the test was to be held, a guard was stationed. This guard was holding a rifle as well as a "no trespassing" sign. The Hillikers knew that tracking was taken seriously here! The tracking committee explained that in hunting season they take no chances on a hunter messing up the tracks.

Westwind Rome-ing Matilda TD, CD earned her title in Auburn, Georgia and was the youngest dog to pass a test at that site. She was six months and two weeks of age. It was somewhat unusual, but the entire gallery ran onto the field when Tilly found the glove. The explanation given for this was that the club president had faithfully laid tracks twice a year for six years, and Tilly was the first dog to pass one of her tracks!

Branscome Penelope TD, CD, CGC was purchased from Doc and Ruth Paule. She became the Hillikers' third successful tracker. Her daughter, Westwind Meg Sarah TD, CGC gave the Hillikers a few gray hairs at some exciting tests. She failed at Orlando with tracks under water, at Atlanta where she flushed a deer, and at the Nationals in Rhode Island where a jogger caught her eye; but in Orlando she kept her nose to the ground and didn't look up.

Westwind Charlie B was sold to Maria Zengion as a puppy and he became Maria's first tracker, attaining his title at the Nationals in Anderson, Indiana, in 1995. His littermate, Westwind Lightfoot Linas TD earned his title in Florida. The Hillikers say he is their best yet.

*A determined Branscombe's Penelope CD TD, CGC.*

**Tracking Note:** The Hillikers have great luck tracking with puppies and they work them on a variety of fields. Because they are babies, the dogs adapt easily.

*Bridi's Ike TDX; Bandit's Just Teddy TDX; Shadowalk's Bayberry Charlie TD; Bridi's I'm Just Ralph TDX; and Bridi's Best Boy Tommy TDX. All are owned and trained by Karen Highley.*

## Jane Jonas, Jonas

Jane is relatively new to tracking, beginning her first tracking dog in May, 1995. Ch. Jonas' Hatty P Hellraiser earned her TD at Mountain States Dog Training Club in Denver five months later. The following year Hatty earned her TDX at the same test.

Hatty's daughter, Ch. Jonas' Madelyn Q Ruffin followed in her mom's footsteps by quickly mastering the tracking concept. She earned her TD after just three months of training. That's quite an accomplishment!

*A mother-daughter combination, Ch. Jonas' Hatty P Hellraiser TD and Ch. Jonas' Madelyn Q Ruffin TD. Breeder-owner-handler, Jane Jonas.*

*Westwind Rome-ing Matilda TD, CD, owned and handled by the Hillikers.*

*Alden Hilliker preparing Westwind Lightfoot Linas TD, at the starting flag.*

## Chris and Sanda Launey, Brierwood

Sanda's first experience with a tracking dog was her Ch. Musicland's Southern Comfort CD, TD, ROM, "Sophie." It proved to be a good exercise for expectant mothers as the bitch was in whelp when she passed her TD in November, 1985. A particular challenge in training Sophie, and for many Southern trackers, is developing strong article indications. The ever-present fire ants swarm over baited training articles as soon as the articles are dropped. Food has to be carried during training so the dog's success can be acknowledged immediately with praise and reward.

In 1987, unusual circumstances allowed Sanda to handle Brierwood's Musical Schooze TDX, as she was earning her TD. Sally Elkins, Music's owner, broke her leg while attending the BHCA Nationals in Colorado. Sally watched from a wheelchair as Sanda handled the bitch in the test. Later, Music earned the TDX with Sally while Sanda and husband Chris proudly watched from the gallery.

In 1988, Judith Bowers, soon to be a tracking judge, asked to borrow the Launey's Musicland's Lily in order to gain experience in tracking with hounds. In January, 1989, Lily and Judith worked their track with such focus on the way to the glove and a TD that they tracked right over a jack rabbit that was hunkered in the grass.

Ch. Brierwood's Zoe TD was trained by Chris. Zoe was a treasured bed dog. One night she growled at Chris when he returned home from an extended trip. Chris began training her to establish a good-working bond with her. She was TDX trained, but died suddenly at the age of five.

Ch. Brierwood's Winter Shadow TD became the next challenge. She was unique in that she lacked desire. Her enthusiasm for tracking was dampened at her first test by a Texas "gully washer." Her pass picture

*Sanda Launey and her Ch. Brierwood's Winter Shadow TD.*

was taken beneath a park sign reading "BEWARE Alligators Exist in this Park."

Dual Champion Branscombe Troubadour TD, VC accomplished his field championship prior to tracking, so rabbits were a big part of his life. On the practice track, a week before his test, "Teddy" went in hot pursuit of a rabbit. He learned a valuable lesson that day, that when in tracking harness the work at hand is tracking! Marking his territory was part of his habit in working a track. As he gained confidence and experience, he marked less and became more competent.

## Virginia Lemieux and Morgan Kiefhaber, Gin Dic

Gin Dic has bred two tracking dogs. "Barney," Am/Can. Ch. Gin Dic's No Show Jones, Am/Can. TD, was the first. He earned both his tracking titles on the first try. At the 1990 BHCA Nationals after his last turn he began wagging his tail vigorously. The hound found not the required glove, but a bunny hole. With a serious tone of voice, the handler gave the command to track, and 15 yards later Barney found his article!

*Am/Can. Ch. Gin Dic's No Show Jones, Am/Can. TD, owned by V. Lemieux and handled here by Morgan Kiefhaber.*

## Cindy Horvath Patrick, Green Mountain

Cindy has three trackers to brag about: a mother, daughter, and granddaughter. Her first tracker was Ch. Bugle Bay's Brunch, who passed at the BHCA Nationals in Fort Worth in 1989. Several years later, Brunch's

*Ch. Green Mountain Wailin' Jenny TD, passing at the San Jacinto K.C. test in December, 1995. Owner-handler, Cindy Horvath Patrick.*

daughter, Ch. Southlake Grn Mtn Cherrybomb, earned her TD in Fort Worth in pouring rain. The bad conditions did not deter "Cherry," even though she had trained for only three months. Ch. Green Mountain Wailin' Jenny, Cherry's daughter, was another quick study, passing at the San Jacinto test after only four months of training.

**Training Note:** Houston is hot, humid, and tough on a tracker, so tracks are laid as the sun rises. Heat tolerance is built slowly through the summer in this manner. Cindy feels tracking is a wonderful confidence builder for youngsters. It does wonders for soft toplines and muscling out of puppy rears.

## Ruth Paule, Branscombe

Ruth Paule has made remarkable achievements with her dogs through the years. Ruth and her husband, Doc, bred and trained numerous trackers, many of which held field and bench championships and obedience titles. They trained 16 trackers and sold 8 other Bassets who earned TDs. Even after Doc's death, Ruth continued breeding and training.

Ch. Branscombe Lochinvar TD, co-owned with Anne Lindsay, was a Basset that loved to bark at people. He sometimes ran a track barking the whole way. His first test, in 1987, was graced by eight inches of snow followed by a cold rain. Lochy decided this wasn't for him and he tracked back to Ruth with no thoughts of walking through the slush. A month later, with kinder weather, he passed without a hitch.

Branscombe Alexander, less than perfect in the beauty department, took to tracking with great enthusiasm and earned his TD at the Western Carolina TD test in 1987.

Field Ch. Branscombe Nightwind, co-owned with Fritz Hager, earned her TD on her first try at the BHCA Nationals in Transfer, Pennsylvania in 1988. She was an excellent tracker, but her first love was hunting. Wendy went on to become a field champion.

Ch. Branscombe Harry Hotspur CD, TD, VC, CGC, a Lochinvar son, also barked at people. He earned his TD at the Winston

*Ch. Branscombe Lochinvar TD, taking the Breed at a conformation show. Owners: Anne Linday and Ruth Paule*

TD trial in 1990 in good style. This redeemed his father's performance, which was still remembered by the club members

## Reed and Becky Pomeroy, Rebec

Reed and Becky Pomeroy of West Salem, Wisconsin have bred two tracking dogs. The first to complete her title was Rebec's P. S. Gitano TD, owned and trained by Marianne Adelmann. Peggy Sue earned her 'T' in October 1988. Rebec's Blues Revival TD, owned by Jane and Robert Sheldon, earned her title in February 1996.

*Rebec's Blues Revival TD, owned by Robert and Jane Sheldon, tracks along a Minnesota lake.*

*What a great retrieve! King Chivas Regal Timmerline CD, TD, was a rescue dog. His owners are Bill and Linda Hutchinson.*

## Rescue Basset

Rescue Basset King Chivas Regal Timmerline CD TD, is owned by Bill and Linda Hutchinson of Minnesota. He earned his TD in 1993. Chivas is a great example of what love and patience can produce in a Basset who otherwise would not have a chance for such an accomplishment.

## Harriet Richman

Ch. Feenrich's Laid Back Jack TD is unique in that he received both a BIS and his tracking certification under the same judge, Miss Dorothy Nickles. Jack took to tracking like the proverbial duck to water. He thoroughly enjoyed the tracking procedure, and neither cross-tracks nor roads were a problem. However, acknowledging the article was a totally different story. Jack was of the opinion that if the tracklayer wanted to leave their belongings on his track, that was their affair and definitely not Jack's! Jack passed his TD on February 28, 1993 (after disdainfully picking up the glove)!

## Theresa Teague, Winsom

Branscombe Winsom Emma was purchased in 1987. With the help of Emma's breeders, Doc and Ruth Paule, Theresa was launched into a new hobby. Emma's big day was at the 1988 National Specialty at Transfer, Pennsylvania. Conditions for that track were exactly what handlers pray they won't be! Emma's track included fog, a downpour, and snow flurries, but Emma did it anyhow!

In 1990, Ch. Winsom Barnstormer CD earned his TD by running the alternative track. Luckily, the two AKC representatives were in attendance. An unusual occurrence took place with electric power line boxes, and this threw the dog off on his originally drawn track. Some believe electro-magnetism may alter a dog's concentration and confuse the dog's scenting ability. After a conference

*Harriet Richman's Ch. Feenrich's Laid Back Jack TD, being certified by judge Dorothy Nickles.*

with judges, representatives, and handler, the dog was put on the alternative track. He tracked it in grand style.

Theresa's third tracker passed her test in 1994 in Tryon, North Carolina. Ch. Branscombe Bramble of Winsom, although a vocal bitch, tracked steadily to her TD.

**Training Note:** Tracking year 'round in all types of weather has paid big dividends for Theresa.

Brierwood's Miles From Home TD acquired his title in four inches of freshly fallen snow. As often happens, test day arrived with new snow, and the dog had never been in snow before. Miles is a fast-paced, air-scenting type and a complete natural. True to form, he galloped at full speed to the glove. The judges were glad Miles was their first dog of the day while they still had the stamina to keep up with him!

*U-CDX Toby Freckled Toes CDX, TD, CGC. Owner, Nicole Turner.*

## Nicole Turner

U-CDX Toby Freckled Toes CDX, TD, CGC is regarded by Nicole as her once-in-a-lifetime dog. All of her dogs earned their titles at Chatfield State Park in Colorado. Brierwood's Movoureen TD was Nicole's second tracker and full of surprises at each turn. Mav had those days when she'd daydream, enjoy the scenery and stroll through the field at her leisure. On her second try, she qualified!

## Dietrich and Florence Voigt, Roadway

The Voigts began their tracking adventures in the Northeast and in later years moved to Tucson in the Southwest. One of their latest trackers was Ch. Roadway's Ramblin' Rogue TDX, Can. TD. "Slugger" earned his TD at 11 months of age in Mass-achusetts on a track with 7 turns. He failed his first TDX test because of briars, but passed two weeks later.

*Billy and Lena Wray have finished 19 hounds in tracking. Shown here is Jagersven Blue Jay TD, who was their number 16 to pass.*

Ch. Branscombe Nomad of Roadway Am/Can. TD earned her "T" at the Virginia Nationals, one week shy of her first birthday. A good, reliable tracker, she earned her Canadian TD the following year.

## Billy and Lena Wray, BeeLee

Lena and Billy Wray have established a most impressive record in the Basset tracking realm, for they have finished 19 hounds. Their first Basset was one of the breed's earliest dual titleholders. Ch. Humphey, Jr. CD TD earned those awards in the 1960s. The BHCA established tracking at the 1970 Nationals and the Wray's Ch. Party Doll's Geraldine scooted right down that track for her "T."

Since 1985, the Wrays have had Jagersven Grace Berry Brown earn the honor of a "T." She did this in a test at the Miami airport, where workers repairing an aircraft hooted, whistled, and hollered at her and her handler. Grace Berry paid no attention to the distractions. Instead, she trotted right down the track to the glove.

In 1993, Ch. Brendan's Stoneybluff Lauren was awarded the coveted TD. Lena, a judge, and Billy, a great tracklayer, have given much time and effort to the Basset world. You'll see them at all the National Specialties and at shows throughout Florida.

*Ch. Roadway's Ramblin Rogue TDX, Can. TD. "Slugger" is shown with his glove by owners Dietrich and Flo Voigt.*

# BASIC AKC TRACKING TITLE ELEMENTS AND REQUIREMENTS

**Tracking Test/TD** is designed to test the dog's ability to follow a track laid by a person under a variety of conditions on moderate terrain and to find a glove or wallet dropped by that person. In order to enter a tracking test, the dog must first satisfactorily pass a certification test under the supervision of an AKC-approved or provisional tracking judge. The certification must be obtained within one year of the test entered. Basic elements of a TD track are 440 to 500 yards in length with scent not less than 30 minutes old or more than two hours old. A combination of left and right turns numbering three to five are included. Two aligned flags provide the handler direction of the starting leg of the track but at least two of the right angle turns will be well out in the open where there are no fences or boundaries to guide the dog. There are no obstacles or change of cover allowed that would be suitable for challenging a dog working the next level of achievement in tracking known as Tracking Dog Excellent. A dog that passes this elementary tracking test is recorded by AKC as a Tracking Dog.

**Tracking Test/TDX** is designed to demonstrate a dog's unquestionable stamina and ability to discriminate and courageously persevere scent under a wide variety of conditions. Therefore the test includes tracks aged longer and tracks that provide a variety of obstacles and challenges. There is only one starting flag for a track that is 800 to 1000 yards long. The scent is not less than three hours nor more than five hours old. More recent "hot-scent" cross-tracks are to be laid by a pair of other persons across the original track in two widely separated places about an hour-and-a-half before the dog is to begin working his TDX track. There are from five to seven turns and four but dissimilar personal articles to indicate along the way. Acute angled turns are allowed as well as obstacles that challenge the dog and handler. Obstacles are designed to test the dog's ability to adapt to changing scenting conditions and to continue scenting while overcoming physical obstacles and difficult handling conditions. The dog and handler may encounter plowed land, gullies, woods, streams and even manmade obstacles such as fences, bridges or lightly traveled roads. A dog that passes this test is recorded by the AKC as a Tracking Dog Excellent.

**Tracking Test/VST** A more recent challenge for tracking dogs is the Variable Surface Tracking test which was designed to measure the credibility of a tracking dog in very public, urban settings. A copy of your AKC TD certificate must be submitted along with your VST test entry form. The variable surface track includes a minimum of three different surfaces to challenge the dog's keenly developed scenting discrimination skills. One-third to one-half of the 600 to 800 yard track must be laid out on other than vegetated surfaces and must include two or more of the following: concrete, asphalt, gravel, hardpan, sand, composition, mulch, et cetera. The track is laid in an area that tolerates multiple-animal, vehicular and pedestrian crosstracks. Articles to be indicated include four dissimilar, common, everyday items of leather, fabric, metal and plastic no smaller than 2 by 5 or larger than 5 by 5 inches and under 8 ounces in weight. These are not necessarily personal articles as required for a TDX track. The VST track is to be three to five hours old and includes four to eight turns, three of which must be right-angle turns. One of the turns on the track must be a right-angle turn in an area devoid of vegetation and allow at least 30 yards before a change of surface. There is some debate as to whether this is 30 yards before the non-vegetated turn, after the turn, or both, and is left to the judge's interpretation. The designers of the VST consider the non-vegetated turn the "moment of truth" concerning the VST tracking dog's credibility. There are no physical obstacles or obstructions on the VST track such as in the TDX test. The urban setting is challenge enough. The addition of the VST to the AKC tracking tests has resulted in challenging tracking enthusiasts to consider and develop new training methods, generated new discussions and debates on the nature of scent, and provided an opportunity to strive to master a different challenge. There is an equality in the working relationship between handler and tracking dog: the harder the work, the deeper the bond. Dogs who become variable surface tracking dogs and have obtained the other tracking titles as well are recorded as an AKC Champion Tracker (CT).

# Field Trialing

Basset Hounds want to hunt!

Time and time again, the Basset Hound reputation as an easygoing, quite comical hound has needed to be revised when that same hound is transformed into a serious and hard-working hunting dog. This hunting ability, however, is exactly that for which the Basset Hound was originally bred. Some have claimed that there were low and heavy hounds bred for scenting ability in ancient Egypt and Greece. We are fairly certain that the origin of the Basset can be traced to hounds bred by St. Hubert. In one description these hounds were described as having "bagging lips" and "hanging ears reaching down both sides of their chappes." Although pack hunting and trials were developed in the US in the 1920s and '30s following the British tradition, a group of people soon became interested in brace trials, which had been developed by Beagle sportsmen in 1890.

Today, the current standard for the breed still begins with this statement, "The Basset Hound possesses in marked degree those characteristics which equip it admirably to follow a trail over and through difficult terrain." That statement is vital to keeping the faith in the Basset as a hunting dog. That statement implies that it is of primary importance that a Basset, in order to maintain trailing characteristics, be equipped with a keen nose, a desire for hunting game, and a sound athletic body. With the quality of *desire*, determination keeps the hound on the trail with eager, deliberate and efficient

*A typical field trial gallery scene.*

*The winner's lineup at a field trial.*

action—and the hound is stubborn, tenacious, and patient. Once he is trailing, the closer he stays to the scent of the trail, the better his chances to keep contact with it. He should be making progress as fast as he can while still maintaining contact with the trail. Thus he is making controlled progress and adjusting the pace to the difficulty of the trail. Though not hunted over as much as in the past, many people are still adhering to the idea of the Basset as a hunter of small game, particularly rabbits, by following the sport of field trialing.

## A HISTORY OF BASSET HOUND FIELD TRIALING

Brace field trialing with Basset Hounds was begun by the BHCA in 1937 in Hastings, Michigan and was judged by approved AKC Beagle judges, Claud Hammond and K. F. Conzetti. To become a champion, a hound needed 25 points (points depended on the number of entries). Hillcrest Peggy, owned by the second president of the Basset Hound Club of America, Emil Seitz, won the first points (10) and went on to become the first field champion in 1938. Emil and Effie Seitz were instrumental in starting field trials in the US. As Effie told it: "To go back to the beginning, we became interested in Bassets in 1930 when it became difficult to replace our 13-year-old Beagle hound for hunting and decided to try a new breed we heard about but never had seen, so we drove over to the Irish Hills in Tipton, Michigan to see what they really looked like...to see a Basset is to want one.... We wound up with a year-old bred bitch, out of a French import. In the meantime, we decided to go to the Detroit Kennel Club dog show to see other Bassets and meet the exhibitors. Carl Nottke and William Fritz were the chief Michigan exhibitors, and there we talked hunting the Basset and were advised that all of their hounds hunted. So it was decided to meet at the home of William Fritz in Detroit (in 1933) to discuss the possibility of organizing a club and having a fun trial to get the Basset before the public in the field to popularize the breed." From 1935 to 1971, the first 10 presidents of the Basset Hound Club of America were all steady

*FC Hillcrest Peggy, the first to attain the field champion title, October, 1938.*

field trialers, as were the 14 charter members of the club.

Eastern field trials began in 1938 at Kimberton, Pennsylvania. At this first Eastern trial there were entrants from 5 states and a total of 32 in the trial. In 1939, the first male Basset to finish a field championship was Irish Hills Senator, owned by James E. Lee, of Battle Creek, Michigan. In 1940, another Eastern field trial was held in Pottersville, New Jersey, with entries of 17 dogs and 13 bitches. The sport was growing, and only slowed temporarily with the advent of World War II. The first Basset Hound Club of America fall Nationals was held at Jackson, Michigan in 1944. This was the year that Consuelo Ford was president and her Bijou Rutile of Banbury became the third field champion. The fourth was Queen

*FC Perry's Marigold, the 1953 Nationals field trial winner.*

Elizabeth. Prior to 1953 these were the only field champions.

In 1953, Hartshead Jet became a field champion, and from that date to 1964, 97 more Bassets finished. The 1953 fall National was held in Dover, Ohio. It was there that Buck LaFollette (Pennsylvania) won with his bitch, Perry's Marigold, a daughter of FC Bose's Melicent Hepsy. Buck was the breeder of a line well known in the 1950s and '60s using the Tulpehocken kennel prefix.

*Johnny Bose and Bose's Red Ace, as a five-month-old puppy in 1954.*

Before 1954 only two trials per year were being held and both were sponsored by the BHCA. They were held in Michigan and Ohio. In that year there was a record entry of 46 at the Ohio trial. Active trialers and breeders, Johnny Bose and current Life Member Norwood Engle were then the president and vice-president of the club with a membership of 66. Ohioans Loren Free (Shellbark), Mike Holly, Elmer Olson, and Ned Aquino were among those who got the Buckeye Basset Hound Club started in 1955. The grounds acquired by the Buckeye club are the only grounds owned by a Basset club to date. The venture was financed by the discovery of oil on the grounds.

Susquehanna Basset Hound Club held its first licensed trial in 1956 at Lykens, Pennsylvania. Bose's Dusty Scarlet, one of many fine hounds and progenitors bred by Johnny Bose, won the champion class. His hounds, especially FC Yoder's Sally Belle, FC Bose's Melicent Hepsy and FC Bose's Royal Knight, were significant in their influence on the breed. One of Royal Knight's outstanding offspring was FC Ed's Jo Jo, owned by Ed Eylander. Ed, and his son, John, bred many outstanding field trial hounds including FC Miss Mitzie.

*Ed Eylander with FC Ed's Jo Jo, John N. Eylander with FC Max's Happy Hunter, and John Eylander, Jr. with Eylander's Shortstop. All hounds owned by John N. Eylander.*

*Field Champions Taber's Solo Sue, Navar's Ears, Navar's Snapper, Navar's Jolly, Navar's Heather, Navar's Jill, and Navar's Ginger.*

A new point system for field championships was adopted in December 1957. The BHCA Nationals were held in the East for the first time in 1959 in Lebanon, Pennsylvania. In the West, the Northern California BHC held a trial in 1959, and then did not have another until the 1970s. A well-known kennel of many field champions in Pennsylvania was the kennel of Joe and Pinkie Navar. Their hounds included descendants of the Tulpehocken line.

In the 1960s, licensed trials were started by the Rancocas BHC in New Jersey, (later discontinued), the Western Michigan BHC, the Kentuckiana BHC, the Valley Forge BHC in Pennsylvania, the Patroon BHC in New York, and at the Pilgrim BHC in Massachusetts (with the trials later being discontinued). Ray and Louise Wells were the mainstays of this regional club and had a number of dual champions. Work was initiated on the Basset Hound field trial procedures, under the chairmanship of Bill Rider, a BHCA Life Member, to review the rules for the sport. The chairmanship was taken over by Life Member Ken McWilliams in 1967, and in 1968 the committee was comprised of a member from each licensed

*Tulpehocken Tip Toe.*

*FC Rosie's Bill, sire of 20 FC offspring.*

field-trial-holding club. This group became known as the Field Trial Advisory Council in 1969.

Also in the 1960s, an outstanding sire, FC Rosie's Bill, (a grandson of FC Bose's Royal Knight), bred by Howard Smith, became well known for his 20 field champion offspring. With Bill's brother, FC Rosie's Sportsman, Howard bred the Rosie (his wife's name) bloodline. In 1968, Illinois was the site for the fall National and the require-

*GFC McWilliams Dixie Belle, one of the first three winners of the Grand Field Champion awards.*

ments for a field champion- ship had been upgraded to one win and 40 points. Ken McWilliam's Dixie Belle won that one and she went on to become one of the three winners of the first Grand Field Champion awards after it was established in 1972. Her sire was McWilliams Buccaneer, a brother to Rosie's Bill.

The '70s saw many advantageous changes in field trialing, in part due to field trialer and Life Member Joe Braun, who served as BHCA president from 1969 to '71. New requirements for championships challenged trialers, more efficient handling of field trial business through the new FTAC (Field Trial Advisory Council), double-header field trials, bigger and better BHCA spring Nationals, and an independent newsletter for trialers, *Basset Babbler*, was started by Jean Spaulding in 1974. At the 1970 fall Nationals in Illinois, Jim and Pat Dohr's handsome hound, Kazoo's Moses The Great, won both the Derby and the Dog class. Moses went on to become the first dual champion Basset. At the same Nationals event, Len Skolnick's Beldean's Slippery Hill Sam was the Absolute Winner. Sam traced back to FC Bose's Snowflake and was bred to FC Slippery Hill Calvin, who traced back to FC Perry's Marigold and also FC Bose's Snowflake. This breeding marked the beginning of the Slippery Hill field trial line.

Other breeders starting a bloodline in the '70s were Tom and Shirley Pettit. They began by winning the Nationals in Kentucky with Van's Fantasy in 1972. Van's Fantasy was also one of the three winners of the first Grand Field Champion award, an award suggested by Tom and established by the BHCA in 1972. The effect of offering this award was to greatly increase entries in the champion class. The Pettit bloodline was based on the Rosie bloodline, but with the addition of FC Dohrshire's Twiggy, all traceable back to FC Bose's Royal Knight and FC Miss Mitzie. The Pettits bred one of the most outstanding field trial hounds of all time. Dual Champion Pettit's Ranger Ric not only became a dual champion, he became a grand field champion and sired a phenomenal 47 field champions. He became a progenitor for nearly all field champions of today. Many lines branched from the Pettit's breeding, including one of the larger kennels, Duncan Creek. These hounds were bred by Joe, Pat and Mike Thomas of Michigan. Tom and Shirley Pettit have retired from active breeding and trialing, but have passed the torch to their son Jeff.

Field trialing grew from 19 to 29 field-trial-holding clubs from 1967 to 1976. Entries at the Nationals grew steadily progressing to 230 in 1976 in Lebanon, Pennsylvania, which is the record to date. 1977 saw the beginning of a three-day spring National trial in the Pittsburgh area. The fall Nationals were held in California with Pierson's Darlin Daisy Mae taking the Absolute. This was the first time that the Nationals field trial was held west of the Mississippi. 1977 also saw the start of the Invitational Stake, a competition between first-place winners of the preceding year. The

*Grand Field Champion Pettit's Ranger Ric, all-time top-producing field trial champion sire. Ric is en route to achieving his conformation championship in 1977.*

first winner of that stake was Dick Spurling's Deepgrass Oliver Wendell. Ollie was the winner of that stake three times and one of the outstanding winners of all time. He was a grandson of DC Pettit's Ranger Ric. The Skolnicks included Oliver Wendell in their bloodline, and his offspring, GFC Slippery Hill Gegenschein also won the Invitational Stake three times. In 1978, field trialer Elsie Tagg became president of BHCA, and in that year the point requirement to finish a field champion went from 40 to 60 points.

For the first time, the Nationals were in Texas in 1980. The Absolute Winner that year was Ken McWilliam's McWilliams Dixie Cup, a hound whose origins could be traced to the bloodlines of Seitz, Bose, Eylander, Smith and Pettit. Dixie Cup won many awards and was a top producer of field champions in the '80s and '90s. The Pacific Northwest was the site of the 1983 Nationals, thereby making a count of six field trials out that way

*Dual Ch. Kazoo's Moses The Great, bred by Kazoo Kennel, Reg., and owned by Jim and Pat Dohr. Moses was the first Basset Hound dual champion.*

*FC Deepgrass Oliver Wendell, one of the all-time outstanding field trial winners.*

Lori Jo continues to accumulate a noteworthy string of field champions. The BHC of Greater Houston started their field trials in 1988 with much interest being provided in that area by Bill and Helen Smith. Bill and Marty Ten Eyck owned the 1988 and 1989 fall Nationals winners. The 1988 winner was Hartshead Good Time Sean, and the winner in 1989 was Red Acres Duke, bred by Barney Linebaugh, from a FC Pettit's Sherlock Holmes son, Friend Book Frank.

Another son of FC Pettit's Sherlock Holmes, bred by Barney Linebaugh, was FC Friend Brook Otto who won the fall Nationals in Michigan in 1990. The BHC of Maryland held its first trial in that same year. A new field-trial-holding club, Looking Glass BHC, in Michigan, was formed in 1991. The New Jersey Nationals that year was won by FC Crooked Sticks Molly, a frequent winner descended from the Pettit bloodline and owned by Vince Yurick. The fall Nationals for 1992 were held in another unusual place, the Carolinas. McWilliams Texas Two Step won the Absolute. The first licensed trial of Looking Glass BHC took place in 1993. Fall Nationals that year were held in California and won by a Texas Basset, Bugle Bay's Anise O Stillhouse, owned by Jim and Marge Cook. The '90s were noteworthy for the new and unusual places for the BHCA fall Nationals. In 1994 they were held in Rhode Island. By this time, a field trialer from the '60s, Fred Atwater was reappearing with hounds descended from the Pettit bloodline. Fred and his wife, Stella, were breeders of the 1994 Nationals winner, Lowries Taffy, owned by Glen Lowrie. Glen owned another winning hound, FC Lowrie's Caesar, another son of FC Pettits's Sherlock Holmes. Caesar was the sire of a top winner in the '90s named FC Lowrie's Casey, owned by Gerry Wardropper. In 1995, in Indiana, fall Nationals Absolute Winner was FC Slippery Hill Kinda Close, a double granddaughter of FC Slippery Hill Gegenschein.

for the year. Those contributing to the spirit of the field trials in the West in the early years were: David Vaughan, Jim Chester, Chuck Pierson, Bud and Diana Rinderneck, Linda Deir, Frank Homar, Roy and Melody Fair, Stan and Sylvia Ellingwood, Steve and Fully Bishop. Arriving on the scene in the '80s were Bob Reynolds (Sanrob), Kaye Cameron and Ted Pulliam, as well as Brian Kinnear, who moved out from Virginia. Field trialing with Bassets was at a peak of interest during the '80s. Among the top winners were FC Pettit's Sherlock Holmes (sire of FC Deepgrass Oliver Wendell) and Pettit's Irish Cheer.

The AKC Centennial year (1984) medallions were awarded at the fall National in Maryland to class winners and to the Absolute Winner, McWilliams Shortcake. 1985 was the 50th Anniversary of the BHCA and the fall National was a large celebration held in the state of origin, Michigan. Effie Seitz, charter member and trialer at the first field trial, was there. GFC Slippery Hill Gegenschein was Absolute Winner. In 1987, the fall Nationals were held in Colorado. The winner there was Shellbark's White Owl, owned by Bill Ashabraner and bred by Lori Jo (Free) Roberts. Lori Jo is a second-generation trialer and daughter of Loren Free.

*A field trial lineup in the early 1990s.*

## Field Trial-Holding Basset Hound Clubs

BERKSHIRE VALLEY BHC;
BHC OF GREATER SEATTLE;
BHC OF MARYLAND, INC.;
BHC OF PORTLAND, OR., INC.;
BHC OF SACRAMENTO;
BUCKEYE BHC (Eastern OH area);
CAPITAL DISTRICT BHC (NY area);
DAL-TEX BHC;
KENTUCKIANA BHC;
LENAPE BHC (NJ area);
LOOKING GLASS BHC (MI area);
MAUMEE VALLEY BHC (Western OH area);
NO. CALIFORNIA BHC;
PATROON BHC (NY area);
SUSQUEHANNA BHC (PA area);
VALLEY FORGE BHC (PA area);
WESTERN MICHIGAN BHC BASSET HOUND CLUB OF AMERICA, INC.

Other clubs that have held field trials in the past, and that could start up again, are: BHC OF GREATER HOUSTON, FT. DEARBORN BHC (Northern IL area), PILGRIM BHC (New England area), POTOMAC BHC (D.C./VA area), and RANCOCAS VALLEY BHC (NJ area).

## The Field Trial Event

Field trials are outdoor events in which individual dogs are given the opportunity to show their qualities in direct competition under actual or simulated natural hunting conditions. Basset Hound field trials are frequently held on Beagle club grounds. Beagle club properties are often farms that have been purchased and fenced with rabbit-proof fencing. Rabbits are restocked, shelters are built, and food plots planted to ensure a good supply of healthy rabbits on which to train and run the dogs. Even in the gundog trials, no rabbits are killed. Seldom can a Basset catch a rabbit, so the latter is safer on field trial grounds than it would be in the wild. Usually Beagle clubs will provide kennels for the participants. These may be fancy concrete runs with chain-link fencing, or the more traditional wire-off-the-ground kenneling. The old farm house is usually altered to suit the needs of the club, or a mobile home or inexpensive building is used. Inexpensive meals are often served.

Basset clubs that hold field trials are either member trials (held by clubs that are members of AKC, such as the BHCA) or licensed trials (held by local breed clubs). Some clubs also hold sanctioned trials where hounds compete, but not for championship points. Most field trials last two days, usually on weekends. Usually the males (Dog class) run on the first day (usually Saturday), along with champions (Champion class). The next day, females (Bitch class) are run. Every hound running in the trial must be individually registered in the AKC Stud Book, or must be part of an AKC-registered litter. Or otherwise, if whelped outside the US and imported by a resident of the US, or owned by a resident of Canada, must have been registered in its country of birth with a foreign registry organization whose pedigrees are acceptable for AKC registration. Castrated dogs or spayed bitches are ineligible for entry.

*An informal photo of a 1938 field trial.*

Field trials usually take place in the spring and fall, when the weather is likely to be moderate. Usually the local clubs hold one trial per season. Larger events, called spring and fall Nationals and regionals, are sponsored by the member club, BHCA. These nearly always draw trialers from more than one region and often have social events, and in the case of the spring National, have an awards dinner and ceremony for outstanding breeders, hounds, etc., of the preceding year. Some of the larger trials may also include a Derby class. The Derby class is for any hound that has not reached its

second birthday on the day the class is scheduled. If you get your name on a master mailing list, you can find out the dates and locations of all the trials. Usually any trialer can see that you get this information.

To become a field champion, a Basset must win a prescribed number of placements at trials and a prescribed number of points based on the number of hounds in competition. Though these requirements do not change frequently, they are occasionally changed and to get up-to-date information on them, it is best to get a copy of *Field Trial Rules and Standard Procedures for Basset Hounds* from the AKC. A grand field championship is awarded by the BHCA to winners from the Champion class after a prescribed number of placements. Information on this award can be obtained from BHCA.

Field trials generally begin precisely at either 7 or 8 a.m. and you should have this information in advance. It is a good idea to get there with enough time to spare to fill out an entry blank and you must remember to bring your hound's registration information. The field trial will begin with the field trial secretary or chairman reading off the names of the entries. Your hound must be on the grounds for this and you should answer for its presence. Then the entries will be closed and a drawing will begin with the purpose of bracing two hounds to run in competition. When all hounds have been paired (two hounds owned by the same person will not be braced together), hounds, handlers, and the two judges will head for the field where the braces will be run in the order in which they were drawn. This is called the "first series." Spectators and waiting handlers, are called "the gallery." These people will beat the bush to drive out a rabbit. The person that sees the rabbit shouts, "Tally-ho" and marks the line that the rabbit takes when it runs. Each brace gets at least one rabbit line and perhaps more, depending on the desire of the judges. The two handlers put their hounds on the line and release them when they seem to be picking up the scent. After this, the hounds may

*Lineup at the Lebanon County Beagle Club.*

not be coached by the handlers and the handlers must remain behind the judges. After all the braces have been run in the first series, the judges will confer and then select, or call back, the best hounds (usually three or four braces), for the second series. From these hounds, placements of first through fourth will win the ribbons and trophies for the trial, and most importantly, the points toward a field championship. Honorary, the fifth-placing hound is awarded NBQ (next best qualifier), but does not earn points toward a field championship. At some trials there is a competition for Absolute Winner. This is determined by competing the winners of all the classes, Dog, Bitch, Champion, and Derby.

## How Field Trials Are Judged

Field trial judges need to have a thorough knowledge of the AKC rules, regulations, and procedures for Basset field trials. Most have attended a seminar to be sure of their familiarity with these rules. Judges should also have plenty of experience with watching hounds in competition. The *Field Trial Rules and Standard Procedures for Basset Hounds* contains the details of hound performance that the judges will consider. Desirable and undesirable qualities are discussed at some length. The good trailing hound uses desire and determination, has accuracy in making controlled progress on the rabbit line, and most importantly, never quits. Speed does not necessarily win, it must be controlled speed. A hound can run faster than he can trail game, but good hounds concentrate on keeping control of the line and pace themselves so that they are able to stay on the scent. Most of the judging at trials is done on the "checks." When a hound loses contact with the trail and must work to find it again, it is called a check. It is in these situations that the intelligent actions and aptitudes (and some of the faults) will show up most dramatically. The best hound not only will cover the distance covered by the rabbit but also will solve the problems created by the rabbit and be able to overcome a variety of scenting conditions. The field trial Basset is judged on his overall performance of this task and the best are those that get the most done in the best manner possible. We deal here with a kind of proportion (as we do also in physical conformation). We want a hound with desire and determination, balanced with steadiness and adaptability. So it is that a judge should have observed and compared quite a number of braces of Bassets to get a solid idea of what the virtues and faults in running look like. Field trials are competitive events in which hounds are rated as compared with each other and, thereby, become breeding tools. The quality of judging and judgments are therefore of primary importance.

## Training for Hunting and Field Trialing

There are many methods and individual approaches to these methods that can be used to start your Basset on trailing rabbits. Most Bassets start between six months and anywhere up to about three or four years of age. The older Bassets are often very hard to start. Also, it could be a disadvantage to start your hound too early because of his lack of maturity. The following are the most common methods of starting a hound:

1. ***Let him start by himself.*** Let him run free in a fenced area that has rabbits, such as a "starting pen" if you are lucky enough to have one easily available for this purpose. In the course of time, he will start himself running rabbits. An undesirable aspect of this is that your hound will not see hunting as a sport that you do together. This may possibly make him harder to manage when you do hunt together. You can, however, take him personally to a starting pen or area with plentiful rabbits, jump rabbits in front of him and try to get him interested in the scent at the "squat." The squat is the place where the rabbit had been hiding. The scent is usually stronger there and you can relate your interest to that scent. Seeing the rabbit can help start some hounds, but it can also hurt some hounds because they may persevere in "sight chasing" the rabbit rather than tracking it by scent. If they do, then a habit is formed that must be broken later.

*A typical field trial entry form.*

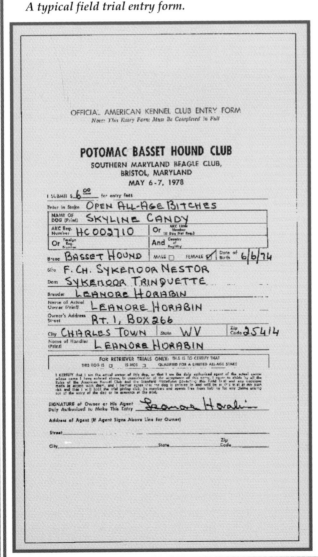

2. ***Let him run with another hound of excellent quality.*** If he can learn from imitation, he will copy a hound with good habits and style. Once you are sure he is taking the line, and not just "running dog," you should run him separately, and with other dogs, to be sure he is running independently. Indeed, one hazard of this method is the danger of the dog becoming dependent. You must run him with a good hound, which will be a reliable hound that will not teach bad habits, but he must then learn to run on his own and he must also learn that all other hounds are not necessarily reliable.

hounds thrive on coming from behind and beating an older dog, others will lose their independence. Some hounds running alone may later become adverse to running or cooperating with other hounds. It is difficult to lay down hard and fast rules. It is true, however, that patience with the hound is always vital. If he seems too immature, try a month later. Don't try to force him to start. Don't be harsh, hunting should be a joy. No matter what method of training you use, it is important to get your hound where the game is. Some hounds start quickly, some do not. Neither type will necessarily develop into a better hunter.

*A typical group of field trial winners Potomac BHC Bitch Stake, in November, 1980.*

3. ***Let him run in a pack with other hounds.*** This is similar to the above method, but the hound is running with a variety of other abilities and styles and there is less chance of becoming dependent. There is, however, more chance of becoming careless, of developing too much speed before a careful method of trailing is learned. It is probably a good idea to run the hound separately from the pack, alone and with one other hound, as soon as he has started. Some hounds have also started after watching others hunt for a while, and then one day they just go and join in.

The method you choose will depend on your particular hound and the type of running you want from the hound. While some

To quote from a prominent Beagler, Jim Hazelwood: "The procedure of starting a pup can take a long time. You may think that 'this dumb pup' will never start. I have known but few hounds that have never run a rabbit. If you have the time, patience, and rabbits, one day that necessary something will click in old Spot's brain."

Gradual, and sometimes quite fast, improvement should be observed once the Basset has been started trailing rabbit. There should be quite a bit of opportunity for your hound to get out and polish up on skill. Usually about two or three times a week will be necessary after starting, and from then on each time that you are attending a competition. Once the skill is established, lighter training with some lay-up periods will be all that is necessary to keep going with your hound for hunting or field trialing. Your Basset can do this for a lifetime. You can see all ages, from Derby age to 13 years old, at the trials. Some older hounds will slow up a bit and some become clever, with practice, at leading a bracemate astray. Very rarely do they ever lose their love for the game. The same can be said for their owners, who, once "hooked," stay with field trialing for decades.

## Field Trialers and the Natural Basset Hound

Basset Hound field trialing is a friendly family sport. Although field trials sustain and perpetuate the priceless heritage of the breed, and are the proving grounds of bloodlines, they are also the occasion for a camaraderie that lasts through the years. Field trialers are young and old, male and female, come from all walks of life and become dedicated to the sport. We know that one of the recurring arguments in the world of purebred dogs is about breeding for "frills of appearance," or glamour, versus breeding of dogs for their original purpose. Today the controversy rages on, sometimes with the contention that some breeds have been ruined, totally changed, and the original physical characteristics exaggerated to the detriment of the character and soundness of the dog. Trialers are determined that the *natural* Basset Hound will endure.

An obstacle for trialers has been that along with the shrinking of habitat for hunters has come the feeling that breeding for hunting quality is a lost cause. For a few years there was a surge in popularity for field trials as a way to test and preserve the original purpose of quite a few breeds, Beagles, Dachshunds, and Bassets among them. Bird dog and Beagle trials became very popular and the people who did it accumulated properties and followed principles of game and habitat preservation with the view to

having testing grounds available for trials. Today, however, some of these clubs and properties are disappearing slowly, similar to the way the naturally occurring habitats have been disappearing.

Today there is still a small core of field trialers "keeping the faith," primarily in the Northeast, Midwest, West, and Southwest. A number of these people have been dedicated to the natural Basset Hound for many years. Breed club support has been the mainstay of their efforts.

There is a strong bond that is enjoyed between the trialer and his Basset Hound. It's the story of a dog doing that special thing he is bred for with that special person he most loves. There is nothing to compare to watching the electrified body and twitching tail, the incomparable delight of a Basset finding the trail, the anxiety of watching him trying to work out a loss, and again the delight at gaining the direction of the scent. Your dog loves you and you love your dog. You have done something wonderful together. He has discovered his *natural* self. You have enjoyed his glorious display. He has proven himself. He is a *natural* Basset Hound. As Bill Rider, a trialer for over 35 years, once wrote: "How many times does a hunter follow his hound over the hill; how much do they endure together, how much excitement and pleasure do they share in competition. Then at the trial they take the breaks of the draw and wait their turn together. Finally, in the actual race, the handler is completely dependent on his hound (and Lady Luck) to get the job done. With such association as this, if the man likes his dog at all, it's just a matter of time until that liking turns to love."

*Then if th' harmonious thunder of the field*
*Delight they revished ears, the deep flew'd hound*
*Breed up with care—strong, heavy, slow but sure:*
*Whose ears down-hanging from his high-peak'd head*
*Shall sweep the morning dew.*
............*Somerville*

# The First 20 Basset Hound Field Champions

1. FC Hillcrest Peggy (Maple Drive Jigilo ex Maple Drive Carmelita)
2. FC Irish Hills Senator (Staridge Pol ex Trompette II)
3. FC Bijou Rutile of Banbury (Ch. Westerby Vintage ex Bijou Sapphire of Banbury)
4. FC Queen Elizabeth (Maple Drive Marlin ex Cooks Bonnie Best)
5. FC Hartshead Jet (Hartshead Masked Knight ex Hartshead Firegirl)
6. FC Perrys Marigold (Hartshead Trigger II ex Boses Melicent Hepsy)
7. FC Pounder II (FC Bose's Royal Knight ex Malone)
8. FC Bose's Royal Knight (Duke of Greenhill ex Boses Melicent Hepsy)
9. FC Yoders Sally Belle (Reisers Tusc O Sport ex Bakers Judy Ann)
10. FC Tulpehocken Peg (Maple Ridge Sandie ex FC Perrys Marigold)
11. FC Eingles Becky (Smiths Major Tempo ex Als Bonnie Girl)
12. FC Boses Neil Theron (Duke of Greenhill ex Boses Melicent Hepsy)
13. FC Boses Exploress (Boses Dapper Dan ex FC Yoders Sally Belle)
14. FC Arrowhead Jody (Belbay Clous ex Lors Majorette)
15. FC Long John Silver (Lord Tietge ex Todles Peggy)
16. FC Boses Dusty Scarlet (Duke of Greenhill ex Boses Melicent Hepsy)
17. FC Behneys Bill (Shaws Brownie Prince ex FC Eingles Becky)
18. FC Boses Alethia (FC Boses Neil Theron ex FC Yoders Sally Belle)
19. FC Miss Mitzie (Rex Cumberland ex Princess Pat Sport)
20. FC Boses Snowflake (Boses Dapper Dan ex FC Yoders Sally Belle)

# The First 20 Grand Field Champions

1. GFC Hamlins Dolly (FC Hamlins Torpedo ex FC Irles Cleopatra) ............................... E. Carhart
2. GFC McWilliams Dixie Belle (McWilliams Buccaneer ex McWilliams Dixie Peach)................................................................................................... K. McWilliams
3. GFC Vans Fantasy (FC Beacon Tick Tock ex Crelins Lady Fair) ........................... T. Pettit
4. GFC Tagg Abouts Pluto (Sandy Hill Homer ex FC Tagabouts Porsche) .............. E. & S. Tagg
5. GFC Slippery Hill Sophie (FC Slippery Hill Calvin ex FC Beldeans Slipper Hill Sam) ...................................................................................................... L. Skolnick
6. GFC Sykemoor Nestor (Dalewell Rambler ex Sykemoor Java) ......................... L. Horabin
7. GFC Mickeys At Last (Azul Rayo ex Crelins Fancy Dancer) ............................. A. Carter
8. GFC Tagg Abouts Jensen (FC Tagg Abouts Pluto ex Brooklines Minn) .............. E. & S. Tagg
9. GFC Campbells Rebel Queen (FC Rosies Bill ex Campbells Cindy Lou) .................... H. Smith
10. GFC Slippery Hill Stub (FC Slippery Hill Calvin ex FC Beldeans Slippery Hill Sam) ...................................................................................................... L. Skolnick
11. GFC Triple R Patricia (Campbells Troubador ex Sues Lucky Lady) ......................................................................... R. Oosterbaan & R. Gargas
12. GFC Sborays Caesar (Ch. Burchs Big Bo ex Boyers Amanda Lee)........................ K. Harvery
13. GFC Candys Viking (Rex of Largo ex Norsemans Cleopatra) ................................. B. Forseth
14. GFC Clancy James (Fouses Clancy Lee ex Horsts Cricket Blake) ...................... T. O'Conner
15. GFC Kenners Duke (FC Sborays Caesar ex FC Miss Fanny II) ............................. E. Beldean
16. Dual Ch./GFC Pettits Ranger Ric (FC Rosies Jeff ex FC Dohrshires Twiggy) ..................................................................................................... T. & S. Pettit
17. GFC Navars Slicker (FC Navars Zekle ex FC Wilsons Mindy Lou) ............................ P. Navar
18. GFC Southern Shots (Oak Shadows Sweetie Pie ex Lady Cleopatra)  Amanda R. Gargas, Jr.
19. GFC Inas Wimpy (FC Carls Little Fellow ex FC Inas Carline) ....................................... D. Dever
20. GFC Sandy Lees Irish Mist (Dual Ch./GFC Pettits Ranger Ric ex FC Dailys Sad Susie)................................................................. R. & S. Quackenbush

# The Dual Champions

| # | Name | Owner | Year |
|---|------|-------|------|
| 1. | Dual Ch. and Can. Ch. Kazoo's Moses The Great | J. & P. Dohr | 1964 |
| 2. | Dual Ch. Helwal's Desire | W. & H. Smith | 1969 |
| 3. | Dual Ch. Braun's Wholly Thursday | J. & M. Braun | 1970 |
| 4. | Dual Ch. Tantivy Daisy's | Dopey W. Luce | 1971 |
| 5. | Dual Ch.-Bda Ch. Double B's Lucky Libertine | L. & R. Wells | 1972 |
| 6. | Dual Ch. Slippery Hill Cinnamon | L. Skolnick | 1974 |
| 7. | Dual Ch./GFC Pettit's Ranger Ric | T. & S. Pettit | 1977 |
| 8. | Dual Ch. Jackson's Samantha Lu | S. Ellingwood | 1977 |
| 9. | Dual Ch. Handyman of Cape Cod | L. & R. Wells | 1978 |
| 10. | Dual Ch. Molly's Mr. Benjamin | B. L. Deir | 1981 |
| 11. | Dual Ch. Custusha's Sobrina of Cape Cod | L. & R. Wells | 1982 |
| 12. | Dual Ch. Branscombe's Troilus | T. D. F. & R. Paule | 1982 |
| 13. | Dual Ch. Branscombe's Man of LaMancha TD, CD | F. & R. Paule | 1983 |
| 14. | Dual Ch. Sanrob's Reginald | R. & S. Reynolds | 1985 |
| 15. | Dual Ch. Sanrob's Shilo | R. & S. Reynolds | 1985 |
| 16. | Dual Ch. Rhinelan's Earnest Pierson | B. & D. Rinderneck | 1988 |
| 17. | Dual Ch. Branscombe Dulcinea CD, TD | R. Paule | 1989 |
| 18. | Dual Ch. Sanrob's Tobias | R. & S. Reynolds | 1989 |
| 19. | Dual Ch. Snifter Red Erica of Cape Cod | L. Wells | 1989 |
| 20. | Dual Ch. Branscombe Bugle Ann TD | R. Paule | 1989 |
| 21. | Dual Ch. Bayrocs O'Mally | H. Farthing | 1991 |
| 22. | Dual Ch. Crabtrees Golden Mystery | H. Farthing | 1992 |
| 23. | Dual Ch. Tailgates Dreamboat Annie | N. & J. Ferris | 1992 |
| 24. | Dual Ch. Stillhouse Alexander | L. & K. Gavin | 1992 |
| 25. | Dual Ch. Branscombe Good Intentions | L. Hager | 1993 |
| 26. | Dual Ch. Bugle Bays Anise O'Stillhouse TD | J. & M. Cook | 1993 |
| 27. | Dual Ch. Branscombe Troubador TD | C. & S. Launey and F. & J. Hager | 1994 |
| 28. | Dual Ch. Tailgate Canis Major | L. Schmidt | 1994 |
| 29. | Dual Ch. Branscombe Trumpeter | R. Paule | 1994 |
| 30. | Dual Ch. Stillhouse Abagail CD, TDX | J. & M. Cook | 1996 |
| 31. | Dual Ch. Branscombe Kachina | Fritz Hager | 1996 |
| 32. | Dual Ch. Tailgate Desert Sands | G. Allen and G. Tankard | 1996 |

# GALLERY OF NATIONAL SPECIALTY FIELD TRIAL WINNERS 1960–1996

*We honor those hounds and their owners who have been awarded at the Basset Hound Club of America annual National Specialty field trial either BW or Absolute Winner, between 1960 and 1998. The reader should be aware that the award of Absolute Winner did not begin until the 1968 Nationals. Prior to that time, BW was the highest award given. Either of these awards is indeed a significant milestone for both the hounds and their owners, and is an achievement sought after by every field trialer in the club. Once again, many aspire, but relatively few achieve, and it is note-worthy that this award is, to some degree, less subjective than the conformation awards.*

## CONGRATULATIONS TO ALL.

### 1962: BEACON TULPEN DUKE
**Owner: Fred Atwater**

### 1964: ROSIE'S SPORTSMAN
**Owner: Howard Smith**

### 1968: FCH. MCWILLIAMS DIXIE BELLE
**Owner: Ken McWilliams**

### 1969: FCH. HI LAWN ROXANNE
**Owner: B. Bennett**

*The title Absolute Winner became effective in 1968; winners from 1960 through 1967 were called Best of Winners.

Photographs not available for the following years and winners:
1960: SHELLBARK'S MICHIE. Owner: Loren Free.
1961: BUSH HILL'S RED DUKE. Owner: No Record.
1963: KRAMER'S MO. Owner: Samuel Bridgers.
1965: FARMER'S NEVER IDLE SALLIE. Owner: Steve Munger.
1966: OLD KENTUCKY BURLEY. Owner: Sam K. Bridgers
1967: BLUE DUCHESS. Owner: Robert Oosterbaan.

**1970: BELDEAN'S SLIPPERY HILL SAM**
Owner: Leonard Skolnick

**1971: FCH. FERGUSON OF BONNIE**
Owner: Robert Segrin

**1972 & 1973: FCH. VANS FANTASY**
Owners: Tom and Shirley Pettit

**1974: FCH. SLIPPERY HILL SOPHIE**
Owner: Leonard Skolnick

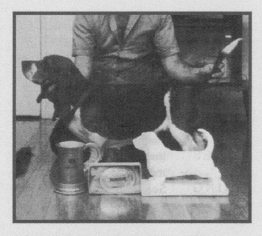

**1975: FCH. CARL'S GIRL**
**Owner: Donald Dever**

**1976: INA'S WIMPY**
**Owner: Donald Dever**

**1977: FCH. PIERSON'S DARLIN DAISY MAE**
**Owners: C. and L. Pierson**

**1978: ROSIE'S DEBBIE**
**Owners: Bill and Mary Rider**

### 1979: FCH. PETTIT'S IRISH CHEER
**Owners: Tom and Shirley Pettit**

### 1980: MCWILLIAMS DIXIE CUP
**Owners: Ken McWilliams**

### 1981: FCH PETTIT'S STAR TRIC
**Owners: Tom and Shirley Pettit**

### 1982: DORSHIRE'S SABRINA
**Owners: Jim and Pat Dohr**

**1983: FCH. PIERSON'S
TROUBLESOME TILLY CD**
Owners: Charles and Linda Pierson

**1984: MCWILLIAMS SHORTCAKE**
Owners: Ken and Mary
McWilliams

**1985: FCH SLIPPERY HILL
GEGENSCHEIN**
Owners: Leonard Skolnick

**1986: MCWILLIAMS MINT JULEP**
Owners: Len and Mary
McWilliams

**1987: SHELLBARK'S WHITE OWL**
Owner: Bill Ashabraner

**1988: HARTSHEAD GOOD TIMES SEAN**
Owner: Bill Ten Eyck

**1989: FCH. RED ACRES DUKE**
Owner: Bill Ten Eyck

**1990: FCH. FRIENDBROOK'S OTTO**
Owners: Barney and Laura Linebaugh

**1991: FCH. CROOKED STICKS MOLLY**
Owners: Vince and Marilyn Urick

**1992: MC WILLIAMS TEXAS TWO STEP**
Owners: Ken and Mary McWilliams

**1993: D.CH. BUGLE BAY'S ANISE O'STILLHOUSE**
Owners: Jim & Marge Cook

**1994: G. FCH. LOWRIE'S CASEY**
Owner: Jerry Wardropper

**1995: FCH. SLIPPERY HILL KINDA CLOSE**
Owner: Leonard Skolnick

**1996: RIDER'S SWEET N LOW**
Owner: Bill and Mary Rider

**1997: FCH. FLEMING'S RED**
**ACRE'S DANA**
Owners: D. Fleming
& B. Ten Eyck

**1998: TAILGATE DESERT DUNES**
Owners: Schmidt/Allen/Tankard

# The Pack Bassets

*The Timber Ridge Basset Hound Pack.*

In 1921 Gerald Livingston started the Kilsyth Pack in Long Island. It was the first known organized Basset Hound pack in America. Mr. Livingston and Mr. Erastus Tefft (Staridge Pack) drafted heavily from the Walhampton Pack in England and imported from France. Eng/Am. Ch. Walhampton Andrew was one of those brought to America. His sire, Walhampton Ferryman, was a fifth generation descendant of "Ada," one of the "Nicholas" ex "Inoculation" offspring (the original Basset to Bloodhound breeding of Sir Everett Millais). It was Mr. Livingston who first brought the "modern" Bassets, both French breeds and English, to America.

Around 1926 Mr. G. W. King (Maple Drive Bassets) started breeding Basset Hounds in Gobles, Michigan. The hounds he bred were from stock gathered from both Erastus Tefft (Staridge) and Gerald Livingston (Kilsyth). Mr. King owned "Staridge Pol," who sired "Maple Drive Marlin." Marlin would figure quite significantly in American pedigrees as he was the sire of Ch. Mon Phillipe of Greenly Hall. Phillipe was out of the bitch hound, Coquette of Greenly Hall and was bred by Mr. and Mrs. Fogleson. The Kilsyth, Staridge, Brandywine, Bijou Bassets, Red Bank, the Rowe House Bassets, and the Stockford Bassets were all hunting packs prior to WWII.

During the same period, Mrs. Consuelo Ford, an early American breeder and owner of the Bijou of Banbury Pack, imported Eng. Ch. Westerby Vintage (Wick Vagabond ex Amayllis of Reynalton), whelped on May 15, 1937. His breeder was Dr. E. F. S. Morrison (not yet a Colonel), the man who would be given distinct honor of being the father of the "English Basset." To all true Basset Hound breeders, he is quite easily the main reason for the crossbred (English Basset) hounds rather than true Basset Hounds being used in most modern pack work in England today.

Mrs. Elizabeth Streeter started pack hunting with AKC Basset Hounds. She remembered that breeders would ask her if she would like to have their "long-haired" hounds since they did not meet the show standard. She preferred these hounds and wanted a whole pack of "long-hairs"; however, they would not breed true. It was Leslie Kelly's contention that these longer-haired hounds came from the breeding done at the Dalby Hall Pack in England, but very near the Scottish border. These hounds, Kelly says, were rugged and a bit rougher in coat and physique. Hounds from the Dalby Hall kennels figured predominately in early Staridge, Maple Drive, and Nottke Basset pedigrees. Mrs. Streeter described these hounds by saying, "They were great hunters!"

Later Mrs. Streeter changed her Skycastle French hounds pack by being the first to import the Petit Basset Griffon Vendéen into America. While they hunted more like Beagles or terriers, they were enjoyable to both Mrs. Streeter and the pack's supporters. I was sorry to see Mrs. Streeter pass away just as her beloved Petit Basset Griffon Vendéen breed was becoming popular in the US. Or, possibly it was a blessing, as what has been sported and catapulted to stardom in the dog game as the Petit breed do not really resemble the true petit-sized Bassets of France and Mrs. Streeter's pack.

In America during the late 1940s, Mr. and Mrs. Andrew Porter of the Upland Pack imported several dog and bitch hounds from the Westerby Pack in England. They were Westerby Dominick, Westerby Gadfly, Westerby Gainful, and Westerby Gaylass. These hounds were still of the pure Basset Hounds within the Westerby Pack. Westerby Dominick became the sire of Ch. Lyn Mar Acres Scalawag who appears in many old pedigrees.

In 1946, Charles R. Rogers's Timber Ridge Bassets became the first recognized pack of Basset Hounds in North America. It was recognized by the National Beagle Club, the organization that oversees all Beagle and Basset pack activities. The pack still hunted until 1989 with its master and huntsman

Amelia F. Rogers. She came to the pack in late 1948. She recalls that: "Charles always said that if he ever found a good whipper-in (and it's a female), he'd marry her." In 1950 Amelia became Mrs. Charles Rogers and joint master of the pack. It was the oldest continuous Basset Hound pack in North America.

Mrs. Amelia (Meena) Rogers and Penny and Randy Frederiksen met because of Ch. Strathalbyn Lugano, a very promising young puppy dog hound that they had acquired from the Strathalbyn Bassets (Mr. and Mrs. Eric and Erica George, MD) kennels. The Timber Ridge Bassets had been taking hounds from Strathalbyn for years, so they were quite interested when they saw him winning the Jr. Sweepstakes at the 1986 BHCA National event. In fact, the pack drafted him into Timber Ridge and for two hunt seasons he was one of the lead hunters in the pack. Lugano was but one of several Ambrican hounds drafted by the pack. Meena and Edward, the pack's honorable secretary and chief whip, abruptly disbanded the pack during 1989, very soon after the death of Eric George.

America's Basset Hound pack activities are not governed or regulated by the AKC or BHCA organizational structure, other than for the individual hound's registration. They do run under the governing rules of the National Beagle Club, thereby, they are recognized, or not recognized by them, as the case may be. Possibly this has come about in the main because many Beagle clubs are actual hunt ground-holding clubs. Some of those packs recognized in the past by the National Beagle Club are: Timber Ridge Bassets, Skycastle French Hounds*, Somerset Bassets, Tewksbury Foots Bassets*, Ashland Bassets, Three Creek Bassets*, Winward Bassets*, Spring Creek Bassets*, Wayne DuPage Foot Bassets, Sandanona Hare Hounds*, Bonniwell Basset Hounds*, Weymouth Bassets, Marlborough Bassets, Strathalbyn Bassets, and Mrs. Cochran's Hounds (not yet recognized). *Those packs noted are not currently purebred Basset Hound packs. A small active family pack named the Poona also hunted and competed during the late '50s and early '60s.

The Basset Hound in the field, doing what comes naturally is a beautiful sight. The Basset Hound as a hunter, however, is *not* about *killing* the quarry, nor is it just about *chasing*. Hunting with the Basset Hound, it seems to me, is what Peter Guy, a hunt supporter in England, has defined as *"The finding and pursuit of a wild hare, in its natural habitat, by hounds, using scent."* Obviously, you can substitute any quarry within the definition but the point is the same.

Most packs are privately owned, but some are supported by subscribers. These subscriptions mean to support the financial end of housing a pack of hounds for the year 'round pleasure of the subscribers and the pack owner. There is always a field master who is responsible for the actions of the field (all the subscribers and their guests). The field master would let you know which way to go and when to stay put, etc. And, there are always some unwritten rules to follow such as: Always closing gates behind you, rolling under fences where possible or climbing a fence at the post areas, moving very quietly near a farmer's stock, silently signaling to the huntsman when the quarry is spotted and not shouting (although some do allow the field to yell "Tally-ho"), being very quiet when the hounds are close to you and working, never overrunning hounds at a check, and being extremely careful with smoking in the fields.

Basseting is a hunting sport. In the States, the quarry of most packs is the cottontail rabbit. We really come to see hounds do their thing. Lest we forget, they are referred to as hounds, not "the" hounds. This was probably picked up from English terminology such as when the English refer to going to hospital... it is never to "the" hospital... just, hospital. No one really knows why, it's just that way.

Randy discloses, "We were fortunate enough to have been involved with several scheduled meets of the Timber Ridge Pack kenneled in Hempsted, Maryland, and mastered by Mrs. Amelia "Meena" Rogers who was also huntsman (she never went along with the term huntswoman). Also, many times she would take us out with the pack on our own private hunts, which were as much for the exercise of hounds as well as ourselves. One of our most memorable hunts was one that I had captured on video tape. What a shot! The actual quarry, hiding in the tall grass, and the subsequent chase scene were captured on film. Another time was when there was snow on the ground and I asked the dumb question about what they did in the winter. The answer soon brought forth heavy clothes and boots and the pack was called to action. Needless to say, layered clothing was in order as you need to be able to peel off the layers as you warm up from the exercise."

As the hunt progresses, hounds are watched as they move into each hedgerow to scare up the quarry. It is usually the bitch hounds that seem to lunge themselves into the thick undergrowth while most of the dog hounds are willing to wait outside. This is serious business and you get the point when watching hounds with their noses to the ground and their sterns feathering with great vigor. Finding the rabbit is a natural thing for hounds and, when they do, their cry is music to your ears. One of the hunt staff's jobs is to make sure that the pack is actually on rabbit scent and not on the scent of a deer because they would be off into the next county before anyone could stop them.

While there is actual historical reasoning for the hunting of rabbits that raid crops and destroy gardens, the real sport is in the chase and in the beautiful work that hounds can do while following the line. Randy adds that "on one private hunt exercise, the scene was absolutely breathtaking when both the Timber Ridge whipper-in, Edward, and I observed the pack from a distant vantage point and saw it move as one whole unit, turning in unison like a flight of birds. It was a sight to behold as 15 couples (30 hounds), at full cry, moved as one. Moments like these are the best and to be enjoyed by all present, because if the actual kill is what you are looking for then a pack of purebred Bassets is not the one to be following. They seldom actually catch the rabbit because it has usually gone to ground way before the hounds could catch them. However, there are times, since rabbits usually circle, that hounds do run upon the quarry and then a kill is made."

When a scent is caught by a hound, and it starts to feather its stern (tail), the huntsman will wait to see if it commits to a line and then sound the hunting horn to summon the other hounds to that line. If it is a good line, and the other hounds pick it up too, then the chase is on. The field is perfectly quiet as the hounds attempt to search the faint line. This is called hold hard, and it is the field master who motions this command to the field. However, if the quarry was to have scampered out the other end of the hedgerow and a member of the field saw it, you would probably then hear "Tally-ho." The huntsman would take the hounds to the spot where the quarry was last spotted so that they could find the line from there. The chase is not only for the hounds

but for the field as well, and when you are through you have really had your exercise for the week.

After a day's hunting, the field is usually invited to stay afterward for some refreshments. Since, at times, a field could consist of up to or more than a hundred persons, these can get to be pretty hefty affairs on the pocketbook. Some fields just meet at the local pub to talk about the hunt and any other such subjects...kind of like the fish tales heard by anglers after a local tournament.

It is obvious that this type of full pack hunting is not for everyone, well at least, the actual financial side of it isn't. Small packs, on the other hand, can be housed in regular home kenneling if they are trained to work as a pack. Even just hunting with one or two hounds, as is done by many hunters after pheasant or snowshoe rabbits, can work extremely well. In fact, in part because of the desire to keep the hunting instinct in the Basset Hound, early enthusiasts designed field trials as a part of the

*The Tantivy Pack receives a blessing prior to the start of a hunt.*

# BASSET PACK HUNTING TERMS:

| | |
|---|---|
| At fault | Hounds have lost the scent. |
| Babble | To give tongue without reason. |
| Cast | An attempt to recover the lost scent. |
| Check | Hounds temporarily lose the scent. |
| Chop | Hounds kill the quarry without a hunt. |
| Colors | The pack's official colors worn only by the hunt staff. |
| Country | The official hunting area the pack calls its own. |
| Couple | Two hounds, hounds are counted in pairs. |
| Doe | Female hare or rabbit. |
| Drag | Artificially laid scent. |
| Draw | Exploration of likely hiding places of quarry. |
| Dwell | When hounds do not drive forward. |
| Feathering | Vigorously wagging the stern to indicate interest. |
| Field | All subscribers and guests. |
| Field master | In charge of the actions of the field during the hunt. |
| Fixture card | A listing of the various meets to be held. |
| Full cry | Chorus of hounds running their quarry with a good scent. |
| Hold hard | Stand still. |
| Honorary secretary | Secretary for the pack. |
| Hound | Proper term for hunting dog or bitch. |
| Huntsman | Person in charge of actual hunt and pack. |
| Jack | Male hare or rabbit. |
| Lead hounds | Those hounds leading the pack. |
| Lift hounds | Moving hounds to a new covert. |
| Line | The line traveled by the quarry. |
| Mark | Indicating the last spot quarry viewed. |
| Mark to ground | Hounds indicating quarry gone to ground (technical kill). |
| Master | Usually owner of the pack (Master of Hounds). |
| Meet | The actual hunting event. |
| Mute | Hound follows scent but does not give tongue. |
| Pack | Generic term for the working unit of hounds. |
| Quarry | Animal being hunted. |
| Riot | Hunting something other than the specific quarry. |
| Scent | Smell left by quarry. |
| Season | The time during the year when hunting is allowed. |
| Stern | Tail of a hound. |
| Tail hounds | Hounds running in rear of pack. |
| Tally-ho | The call made when quarry is viewed. |
| Whipper-in | Part of hunt staff to help guide hounds. |
| Worry | Hounds fighting over quarry kill. |

Basseting sport. And, from this beginning came the Basset Hound Club of America. In England, the club decided to take an actual pack under its protection and support for the hunting qualities of the Basset Hound to be preserved. The pack is called the Albany Pack.

In America, as in England, the old packs had gone (Kilsyth Bassets, Bijou Bassets, and the Starridge Bassets) or changed over to crossbred hounds, but still there are a few purebred Basset Hound packs to be found; The Marborough (PA), Springcreek (IL), Weymouth (NC), Somerset Bassets (VA), Ashland Bassets (VA), Southern Illinois Foot Bassets (IL), and the Three Creek Pack (the reorganized Strathalbyn). Historically recently fallen names are: Timber Ridge (MD) which ended its 43 year run in 1989, as did the Wayne Du Page Hunt (IL) of Dr. and Mrs. Ted Kjellstrom. Mr. Joseph J. McKenna's

Cold Stream Pack no longer hunts and neither do the Flint Hill Bassets, the Strathalbyn Bassets, the Tantivy Bassets, or the Bridlespur Bassets. The Tewksbury Foot Bassets is no longer a purebred Basset Hound pack.

The act of hunting with a pack does, in fact, combine some of the disciplines of tracking and field trialing, but with the added confinement of teamwork among the pack individuals. As hunting goes, pack Basseting is more action packed than the field trialing or tracking experiences. It is a most inspiring sight, that of hounds casting and running a line in a very wide pattern at first but then bringing it all together once the scent is strong. There are few who would call this an amble through the countryside. All in all, the comradeship at the local pub, clubhouse, or at someone's home is certainly a great way to end the day.

*Just a brace of Bassets on the scent of a rabbit...the beginning of something wonderful!*

*"Happy the man, who with unrivall'd speed*
*Can pass his fellows, and with pleasure view*
*The struggling pack; how in the rapid chase*
*Alternate the preside, and jostling push*
*To guide the dubious scent; how giddy youth*
*Oft babbling errs, by wiser age reprov'd*
*How, niggard of his strength, the wise old hound*
*Hangs in the rear, till some important point*
*Rouse all his diligence, or till the chase*
*Sinking he finds; then to the head he springs*
*With thirst of glory fit'd, and wins the prize."*
***Author Unknown***

# Health and the Basset Hound

## INTRODUCTION

This section on the health of the Basset Hound is written for the breeder and/or owner of a Basset as an aid in maximizing his ability to deal with the health problems he encounters. It is not intended to be a general health guide, nor is it intended to supplant the veterinarian's expertise. It covers four areas that should be of concern to breeders and pet owners. The first section discusses the importance of observation, or looking versus seeing. It is followed by some tips for selecting a veterinarian. Next comes a description of the reproduction problems that the breeder may encounter. The final section contains a list of the genetic diseases and disorders that have been identified in the Basset with a short description of each.

## WHAT TO LOOK FOR

By far, the most important tool the breeder has for ensuring the health of his animals is his skill in observation. Knowing what is normal and what is not for a particular animal can help to identify health problems before they become significant. What the owner sees is not the problem, but rather a symptom of the problem. It is this information that will help the veterinarian in making a diagnosis, should it be necessary to seek medical assistance.

Taking notes on things you see that "aren't quite right" is an excellent way to discover potential problems. Each observation should include date and time, and what took place with any ideas you have about why you're seeing what you're seeing. What you are doing in performing this exercise is documenting patterns of symptoms or behaviors. The patterns may not make sense to you, but may provide great assistance to the veterinarian in making a diagnosis.

**Elimination:** Stools should be examined at least once a day. Are they firm and of normal color? Are they loose or runny? Do they contain blood or mucous? Do they contain foreign objects such as rocks, pieces of wood, etc.? Are there as many as usual? Is the dog urinating more or less frequently than usual and how does this relate to his consumption of water? Is there any blood in the urine? Is it much darker in color than normal? Is he relieving himself in a place that is not usual?

**Eating:** Are the dog's eating habits normal for him? Is he eating the usual quantity? Is he eager to eat? Is he going through the same eating ritual with each feeding? For one dog that may mean dumping his food on the floor before consuming it daintily, while for another it may mean inhaling it.

**Cycle consistency:** Are the bitch's seasons totally predictable? Is it approximately the same number of days between seasons over the years? Do they last for approximately the same number of days? Is the flow heavier or lighter than normal? If you're not recording the dates and length of each season, you should be.

**Attitude:** Is the dog's attitude the same as usual? Is he as interested in his toys as he usually is? Does he show the same excitement when he sees the van being packed for a show? Does he show the same remorse when he knows he's committed a *faux pas*?

**Coat:** Is the coat as shiny and smooth as usual? Has his coat changed to a rough or dry-feeling coat? Is he shedding more than usual for the time of year? Is he losing hair down the top of his back or is it occurring in one location? Is the skin healthy looking?

**Eyes:** Are his eyes bright and shiny? Is there evidence of scratches, abrasions or cloudiness apparent in the eye? Are you sure he can see you well? Are his eyes filled with matter or mucous? If his eyes are clear, are they really clear, or does he have a kennelmate who cleans him regularly? Is the sclera (the white part of the eye) as white as normal?

**Alertness:** While we don't measure Basset IQ, it's obvious that some hounds are more intelligent than others. Is your dog as alert as usual? Does he have periods where he looks "spacey" or seems not to recognize you? Does he suddenly growl at you when he's never done it before and there is no apparent reason? Does he pace when he doesn't normally do that?

**Ears**: While it's a known fact that Bassets practice selective hearing ("Cookie" is always heard, "Get off the sofa" isn't), dogs can have legitimate hearing problems. Does your dog come when called as he always has or is he starting to miss on occasion? Do you know that he is responding to your voice, or is he responding to the vibration he feels when you clap and call his name? Are his ears as clean as normal? Sniff them. Do they smell unusual? Are they unusually dirty or are they filled with wax?

**Temperature**: You should check your dog's temperature when you know all is well with him so that you know when he has a fever or is subnormal.

**Lameness**: If the dog is not moving normally, try to determine why. Start with the foot: Is the pad injured? Has a toenail broken off or pulled out? Does the wrist flex normally with no evidence of pain when you move it? What about the elbow? Is there any sign of injury to the leg itself? If he is lame on the left rear leg today, was he lame on the right rear leg last week? Has he been crated or kept in a small confined area for several days with no apparent improvement?

**Stress:** Sometimes the unusual thing you see is not a health problem at all, but may be the result of what is going on in the dog's "world." The death of a kennelmate may leave a dog very depressed. He may seem lethargic and not want to eat or play. A dog going to a new home will require a period of adjustment. He may require a refresher course in housebreaking. Prolonged absence of a family member or other stress in the family may have its effect on the dog. Airplane travel can cause stress.

**The hands-on approach:** Dogs love to be touched and lucky for them this is another of your observation tools. You should touch your dog at least once a day. As you run your hands over him you are feeling for anything that doesn't seem normal. Does he have flea nests or lumps? Is his skin of normal color without signs of inflammation, rash or injury? Are there any areas that seem to be tender to the touch? Does the coat feel normal? Are there signs of fungal growth between the toes? Is the skin moist in any area? Do the ears look clean? Is the gumline pink and healthy or is it inflamed and red where it meets the teeth? Are the teeth clean or are they covered with tartar, crud, and the like? Is there any discharge visible?

**Summary:** When you seek help from your veterinarian your input is essential. Any observations you have made may make the difference between a correct diagnosis (and resolution) of a problem and an incorrect diagnosis.

## HOW TO SELECT A VETERINARIAN

You want a veterinarian who is willing to communicate both with you and with others. Obviously, no one person is going to be expert in all areas, so you must find someone who is willing to consult with others when the need arises. Using fax, phone and e-mail makes consultation relatively easy for your veterinarian today.

When you are looking for a new veterinarian, either because you're new in the area or because you and your current veterinarian have had a parting of the ways, you should interview people. Start with those veterinarians who come recommended by breeders in your area, or call the local veterinary medical association for a recommendation. They're listed in the phone book. And check out the office staff too. Do they seem to care about your animal? Are they careful to follow the veterinarian's instructions? Do they seem easy to work with?

Take one of your dogs in for routine care, and tell them what you're looking for. Be completely honest and open. Tell them what you expect of a veterinarian, how you expect to follow through with their advice, and what your needs are. You want to establish a relationship based on honesty and mutual respect. If none of the first few you consult seem to be what you're looking for, you might ask yourself if you are being realistic and reasonable.

## SPECIAL PROBLEMS RELATED TO BREEDING

When one takes the leap from owning a Basset to breeding it, it's somewhat akin to jumping across the Atlantic. While the Basset is thought of as an "easy keeper," breeding this hound can be fraught with problems and only those who are thoroughly prepared and knowledgeable about the familial lines, the potential problems, and the genetic implications should attempt it.

For the typical pet owner, spaying or neutering the animal is the recommended course. Breeding can be filled with heartache not to mention financial problems. Only those animals that can contribute to the improvement of the breed should be bred.

Assuming the bitch is worthy of breeding, the breeder should be aware of the following problems that can occur. Each problem is described very briefly and the descriptions are not meant to be complete. If a breeder suspects that any of these problems is present, a veterinarian should be consulted.

The problems described here are all possibilities when breeding is attempted. Some of them are seldom seen and others not uncommon.[4, 5]

**Adrenal failure:** Adrenal failure may be seen within a few weeks prior to or following whelping. Vomiting and diarrhea may be seen and the bitch will be weak. It is seen most often in large litters or in litters with large pups.

**Brucellosis:** Brucellosis is an infection that can pass from one animal to another in the kennel. All breeding animals should be tested for it prior to mating regardless of their breeding history. Abortions during late pregnancy or stillbirths may result from the disease. There may be long-term implications.

**Detached placenta:** The sign of a detached placenta is usually a green discharge, or in worst cases it may be very dark and thick. This is an emergency situation.

**Eclampsia:** Eclampsia may be seen within a week or so of whelping, but may also be seen in the week before parturition if the bitch has a lot of milk. It is caused by a drop in the calcium serum level in the blood. The bitch has muscle spasms that you will first see as a quivering sensation in her shoulders. Left untreated, eclampsia is fatal.

**False pregnancy:** Bitches have been known to show all the signs of pregnancy including milk production and nesting, only to produce nothing but disappointment.

**Hemorrhage:** There are a number of conditions that may cause the bitch to hemorrhage following the whelping of her pups. Hemorrhaging is not normal and a veterinarian's advice should be sought. Treatment will depend upon the cause.

**Mastitis:** Mastitis is an infection of one or more of the mammary glands. The breeder will see unusual redness and the breast will feel warmer and firmer than normal. The milk expressed may be thick and yellow, or even have blood in it. Puppies should not be allowed to nurse unless and until a veterinarian has examined the bitch.

**Metritis:** Metritis is a bacterial infection of the uterus. It may lead to pyometra. There may be a strong odor during the whelping or in the days following. A veterinarian should be consulted if it is suspected.

**Pyometra:** One or both of the uterine horns will be filled with pus. It normally results in abortion or stillborn pups if the bitch is pregnant when it occurs, but if pups survive there will likely be deformities. When it occurs, it is usually seen in bitches over five years of age. There will be a strong odor. The bitch may vomit and show signs of depression, becoming weaker and weaker as it progresses. A veterinarian should be consulted immediately.

**Resorption:** Resorption is a condition in which the fetal tissue is "absorbed" back into the bitch's body. It may be caused by hormonal irregularity or by stress. The breeder may see signs of depression, but may notice nothing else.

**Retained placentas:** Retained placentas are those sacs not delivered following presentation of the puppy. The condition can lead to metritis or pyometra if they remain. A "pit shot" (oxytocin) is usually administered following whelping to prevent this.

**Torsion of the uterus:** One of the horns of the uterus may twist. If it occurs it is usually seen near the time of whelping. This is an emergency situation and requires immediate attention by the veterinarian.

**Toxins:** Pregnant bitches may eat things that they wouldn't ordinarily consider. Toxins cannot be ignored as the cause of panting, watery eyes, etc. Bitches have even been known to eat rocks during pregnancy only to end up with an intestinal blockage requiring surgery. Lethargy and depression are typically seen in this case. A veterinarian should be consulted immediately.

**Vaginitis:** Vaginitis is an inflammation of the vagina. There may be a discharge. The bitch may lick herself, and the vulva may be swollen. Keeping the long hair on the vulva trimmed may help to prevent it.

***Summary:*** It is important that the breeder not try to diagnose problems in the pregnant or lactating bitch, but rather consult a veterinarian when any of the above problems is suspected.

## GENETIC DISEASES AND DISORDERS

There are a number of genetic diseases and disorders that are known in the Basset Hound. Most of them are found in at least a few other breeds. Information on all the diseases and disorders described in the following paragraphs including breeding recommendations comes from the University of Pennsylvania's Canine Genetic Data Base unless otherwise noted.[7]

**Acute gastric dilatation:** *See* Bloat.

**Avian tuberculosis (avian myco-bacteriosus):** This form of TB is known to occur in Bassets where there is a suspected primary immune deficiency. Dogs kept in areas where they are exposed to poultry feces have been known to become infected. This disease can be transmitted to man, and because of this is dangerous. There is no known effective treatment. It is an autosomal (found in both sexes) recessive trait.

**Bird Tongue (glossopharyngeal defect):** Bird tongue is a condition in which affected puppies cannot (or do not attempt to) suck because of the shape of the tongue and die from starvation as a result. The tongue is narrower than normal, especially toward the tip, and there is an inward folding of the outer edges of the tongue. It is an autosomal recessive trait and parents should not continue to be used in a breeding program.

**Bloat (acute gastric dilatation):** This is a severe accumulation of gas in the stomach. The stomach may twist. The abdomen is distended and may feel very hard to the touch. Bloat is a life-threatening emergency that requires immediate veterinary attention. Data from the University of Pennsylvania Canine Genetic Disease Data Base states, "the offspring of affected dogs should be considered at increased risk" for developing it.

**Caudal cervical spondylopathy:** *See* Wobbler's syndrome.

**Cryptorchidism:** Cryptorchidism is a sex-linked recessive condition in which one of the testicles is retained within the abdominal cavity.[6]

**Cystinuria:** Cystinuria is a kidney defect found more frequently in dogs than in bitches. It can be seen as early as six months of age. Stones form in the kidney, bladder and/or ureter. The mode of inheritance is listed as autosomal recessive and breeders are cautioned not to breed affected dogs or their parents except for the purpose of test mating for carriers since there is currently no test for the carrier state.

**Ectodermal dysplasia:** This is an X-linked recessive trait in which pups are born with a symmetrical lack of normal hair on various parts of the body. They remain partially bald and often teeth are missing or abnormally formed. There is currently no reliable test for carriers and it is not recommended that affected dogs be used for breeding. The carrier state of the dam may be ruled out on statistical grounds if only one male in a large litter of males is affected.

**Ectropion:** Ectropion is an out rolling of the lower eyelids. The conjunctiva shows signs of redness and the eyes may be watery or have a mucous discharge.[3]

**Elbow dysplasia:** This term refers to a group of abnormalities associated with the development of the elbow joint. Symptoms are usually seen before six months of age and include an abnormal gait, lameness, and tenderness. The elbow may become arthritic with age.

**Entropion:** Entropion is an in rolling of the upper or lower eyelids and is usually associated with the pagoda eyelid condition. Characterized by tearing, it is painful for the dog and he will rub his eyes.[3]

**Epilepsy:** *See* Laforas disease

**Fading puppy syndrome (FPS):** FPS is not one disease but a name given to a pattern of increasing weakness, lack of vigor in nursing, hypothermia, and death. The puppy seems to "fade away." In Bassets it is usually seen in the first week or so of life. There may be any number of diseases that underlie FPS and some of them have a genetic basis. There is evidence that it is more frequently seen with inbreeding than with other types of breeding practices, and in these cases, repeated inbreeding should be avoided.

**Familial autoimmune thyroid disease:** This form of thyroid disease leads to hypothyroidism. It is often associated with the acquired form of vWD. Some of the clinical signs include lethargy or reduced activity level and poor coat.[1]

**Fear biting:** Fear biting is a behavioral abnormality and is considered an autosomal dominant trait. Affected dogs should not be used for breeding.

**Glaucoma:** Glaucoma is a syndrome produced by more than one cause in other breeds, but in the Basset Hound is thought to be a primary disease, occurring usually in

five- to seven-year-old dogs or bitches. It is characterized by elevated introocular pressures as a result of impaired outflow of aqueous fluid through the iridocorneal angle. This angle abnormality is termed "goniodysgenesis." Glaucoma results in permanent blindness, enlarged eyes, and corneal ulceration. It can be painful to the animal. There is no successful treatment and surgery is recommended. The pattern of inheritance is not known but it is recommended that dogs with glaucoma and their offspring, as related to goniodysgenesis, not be used for breeding.[3]

**Glossopharyngeal defect:** *See* Bird tongue.

**Goniodysgenesis:** Dogs with this angle abnormality (described in Glaucoma) have a much greater than average chance of developing glaucoma.[3]

**Hemangiosarcoma, susceptibility to:** This is a predisposition to develop a type of cancer often involving the spleen. Its method of inheritance is not completely defined.

**Hypertrophic osteodystrophy:** Symptoms of this disease include fever and swelling in areas of the long bones. The dog may show signs of lameness. It usually runs its course and may not need treatment. Excessive diet supplementation has been investigated as a cause, but the results are not clear.

**Inguinal hernia:** An inguinal hernia occurs when loops of the intestine descend through the inguinal canal. The owner will see a "lump" in the groin. Bassets are at an above average risk for developing the condition. Affected dogs should not be used for breeding.[2]

**Laforas disease:** Laforas disease is caused by an accumulation of glycoproteins within the nervous system. Dogs who have it develop a progressive form of epilepsy that eventually cannot be controlled with medication. Clinical signs include lack of coordination and seizures. The mode of inheritance is not completely defined. Affected dogs and their parents should not be used for breeding.

**Methylmalonic aciduria:** This is a metabolic disturbance in which there is an excretion of methlmalonic acid in the urine. There may be seizures, lethargy, and growth failure. The mode of inheritance is incompletely defined. Affected dogs, their parents and their offspring should not be used for breeding.

**Multiple cartilaginous exostoses:** Abnormal growths of bone and cartilage have been seen in pups from one to four months of age. They may cause pain or lack of function if tissues are affected by these growths. It is an autosomal dominant trait. It is recommended that affected dogs not be used for breeding.

**Pagoda eyelids:** "Pagoda eyelid shape describes a diamond shape to the eyelid opening. It is "characterized by the presence of a kink in the central portion of the upper and lower lids ... which leads to the development of ectropion (out rolling) in the area of the kink and entropion (in rolling) medial and lateral to the kink."[3]

**Persistent mullerian duct syndrome:** This is a condition in which internal reproductive organs of the female occur in otherwise normal males. The males may be sterile or nearly so, and they may have retained testicles. It is considered an autosomal recessive trait. It is recommended that affected dogs and their parents not be used for breeding.

**Primary seborrhea:** This is a disease of the skin in which the mode of inheritance is incompletely defined. The skin is excessively oily and has an unpleasant odor. There may be reddish patches on the skin with hair loss.

**Progressive retinal atrophy (PRA):** There are two forms of PRA in the Basset. One occurs by three years of age, the other not until six to eight years of age. PRA is a degenerative disease of the retina that leads to blindness. The presumption is that the condition is recessive.[3]

**Temperomandibular dysplasia:** This is an abnormality of the jaw. The dog may have difficulty closing its mouth The mode of inheritance is incompletely defined.

**Thrombopathia:** Thrombopathia is a severe platelet dysfunction in which there is strong tendency to bleed. Bleeding from the mucosal surfaces is common. Petechia, small measle-like red spots, may be seen on the abdomen. These dogs are at risk for any kind of surgery. According to Bell *et al,* 1984, it is an autosomal recessive trait. There is no reliable test for the carrier state. Affected dogs, their parents and their offspring should not be used for breeding. Test mating can be used to determine the carrier state.

**Von Willebrand's disease:** vWD is the most common canine inherited bleeding disorder. It may be inherited or may be acquired. The inherited form is considered to be an autosomal dominant trait. The symptoms include abnormal bleeding times. The owner may notice longer than usual bleeding time when nails are trimmed, particularly long or intense seasons, excessive bleeding when deciduous teeth are lost, blood in the urine, red spots on the tummy of a puppy (petechia), etc. The animal is a poor risk for surgery. The acquired form is usually associated with thyroid insufficiency.

**Wobbler's syndrome (caudal cervical spondylopathy):** Seen normally in middle-age dogs, Wobbler's can also occur in very young or old dogs as well. There is a progressive weakness and lack of coordination in the hindquarters. The mode of inheritance in the Basset is incompletely defined, but breeders are cautioned not to breed affected animals, their parents or siblings.

**X-linked severe combined immunodeficiency:** This is a recessive defect of the immune system affecting only males. The growth rate is not normal and puppies usually die within five months from a viral or bacterial infection. The dams of affected pups are carriers and should not be used for breeding.

1.Dodds, W. Jean, DVM, "Importance of Genetic Screening for Health and Longevity of Purebred Dogs," 1993.
2.Hutt, Frederick B., *Genetics for Dog Breeders,* 1979.
3.Maurer, Grant D., DVM, MS, Diplomate, American College of Veterinary Ophthalmologists, in a presentation to the Basset Hound Club of Portland, Oregon, 1995.
4.McConnell, Aura, DVM, unpublished works.
5.*Merck Veterinary Manual,* Merck & Co., Inc. 1979.
6.Moon, Calvin, VMD, "Veterinary Aspects and Breeding of the Basset Hound," in The New Basset Hound, 1993.
7.University of Pennsylvania, Canine Genetic Disease Information System, 1994.

# Getting Your
# Very Own Basset

"So many questions, so little time!" "Got to have one, *now!*" This seems the prevailing mentality once someone has made up his mind that he must have a Basset Hound of his very own!

Probably the very first thing to be decided is why you want the animal in the first place. What is its purpose to be? Are you looking for "just a pet," as most are prone to say? Others may want this breed of dog because they plan to become active in their local all-breed dog club, either to work in obedience or to exhibit in conformation shows. In certain instances, you may even want one for hunting! The most likely scenario, however, is you want a Basset Hound for "just a pet!"

Depending on the area of the country that you are living in, finding a Basset Hound may be as simple as turning to the classified section of your local newspaper, or even visiting the pet store in your major metropolitan shopping mall. Note that I said, "finding one," but I've made no mention of "finding a *good* one!" in this manner. While sometimes readily available in this fashion, neither of these sources can be recommended by this writer. As an example, living on the outskirts of a major city, I decided to check today's paper for Basset Hounds. Surprisingly, there were none of this breed listed in the pet store ad, so we may be making headway, after all, on putting the "puppy mill" types out of business. There are, however, four ads by individuals for Basset pups, and two more for Basset/Beagle mixes! Why do we not want to respond to these ads, you may ask. If you skipped over the first part of this book, entitled, "About the Author," turn back there now and read the first page of that section. That will explain that!

Let's talk a little bit about some ways to help you beat the odds on getting the best Basset for your particular purpose the first time out. Reading this book and finding someone to help you understand the section on the standard in particular will be a giant step in the right direction. Looking at the many photos of the excellent dogs contained in this book should also help your understanding to a great degree. You might also want to purchase the AKC (American Kennel Club) breed video, *The Basset Hound*. It can be ordered, and charged by phone, at 1-919-233-9767. It is an excellent breed reference, filmed in 1991, the weekend before the 1991 National Specialty show was held in the same general area, so many of our top Basset Hounds were there for the show and participated in the filming. Also available through the Basset Hound Club of America is the booklet, *The Basset Hound Illustrated Standard*. This booklet, completed in 1996, is well worth its reasonable selling price and it is essentially the printed standard for the breed with accompanying drawings of what is correct, and what is not, including skeletal so that you may learn what is actually underneath all that skin.

The next step would be to find a breeder and visit their kennel, armed with the knowledge that you will already have gained in those first educational steps. Can't find a breeder? Once again, call the American Kennel Club, this time for free! 1-800-252-8355 will get you through to AKC's Public Education Department. They in turn can give you a telephone number for the current Basset Hound Club of America's telephone representative for breeder contact. The BHCA representative can give you the name

*Three very nice ten-week-old pups of the type and quality that any good, reliable breeder would be proud to offer for sale. Photograph furnished by Castlehill kennel.*

of the closest BHCA member breeder to your area and the contact for the closest local Basset Hound Club, as well. It is possible to get some of these questions answered via the email process by contacting AKC at <info@akc.org>. You can also gain considerable information on the Basset Hound Club of America and the Basset Hound breed by going to the BHCA website at http://www.basset-bhca.org/. If these steps don't get you started on the right foot, nothing will! It's also a good idea to visit a dog show, or two, to see more of the breed "in the flesh!" Any of the foregoing breed people can help you with how to find the date and location of the next dog show in your area.

It has been my experience that most who want a Basset Hound have been drawn to it as a result of having observed its rather

unique breed characteristics: In particular, its long ears, loose skin, heavy bone and soft, rather sad expression. Be forewarned, however, that between 8 and 12 weeks, most any Basset Hound puppy is pretty cute and can easily steal your heart. Except for the very badly bred ones, all seem to have what appears to be a reasonable measure of these very characteristics, known as "breed type." Only the well-bred ones, however, maintain those characteristics into maturity. I can't begin to tell you how many times over the past 30 years that someone, with what has turned out to be his poorly bred pet, has been sent to my kennel to show me his pup (usually at about six months of age), and asks if this is what a pup should look like. In the past, we've usually had something about the same age that we could show. You've heard the old adage, "A picture is worth a thousand words." The difference has always been dramatic, to say the least. The disappointed owner sees it immediately and is always, to some degree, devastated. By then, however, the individual is quite emotionally attached to the pet and, unless he is prepared to have two dogs, spends the next ten years with one that is "not quite what he had really wanted!"

In all of these cases, these were pups that had been "impulse buys" from either the newspaper or pet shops. And in many, many cases, they were purchased at prices exceeding what most reputable breeders would have charged.

Before we go to the next step, which is essentially a little breeder evaluation, let's mention one or two other avenues for obtaining good pets. Perhaps you don't really want or need to have a "puppy." Sometimes one can find an adult dog at a lesser price, or even at no cost, to say nothing of a lot less work in housebreaking, etc. Most local or regional Basset Hound Clubs have some type of Basset Hound rescue program where they rehome dogs that have been abandoned, or for some other reasons are in need of loving homes. In other cases, they are aware of breeders wanting to place some of their mature dogs in a family environment when they no longer intend to use them in their breeding programs. Do not believe the old wives' tale about older dogs not adjusting. I've never had one fail to do so. I know one family who has its third Basset from my kennel, all at no initial cost to them. And two of those were champions, with one having been listed in the BHCA Register of Merit. These were special dogs and they are a special family!

Assuming that you've now located a breeder within a reasonable distance, make arrangements to visit the kennel and see the adult dogs. Do not be overly disappointed if there are no puppies immediately available for sale. Conversely, be suspicious if there are numerous puppies from numerous litters available! Most

good breeders are lucky to average two litters per year, though there are rare exceptions. Look around at the facilities. Are they clean? Are the dogs friendly and outgoing? Can the breeder show you the sire and the dam, or if the sire is not on the premises, is there a picture of him available? Can the breeder furnish references from other satisfied owners of his stock? Is the breeder a member of the Basset Hound Club of America? (All serious Basset Hound breeders should be!)

The good breeder will not be overly anxious to sell you a puppy, should he have one available. He will want to size you up, just like you have been advised to size him up! How did you find me? Why do you want a Basset Hound? He may ask about your home situation. Where do you live, city or suburbs, apartment or single family home? Do you have a secure area for the dog, fenced in for exercise? Will someone be at home with the dog most of the time? Is this your first dog? What do you know about this breed? Are you looking for a male or a female?

If, eventually, an agreement can be reached on obtaining a puppy, depending upon your purpose for purchasing it, do not be surprised if you are advised that the dog will be sold to you on a Limited Registration or that you may be required to sign a spay/neuter agreement, or both! Most good breeders are not in the habit of selling dogs for the purpose of reproduction unless they are quite exceptional specimens. While this writer has, upon occasion, been fortunate to produce litters with multiple championship-quality get, it is rather the exception than the rule. Additionally, it is not the purpose of this book to provide instruction relative to the breeding of Basset Hounds. Suffice it to say that no one should consider becoming involved in the breeding of these animals without considerably more experience than can be provided by written instruction. This is, at best, a difficult breed in which to produce consistently worthy specimens and it is an undertaking that should not be entered into lightly. I would think that a minimum of two or three years of intense association with the breed would be the minimum requirement before entering into the breeding arena. And then, it should be undertaken only with the help and encouragement of other qualified breeders. In addition to any agreements, you should also expect written instruction on care and feeding, a record of the worming that has been accomplished, and a record of all inoculations to date, as well as advice with respect to future requirements in this area. I generally advise the new owner of my choice of inoculations and their scheduled times, stressing however, that most vets have their own favorite regimen to follow and that that is usually the best course to follow. I also insist that the animal be taken to a veterinarian of their choice within 48 hours for a health check. It is also very important that the breeder provide you with a phone number that you may call at anytime you may have a question and most will encourage you to return for a future visit or two. Hopefully, if you are successful in your quest for a fine-quality pet, you will have gotten something that will look quite similar to the pups illustrated in this book. If you see any really significant differences, keep on looking!

*Santa Claus (Doug Taylor) and two friends.*

# The Basset Hound

The funny old Basset Hound's low to the ground;
He's bench-legged and crook-kneed, but every bit hound.
He's half-a-dog tall, and a dog-and-a-half long;
He's heavy of bone, and he's solid, and strong.
His underslung chassis makes him a bit slow,
But he goes right along where the rabbits can go.
He has ears like an elephant, voice like a bell;
Both in couples and pack, how their fine voices swell!
Tho especially for rabbits, he hunts pheasants, too;
Both routing and retrieving are things he can do.
He's good after "snowshoes," and also for grouse;
An he makes a fine pet just to have 'round the house.
He has good disposition, his manners the same;
Can especially be trained for both small or large game.
His colors are tri-color, or just red an white;
His hair is quite smooth, and the colors are bright.
He has wrinkles like bloodhounds, and nose most as good.
He's a keen scented hunter for fields, swamps, or wood.
A Basset pack makes the whole hillside resound,
There's a lot of good sport in this quaint little hound.
He's not fast on the hills, and not fast on the level;
But he keeps right on coming, and hunts like the devil!

Carl E. Smith

# Epilogue

Even though the writer has had in excess of 30 years of association with the Basset Hound, and nearly as many years of judging it and other breeds as well, considerable additional research was required to complete this book. One never realizes all of the work, and all of the accomplishments, attributable to the many individuals within the breed, until a detailed review has been made. Without these dedicated fanciers, the world of the Basset Hound, and the world of the dog sport, would not be the same.

While you have been provided with information relating to the development and history of the breed, certainly things are no longer the same as they once were. There is significant change, for example, just since the Basset Hound Club of America was formed, as well as where the majority emphasis in the breed lies today. Those who started us along the road that we travel today were dedicated primarily to using the Basset Hound for its intended purpose of hunting small game on foot. Fortunately, there are those who are still dedicated to that endeavor today. The additional disciplines that have been added over the years, hopefully, have not taken away from our hound's intended purpose. It is doubtful that they have, since every discipline has its roots in the original function of the breed. What has changed is simply that, for other than pure sport, no one needs the help of a hound to put the meal on the table, consequently, other challenges have been established to keep the breed and its owners otherwise occupied.

Those new to the sport often do not know what makes a breed, a breeder, or a parent breed club. Much of what has been written here has been written about those of another era in other books. The breeders who are mentioned in this book, like those who have gone before them, did not achieve their status in a year or two, or necessarily in five or ten. It has taken them years and years to establish their lines, or their style of hound, and to become recognized as having a kennel that produces winning dogs, whatever their discipline. I recently asked Mary Jo Shields, the breeder that helped me get started in the breed back in the early 1960s, "How many of those whom you helped get started back then are still in it today?" Her answer was, "Just you, I think!" But, as mentioned, times change and things are different today. New young faces in the breed are somewhat scarce to come by, but sorely needed. Perhaps this is because this has gotten to be a very expensive sport. Perhaps it is because there are simply fewer "true breeders" today. As in other aspects of life, some people just want the "easy win," and lack the dedication that it takes to achieve consistently in the sport of dogs.

The real dog person is the one who stays with it for a lifetime, and never stops learning, whether it be about Basset Hounds, or the other breeds as well. It is that lifelong dedication to the sport that is the most consistent ingredient among the majority of "real dog people" whom I have known and continue to respect. And, as Merce Braun pointed out, they are the kind of Basset Hound breeders to whom the Basset of tomorrow is more important than the win of today. I thank them for sharing their knowledge with me and for the pleasure of having known them. I salute them: they have made my life all the richer.

# Bibliography

American Kennel Club, *The Complete Dog Book,* Howell Book House, Inc., New York, NY, USA, 1992

Appelton, Douglas A., *The Basset Hound Handbook*, Nicholson & Watson, London, UK, 1960

Barton, Frank Townsend, *Sporting Dogs*, R. A. Everett & Co., Ltd., London, UK, 1905
——. *Hounds*, John Long, Ltd., London, UK, circa 1900

Braun, Mercedes, *The New Complete Basset Hound*, Howell Book House, Inc., New York, NY, USA, (first published in 1965 under the title: *The Complete Basset Hound*).

Buchanan-Jardine, Sir John, *Hounds of the World*, Graylings Books, Cumbria, UK, 1937, Ltd. Ed. 1979

Canadian Kennel Club, *The Canadian Kennel Club Book of Dogs*, General Publishing Co., Ltd., Toronto, Ontario, Canada, 1982

Croxton-Smith, A., *Hounds & Dogs*, Seeley, Service & Co., Ltd., London, UK, 1906
——. *Everyman's Book of the Dog*, Hodder & Strughton, London, UK, circa 1935

Daglish, E. Fitch, *The Basset Hound*, W & G Foyle, Ltd., London, UK, 1964

Foy, Marcia A. & Anna K. Nicholas, *The Basset Hound*, TFH Publications, Inc., Neptune City, NJ, USA 1985

# Bibliography

Frederiksen, R. W., *Basset Hound, A World History*, Collector's Press, Joshua, Texas, USA, 1987

Gilbert & Brown, *K-9 Structure & Terminology*, Howell Book House, New York, NY, USA, 1995

Hutchison, Walter, *Hutchinson's Popular & Illustrated Dog Encyclopedia*, Hutchinson & Co., London, UK, circa 1935. (Article included by: Lt. Col. Christopher Heseltine).

Johns, Jeanne Rowett, *All About the Basset Hound*, Pelham Books, Ltd., 1973

Johnston, George & Maria Ericson, *Hounds of France*, Spur Publishing Co., Ltd., Hindhead, UK, 1979

Johnston, George, *The Basset Hound*, Popular Dogs Publishing Co., Ltd., London, UK, 1968

Smith, Carl E. *Training The Rabbit Hound*, The Hunter-Trapper-Trader Co. (Publishers), Columbus, OH, USA, 1926

Venzins, Comte Elie de, *Hounds for the Pack*, Translated by Lionel R. Woolner, first published in France in 1882, English translation published in 1974, J. A. Allen & Co., London, UK

Walton, Margaret S., *The New Basset Hound*, Howell Book House, New York, NY, USA, 1993

Wells-Meacham, Joan, *The Basset Hound*, John Bartholomew & Son, Ltd., Edinburgh, UK, 1980

# Index